Nikon® D5300™ For Dummies®

A Wiley Brand

by Julie Adair King

For Dummies®
A Wiley Brand

Nikon® D5300™ For Dummies®

Published by: **John Wiley & Sons, Inc.,** 111 River Street, Hoboken, NJ 07030-5774, www.wiley.com

Published simultaneously in Canada

For general information on our other products and services, please contact our Customer Care Department within the U.S. at 877-762-2974, outside the U.S. at 317-572-3993, or fax 317-572-4002. For technical support, please visit www.wiley.com/techsupport.

Wiley publishes in a variety of print and electronic formats and by print-on-demand. Some material included with standard print versions of this book may not be included in e-books or in print-on-demand. If this book refers to media such as a CD or DVD that is not included in the version you purchased, you may download this material at http://booksupport.wiley.com. For more information about Wiley products, visit www.wiley.com.

Library of Congress Control Number: 2013957978

ISBN 978-1-118-87214-7 (pbk); ISBN 978-1-118-87218-5 (ebk); ISBN 978-1-118-87254-3 (ebk)

Manufactured in the United States of America

10 9 8 7 6 5 4 3 2 1

Contents at a Glance

Table of Contents

Introduction

Nikon. The name has been associated with top-flight photography equipment for generations. And the introduction of the D5300 has only enriched Nikon's well-deserved reputation, offering all the control that a diehard photography enthusiast could want while providing easy-to-use, point-and-shoot features for the beginner.

In fact, the D5300 offers so *many* features that sorting them all out can be more than a little confusing, especially if you're new to digital photography, SLR photography, or both. For starters, you may not even be sure what SLR means or how it affects your picture-taking, let alone have a clue about all the other techie terms you encounter in your camera manual — *resolution, aperture, white balance,* and so on. And if you're like many people, you may be so overwhelmed by all the controls on your camera that you haven't yet ventured beyond fully automatic picture-taking mode.

Therein lies the point of *Nikon D5300 For Dummies.* Throughout this book, you can discover not just what each bell and whistle on your camera does but also when, where, why, and how to put it to best use. Unlike many photography books, this one doesn't require any previous knowledge of photography or digital imaging to make sense of things, either. In classic *For Dummies* style, everything is explained in easy-to-understand language, with lots of illustrations to help clear up any confusion.

In short, what you have in your hands is the paperback version of an in-depth photography workshop tailored specifically to your Nikon picture-taking powerhouse.

A Quick Look at What's Ahead

This book is organized into four parts, each devoted to a different aspect of using your camera. Although chapters flow in a sequence that's designed to take you from absolute beginner to experienced user, I've also tried to make each chapter as self-standing as possible so that you can explore the topics that interest you in any order you please.

Here's a brief preview of what you can find in each part of the book:

- **Part I: Fast Track to Super Snaps:** Part I contains two chapters to help you get up and running. Chapter 1 guides you through initial camera setup, shows you how to view and adjust camera settings, and walks you through the steps of taking your first pictures using the Auto exposure mode. Chapter 2 introduces you to other exposure modes and also explains basic picture options such as Flash mode, Shutter Release mode, Image Size (resolution), and Image Quality (JPEG or Raw).

- **Part II: Taking Creative Control:** Chapters in this part help you unleash the full creative power of your camera by detailing the advanced shooting modes (P, S, A, and M). Chapter 3 covers the critical topic of exposure; Chapter 4 explains how to manipulate focus; and Chapter 5 discusses color controls. Chapter 6 summarizes techniques explained in earlier chapters, providing a quick-reference guide to the camera settings and shooting strategies that produce the best results for portraits, action shots, landscape scenes, and close-ups. Chapter 7 shifts gears, moving from still photography to HD movie recording with your D5300.
- **Part III: After the Shot:** This part offers two chapters, both dedicated to tasks you do after you press the shutter button. Chapter 8 explains how to review your pictures on the camera monitor, create an in-camera slide show, and connect your camera to a TV for large-screen playback. Chapter 9 topics include rating, deleting, and protecting photos, downloading images to your computer or to a tablet or smartphone, processing Raw files, and preparing pictures for online sharing.
- **Part IV: The Part of Tens:** In famous *For Dummies* tradition, the book concludes with two top-ten lists containing additional bits of information and advice. Chapter 10 covers the photo-editing and effects tools found on the camera's Retouch menu and also shows you how to use the Effects exposure mode to add special effects to movies and photos as you record them. Chapter 11 wraps up the book by detailing some camera features that, although not found on most "Top Ten Reasons I Bought My Nikon D5300" lists, are nonetheless interesting, useful on occasion, or a bit of both.

Icons and Other Stuff to Note

If this isn't your first *For Dummies* book, you may be familiar with the large, round icons that decorate its margins. If not, here's your very own icon-decoder ring:

TIP

The Tip icon flags information that will save you time, effort, money, or some other valuable resource, including your sanity. Tips also point out techniques that help you get the best results from specific camera features.

WARNING!

When you see this icon, look alive. It indicates a potential danger zone that can result in much wailing and teeth-gnashing if ignored. In other words, this is stuff that you really don't want to learn the hard way.

Lots of information in this book is of a technical nature — digital photography is a technical animal, after all. But if I present a detail that is useful mainly for impressing your technology-geek friends, I mark it with this icon.

I apply this icon either to introduce information that is especially worth storing in your brain's long-term memory or to remind you of a fact that may have been displaced from that memory by another pressing fact.

Additionally, I need to point out these extra details that will help you use this book effectively:

- **Other margin art:** Replicas of some of your camera's buttons and onscreen symbols also appear in the margins of some paragraphs. I include these to provide a quick reminder of the appearance of the button or feature being discussed.
- **Software menu commands:** In sections that cover software, a series of words connected by an arrow indicates commands that you choose from the program menus. For example, if a step tells you to "Choose File⇨Convert Files," click the File menu to unfurl it and then click the Convert Files command on the menu.

eCheat Sheet

For a little bonus, you can find an electronic version of the famous *For Dummies* eCheat Sheet at `www.dummies.com/cheatsheet/nikond5300`. The eCheat Sheet contains a quick-reference guide to all the buttons, dials, switches, and exposure modes on your camera. Log on, print it out, and tuck it in your camera bag for times when you don't want to carry this book with you.

Practice, Be Patient, and Have Fun!

To wrap up this preamble, I want to stress that if you initially think that digital photography is too confusing or too technical for you, you're in very good company. *Everyone* finds this stuff mind-boggling at first. So take it slowly, experimenting with just one or two new camera settings or techniques at first. Then, every time you go on a photo outing, make it a point to add one or two more shooting skills to your repertoire.

I know that it's hard to believe when you're just starting out, but it really won't be long before everything starts to come together. With some time, patience, and practice, you'll soon wield your camera like a pro, dialing in the necessary settings to capture your creative vision almost instinctively.

So without further ado, I invite you to grab your camera, a cup of whatever it is you prefer to sip while you read, and start exploring the rest of this book. Your D5300 is the perfect partner for your photographic journey, and I thank you for allowing me, through this book, to serve as your tour guide.

REMEMBER

Occasionally, Wiley's technology books are updated. If this book has technical updates, they'll be posted at `www.dummies.com/go/nikond5300updates`.

Part I
Fast Track to Super Snaps

getting started with your Nikon D5300

web extras

Visit `www.dummies.com` for more great *For Dummies* content online.

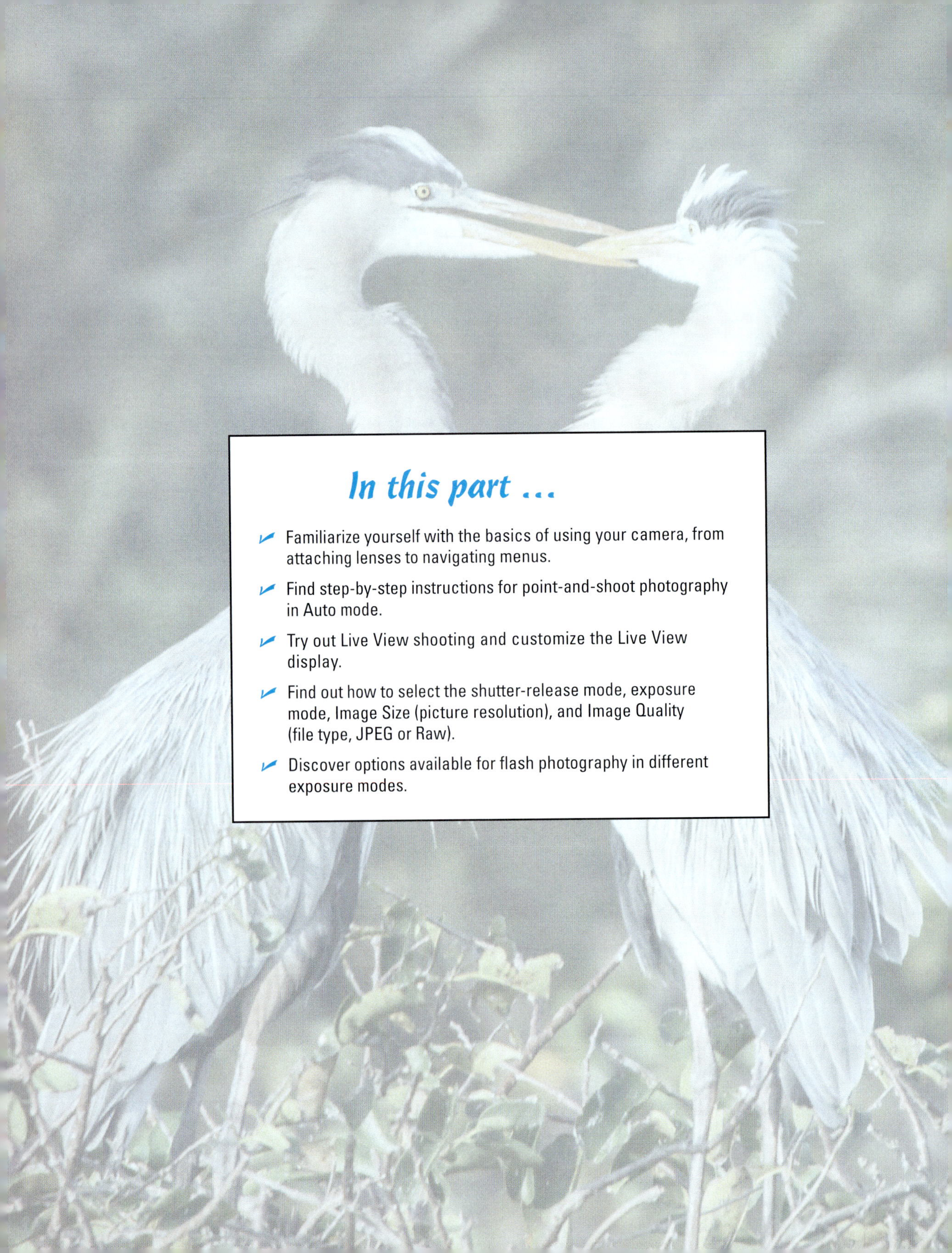

In this part ...

- Familiarize yourself with the basics of using your camera, from attaching lenses to navigating menus.
- Find step-by-step instructions for point-and-shoot photography in Auto mode.
- Try out Live View shooting and customize the Live View display.
- Find out how to select the shutter-release mode, exposure mode, Image Size (picture resolution), and Image Quality (file type, JPEG or Raw).
- Discover options available for flash photography in different exposure modes.

1

Getting Up and Running

In This Chapter

- Preparing the camera for its first outing
- Getting acquainted with camera features
- Viewing and adjusting camera settings
- Setting a few basic preferences
- Returning your camera to its original state
- Taking a picture in Auto mode

Shooting for the first time with a camera as sophisticated as the Nikon D5300 can produce a blend of excitement and anxiety. On one hand, you can't wait to start using your new equipment, but on the other, you're a little intimidated by all its buttons, dials, and menu options.

Well, fear not: This chapter provides the information you need to start getting comfortable with your D5300. The first section walks you through initial camera setup; following that, you can get an overview of camera controls, discover how to view and adjust camera settings, and get my take on some basic setup options. At the end of the chapter, I walk you step-by-step through taking your first pictures using Auto mode, which offers point-and-shoot simplicity until you're ready to step up to more advanced options.

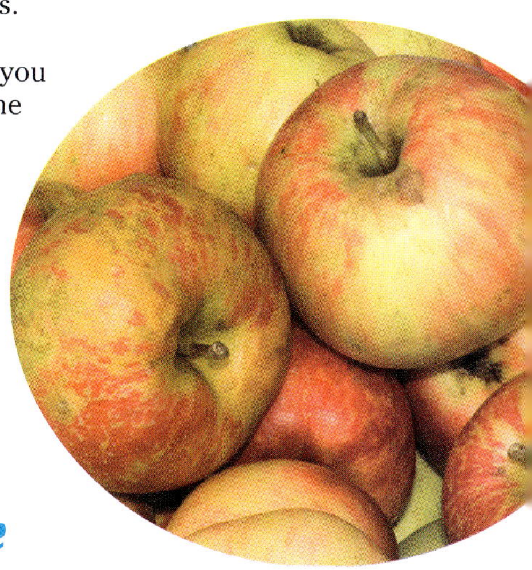

Preparing the Camera for Initial Use

After unpacking your camera, you have to assemble a few parts. In addition to the camera body and the supplied battery (be sure to charge it before the first use), you need a lens and a memory card. Later sections in this chapter provide details about working with lenses and memory cards, but here's what you need to know up front:

- **Lens:** You can mount a wide range of lenses on your D5300, but some aren't compatible with all camera features. For example, to enjoy autofocusing, you need an AF-S or AF-I lens. Your camera manual offers details about lens compatibility.

  The *AF* in AF-S stands for *autofocus,* and the *S* stands for *silent wave,* a Nikon autofocus technology. AF-I lenses are older, professional-grade (expensive) lenses that are no longer made but may be available on the secondhand market.

  If you don't yet own a lens, the website for this book offers a short buying guide. Go to `www.dummies.com/extras/nikon`.

- **SD (Secure Digital) memory card:** Your camera accepts only this type of card. Most SD cards carry the designation SDHC (for *High Capacity*) or SDXC (for *eXtended Capacity*), depending on how many gigabytes (GB) of data they hold. SDHC cards hold from 4GB to 32GB of data; the SDXC moniker is assigned to cards with capacities greater than 32GB.

  Cards are also assigned a speed rating from 2 to 10, with a higher number indicating a faster data-transfer rate. The industry recently added a new speed rating: Ultra High Speed (UHS). UHS cards also carry a number designation; at present, there is only one class of UHS card — UHS 1. These cards currently are the fastest the planet has to offer. Of course, a faster card means a more expensive card. But to maximize your camera's performance, I recommend Class 10 or UHS 1 cards.

  A faster card translates to smoother movie recording and playback and also can improve performance when you're shooting a burst of images using the camera's continuous capture feature.

With camera, lens, battery, and card within reach, take these steps:

1. **Turn the camera off.**
2. **Install the battery into the compartment on the bottom of the camera.**
3. **Attach a lens.**

   First, remove the caps that cover the front of the camera and the back of the lens. Then align the *mounting index* (white dot) on the lens with the one on the camera body, as shown in Figure 1-1. After placing the lens on the camera mount, rotate the lens toward the shutter-button side of the camera. You should feel a solid click as the lens locks into place.

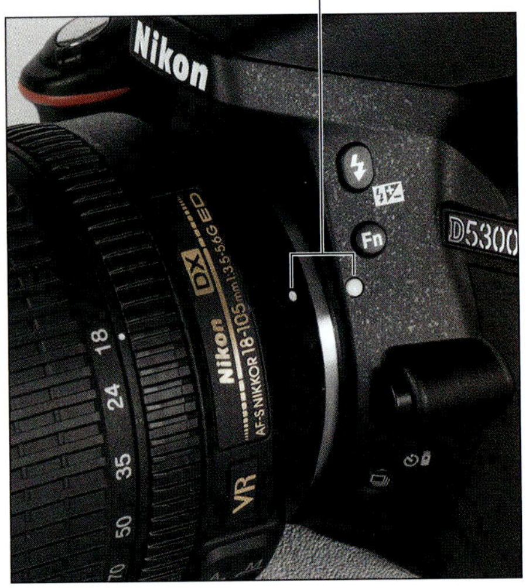

Figure 1-1: Align the white dot on the lens with the one on the camera body.

4. **Insert a memory card.**

   Open the card-slot cover on the right side of the camera and orient the card as shown in Figure 1-2 (the label faces the back of the camera). Push the card gently into the slot and close the cover. The memory-card access light, labeled in the figure, illuminates briefly to let you know that the camera recognizes the card.

5. **Rotate the monitor to the desired viewing position.**

   When you first take the camera out of its box, the monitor is positioned with the screen facing inward, protecting it from scratches and smudges. Use your fingertip to gently lift the right side of the monitor up and away from the camera back. You can then rotate the monitor to move it into the traditional position on the camera back, as shown on the left in Figure 1-3, or swing the monitor out and away from the camera and adjust it to find the best viewing angle, as shown on the right.

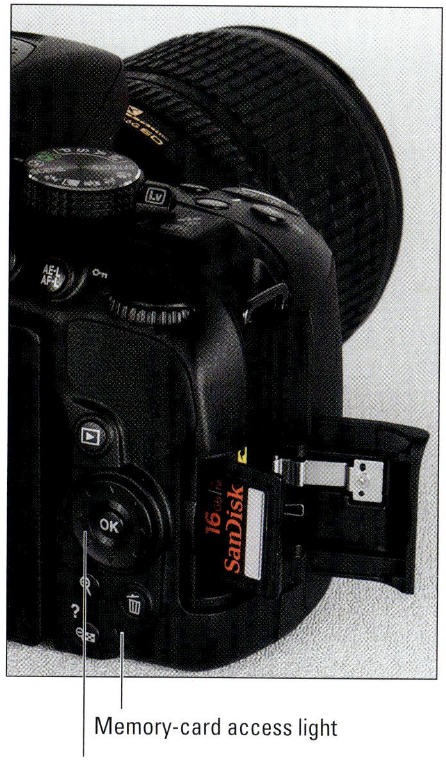

Figure 1-2: Insert the memory card with the label facing the back of the camera.

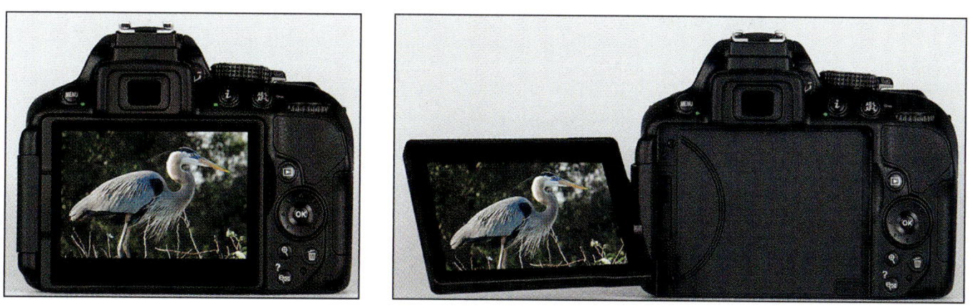

Figure 1-3: Here are just two of the possible monitor positions.

6. **Turn the camera on.**

   The chances are slim, but you may see a message on the monitor telling you to format the memory card. Continue with these setup steps and then skip to the section "Working with memory cards" to find out about formatting.

7. **Adjust the viewfinder to your eyesight.**

   Tucked behind the right side of the rubber eyepiece that surrounds the viewfinder is a *diopter adjustment* dial that enables you to adjust the viewfinder focus to accommodate your eyesight. I highlighted the dial in Figure 1-4.

   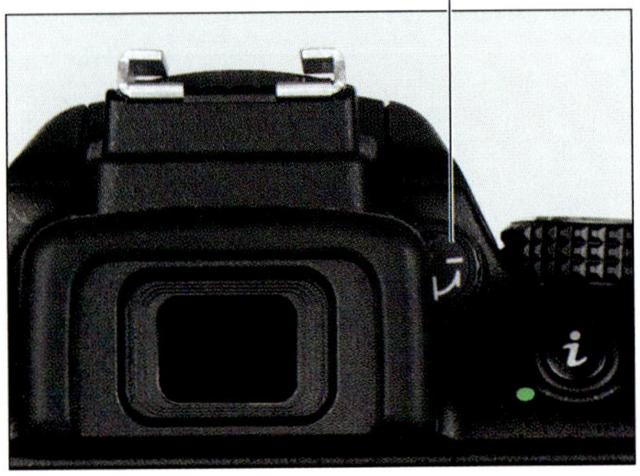

   Figure 1-4: Rotate this dial to set the viewfinder focus for your eyesight.

   To take this step, remove the lens cap, look through the viewfinder, and press the shutter button halfway to display data at the bottom of the viewfinder. (In dim lighting, the flash may pop up; ignore it for now and close the unit after you adjust the viewfinder.) Now rotate the dial until the data appears sharpest. The markings in the center of the viewfinder, which relate to autofocusing, also become more or less sharp.

8. **Set the camera language, time zone, date, and time.**

   When you power up the camera for the first time, the monitor displays a message asking you to select the menu language and set the time zone, date, and time. Navigate the screens and adjust the settings by using the Multi Selector and the OK button (refer to Figure 1-2):

   - Press the edge of the Multi Selector up and down to scroll the screen vertically; press right/left to travel horizontally.
   - After making your selections, press OK to finalize things.

   (The later section "Ordering from camera menus" provides more help with using menus.)

   The date/time information is included as *metadata* (hidden data) in the picture file. You can view metadata in some playback display modes (see Chapter 8) and in certain photo programs, including Nikon ViewNX 2 (refer to Chapter 9).

That's all there is to it — the camera is now ready to go. From here, my recommendation is that you keep reading this chapter to familiarize yourself with the main camera features and basic operation. But if you're anxious to take a picture right away, I won't think any less of you if you skip to the very last section of the chapter, which guides you through the process. Just promise that at some point, you'll read the pages in between, because they actually do contain important information.

Exploring Basic Camera Features

If you're new to dSLR photography, some aspects of using your camera, such as working with the lens, may be unfamiliar to you. But even if you're an old pro — check that, even if you're a *seasoned* pro — it pays to take some time before your first shoot with a new camera to get familiar with its controls. To that end, the upcoming pages provide a quick overview of the D5300's main features and also offer a primer on working with lenses and memory cards.

Exploring external camera controls

Scattered across your camera's exterior are numerous controls that you use to change picture-taking settings, review your photos, and perform various other operations. In later chapters, I discuss all your camera's functions in detail and provide the exact steps to follow to access them. This section provides just a basic "what's this thing do?" guide to each control. (Don't worry about memorizing the button names; throughout the book, I show pictures of buttons in the page margins to help you know exactly which one to press.)

Topside controls

Your virtual tour begins with the bird's-eye view shown in Figure 1-5. There are a number of features of note here:

- **On/Off switch and shutter button:** Okay, I'm pretty sure you've already figured out this combo button. But you may not be aware that you need to press the shutter button in two stages: Press and hold the button halfway and wait for the camera to initiate exposure metering and, if you're using autofocusing, to set the focusing distance. Then press the button the rest of the way to take the picture.

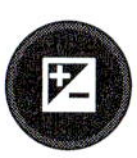

- **Exposure Compensation button:** This button activates Exposure Compensation, a feature that enables you to tweak exposure when working in the P (programmed autoexposure), A (aperture-priority autoexposure), or S (shutter-priority autoexposure) modes. (I cover this feature in Chapter 3.) Press the button while rotating the Command dial (in back of the camera; see Figure 1-6, in the next section) to set the amount of Exposure Compensation. In M (manual exposure) mode, press this button while rotating the Command dial to adjust the aperture setting.

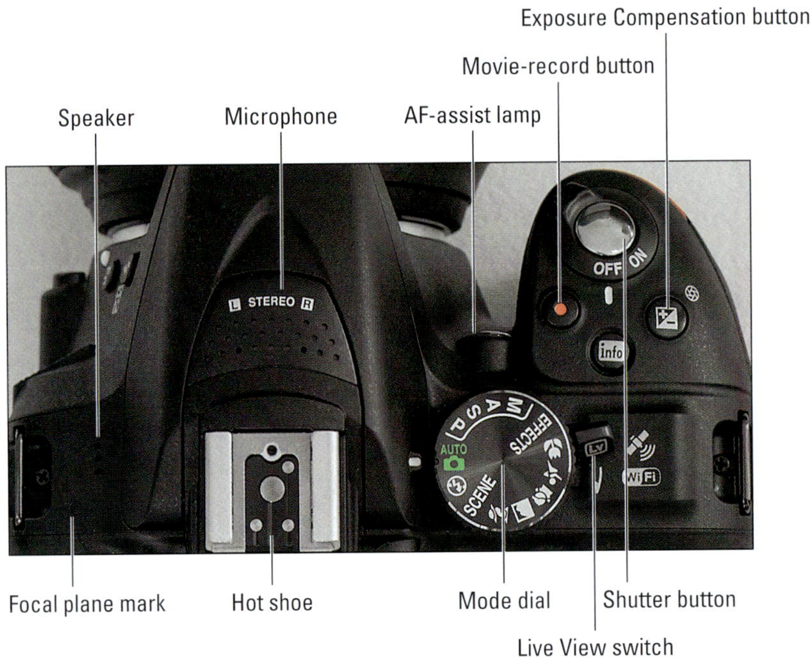

Figure 1-5: Rotate the Live View switch to shift from viewfinder to Live View photography.

- **Info button:** Press this button to display the Information screen on the camera monitor. The screen enables you to not only view current picture settings but also adjust some settings more quickly than by using the camera menus. (Look for details later in this chapter, in the section "Adjusting settings via the Information display control strip"). To turn off the screen, press the Info button again.

  You also can display the screen by pressing the shutter button halfway and releasing it.

- **Live View switch:** As its name implies, this switch turns Live View on and off. In Live View mode, the scene in front of the lens appears on the monitor, and you can't see anything through the viewfinder. You then can compose a still photo using the monitor or begin recording a movie. The last section of this chapter introduces you to Live View photography; see Chapter 7 for help with movie making.

  To the right of the switch, you see symbols representing the GPS (Global Satellite Positioning) and Wi-Fi features. These labels are decorative only; rotating the Live View switch doesn't have any impact on either feature. Instead, you control them both via the Setup menu. Chapter 11 details the GPS feature; Chapter 9, the Wi-Fi feature.

- **Movie-record button:** After shifting to Live View mode, press this button to start recording a movie. Press again to stop recording.
- **Mode dial:** With this dial, you set the camera to fully automatic, semiautomatic, or manual exposure mode. Setting the dial to Effects enables you to apply special effects as the image or movie is captured. Chapter 2 introduces you to each exposure mode.
- **AF-assist lamp:** When you use autofocusing, the camera may emit a beam of light from this lamp in dim lighting; the light helps the camera find its focus target. The lamp also lights when you use red-eye reduction flash and the Self-Timer shutter-release mode, both covered in Chapter 2.
- **Flash hot shoe:** A *hot shoe* is a connection for attaching an external flash head. When not in use, the contacts on the shoe are protected by a black cover; remove the cover to expose the contacts (refer to Figure 1-5) to attach the external flash.
- **Microphone:** The holes labeled *microphone* in the figure lead to the camera's internal microphone.
- **Speaker:** When you play a movie, the sound comes wafting out of these holes (refer to Figure 1-5).
- **Focal plane indicator:** When you need to know the exact distance between your subject and the camera, the focal plane mark (refer to Figure 1-5) is the key. The mark indicates the plane at which light coming through the lens is focused onto the camera's image sensor. Basing your measurement on this mark produces a more accurate camera-to-subject distance than using the end of the lens or another external point on the camera body as your reference point.

Back-of-the-body controls

On the back of the camera, shown in Figure 1-6, you find these features:

- **Infrared receiver:** Labeled in Figure 1-6, this is one of two receivers that picks up the infrared signal from the optional ML-L3 wireless remote control. The other receiver is on the front-right side of the camera, near the middle of the hand grip.
- **Menu button:** Press this button to access menus of camera options. See "Ordering from camera menus," later in this chapter, for details.
- **Viewfinder adjustment dial:** Rotate this dial to adjust the viewfinder focus to your eyesight; see the first section of this chapter for details.
- ***i* button:** Pressing this button activates the control strip at the bottom of the Information display, enabling quick access to certain picture settings. Use the Multi Selector to highlight an option and press OK to display a screen that offers the settings for that option. Press the ***i*** button again to exit the control strip.

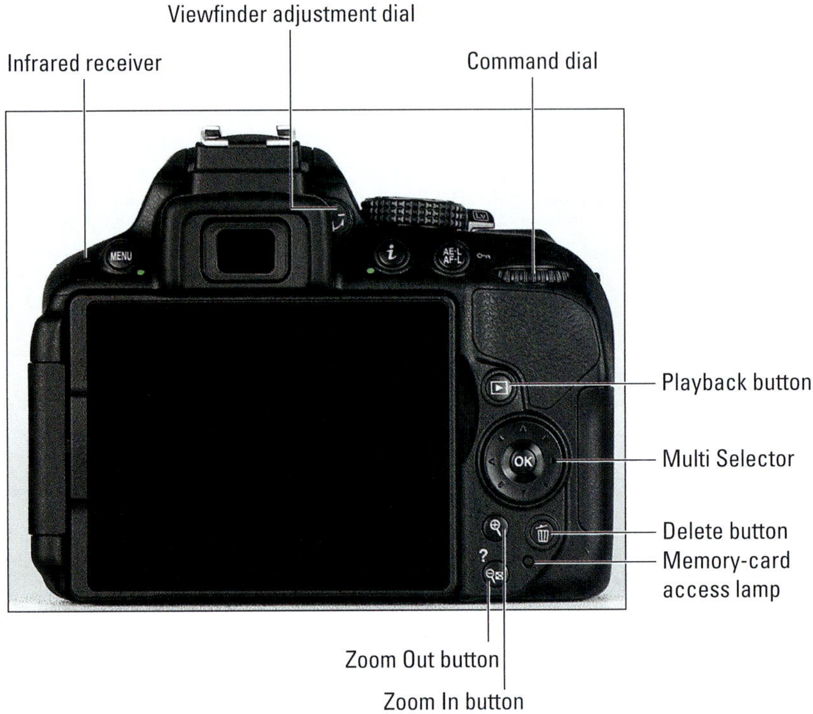

Figure 1-6: Use the Multi Selector to navigate menus and access certain other camera options.

- **Command dial:** After you activate certain camera features, you rotate this dial to select a setting. For example, to choose a shutter speed when shooting in shutter-priority (S) mode, you rotate the Command dial.
- **AE-L/AF-L button:** Pressing this button initiates autoexposure lock (AE-L) and autofocus lock (AF-L). Chapter 3 explains autoexposure lock; Chapter 4 talks about autofocus lock.

  In playback mode, pressing the button activates the Protect feature, which locks the picture file — hence the little key symbol that appears above the button — so that it isn't erased if you use the picture-delete functions. See Chapter 9 for details. (The picture *is* erased if you format the memory card, however.)
- **Multi Selector/OK button:** This dual-natured control plays a role in many camera functions. You press the outer edges of the Multi Selector left, right, up, or down to navigate camera menus and access certain other options. At the center of the control is the OK button, which you press to finalize a menu selection or another camera adjustment.

In this book, the instruction "Press the Multi Selector left" simply means to press the left edge of the control. "Press the Multi Selector right" means to press the right edge, and so on.

- **Playback button:** Press this button to switch the camera into picture review mode. Chapter 8 details playback features.
- **Delete button:** Sporting a trash can icon, the universal symbol for delete, this button enables you to erase pictures from your memory card. Chapter 9 explains the steps.
- **Zoom In button:** In playback mode, pressing this button magnifies the currently displayed image and also reduces the number of thumbnails displayed at a time. Note the plus sign in the middle of the magnifying glass — plus means enlarge.
- **Zoom Out button:** As you can probably deduce from the three symbols that mark this button, it has not one, but *three* primary functions:
    - *Display help screens:* The little question mark symbol above the button is a reminder that you can press this button to display helpful information about certain menu options. See the sidebar "Displaying Help screens," later in this chapter, for details.
    - *Display thumbnails during playback:* In playback mode, pressing the button enables you to display multiple image thumbnails on the screen; thus the little thumbnail grid on the button face.
    - *Reduce image magnification during playback:* If you magnify an image during playback, pressing the button reduces the magnification amount. The magnifying glass with the minus sign tips you off to this function.

Front-left features

The front-left side of the camera, shown in Figure 1-7, sports these features:

- **Flash button:** In the advanced exposure modes (P, S, A, and M), as well as in Food Scene mode, pressing this button raises the built-in flash. (In other modes, the camera decides whether the flash is needed.) By holding the button down and rotating the Command dial, you can adjust the Flash mode (fill flash, red-eye reduction, and so on). In advanced exposure modes, you also can adjust the flash power by pressing the button while simultaneously pressing the Exposure Compensation button and rotating the Command dial. The little plus/minus symbol that appears below the button — the same symbol that's on the Exposure Compensation button — is a reminder of the button's role in flash-power adjustment.

  Check out Chapter 2 for details on flash options.

- **Function (Fn) button:** By default, this button gives you quick access to the ISO setting, which controls the camera's sensitivity to light. (Chapter 3 explains.) If you don't adjust that setting often, you can use the button to perform a variety of other operations. Chapter 11 shows you how to change the button's purpose. (***Note:*** All instructions in this book assume that you haven't changed the function.)
- **Lens-release button:** Press this button to disengage the lens from the camera's lens mount so that you can remove the lens.
- **Release Mode button:** Press this button to display a screen where you can select the shutter-release mode. By default, the option is set to Single Frame, which results in one picture each time you press the shutter button. You can explore other options in Chapter 2.

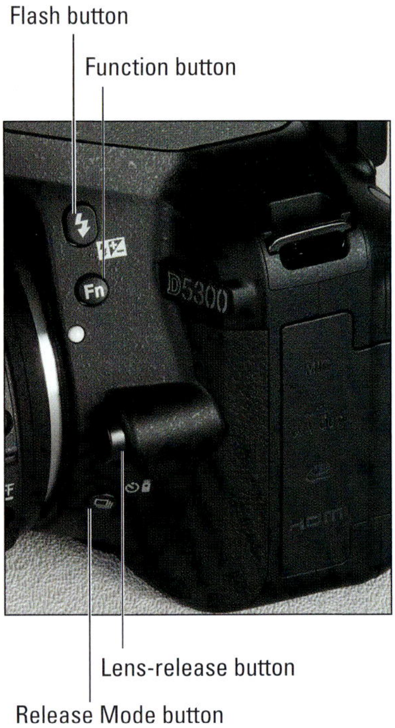

Figure 1-7: Press the Flash button to use the built-in flash in P, S, A, or M mode.

Hidden connections

Hidden under cover on the left side of the camera are the following connection ports, labeled in Figure 1-8:

- **Microphone jack:** If you're not happy with the audio quality provided by the internal microphone, you can plug in the optional ME-1 stereo microphone here.
- **USB and A/V port:** Through this port, you can connect your camera to your computer via USB connection for picture downloading. The same port enables you to connect the camera to a television via an A/V cable for picture playback. Nikon supplies the cables you need for both connections in the camera box; see Chapter 8 for information on television connections and Chapter 9 for help with downloading pictures.
- **Accessory terminal:** This terminal accepts the following accessories: Nikon MC-DC2 remote shutter-release cable; WR-1 and WR-R10 wireless remote controllers; and GP-1/GP-1A GPS units. I don't cover these optional accessories, but the manual that comes with each device can get you up and running.

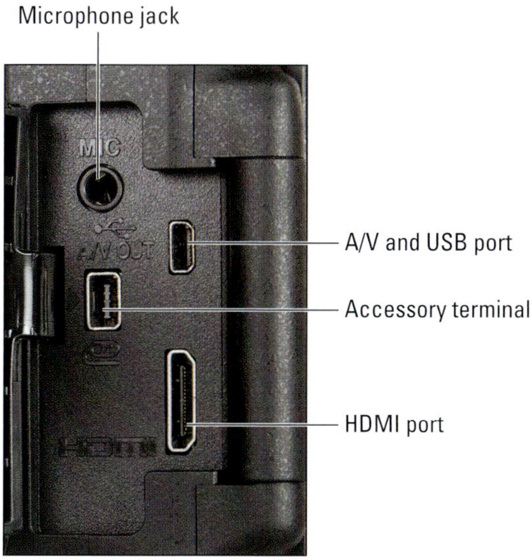

Figure 1-8: Open the cover on the side of the camera to reveal these connections.

You can't connect a wireless remote controller while the ME-1 stereo microphone is attached.

- **HDMI port:** You can use this port to connect your camera to a high-definition TV, but you need to buy an HDMI cable to do so. Look for a Type C mini-pin cable. Chapter 8 offers details on television playback.

If you turn the camera over, you find a tripod socket, which enables you to mount the camera on a tripod that uses a ¼-inch screw, plus the battery chamber.

Ordering from camera menus

When you press the Menu button, you see a screen similar to the one shown on the left in Figure 1-9. The icons along the left side of the screen represent the available menus, each of which is loaded with shooting, playback, and customization settings; Table 1-1 offers an icon decoder ring. On the menu screens, the icon that's highlighted is the active menu; options on that menu automatically appear to the right. In the figure, the Shooting menu is active, for example.

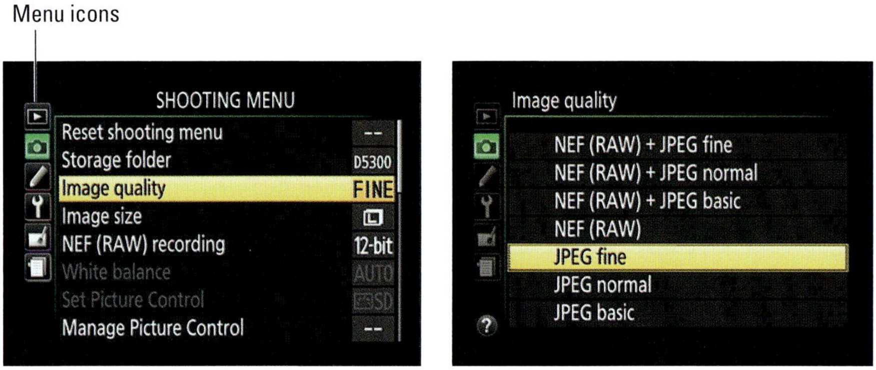

Figure 1-9: Highlight a menu in the left column to display its contents.

Table 1-1 D5300 Menus

Symbol		*Open This Menu . . .*	*To Access These Functions*
		Playback	Viewing, deleting, and protecting pictures
		Shooting	Basic photography settings
		Custom Setting	Advanced photog-raphy options and some basic camera operations
		Setup	Additional basic camera operations
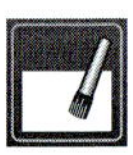		Retouch	Photo and movie editing options
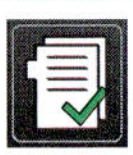		My Menu/Recent Settings	Your custom menu or 20 most recently used menu options

To select menu options, use the Multi Selector and OK button, as follows:

- **To select a different menu:** Press the Multi Selector left to jump to the column containing the menu icons. Then press up or down to highlight the menu you want to display. Finally, press right to jump over to the options on the menu.
- **To select and adjust a function on the current menu:** Again, use the Multi Selector to scroll up or down the list of options to highlight the feature you want to adjust and then press OK. Settings available for the selected item then appear. For example, if you select the Image Quality item from the Shooting menu (refer to the left side of Figure 1-9) and press OK, the available Image Quality options appear, as shown on the right. Repeat the old up-and-down scroll routine until the choice you prefer is highlighted. Then press OK.

  In some cases, a right-pointing triangle appears next to a menu item. That's your cue to press the Multi Selector right to display a submenu.

  REMEMBER

  Items that are dimmed aren't available in the current exposure mode. For access to all settings, set the Mode dial to P, S, A, or M.
- **To select items from the Custom Setting menu:** Displaying the Custom Setting menu takes you to a screen that contains six submenus that carry the labels A through F, as shown in Figure 1-10. Each submenu holds clusters of options related to a specific aspect of the camera's operation. Highlight a submenu and press OK to get to those options.

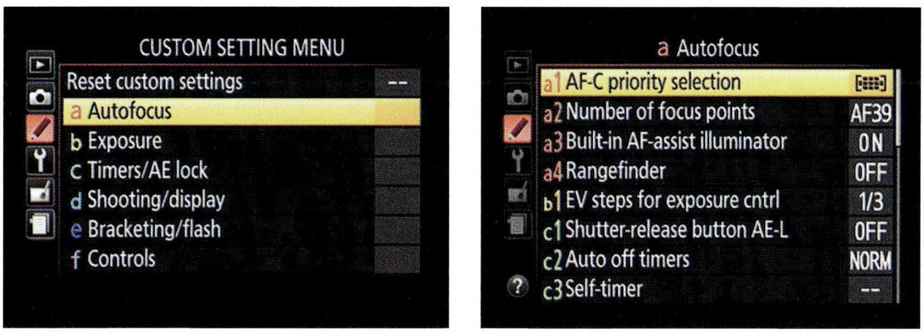

Figure 1-10: The Custom Setting menu contains six submenus of advanced options.

In the Nikon manual, instructions reference the Custom Setting menu items by a menu letter and number. For example, "Custom Setting a1" refers to the first option on the a (Autofocus) submenu. I try to be more specific, however, so I use the actual setting names. (Really, we all have enough numbers to remember, don't you think?)

TIP

After you jump to the first submenu, you can simply scroll up and down the list to view options from other submenus. You don't have to keep going back to the initial menu screen, selecting the submenu, pressing OK, and so on.

- **Create a custom menu or view your 20 most recently adjusted menu items:** The sixth menu is actually two menus that share an apartment: Recent Settings and My Menu, both shown in Figure 1-11. Each menu contains a Choose Tab option; select this option and press OK to shift between the two menus.

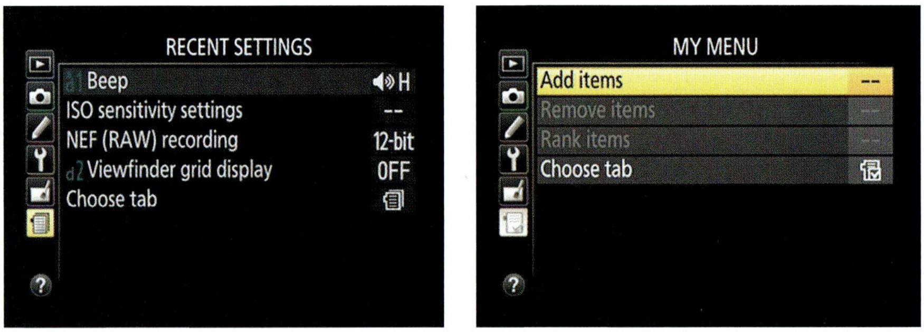

Figure 1-11: The Recent Settings menu offers quick access to the last 20 menu options you selected; the My Menu menu enables you to design a custom menu.

Here's what the two menus offer:

- *Recent Settings:* This screen lists the 20 menu items you ordered most recently. To adjust those settings, you don't have to wade through all the other menus to look for them — just head to the Recent Settings menu instead.

  To remove an item from the Recent Settings menu, highlight the item and press Delete. Press again to confirm your decision.

- *My Menu:* From this screen, you can create a custom menu that contains your favorite options. Chapter 11 details the steps.

Displaying Help screens

If you see a small question mark in the lower-left corner of a menu, as shown in the left figure in this sidebar, press and hold the Zoom Out button — note the question-mark label above the button — to display information about the current menu option. For example, the right screen here shows the Help screen associated with the White Balance setting. To scroll the screen, keep the button depressed and press the Multi Selector up and down.

You may spot the question-mark symbol blinking in the lower-left corner of the Information display; in this case, the camera's alerting you to a potential shooting problem. Again, just press the Zoom Out button to see what solution the camera suggests. When the symbol isn't blinking, pressing the button displays a screen that explains the current exposure mode.

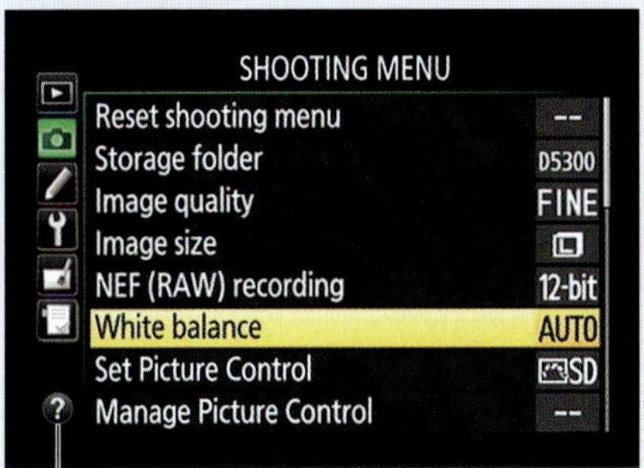

Help symbol

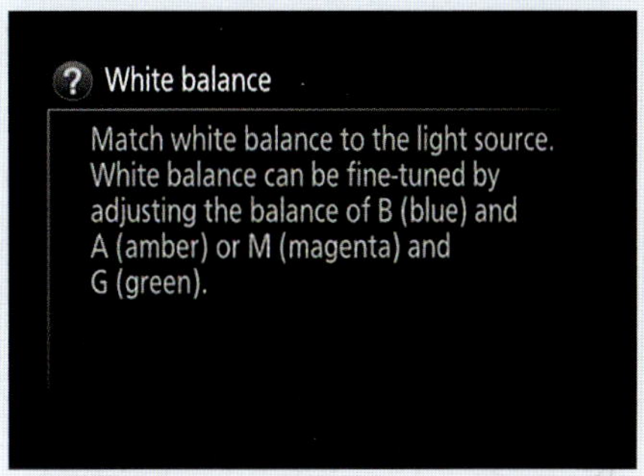

Viewing critical picture settings

Your D5300 gives you the following ways to monitor the most important picture-taking settings:

- **Information display:** The left screen in Figure 1-12 gives you a look at this display, which appears when you first turn on the camera and then disappears after a few seconds. To redisplay it, take any of these steps:
  - *Press the Info button.* Press once to display the screen; press again to turn off the monitor.
  - *Press the shutter button halfway and release it.* Pressing and holding the button halfway down turns off the screen and fires up the autofocusing and exposure metering systems. Because those two systems use battery power, you may want to avoid this technique when the battery is running low.

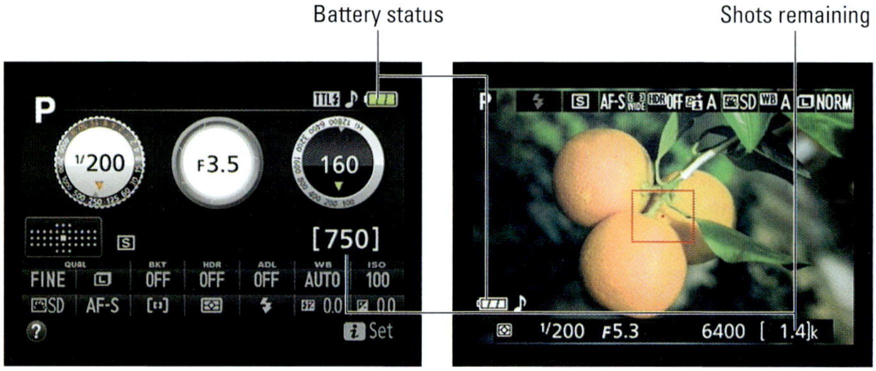

Figure 1-12: Press the Info button to view picture-taking settings on the monitor.

In this book, I explain the display as it works by default. But you can modify its behavior via the Setup menu; look for details in Chapter 11.

Also note that this display is available for viewfinder shooting only; in Live View mode, where you compose pictures using the monitor, the shooting data appears atop the live preview (refer to the right side of Figure 1-12).

TIP

You can vary the type of data displayed on the Live View screen by pressing the Info button. In fact, you can choose from five different display styles; see the last section of this chapter for information about this issue and about Live View shooting in general. Figure 1-12 shows the default display style.

- **Viewfinder:** You also can view some settings at the bottom of the viewfinder, as shown on the left in Figure 1-13. The information that appears depends on the exposure mode.

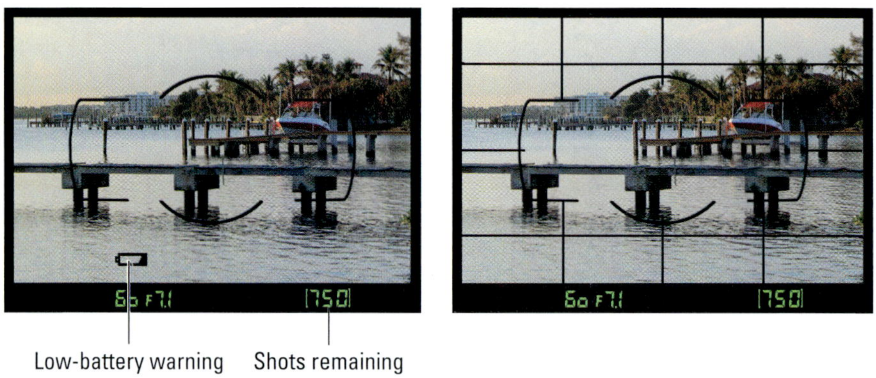

Figure 1-13: Picture settings also appear at the bottom of the viewfinder (left); enable the grid for help with aligning objects in the frame (right).

You can display gridlines in the viewfinder, as shown on the right in the figure, by visiting the Shooting/Display section of the Custom Setting menu and turning on the Viewfinder Grid Display option. The gridlines help you ensure the alignment of objects in your photo — for example, to make sure that the horizon is level in a landscape.

If what you see in Figures 1-12 and 1-13 looks like a confusing mess, don't worry. Many settings relate to options that won't mean anything to you until you explore the advanced exposure modes (P, S, A, and M). But make note of the following bits of data that are helpful in any exposure mode:

- **Battery status indicator:** A full-battery icon (refer to Figure 1-12) shows that the battery is fully charged; if the icon appears empty, look for your battery charger.

  Just for good measure, the camera also displays a low-battery symbol in the viewfinder (refer to the left image in Figure 1-13). If the symbol blinks, the camera won't take more pictures until you charge the battery.

- **Shots remaining:** Labeled in Figures 1-12 and 1-13, this value indicates how many more pictures you can store on the memory card. If the number exceeds 999, the initial *K* appears, to indicate that the value is in the thousands. For example, 1.0K means that you can store 1,000 more pictures (*K* is a universally accepted symbol indicating 1,000 units). The number is rounded down to the nearest hundred. So if the card has room for, say, 1,230 more pictures, the value reads 1.2K.

Adjusting settings via the Information display control strip

The Information display isn't just for checking current picture-taking settings; it also gives you quick access to some of the most critical of those settings. The key to this feature is the ***i*** button. Here's how it works:

1. **Press the *i* button.**

   During viewfinder photography, the Information display appears as shown in Figure 1-14. The top part of the display dims, and the two rows of settings at the bottom of the screen become accessible. The currently selected setting appears highlighted, and its name is displayed at the bottom of the screen. For example, in the left screen in Figure 1-14, the Image Quality option is selected.

   For expediency's sake, I refer to this part of the Information display as the *control strip.*

   In Live View mode, the control strip appears in the middle of the live preview.

2. **Use the Multi Selector to highlight the setting you want to change.**

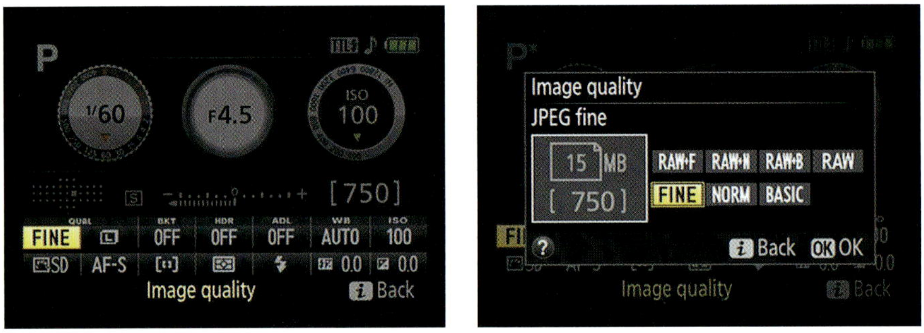

Figure 1-14: Press the *i* button to activate the control strip (left); highlight the option you want to adjust and press OK to display the available settings (right).

3. **Press OK.**

   A screen displays the available settings for the option (refer to the right side of Figure 1-14).

4. **Use the Multi Selector to highlight the desired option, and press OK.**

   You're returned to the control strip. You can then adjust another setting, if needed.

5. **To exit the control strip, press the *i* button again.**

   Or just give the shutter button a quick half-press and release it. The Information display returns to its normal appearance.

Familiarizing yourself with the lens

Because I don't know which lens you're using, I can't give you full instructions on its operation. But the following basics apply to most Nikon AF-S lenses as well as to certain other lenses that support autofocusing — you should explore the lens manual for specifics, of course:

- **Focusing:** First, set the lens to automatic or manual focusing by moving the focus-method switch on the lens. For example, Figure 1-15 shows the switch as it appears on the popular Nikon 18–105mm AF-S lens, which sports the same controls as the 18–140mm lens that's available as a bundle with the D5300. On both lenses, move the switch to the A position for autofocusing and to M for manual focusing.
  - *Autofocusing:* Press and hold the shutter button halfway. See the last section of this chapter for details on autofocusing in the Auto exposure mode; visit Chapter 4 for details on controlling the autofocusing system.
  - *Manual focusing:* Rotate the focusing ring on the lens barrel. The position of the focusing ring varies depending on the lens; I labeled the one found on the 18–105mm lens in Figure 1-15. Chapter 4 has additional tips on manual focusing, too.

Focal-length indicator

Zoom ring

Focusing ring

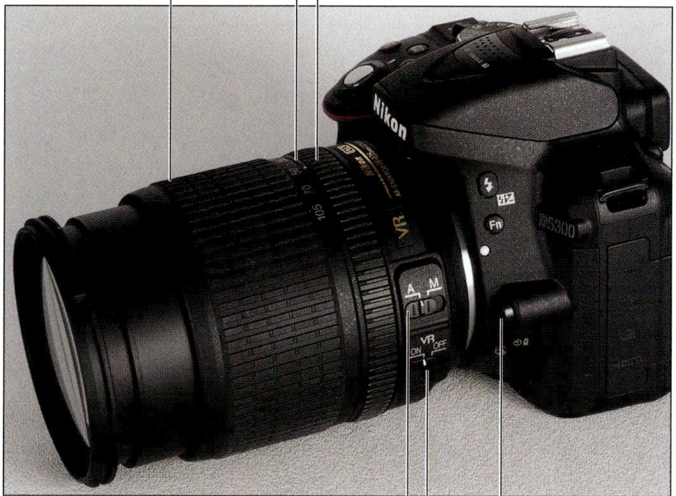

Auto/Manual focus switch

Lens-release button

Vibration Reduction switch

Figure 1-15: Here are a few features that may be found on your lens.

- **Zooming:** If you bought a zoom lens, it has a movable *zoom ring*. The location of the zoom ring on my 18–105mm lens is shown in Figure 1-15. To zoom in or out, rotate the ring.

  TIP

  You can determine the current focal length of the lens by looking at the number that's aligned with the white dot labeled *focal-length indicator* in Figure 1-15. (If you're new to the term *focal length,* the sidebar "Focal length and the crop factor," elsewhere in this chapter, explains the subject.)

- **Enabling Vibration Reduction:** Many Nikon lenses offer *Vibration Reduction,* which compensates for small amounts of camera shake that can occur when you handhold the camera. Camera movement during the exposure can produce blurry images, so turning on Vibration Reduction can help you get sharper handheld shots. When you use a tripod, however, turn the feature off so that the camera doesn't try to compensate for movement that isn't occurring. Turn Vibration Reduction on or off by using the VR switch (refer to Figure 1-15). The available settings vary depending on the lens, so again, see the lens manual for details.

TIP

Focal length and the crop factor

The angle of view that a lens can capture is determined by its *focal length,* or in the case of a zoom lens, the range of focal lengths it offers. Focal length is measured in millimeters.

According to photography tradition, a focal length of 50mm is described as a "normal" lens. Most point-and-shoot cameras feature this focal length, which is a medium-range lens that works well for the type of snapshots that users of those kinds of cameras are likely to shoot.

A lens with a focal length under 35mm is characterized as a *wide-angle* lens because at that focal length, the camera has a wide angle of view, making it good for landscape photography. A short focal length also has the effect of making objects seem smaller and farther away. At the other end of the spectrum, a lens with a focal length longer than 80mm is considered a *telephoto* lens and is often referred to as a *long lens.* With a long lens, the angle of view narrows and faraway subjects appear closer and larger, which is ideal for wildlife and sports photographers.

Note, however, that the focal lengths stated here and elsewhere in the book are *35mm equivalent* focal lengths. Here's the deal: For reasons that aren't really important, when you put a standard lens on most digital cameras, including the D5300, the available frame area is reduced, as if you took a picture on a camera that uses 35mm film negatives and cropped it.

This *crop factor* varies depending on the camera, which is why the photo industry adopted the 35mm-equivalent measuring stick as a standard. With the D5300, the crop factor is roughly 1.5. In the figure here, the red line indicates the image area that results from the 1.5 crop factor.

When shopping for a lens, it's important to remember this crop factor to make sure that you get the focal length designed for the type of pictures you want to take. Just multiply the lens focal length by 1.5 to determine the actual angle of view. Not sure which focal length to choose? Point your web browser to `http://imaging.nikon.com`, click the link for Nikkor lenses, and then click the link for the Nikkor Lenses Simulator. Using this interactive tool, you can see exactly how different focal-length lenses capture the same scene.

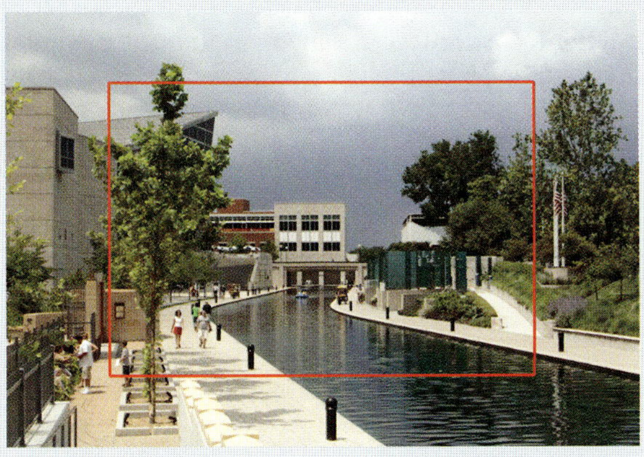

TIP

Vibration Reduction is initiated when you depress the shutter button halfway. If you pay close attention, the image in the viewfinder may appear to be a little blurry immediately after you take the picture. That's a normal result of the Vibration Reduction operation and doesn't indicate a problem with your camera or focus.

- **Removing a lens:** After turning the camera off, press the lens-release button (refer to Figure 1-15), and turn the lens toward that button until it detaches from the lens mount. Put the rear protective cap onto the back of the lens and, if you aren't putting another lens on the camera, cover the lens mount with its cap, too.

WARNING!

Always switch lenses in a clean environment to reduce the risk of getting dust, dirt, and other contaminants inside the camera or lens. Changing lenses on a sandy beach, for example, isn't a good idea. For added safety, point the camera body slightly down when performing this maneuver; doing so helps prevent any flotsam in the air from being drawn into the camera by gravity.

Working with memory cards

As the medium that stores your picture files, the memory card is a critical component of your camera. See the steps at the start of this chapter for help installing a card; follow these tips for buying and maintaining cards:

- **Formatting a card:** The first time you use a new memory card or insert a card that's been used in other devices, you need to *format* it to prepare it to record your pictures. You also need to format the card if you see the blinking letters *FOR* in the viewfinder or if the monitor displays a message requesting formatting.

WARNING!

Formatting erases everything on your memory card. So before you format a card, be sure that you've copied any data on it to your computer. After doing so, get the formatting job done by selecting Format Memory Card from the Setup menu.

- **Removing a card:** After making sure that the memory card access light is off, indicating that the camera has finished recording your most recent photo, turn off the camera. Open the memory card door, depress the memory card slightly, and then let go. The card pops halfway out of the slot, enabling you to grab it by the tail and remove it.

REMEMBER

If you turn on the camera when no card is installed, the symbol [-E-] appears in the lower-right corner of the viewfinder, and the image area of the viewfinder displays a blinking memory card symbol. A message on the monitor also nudges you to insert a memory card. If you have a card in the camera and you get these messages, try taking out the card and reinserting it.

- **Handling cards:** Don't touch the gold contacts on the back of the card. (See the right card in Figure 1-16.) When cards aren't in use, store them in the protective cases they came in or in a memory card wallet. Keep cards away from extreme heat and cold as well.

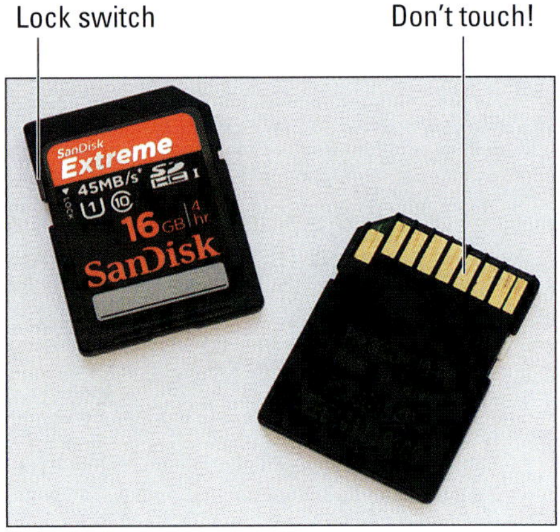

Figure 1-16: Avoid touching the gold contacts on the card.

- **Locking cards:** The tiny switch on the side of the card, labeled *Lock switch* in Figure 1-16, enables you to lock your card, which prevents any data from being erased or recorded to the card. If you insert a locked card into the camera, a message on the monitor alerts you, and the symbol [d blinks in the viewfinder.

  You can protect individual images from accidental erasure by using the camera's Protect feature, which I cover in Chapter 9. Note, though, that formatting the card *does* erase even protected pictures; the safety feature prevents erasure only when you use the camera's Delete function.

- **Using Eye-Fi memory cards:** Your camera works with *Eye-Fi memory cards,* which are special cards that enable you to transmit your files wirelessly to your computer and other devices. That's a cool feature, but, unfortunately, the cards themselves are more expensive than regular cards and require some configuring that I don't have room to cover in this book. For more details, visit `www.eye.fi`.

  If you do use Eye-Fi cards, enable and disable wireless transmission via the Eye-Fi Upload option on the Setup menu. When no Eye-Fi card is installed in the camera, this menu option disappears.

  Of course, for transferring files to a smartphone or tablet, you can instead use the camera's built-in Wi-Fi feature. Chapter 9 shows you how. This feature doesn't permit transferring files to a computer, however.

Taking a Few Final Setup Steps

Your camera offers scads of options for customizing its performance. Later chapters explain settings related to actual picture-taking, such as those that affect flash behavior and autofocusing, and Chapter 11 talks about some options that are better left at their default settings until you're fully familiar with your camera. That leaves just the handful of options covered in the next two sections that I recommend you consider at the get-go.

Cruising the Setup menu

The following options live on the Setup menu, which is the one marked with the little wrench icon. The menu, which appears in Figure 1-17, is a three-page affair (only Page 1 is visible in the figure); use the Multi Selector to scroll the pages up and down and access these settings:

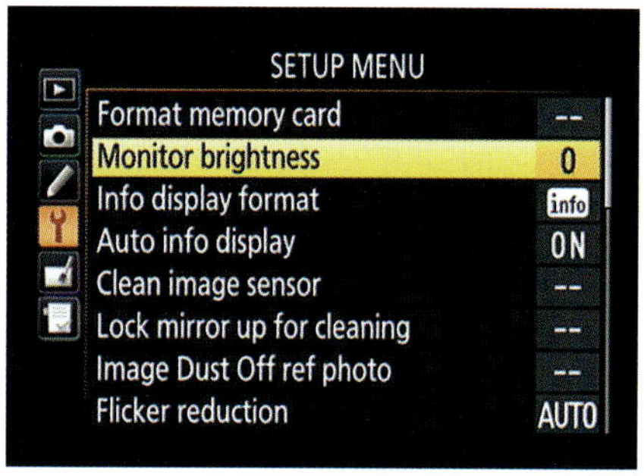

Figure 1-17: Visit the Setup menu to customize the camera's basic operation.

- **Monitor Brightness:** This option enables you to make the display brighter or darker. But if you take this step, what you see on the monitor may not be an accurate rendition of the picture exposure. I recommend that you keep the brightness at the default setting (0).
- **Location Data:** This option controls the built-in GPS feature, which tags your photos with data that indicates where you were when you took the picture. The feature is turned off by default; to enable it, see Chapter 11 for details.
- **Wi-Fi:** Select this option to enable the built-in Wi-Fi transmitter, which enables you to connect the camera to a smartphone or tablet. See Chapter 9 for information about this feature.

  WARNING! To save battery power, keep the Wi-Fi feature turned off, as it is by default, until you're ready to connect the camera to your smart device.
- **Conformity Marking:** I bring this one up just so that you know you can ignore it: When you select the option, you see logos indicating that the camera conforms with certain camera-industry standards. I know you'll sleep better at night with that information.
- **Firmware Version:** Select this option and press OK to view which version of the camera *firmware,* or internal software, your camera runs. You see the firmware items C and L. At the time this book was written, C was version 1.00; L was 2.00.

  WARNING! Keeping your camera firmware up to date is important, so visit the Nikon website (`www.nikon.com`) regularly to find out whether your camera sports the latest version. You can find detailed instructions at the site on how to download and install any firmware updates.

Custom Setting options

Check the status of these Custom Setting menu options before you shoot your first pictures:

- **Beep:** By default, your camera beeps after certain operations, such as after it sets focus when you shoot in autofocus mode. If you need the camera to hush up, open the Custom Setting menu, select the Shooting/Display submenu, and then turn off the Beep option. You can also adjust the volume of the beep through the same menu option. On the Information display, a little musical note icon appears near the top-right corner of the screen when the beep is enabled. Turn off the beep, and the icon appears in a circle with a slash through it.
- **File Number Sequence:** This option, found on the Shooting/Display submenu and highlighted in Figure 1-18, controls how the camera names your picture files. When the option is set to Off, as it is by default, the camera restarts file numbering at 0001 every time you format the memory card or insert a new memory card. Numbering is also restarted if a new image-storage folder is created. (Chapter 11 explains folders.)

  This setup can cause problems over time, creating a scenario where you wind up with multiple images that have the same filename — not on the current memory card, but when you download images to your computer. So set the option to On (refer to Figure 1-18). Note that when you get to picture number 9999, file numbering is still reset to 0001, however. The camera automatically creates a new folder to hold your next 9,999 images.

  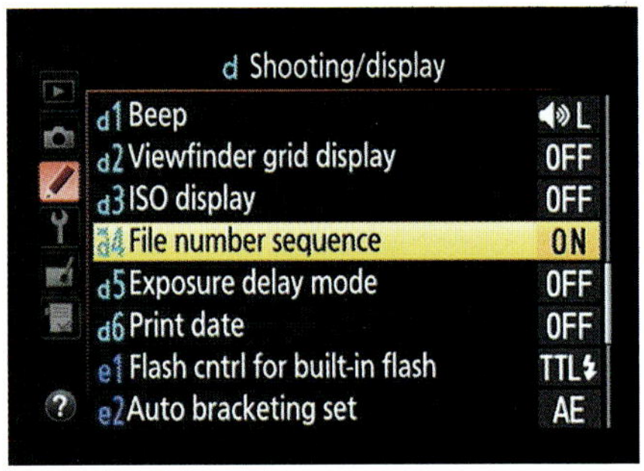

  Figure 1-18: Danger, Will Robinson! Change the File Number Sequence option to On to avoid winding up with multiple pictures that have the same filename.

  As for the Reset option, it enables you to assign the first file number (which ends in 0001) to the next picture you shoot. Then the camera behaves as if you selected the On setting.

  Should you be a really, *really* prolific shooter and snap enough pictures to reach image 9999 in folder 999, the camera will refuse to take another photo until you choose that Reset option and either format the memory card or insert a brand-new one.

- **Print Date:** Using this option, you can imprint on the photo the shooting date, the date and time, or the number of days between the day you took the picture and another date that you specify. This feature works only with pictures that you shoot in the JPEG file format; see the Chapter 2 section related to the Image Quality setting for details about file formats.

  The default Print Date setting, Off, is the way to go; you don't need to permanently mar your photos to find out when you took them. Every picture file includes a hidden vat of text data, or *metadata,* that records the shooting date and time as well as all the camera settings you used — f-stop, shutter speed, and lots more. You can view this data during playback and, after downloading, in the free software provided with your camera as well as in many photo programs.

- **Slot Empty Release Lock:** This cryptically named feature, found on the Controls section of the Custom Setting menu, determines whether the camera lets you take a picture when no memory card is installed in the camera. If you set it to Enable Release, the camera no longer warns you if a memory card isn't installed. You can take a temporary picture, which appears in the monitor with the word *Demo* but isn't recorded anywhere. The feature is provided mainly for use in camera stores, enabling salespeople to demonstrate the camera without having to keep a memory card installed. I can think of no good reason why anyone else would change the setting from the default, Release Locked.

Restoring Default Settings

Should you ever want to return your camera to its original, out-of-the-box state, the camera manual contains a complete list of most of the default settings. Look on the pages that introduce each of the menus.

You can also partially restore default settings by taking these steps:

- **Reset all Shooting Menu options:** Open the Shooting menu, choose Reset Shooting Menu, and press OK. Note that resetting the menu does not affect the Storage Folder option, which is a concern only if you create custom folders, as outlined in Chapter 11.
- **Reset all Custom Setting Menu options:** Choose Reset Custom Settings at the top of the Custom Setting menu.

  Resetting the Custom Setting menu restores the File Number Sequence option to its default, Off, which is most definitely Not a Good Thing. If you restore the menu defaults, be *sure* that you revisit that option and return it to the On setting. See the preceding section for details.

- **Restore critical picture-taking settings *without* affecting all options on the Custom Setting menu:** Use the two-button reset method: Press and hold the Menu button and the ***i*** button simultaneously for longer than 2 seconds. (The little green dots near these two buttons are a reminder of this function.) See the camera manual for a list of exactly which settings are restored.

TIP

One last tip with regard to Custom Setting menu defaults: When you choose a setting other than the default, an asterisk appears above the number of the menu item.

Shooting Your First Pictures in Auto Mode

Your camera is loaded with features for the advanced photographer, enabling you to exert precise control over options such as f-stop, shutter speed, ISO, flash power, and much more. But you don't have to wait until you master those topics to take great pictures, because your camera also offers point-and-shoot simplicity through its Auto exposure mode.

The next two sections walk you through the process of taking a picture in Auto mode using autofocusing and the default picture settings. (Before taking these steps, you may want to visit the preceding section and follow the instructions there for returning the camera to its default state.) The first section explains normal, through-the-viewfinder shooting; the second section shows you how to take a picture in Live View mode.

Viewfinder photography in Auto mode

When you use the viewfinder to frame photos, follow these steps to take a picture:

1. **Set the Mode dial to Auto, as shown in Figure 1-19.**

2. **Set the lens focusing method to auto.**

   As outlined earlier, you make this shift using a switch on the side of the lens. On the lens featured in this book, as well as with the 18–140 mm kit lens, set the switch to A.

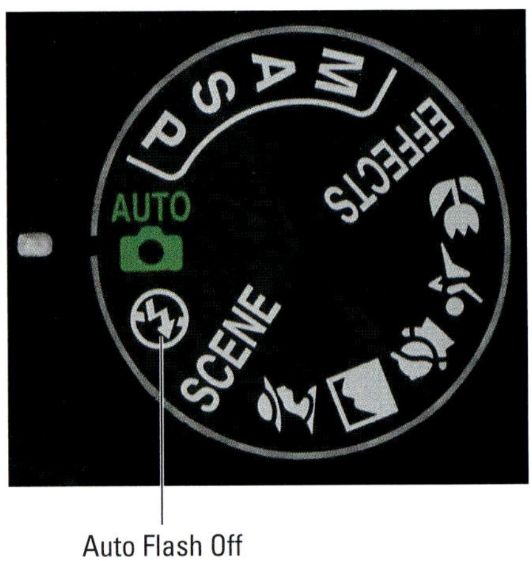

Figure 1-19: Set the Mode dial to Auto for point-and-shoot simplicity.

3. **Looking through the viewfinder, frame your subject so that it appears within the autofocus brackets, labeled in Figure 1-20.**

4. **Press and hold the shutter button halfway down.**

   At this point, the following occurs:

   - *Exposure metering begins.* The autoexposure meter analyzes the light and selects the initial exposure settings. The camera continues monitoring the light up to the time you take the picture, however, and may adjust the exposure settings if lighting conditions change.
   - *The built-in flash pops up if the camera thinks additional light is needed.* If you're in a situation where flash is prohibited, return to Step 1 and change the Mode dial setting from Auto to Auto Flash Off (refer to Figure 1-19). This shooting mode does the same thing as Auto but disables flash.
   - *The autofocus system begins to do its thing.* In dim light, the AF-assist lamp may shoot out a beam of light to help the camera measure the distance between your subject and the lens so that it can better establish focus.

Autofocus brackets

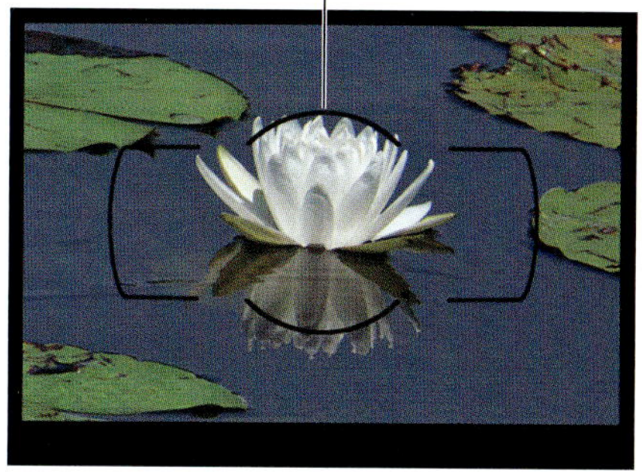

Figure 1-20: Frame your subject so that it's within the area surrounded by the autofocus brackets.

5. **Check the focus indicators in the viewfinder.**

   When the camera has established focus, one or more of the focus points turns red for a split second. The red focus points represent the areas of the frame used to set the focusing distance. (Typically, the camera focuses on the object closest to you.) Then a single black focus point appears, as shown in Figure 1-21. At the bottom of the viewfinder, the focus indicator, labeled in the figure, lights to give you further notice that focus has been achieved.

   If the subject isn't moving, autofocus remains locked as long as you hold the shutter button

Selected focus point

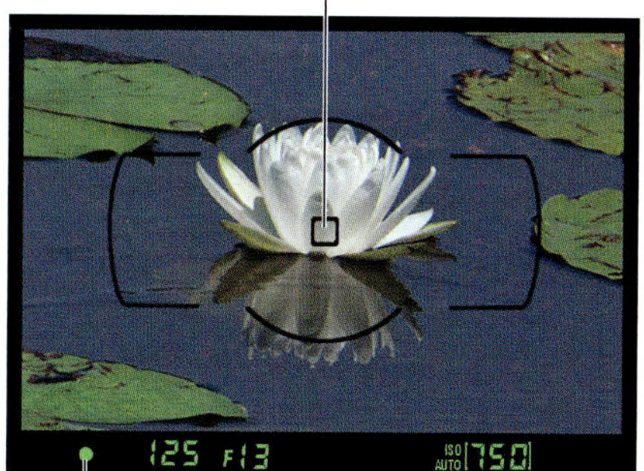

Focus indicator light

Figure 1-21: The green light indicates that the camera locked focus on the object under the focus point.

halfway down. But if the camera detects subject motion, it adjusts focus up to the time you press the button fully to record the picture. As your subject moves, keep it within the autofocus brackets to ensure correct focusing.

6. **Press the shutter button the rest of the way to record the image.**

   TIP

   If the camera refuses to take the picture, don't panic: This error is likely related to autofocusing. By default, the camera insists on achieving focus before it releases the shutter to take a picture. You can press the shutter button all day, and the camera just ignores you if it can't set focus.

   Try backing away from your subject a little — you may be exceeding the minimum focusing distance of the lens. If that doesn't work, the subject just may not be conducive to autofocusing. Highly reflective objects, scenes with very little contrast, and subjects behind fences are some of the troublemakers. The easiest solution? Switch to manual focusing and set focus yourself.

WARNING!

While the camera sends the image data to the memory card, the memory card access lamp lights. Don't turn off the camera or remove the memory card while the lamp is lit or else you may damage both camera and card.

When the recording process is finished, the picture appears briefly on the camera monitor. If the picture doesn't appear or you want to take a longer look at the image, see Chapter 8, which covers picture playback.

Live View photography in Auto mode

Most aspects of shooting in Live View are the same as for viewfinder photography. Autofocusing, however, works quite differently. Here are the steps to take a picture in the Auto Exposure mode using the default settings:

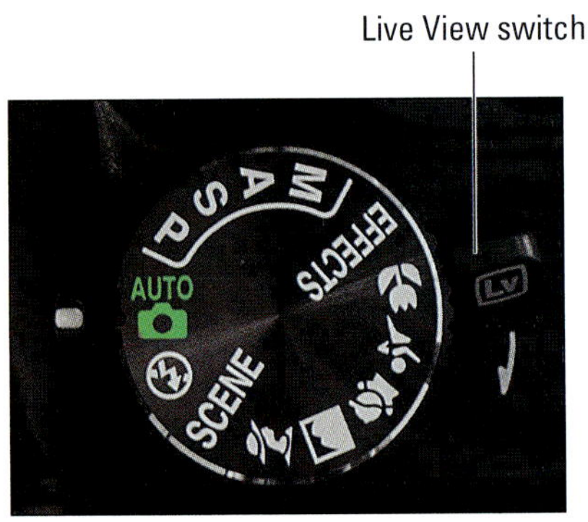

Figure 1-22: Rotate the Live View switch once to enter Live View mode; rotate a second time to return to viewfinder shooting.

1. **Set the Mode dial to Auto, as shown in Figure 1-22.**
2. **To engage Live View, rotate the Live View switch (refer to Figure 1-22).**

   The viewfinder goes dark, and the scene in front of the lens appears on the monitor, along with some shooting data, as shown in Figure 1-23. The figures show the default Live View display; see the tips at the end of this step list for other display options.

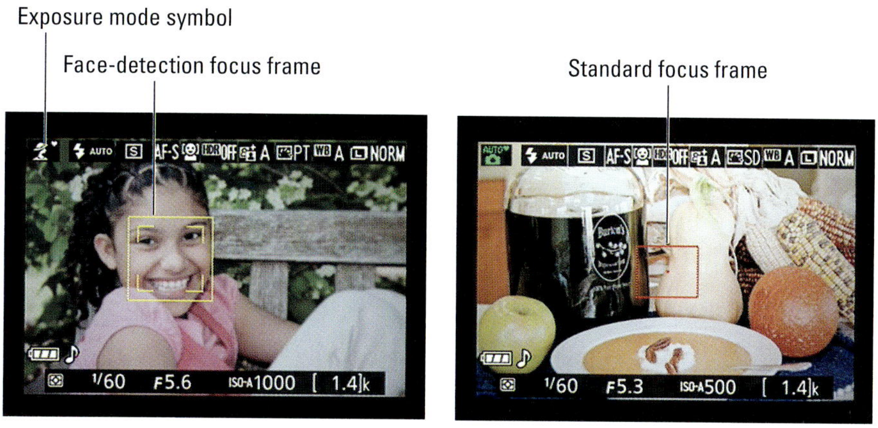

Figure 1-23: For portraits, a focus box appears automatically over the subject's face (left); otherwise, you see a focus box in the center of the screen (right).

3. **Frame your subject in the monitor.**
4. **Check the position of the focusing frame; if necessary, recompose or adjust the frame so that it's over your subject.**

   The autofocus frame that appears depends on your subject:

   - *Portraits:* By default, the camera uses an autofocusing option called Face Priority AF-area mode. If it detects a face, it displays a yellow focus box over it (refer to the left side of Figure 1-23). In a group portrait, you may see several boxes: The one that includes the interior corner marks (refer to the figure) indicates the face that will be used to set the focusing distance. You can use the Multi Selector to move the box over a different face, which is then used to determine the focusing distance.
   - *Other subjects:* Anytime the camera can't detect a face, it switches to Wide Area AF-area mode, with the focus point indicated by a red box in the center of the screen (refer to the right side of Figure 1-23). Again, you can use the Multi Selector to move the focus box over your subject. Press OK to move the focus box quickly back to the center of the frame.

5. **Press the shutter button halfway to set focus and initiate exposure metering.**

   When focus is set, the focus box turns green and you hear a beep (assuming that you didn't disable it via the Custom Setting menu). In dim lighting, the built-in flash pops up.

   In Live View mode, the camera always locks focus when you press the shutter button halfway, even if the subject is moving. If you want the camera to track focus on a moving subject, you must shift from the default Focus mode option AF-S (for single-servo autofocus) to AF-F (full-time servo) mode. Chapter 4 explains the details.

What does [r 24] in the display mean?

When you look through the viewfinder, the initial value in brackets at the right end of the data display indicates the number of additional pictures that can fit on your memory card. For example, in the left image in this sidebar, the value shows that the card can hold 856 more images. The same value appears in the lower-right corner of the Live View display.

As soon as you press the shutter button halfway, which kicks the autofocus and exposure mechanisms into action, that value changes to show you how many pictures can fit in the camera's *memory buffer,* which is a temporary storage tank where the camera stores picture data until it has time to record that data to the memory card. In the right image here, for example, the r 24 value tells you that the buffer can hold 24 pictures. This system exists so that you can take a continuous series of pictures without waiting between shots until each image is written to the card. When the buffer is full, you can't take another picture until the camera catches up with its recording work.

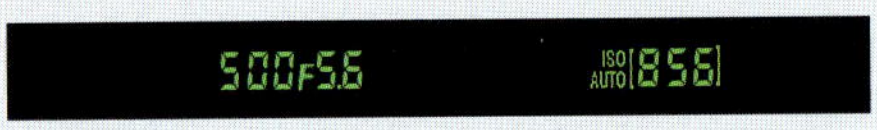

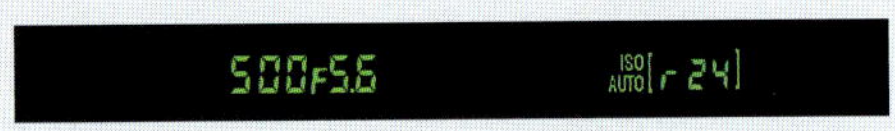

6. **Press the shutter button all the way down to record the picture.**

   The photo appears briefly on the monitor, and then the live preview reappears.

After you press the shutter button halfway, the camera may shift automatically to one of four Scene modes that are designed to capture specific types of subjects. The exposure-mode symbol labeled in Figure 1-23 is your cue that this switch was made. For example, in the left screen in the figure, the camera shifted to Portrait mode, represented by the lady with a hat. The other three Scene modes that the camera may select are Landscape (mountain symbol); Close Up (flower symbol); and Night Portrait (head-and-shoulders with a star). If you see the word *Auto* with a heart, as on the right screen of the figure, the camera is sticking with ordinary Auto mode. If you prefer to select a Scene type directly, see the first section of Chapter 2.

To close out this chapter, here are a few important pointers to remember when you use Live View mode, whether you're shooting photos or movies:

- **Press the Info button to change the type of data that's displayed on the monitor.** You can choose from five displays:
  - *Show Photo Indicators:* Reveals extensive shooting data for still photography (refer to Figure 1-23). The display uses this mode by default. (I detail each value or symbol as I explain the relevant features later in the book.)

- *Show Movie Indicators:* Displays data related to movie recording, as shown on the first screen in Figure 1-24. The transparent gray bar that appears along the top and bottom of the screen shows how much of the vertical image area is excluded from the frame if you set the movie resolution to a setting that produces a 16:9 frame aspect ratio. (The only setting that doesn't produce this ratio is 640 x 424, which captures a 3:2 frame, the same as a still photo.) I discuss this option, along with other movie-recording topics, in Chapter 7.

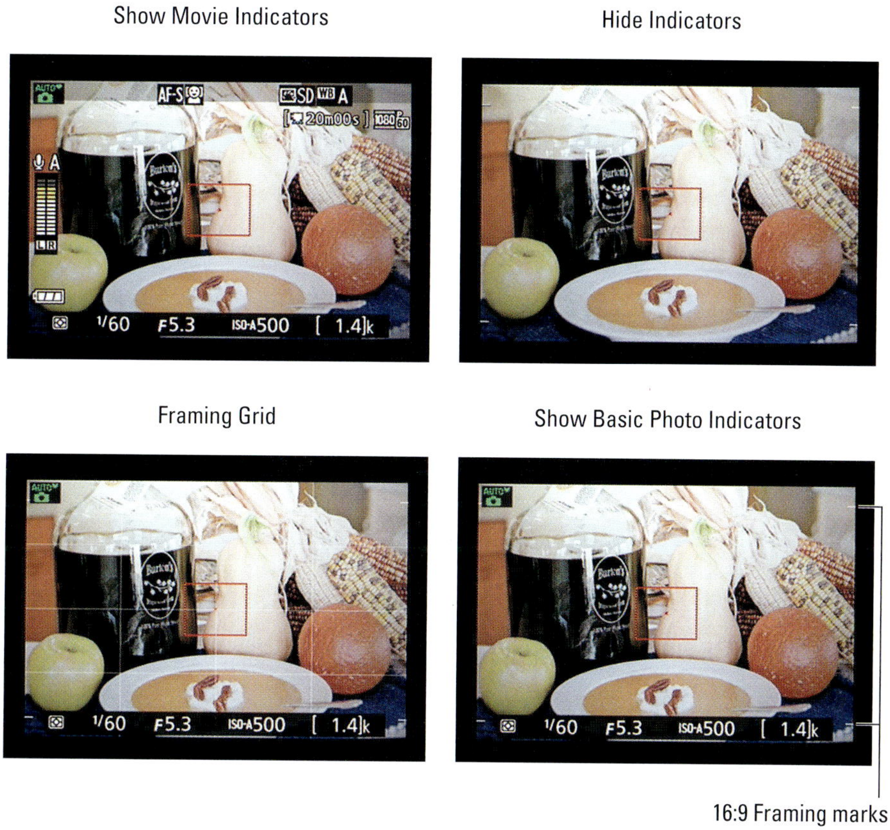

Figure 1-24: Press the Info button to change the Live View display style.

- *Hide Indicators*: Displays only the markings shown in the upper-right corner in Figure 1-24.

  In this display mode, as well as in the two described next, you may see four tiny, horizontal markers near the corners of the display. They take the place of the shaded bars indicating the 16:9 frame area that appears in Show Movie Indicators mode. I labeled two of the markers in Figure 1-24.

- *Framing Grid:* Adds a grid and the 16:9 framing marks (refer to the lower-left corner of Figure 1-24).
- *Show Basic Photo Indicators:* Presents only the basic exposure settings plus the aforementioned movie frame-area markers, as shown in the lower-right corner in the figure.

- **Cover the viewfinder to prevent light from seeping into the camera and affecting exposure.** The camera ships with a cover designed for this purpose. Slide the rubber eyecup that surrounds the viewfinder up and out of the groove that holds it in place; then slide the cover down into the groove. (Orient the cover so that the Nikon label faces the viewfinder.)
- **The monitor turns off by default after ten minutes of inactivity.** When monitor shutdown is 30 seconds away, a countdown timer appears in the upper-left corner of the screen. You can adjust the shutdown timing via the Auto Off Timers option on the Custom Setting menu; Chapter 11 has details.
- **Using Live View for an extended period can harm your pictures and the camera.** In Live View mode, the camera's innards heat up more than usual, and that extra heat can create the proper electronic conditions for *noise,* a defect that gives your pictures a speckled look. Perhaps more importantly, the increased temperatures can damage the camera. For that reason, Live View is automatically disabled if the camera detects a critical heat level. In extremely warm environments, you may not be able to use Live View mode for long before the system shuts down.

  When the camera is 30 seconds or fewer from shutting down, the countdown timer appears in order to let you know how many seconds remain for shooting. The warning doesn't appear during picture playback or when menus are active, however.
- **Aiming the lens at the sun or another bright light also can damage the camera.** Of course, you can cause problems by doing this even during viewfinder shooting, but the possibilities increase when you use Live View. You can harm not only the camera's internal components but also the monitor (not to mention your eyes).
- **Some lights may interfere with the Live View display.** The operating frequency of some types of lights, including fluorescent and mercury-vapor lamps, can create electronic interference that causes the monitor display to flicker or exhibit odd color banding. Changing the Flicker Reduction option on the Setup menu may resolve this issue. At the default setting, Auto, the camera gauges the light and chooses the right setting for you. But you also can choose from two specific frequencies: 50 Hz and 60 Hz. (In the United States and Canada, the standard frequency is 60 Hz; in Europe, it's 50 Hz.)

2

Reviewing Five Essential Picture-Taking Options

In This Chapter

- Selecting an exposure mode
- Changing the shutter-release mode
- Choosing the right Image Size (resolution) setting
- Understanding the Image Quality setting: JPEG or Raw?
- Adding flash

Every camera manufacturer strives to ensure that your initial encounter with the camera is a happy one. To that end, the D5300's default settings are designed to make it easy to take a good picture the first time you press the shutter button. The camera is set to the Auto exposure mode, which means that all you need to do is frame, focus, and shoot, as outlined at the end of Chapter 1.

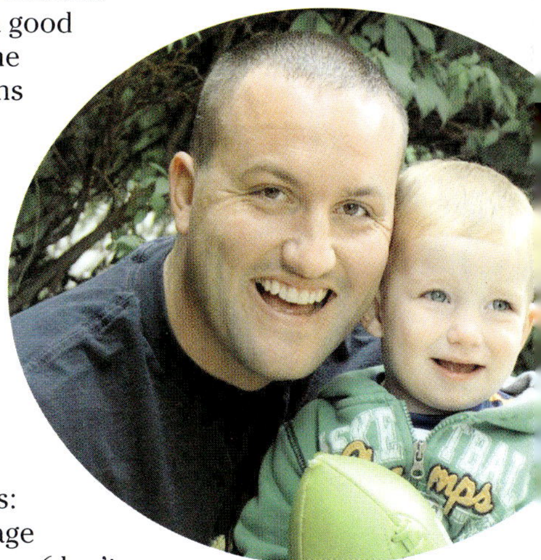

Although the default settings deliver acceptable pictures in many cases, they don't produce optimal results in every situation. You may be able to take a decent portrait in Auto mode, for example, but by tweaking a few settings, you can turn that decent portrait into a stunning one.

This chapter helps you start fine-tuning the camera settings by explaining five basic picture-taking options: exposure mode, shutter-release mode, image size, image quality, and flash. They're not the most exciting features (don't think I didn't notice you stifling a yawn), but they make a big difference in how easily you can capture the photo you have in mind. You should review these settings before each photo outing.

Choosing an Exposure Mode

The first setting to consider is the exposure mode, which you select via the Mode dial, shown in Figure 2-1. Your choice determines how much control you have over two critical exposure settings — aperture and shutter speed — as well as many other options, including those related to color settings and flash photography.

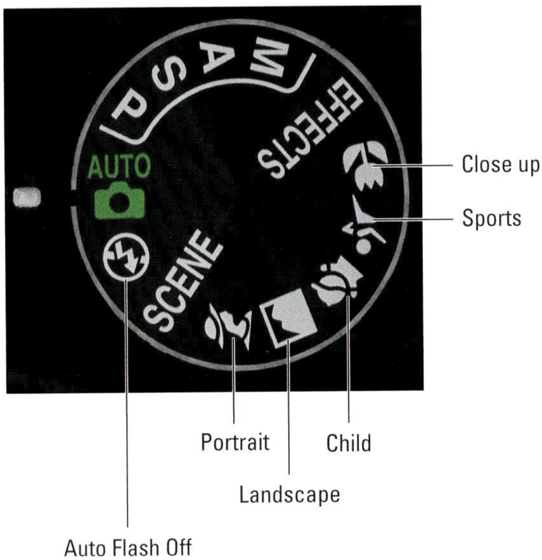

Figure 2-1: The Mode dial determines how much input you have over exposure, color, and other picture options.

Your choices fall into three categories: fully automatic; semiautomatic; and full manual. The next three sections provide the background you need to choose the option.

Fully automatic exposure modes

My guess is that you bought this book for help with using the camera's advanced exposure modes, so that's what the rest of this book covers. But until you have time to digest that information — or if you just need a break from thinking about the advanced options — you can always take advantage of the following point-and-shoot modes:

- **Auto and Auto Flash Off:** The camera analyzes the scene and selects what it considers the most appropriate settings to capture the image. The only difference between the two modes is that Auto Flash Off disables flash; in Auto mode, you can choose from three Flash modes, which I detail later in this chapter. Again, Chapter 1 shows you how to take a picture using both Auto and Auto Flash Off modes.

- **Scene modes:** You also get a batch of automatic modes designed to capture specific subjects in ways deemed best according to photography tradition. For example, in Portrait mode, skin tones are manipulated to appear warmer and softer, and the background appears blurry to bring attention to your subject, as shown on the left in Figure 2-2; in Landscape mode, greens and blues are intensified, and the camera tries to maintain sharpness in both near and distant objects, as shown on the right in the figure.

Portrait mode Landscape mode

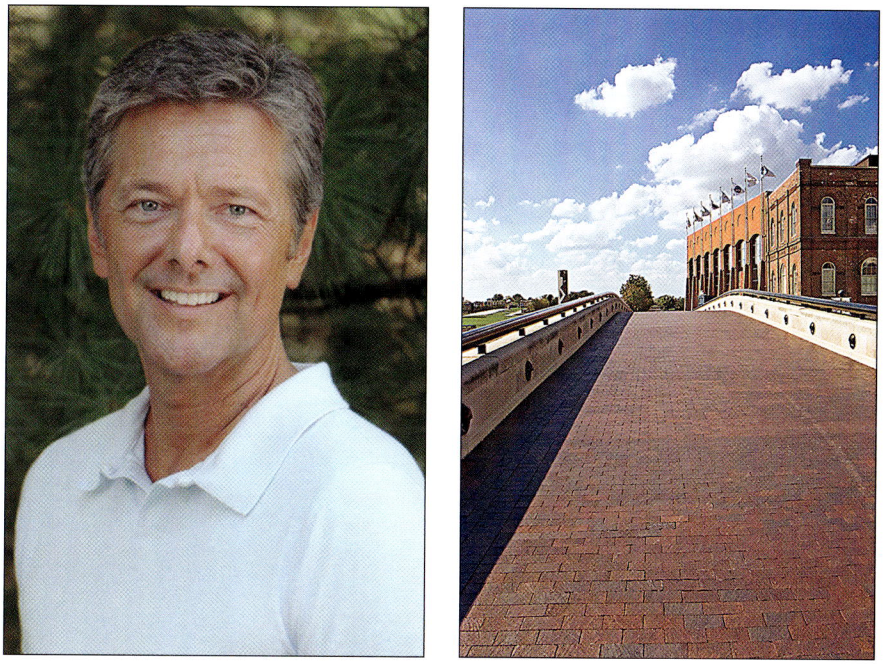

Figure 2-2: Portrait mode produces pleasant skin tones and a soft background; Landscape mode delivers vivid colors and keeps both foreground and background objects sharp.

REMEMBER

Five Scene modes have their own positions on the Mode dial (refer to Figure 2-1). To use these modes, just rotate the Mode dial to your desired setting.

To access the other Scene mode options, set the Mode dial to Scene. An icon representing the current Scene mode appears in the upper-left corner of the screen, as shown on the left in Figure 2-3. Rotate the Command dial to shift to the scene selection screen, as shown on the right; keep spinning the dial to cycle through the Scene types. (The figures show how things look when you're using the viewfinder to frame shots; the display looks slightly different in Live View mode, but you adjust the setting using the same technique.)

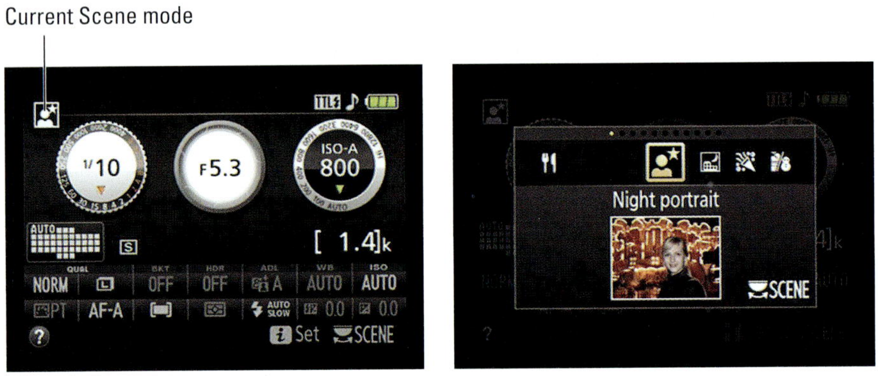

Figure 2-3: After setting the Mode dial to Scene, rotate the Command dial to scroll through additional Scene types.

After you exit the selection screen, you can press the Zoom Out button to display a Help screen with more information about the chosen mode.

For the most part, the process of taking pictures in the Scene modes is the same as for shooting in Auto mode. For a few Scene modes, however, some variations come into play:

- *Close Up, Candlelight, and Food:* In Auto mode (and in most Scene modes), the camera selects the focus point, typically focusing on the object closest to the lens. But in these three modes, the center focus point is used by default, so frame the picture with your subject under that point. Or you can press the Multi Selector to choose a different focus point. (You may need to give the shutter button a quick half-press to wake up the camera before you can do so.)
- *Sports and Pet Portrait:* Again, the center focus point is selected by default, and you can choose a different point by using the Multi Selector. Start by framing your subject under the focus point, and then press and hold the shutter button halfway. If the subject leaves the selected focus point, the camera looks to the other available focus points for focusing information, adjusting focus as necessary up to the time you press the button the rest of the way to take the shot.

  Sports mode and Pet Portrait mode also use the Continuous High shutter-release setting, which means that the camera records a burst of images as long as you hold down the shutter button. See the later section "Setting the Release Mode" for more about this setting.

- **Effects:** This mode works like Auto except that the camera applies one of nine special effects to the picture. Chapter 10 provides details on Effects mode and also explains how you can apply effects to existing pictures by using options on the Retouch menu.

WARNING!

Because all these modes are designed to make picture-taking simple, they prevent you from accessing many camera features. You can control the rest of the settings covered in this chapter and also adjust certain aspects of the camera's autofocusing behavior (Chapter 4 tells you how), but that's about it. Options that are off-limits appear dimmed on the menus and Information and Live View displays. If you press a button that leads to an advanced setting, the monitor displays a message telling you that the option is unavailable.

TIP

Scene modes in focus (or not)

When you focus the camera, you determine the point of sharpest focus. The distance to which the focus zone extends from that point — photographers call it *depth of field* — depends in part on the *aperture setting,* or *f-stop,* which is an exposure control. Some Scene modes are designed to choose aperture settings that deliver a certain depth of field. The Portrait, Child, and Close Up modes, for example, try to use a wide aperture (low f-stop number) because doing so shortens the depth of field, rendering backgrounds softly focused — an artistic choice that most people prefer for those types of shots. On the flip side, Landscape mode tries to use a small aperture (high f-stop number), which produces a large depth of field, maintaining sharpness in both foreground and background objects.

However, the range of apertures that the camera can select varies, depending on the light. In dim lighting, an open aperture is needed in order to properly expose the picture, and in bright light, a small aperture may be required in order to avoid overexposing the picture. Additionally, the range of available aperture settings varies from lens to lens, and the amount of background blurring also increases as the distance between your subject and the background grows. Depth of field is affected by the lens focal length and the subject-to-camera distance, too. Long story short: How much depth of field any Scene mode produces varies from shot to shot.

Another exposure-related control, *shutter speed,* affects how sharp moving subjects appear. At slow shutter speeds, moving objects appear blurry; at fast shutter speeds, they appear sharp.

In Sports and Pet Portrait modes, the camera tries to select a shutter speed fast enough to freeze action, but in dim lighting, that may not be possible: The less light that's available, the slower the shutter speed that's needed to expose the photo — so even in these two modes, a moving subject may appear blurry. Additionally, some Scene modes, such as Night Portrait, Night Landscape, and Candlelight, purposely choose a slow shutter speed to cope with the dark settings. For these modes, it's critical to use a tripod because any camera movement during the exposure can also blur the image.

To fully understand these issues — and to find out how to control the focus and depth of field to a greater extent than the Scene modes allow — visit Chapters 3 and 4.

Semiautomatic exposure modes (P, S, and A)

To take more creative control but still get some exposure assistance from the camera, choose one of these exposure modes, all detailed in Chapter 3:

- **P (programmed autoexposure):** The camera selects the aperture and shutter speed necessary to ensure a good exposure. But you can rotate the Command dial to choose from different combinations of the two to vary the creative results. For example, you might use a fast shutter speed to freeze action, or you might go in the other direction, choosing a shutter speed slow enough to blur the action, which creates a heightened sense of motion.
- **S (shutter-priority autoexposure):** You rotate the Command dial to select the shutter speed, and the camera selects the proper aperture to properly expose the image. This mode is ideal for capturing moving subjects because it gives you direct control over the shutter speed.
- **A (aperture-priority autoexposure):** In this mode, you rotate the Command dial to choose the aperture, and the camera automatically chooses a shutter speed to properly expose the image. Because aperture affects depth of field (the distance over which objects in a scene remain acceptably sharp), this setting works well for portraits because you can select an aperture that results in a soft, blurry background, putting the emphasis on your subject. For landscape shots, on the other hand, you might choose an aperture that keeps the entire scene sharply focused so that both near and distant objects have equal visual weight.

TIP

These modes give you access to all camera features. So even if you're not ready to explore aperture and shutter speed, go ahead and set the Mode dial to P if you need to access a setting that's off-limits in the fully automated modes. The camera then operates pretty much as it does in Auto mode but doesn't limit you to the most basic picture-taking settings.

Manual exposure mode (M)

In Manual mode, you take the exposure reins completely, selecting both aperture and shutter speed as follows:

- **To set the shutter speed:** Rotate the Command dial.
- **To set the aperture:** Press the Exposure Compensation button while rotating the Command dial.

Even in this mode, the camera offers an assist by displaying an exposure meter to help you dial in the right settings. (See Chapter 3 for details.) You have complete control over all other picture settings, too.

REMEMBER

One important and often misunderstood aspect of Manual exposure mode: Setting the Mode dial to M has no bearing on focusing. You can still choose manual focusing or autofocusing, assuming that your lens offers autofocusing. Just set the lens switch to the focusing method you prefer.

Setting the Release Mode

By using the Release mode setting, you tell the camera whether to capture a single image each time you press the shutter button; to record a burst of photos as long as you hold down the shutter button; or to use Self-Timer mode, which delays the image capture until a few seconds after you press the shutter button. You also get two options related to wireless remote control shooting and Quiet Shutter mode, which dampens the normal shutter-release sounds.

Why *Release mode?* It's short for *shutter-release mode.* Pressing the shutter button tells the camera to release the *shutter* — an internal light-control mechanism — so that light can strike the image sensor and expose the image. Your choice of Release mode determines when and how that action occurs.

On the Information screen and Live View display, the current Release mode is indicated by the icons labeled in Figure 2-4. (See the next several sections for a look at the icon representing each mode.) Note that the Live View screen in the figure shows the default data-display mode; if your screen shows a different assortment of data, press the Info button to cycle through the available display modes.

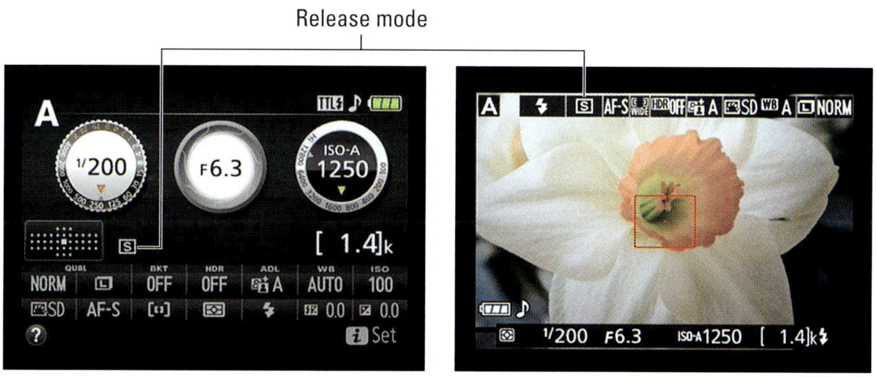

Figure 2-4: This S represents the Single Frame shutter-release option, which produces one picture for each press of the shutter button.

To adjust the Release mode setting, use these methods:

- **Release Mode button:** Press this button, labeled in Figure 2-5, to display the selection screen shown in Figure 2-6. Use the Multi Selector to highlight the setting you want to use and then press OK.

- **Shooting menu:** Scroll to the second page of the menu to find the setting, as shown in Figure 2-7.

With those basics out of the way, the next few sections explain how each Release mode works.

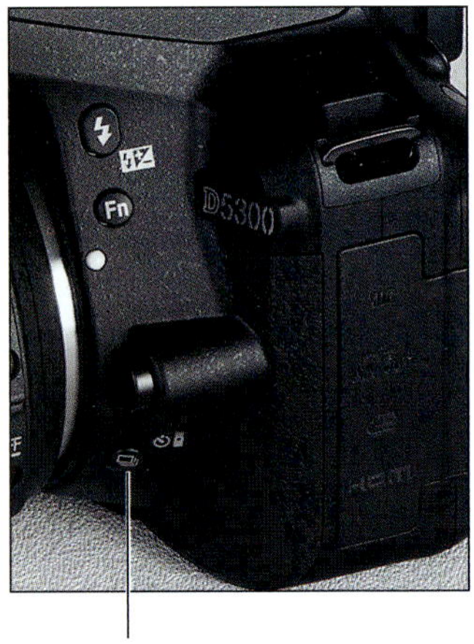

Figure 2-5: The Release Mode button offers the fastest access to the setting.

Single Frame and Quiet Shutter Release modes

Single Frame Release mode captures one picture each time you press the shutter button. It's the default setting for all exposure modes except the Sports and Pet Portrait Scene modes.

Quiet Shutter mode works just like Single Frame mode but makes less noise as it goes about its business. First, the camera disables the beep that it emits by default when it achieves focus. (You can turn off the beep for other Release modes via the Beep option, found in the Shooting/Display section of the Custom Setting menu.)

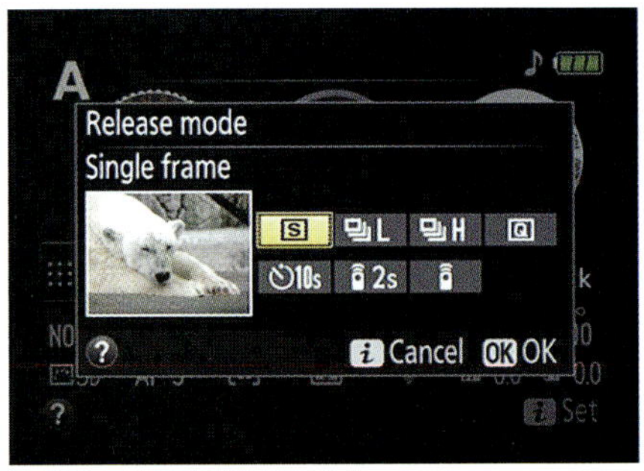

Figure 2-6: Use the Multi Selector to highlight your choice and press OK.

Additionally, Quiet Shutter mode affects the operation of the internal mirror that causes the scene coming through the lens to be visible in the viewfinder. Normally, the mirror flips up when you press the shutter button and then flips back down after the shutter opens and closes. This mirror movement makes some noise. In Quiet Shutter mode, you can prevent the mirror from flipping back down by keeping the shutter button fully pressed after the shot. This way, you can delay the sound made by the final mirror movement to a moment when the noise won't be objectionable.

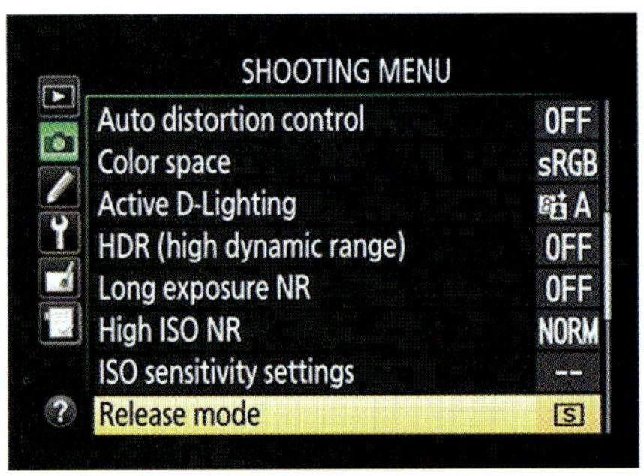

Figure 2-7: The Release Mode option is also found on the Shooting menu.

Continuous (burst mode) shooting

Continuous Low and Continuous High enable *burst mode* shooting. That is, the camera records a continuous series of images for as long as you hold down the shutter button, making it easier to capture fast-paced action.

Here's how the two modes differ:

- **Continuous Low:** The camera can capture as many as 3 frames per second (fps).
- **Continuous High:** Records as many as 5 fps, depending on the Image Quality setting, which I cover later in this chapter. If you select the Image Quality setting that produces 14-bit RAW (NEF) files, the maximum frame rate is 4 fps.

A few critical details about these two Release modes:

- **You can't use flash.** Continuous mode doesn't work with flash because the time that the flash needs to recycle between shots slows down the capture rate too much. If flash is enabled, you get one shot per each press of the shutter button, as in Single Frame mode.
- **Images are stored temporarily in the memory buffer.** The camera has some internal memory — a *buffer* — where it stores picture data until it has time to record all the photos in a burst of shots to the memory card. The number of pictures the buffer can hold depends on certain camera settings, such as Image Quality. When you press the shutter button halfway, the shots remaining value in the lower-right corner of the viewfinder and Live View display changes to show an estimate of how many pictures will fit in the buffer.

  WARNING! After shooting a burst of images, wait for the memory card access light to go out before turning off the camera. (The light is in the lower-right corner of the camera back, just below the Delete button.) That's your signal that the camera has moved all data from the buffer to the memory card. Turning off the camera before that happens may corrupt the image file.
- **Your mileage may vary.** The number of frames per second depends on several factors, including shutter speed. To achieve the highest rate, the shutter speed must be 1/250 second or faster. Additionally, although you can capture as many as 100 frames in a single burst, the frame rate can drop if the buffer gets full.
- TIP **Continuous Low is enough for all but the fastest action.** Unless you're shooting a subject that's moving at a really fast pace, not too much changes between frames when you shoot at 5 fps. So, when you use Continuous High, you typically wind up with lots of shots that show the exact same thing, wasting space on your memory card. Continuous Low usually gives you plenty of frames to capture the shot without the unnecessary file bloat.

Self-timer shooting

You're no doubt familiar with Self-Timer mode, which delays the shutter release for a few seconds after you press the shutter button, giving you time to dash into the picture. Here's how it works on the D5300: After you press the shutter button, the AF-assist lamp on the front of the camera starts to blink, and the camera emits a series of beeps (assuming that you didn't disable its voice via the Beep option on the Custom Setting menu). A few seconds later, the camera captures the image.

By default, the camera waits ten seconds after you press the shutter button and then records a single image. But you can tweak the delay time and capture as many as nine shots at a time. Set your preferences by using the Self-Timer option, found in the Timers/AE Lock section of the Custom Setting menu and shown in Figure 2-8. Here's what you need to know about the two settings:

- **Self-Timer Delay:** Choose a delay time of 2, 5, 10, or 20 seconds. The selected delay time appears with the Self-Timer symbol in the Information and Live View displays. (Refer to Figure 2-4 for help locating the symbol in the displays.)
- **Number of Shots:** Specify how many frames you want to capture with each press of the shutter button; the maximum is nine. When you record multiple frames, shots are taken at 4-second intervals.

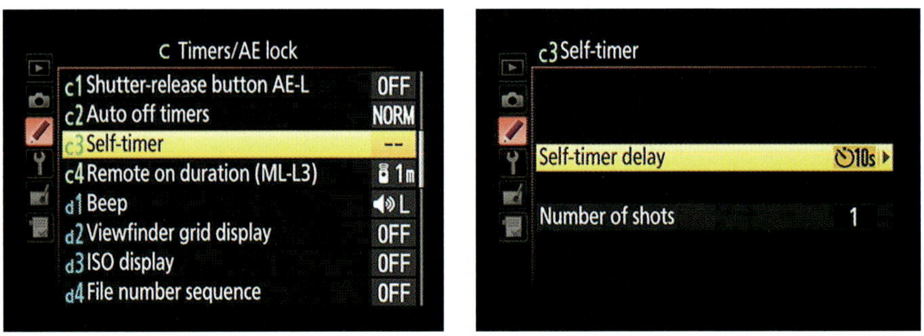

Figure 2-8: You can adjust the self-timer capture delay and the number of frames taken with each press of the shutter button.

Two more points about self-timer shooting:

- **After the specified number of shots are captured, the camera resets the Release mode to Single Frame, Quiet, or Continuous Low or High.** Turning off the camera also resets the Release mode. Either way, the camera selects the Release mode you used before Self-Timer mode.
- **Cover the viewfinder during self-timer shooting.** Otherwise, light may seep into the camera through the viewfinder and affect exposure. Your

camera comes with a cover made just for this purpose. Remove the rubber eyepiece that surrounds the viewfinder, and then insert the cover in its place.

Wireless remote control modes

Two other Release mode settings relate to the Nikon ML-L3 wireless remote control and work as follows:

- **Delayed Remote:** After you press the shutter-release button on the remote unit, the AF-assist lamp blinks for about two seconds, and then the camera takes the picture.
- **Quick Response Remote:** The image is captured immediately. In this mode, the AF-assist lamp blinks after the shot is taken.

Normally, the camera cancels out of the remote control modes if it doesn't receive a signal from the remote after about one minute. You can adjust this timing by using the Remote On Duration option, located on the Timers/AE Lock submenu of the Custom Setting menu. The maximum delay time is 15 minutes; keep in mind that a shorter delay time saves battery life. After the delay time expires, the camera resets itself to either Single Frame, Quiet Shutter, or Continuous Low or Continuous High mode, depending on which mode you last used. The Release mode is also reset to one of those modes if you turn off the camera.

As with self-timer shooting, it's a good idea to cover the viewfinder when you're using these modes, to prevent exposure problems that can be caused by light entering the camera through the viewfinder.

These Release modes are not meant to be used with a wired remote control. Select one of the other Release mode settings, and then press the shutter-release button on the remote to trigger the shutter. Wired or wireless, see your remote's operating guide for more details on using the unit.

Investigating other shutter-release options

In addition to the official Release mode setting, your camera offers two other features related to triggering the shutter release: Exposure Delay Mode and Interval Timer Shooting. Check 'em out in the next two sections.

Exposure Delay Mode

One component of a dSLR camera is a mirror that moves every time you press the shutter button. The vibration caused by the mirror action can cause a small amount of blur when you use a very slow shutter speed, shoot with a long telephoto lens, or take extreme close-ups.

To cope with that issue, some cameras offer *mirror-lockup* shooting, which delays opening the shutter until after the mirror movement is complete. Although the D5300 doesn't offer mirror-lockup shooting — its mirror-lockup function is provided solely for the purpose of accessing the sensor for cleaning — it does offer another solution: Exposure Delay Mode. When you enable this feature, the camera waits about 1 second after the mirror is raised to release the shutter, ensuring that the mirror movement is complete before the image is recorded.

Look for the Exposure Delay Mode option on the Shooting/Display block of the Custom Setting menu, as shown in Figure 2-9. You can use Exposure Delay Mode with any Release mode. Just don't forget that you enabled the feature or else you'll drive yourself batty trying to figure out why the camera isn't responding to your shutter-button finger. I say this from experience. . . .

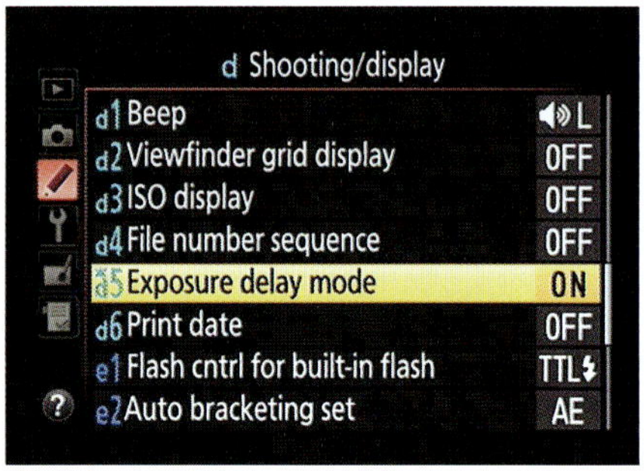

Figure 2-9: Exposure Delay Mode helps ensure that the movement of the camera's internal mirror doesn't create image blur.

Interval Timer Shooting

With Interval Timer Shooting, you can set the camera to automatically release the shutter at intervals ranging from seconds to hours apart. This feature enables you to capture a subject as it changes over time — a technique commonly known as *time-lapse photography* — without having to stand around pressing the shutter button the whole time. Here's how to take advantage of this feature:

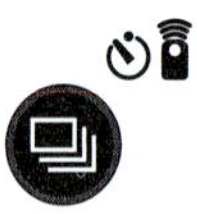

1. **Set the Release mode to Single Frame or Quiet Shutter.**

   The fastest way to access the setting is to press the Release Mode button on the front-left side of the camera.

2. **Display the Shooting menu, highlight Interval Timer Shooting (as shown on the left in Figure 2-10), and press OK.**

   The screen on the right in Figure 2-10 appears.

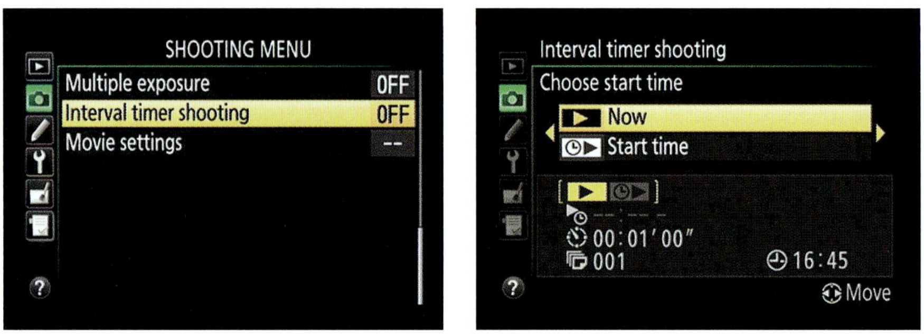

Figure 2-10: The Interval Timer Shooting feature enables you to do time-lapse photography.

3. **To begin setting up your capture session, highlight Now or Start Time:**

   - To start the captures right away, highlight Now.
   - To set a later start time, highlight Start Time.

4. **Press the Multi Selector right to display the capture-setup screen.**

   If you selected Start Time in Step 3, the screen looks like the one shown in Figure 2-11. At the bottom of the screen, values appear for three available options: Start Time, Interval (time between shots), and Number of Times (total number of frames recorded). I labeled these values in the figure. Note that if you selected Now in Step 3, the Start Time option is dimmed and the Interval option is highlighted instead.

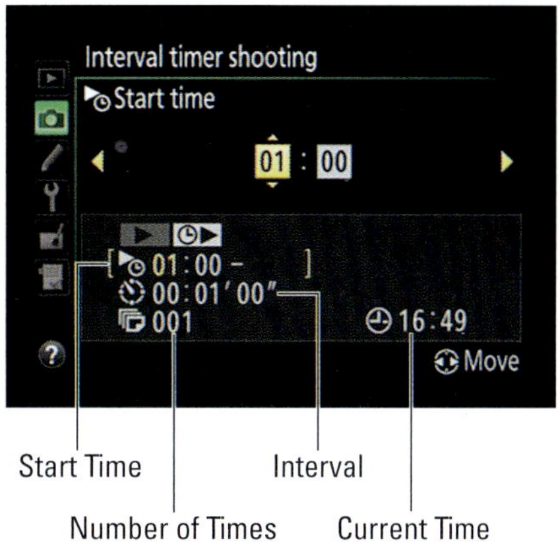

Figure 2-11: Press the Multi Selector right or left to cycle through the setup options; press up or down to change the highlighted value.

5. **Set up your recording session.**

   At the top of the screen, little value boxes appear. The highlighted box is the active option and relates to the setting that's highlighted at the bottom of the screen. For example, in the figure, the hour box for the Start Time setting is active. Press the Multi Selector right or left to cycle through the value boxes; to change the value in a box, press the Multi Selector up or down.

   A few notes about these options:

   - *The Interval and Start Time options are based on a 24-hour clock.* The current time appears in the lower-right corner of the screen and is based on the date/time information you entered when setting up the camera.
   - *In the Interval option, the left column box is for the hour setting; the middle, minutes; and the right, seconds.* Make sure that the value you enter is for a longer time than the shutter speed you plan to use.
   - *For the Start Time option, you can set only the hour and minute values.* Again, the Start Time option is available only if you selected Start Time in Step 3.

6. **After setting the capture options, press the Multi Selector right until you see the On and Off options on the screen, as shown in Figure 2-12.**

7. **Highlight On and press OK.**

   If you selected Now as the Start Time option in Step 3, the first shot is recorded about 3 seconds later. If you set a delayed start time, the camera displays the message *Timer Active* for a few seconds.

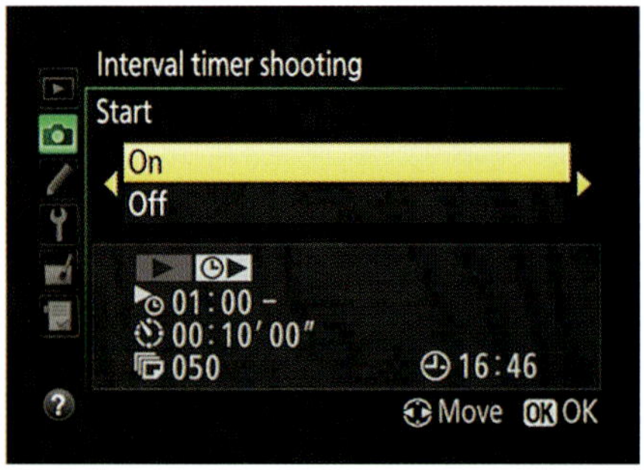

Figure 2-12: Highlight On and press OK to finalize the Interval Timer Shooting setup.

A few final factoids:

- **Interval Timer Shooting isn't available for Live View photography or Effects exposure mode.** The menu option is disabled any time Live View is enabled or the Mode dial is set to Effects.
- **The card access light blinks while Interval Timer Shooting is in progress.** It's the little light just above the Delete button on the back of the camera.
- **To interrupt Interval Timer Shooting, turn off the camera.** Or move the Mode dial to a different setting.
- **You can't adjust camera settings while the interval sequence is in progress.** Make sure that everything is set up to your liking before you begin the interval-shooting session.
- **Autobracketing, high dynamic range (HDR), and multiple-exposure are disabled.** Chapter 3 explains the first two features; Chapter 10 covers the third.
- **If you're autofocusing, be sure that the camera can focus on your subject.** The camera initiates focusing before each shot. See Chapter 4 for details about autofocusing.
- **To prevent exposure miscues, cover the viewfinder.** This prevents light from entering the viewfinder and fooling the exposure meter. Root around in your camera box for the viewfinder cover; then remove the viewfinder's rubber eyepiece and install the cover in its place.
- **When the interval sequence is complete, the Interval Timer Shooting menu option is reset to Off.** The card access light stops blinking shortly after the final image is recorded to the memory card.

One final piece of advice for this section: The camera battery may not contain enough juice for time-lapse photography sessions that span many hours. If you do a lot of this kind of shooting, you may want to invest in the AC power supply.

Checking Image Size and Image Quality

Your preflight camera check should also include a look at the Image Size and Image Quality settings. The first option sets picture resolution; the second, file type.

The names of these settings are a little misleading, though, because the Image Size setting also contributes to picture quality, and the Image Quality setting affects the file size of the picture. Because the two work in tandem to determine quality and size, it's important to consider them together. The next few sections explain each option; following that, I offer a few final tips and show you how to select the settings you want to use.

REMEMBER

Also check out the section related to ISO in Chapter 3; very high ISO settings can also reduce image quality. In this case, a defect known as *noise* can give the picture a speckled appearance.

Considering the Image Size setting (resolution)

The Image Size setting determines how many pixels are used to create your photo. *Pixels* are the square tiles from which digital images are made; you can see some pixels close up in the right image in Figure 2-13, which shows a greatly magnified view of the eye area in the left image.

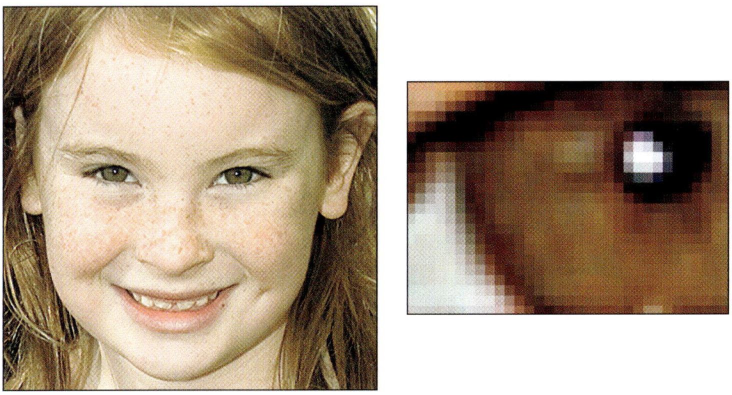

Figure 2-13: Pixels are the building blocks of digital photos.

TECHNICAL STUFF

Pixel is short for *picture element.*

The number of pixels in an image is referred to as *resolution.* You can define resolution in terms of either the *pixel dimensions* — the number of horizontal pixels and vertical pixels — or total resolution, which you get by multiplying those two values. This number is usually stated in *megapixels* (or MP, for short), with one megapixel equal to 1 million pixels.

Your camera offers three Image Size options: Large, Medium, and Small. Table 2-1 lists the resolution values for each setting. (Megapixel values are rounded off.)

Table 2-1 Image Size (Resolution) Options

Setting	*Resolution*
Large	6000 x 4000 (24.0MP)
Medium	4496 x 3000 (13.5MP)
Small	2992 x 2000 (6.0MP)

REMEMBER However, if you select Raw (NEF) as the Image Quality setting, images are captured at the Large setting. You can vary the resolution only for pictures taken in the JPEG format. The upcoming section "Understanding Image Quality options (JPEG or Raw)" explains file formats.

To choose the right Image Size setting, you need to understand the three ways that resolution affects your pictures:

- **Print size:** Pixel count determines the size at which you can produce a high-quality print. When an image contains too few pixels, details appear muddy, and curved and diagonal lines appear jagged. Such pictures are said to exhibit *pixelation.*

  Depending on your photo printer, you typically need anywhere from 200 to 300 pixels per linear inch, or *ppi,* for good print quality. To produce an 8 x 10 print at 200 ppi, for example, you need a pixel count of 1600 x 2000, or about 3.2 megapixels.

  WARNING! Even though many photo-editing programs enable you to add pixels to an existing image — known as *upsampling* — doing so doesn't enable you to successfully enlarge your photo. In fact, upsampling typically makes matters worse.

  To give you a better idea of the impact of resolution on print quality, Figures 2-14, 2-15, and 2-16 show you the same image at 300 ppi, at 50 ppi, and then resampled from 50 ppi to 300 ppi (respectively). As you can see, there's no way around the rule: If you want quality prints, you need the right pixel count from the get-go.

300 ppi

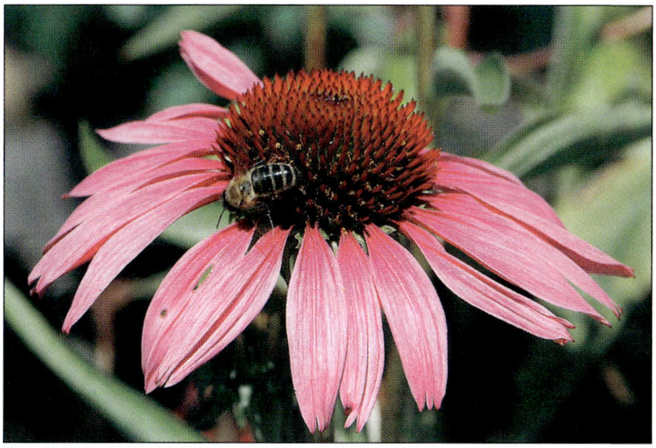

Figure 2-14: A high-quality print depends on a high-resolution original.

50 ppi

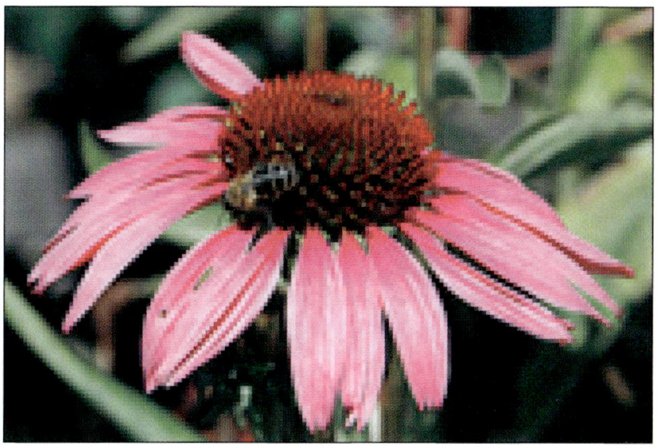

Figure 2-15: At 50 ppi, the image has a jagged, pixelated look.

- **Screen display size:** Resolution doesn't affect the quality of images viewed on a monitor or television or another screen device the way it does for printed photos. Instead, resolution determines the *size* at which the image appears. This issue is one of the most misunderstood aspects of digital photography, so I explain it thoroughly in Chapter 9. For now, just know that you need *way* fewer pixels for onscreen photos than you do for prints. In fact, even the Small resolution setting creates a picture too big to be viewed in its entirety in many e-mail programs.
- **File size:** Every pixel increases the amount of data required to create the picture file. So a higher-resolution image has a larger file size than a low-resolution image.

50 ppi resampled to 300 ppi

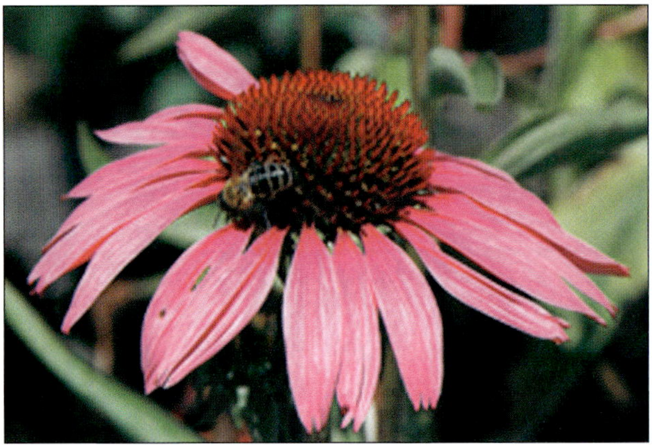

Figure 2-16: Adding pixels in a photo editor doesn't rescue a low-resolution original.

WARNING!

Large files present several problems:

- You can store fewer images on the memory card, on your computer's hard drive, and on removable storage media such as DVDs.
- The camera needs more time to process and store the image data on the memory card after you press the shutter button. This extra time can hamper fast-action shooting.
- When you share photos online, larger files take longer to upload and download.
- When you edit photos in your photo software, your computer needs more resources and time to process large files.

TIP

As you can see, resolution is a bit of a sticky wicket. What if you aren't sure how large you want to print your images? What if you want to print your photos *and* share them online? I take the better-safe-than-sorry route, which leads to the following recommendations:

- **Always shoot at a resolution suitable for print.** You then can create a low-resolution copy of the image for use online. In fact, your camera offers a built-in resizing option that I cover in Chapter 9.
- **For everyday images, Medium is a good choice.** I find Large to be overkill for casual shooting, creating huge files for no good reason. Keep in mind that even at the Small setting, the pixel count (2992 x 2000) gives you enough resolution to produce an 8 x 10-inch print at 200 ppi.

TIP

- **Choose Large for an image that you plan to crop or print very large, or both.** The benefit of maxing out the resolution is that you have the flexibility to crop your photo and still generate a decently sized print of the remaining image. Figure 2-17 offers an example. When I was shooting this photograph, I couldn't get close enough to fill the frame with my main interest — the two juvenile herons at the center of the scene. But because I had the resolution cranked up to Large, I could later crop the shot to the composition you see on the right and still produce a great-looking print. In fact, I could have printed the cropped image at a much larger size than fits here.

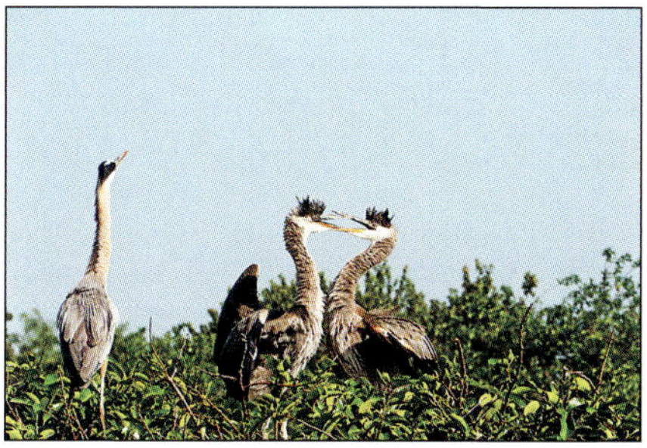

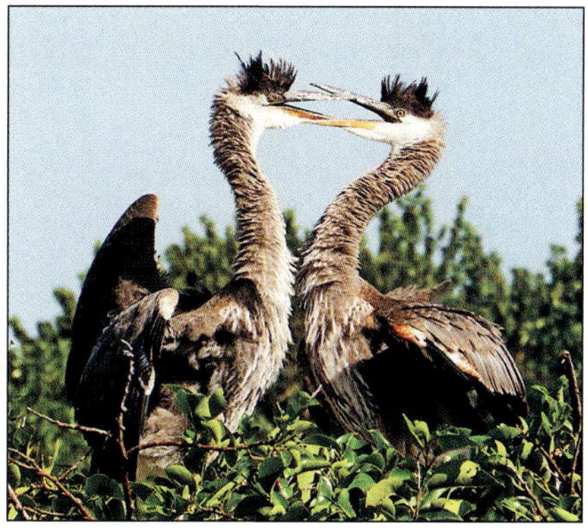

Figure 2-17: A high-resolution original (left) enabled me to crop the photo and still have enough pixels to produce a quality print (right).

- **Reduce resolution if shooting speed is paramount.** If the camera takes too long after you take one shot before it lets you take another, dialing down the resolution may help.

Understanding Image Quality options (JPEG or Raw)

If I had my druthers, the Image Quality option would instead be called File Type because that's what the setting controls. Here's the deal: The file type, sometimes also known as a file *format,* determines how your picture data is recorded and stored. Your choice does affect picture quality, but so does the Image Size setting, as described in the preceding section, and the ISO setting, covered in the next chapter. In addition, your choice of file type has ramifications beyond picture quality.

At any rate, your camera offers two file types: JPEG and Camera Raw — or Raw, for short, which goes by the specific moniker NEF (Nikon Electronic Format) on Nikon cameras. The next couple of sections explain the pros and cons of each format. If your mind is already made up, skip ahead to the section "Setting Image Size and Image Quality," to find out how to make your selection.

Don't confuse *file format* with the Format Memory Card option on the Setup menu. That option erases all data on your memory card; see Chapter 1 for details.

JPEG: The imaging (and web) standard

Pronounced "jay-peg," this format is the default setting on your D5300, as it is on most digital cameras. JPEG is popular for two main reasons:

- **Immediate usability:** All web browsers and e-mail programs can display JPEG files, so you can share pictures online immediately after you shoot them. You also can get a JPEG file printed at any retail photo outlet. The same can't be said for Raw (NEF) files, which must be converted to JPEG for online sharing and to JPEG or another standard format, such as TIFF, for retail printing.
- **Small files:** JPEG files are smaller than Raw files. And smaller files consume less room on your camera memory card and in your computer's storage tank.

The downside (you knew there had to be one) is that JPEG creates smaller files by applying *lossy compression.* This process actually throws away some image data. Too much compression produces a defect called *JPEG artifacting.* Figure 2-18 compares a high-quality original (left photo) with a heavily compressed version that exhibits artifacting (right photo).

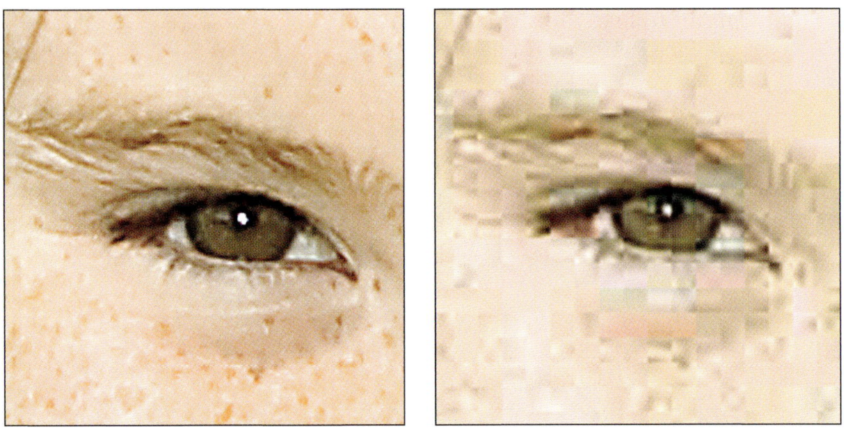

Figure 2-18: The reduced quality of the right image is caused by excessive JPEG compression.

Fortunately, your camera enables you to specify how much compression you're willing to accept. You can choose from three JPEG settings, which produce the following results:

- **JPEG Fine:** The compression ratio is 1:4 — that is, the file is four times smaller than it would otherwise be. Because very little compression is applied, you shouldn't see many compression artifacts, if any.
- **JPEG Normal:** The compression ratio rises to 1:8. The chance of seeing some artifacting increases as well. This setting is the default.
- **JPEG Basic:** The compression ratio jumps to 1:16. That's a substantial amount of compression that brings with it a lot more risk of artifacting.

Note, though, that even the Basic setting doesn't result in anywhere near the level of artifacting you see in the right image in Figure 2-18. I've exaggerated the defect in that example to help you recognize artifacting and understand how it differs from the quality loss that occurs when you have too few pixels (refer to Figures 2-14 through 2-16). In fact, if you keep the image print or display size small, you aren't likely to notice a great deal of quality difference between the Fine, Normal, and Basic compression levels. It's only when you greatly enlarge a photo that the differences become apparent.

TIP

Given that the differences between the compression settings aren't that easy to spot until you enlarge the photo, is it okay to stick with the default setting — Normal — or even drop down to Basic to capture smaller files? Well, only you can decide what level of quality your pictures demand. For me, the added file sizes produced by the Fine setting aren't a huge concern, given that the prices of memory cards fall all the time. Long-term storage is more of an issue; the larger your files, the faster you fill your computer's hard drive and the more DVDs or CDs you need for archiving purposes. But in the end, I prefer to take the storage hit in exchange for the lower compression level of the Fine setting. You never know when a casual snapshot will be so great that you want to print or display it large enough that even minor quality loss becomes a concern. And of all the defects that you can correct in a photo editor, artifacting is one of the hardest to remove.

If you don't want *any* risk of artifacting, change the file type to Raw (NEF). Or consider your other option, which is to record two versions of each file — one Raw and one JPEG. The next section offers details.

Raw (NEF): The purist's choice

The other picture file type you can create is *Camera Raw,* or just *Raw* (as in uncooked), for short.

Each manufacturer has its own flavor of Raw. Nikon's is NEF, for Nikon Electronic Format, so you see the three-letter extension NEF at the end of Raw filenames.

Raw is popular with advanced, very demanding photographers for three reasons:

- **Greater creative control:** With JPEG, internal camera software tweaks your images, adjusting color, exposure, and sharpness as needed to produce the results that Nikon believes its customers prefer. With Raw, the camera simply records the original, unprocessed image data. The photographer then copies the image file to the computer and uses special software known as a *Raw converter* to produce the actual image, making decisions about color, exposure, and so on at that point. Nikon ViewNX 2, which ships with your camera, offers a Raw converter, and the D5300 also has a built-in Raw converter. I cover both options in Chapter 9.
- **Higher bit depth:** *Bit depth* is a measure of how many distinct color values an image file can contain. JPEG files restrict you to 8 bits each for the red, blue, and green color components, or *channels,* that make up a digital image, for a total of 24 bits. That translates to roughly 16.7 million possible colors. On the D5300, you can set the camera to capture either 12 or 14 bits per channel when you shoot in the Raw format.

  Although jumping from 8 to 12 or 14 bits sounds like a huge difference, you may never notice any difference in your photos — that 8-bit palette of 16.7 million values is more than enough for superb images. Where the extra bits can come in handy is if you adjust exposure, contrast, or color in your photo-editing program. When you apply extreme adjustments, the extra bits sometimes help avoid a problem known as *banding* or *posterization,* which creates abrupt color breaks where you should see smooth, seamless transitions. (A higher bit depth doesn't always prevent this problem, however.)
- **Best picture quality:** Because Raw doesn't apply the destructive compression associated with JPEG, you don't run the risk of the artifacting that can occur with JPEG.

But Raw isn't without its disadvantages:

- **You can't do much with your pictures until you process them in a Raw converter.** You can't share them online or put them into a text document or multimedia presentation. You can view and print them immediately if you use the Nikon ViewNX 2 software that ships with the camera, but most other photo programs require you to convert the Raw files to a standard format first, such as JPEG or TIFF. Ditto for retail photo printing.
- **Raw files are larger than JPEGs.** Unlike JPEG, Raw doesn't apply lossy compression to shrink files. In addition, Raw files are always captured at the maximum resolution. For both reasons, Raw files are significantly larger than JPEGs, so they take up more room on your memory card and on your computer's hard drive or other picture-storage device.

Whether the upside of Raw outweighs the down is a decision that you need to ponder based on your photographic needs and on whether you have the time to, and interest in, converting Raw files.

TIP

You do have the option to capture a picture in the Raw and JPEG format at the same time; see the section "Setting Image Size and Image Quality" for details. I often take this route when I'm shooting pictures I want to share right away with people who don't have software for viewing Raw files. I upload the JPEGs to a photo-sharing site where everyone can view them, and then I process the Raw versions when I have time.

My take: Choose JPEG Fine or Raw (NEF)

At this point, you may be finding all this technical goop a bit overwhelming, so allow me to simplify things for you. Until you have the time or energy to completely digest all the ramifications of JPEG versus Raw, here's a quick summary of my thoughts on the matter:

- If you require the absolute best image quality and have the time and interest in doing the Raw conversion, shoot Raw.
- If great photo quality is good enough and you don't have time to spend processing images, stick with JPEG Fine.
- If you don't mind the added file-storage space requirement and want the flexibility of both formats, choose the Raw+JPEG Fine option, which stores one copy of the image in each format.
- If you go with JPEG only, stay away from JPEG Normal and Basic. (Remember, Normal is the default setting on your camera.) The trade-off for smaller files isn't, in my opinion, worth the risk of compression artifacts.

Setting Image Size and Image Quality

REMEMBER

To sum up the Image Size and Image Quality information laid out in the preceding sections:

- Both options affect picture quality and file size.
- Choose a high Image Quality setting — Raw (NEF) or JPEG Fine — and the maximum Image Size setting (Large) for top-quality pictures and large file sizes.
- Combining the lowest Quality setting (JPEG Basic) with the lowest Size setting (Small) greatly shrinks files, enabling you to fit lots more pictures on your memory card, but it also increases the chances that you'll be disappointed with the quality of those pictures, especially if you make large prints.

Now for the lowdown on how to monitor and adjust the setting: First, to see which options are currently in force, check the Information screen or Live View display, in the areas labeled in Figure 2-19.

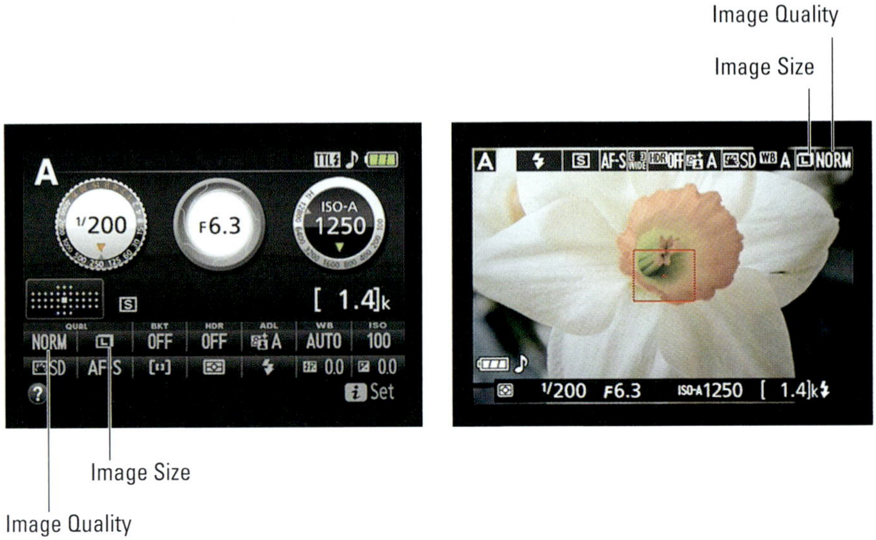

Figure 2-19: The current Image Quality and Image Size settings appear here.

To adjust the settings, you have the following choices:

- ***i* button:** Press the button to access the display control strip, highlight one of the two options, and then press OK to view the screen where you can select the setting you want to use. Figure 2-20 illustrates the process of setting the Image Quality option.

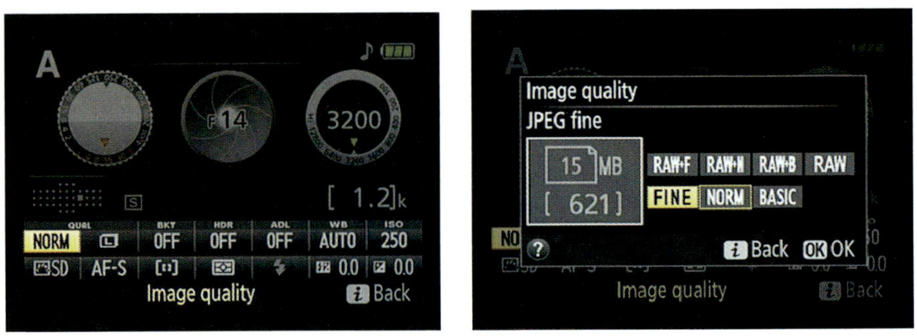

Figure 2-20: Press the *i* button to access the Image Size and Quality settings quickly.

- Notice that in the screen shown on the right in Figure 2-20, the left side of the display shows the file size that will result from your selected setting along with the number of pictures that will fit on the memory card at that size (15MB and 621 images, in the figure). Keep in mind that certain other factors also affect the file size, such as the level of detail and color in the subject.

- **Shooting menu:** As an alternative, you can adjust the settings via the Shooting menu, as shown in Figure 2-21. If you select the Image Size setting from the menu, the options screen shows the pixel counts for each setting, as shown on the right in the figure.

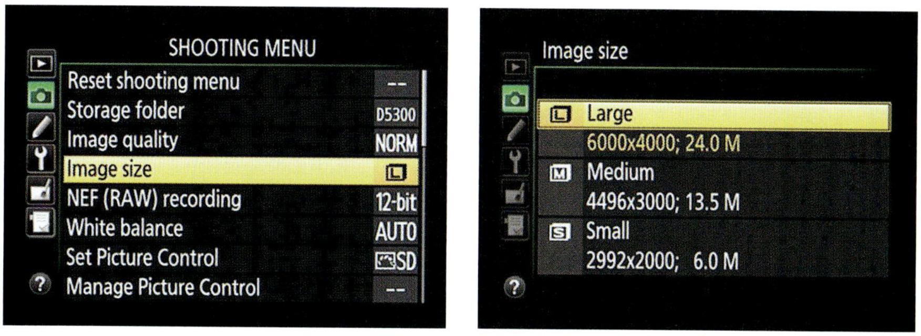

Figure 2-21: You also can set Image Size and Image Quality via the Shooting menu.

REMEMBER

When you choose the Raw (NEF) option, all pictures are automatically captured at the Large resolution setting. However, if you choose Raw+JPEG, the JPEG version is captured at the selected Image Size setting.

In addition, you can specify the bit depth of Raw files. Make the call through the NEF (RAW) Recording option on the Shooting menu, as shown in Figure 2-22. The default setting is 12 bits, which is typically more than adequate. If you opt for 14 bits, which enables the file to contain more color data, understand that doing so increases the file size. A 12-bit Raw file has a size of 19.0MB; a 14-bit file, 23.8MB. See the earlier section "Raw (NEF): The purist's choice" for more information about bit depth.

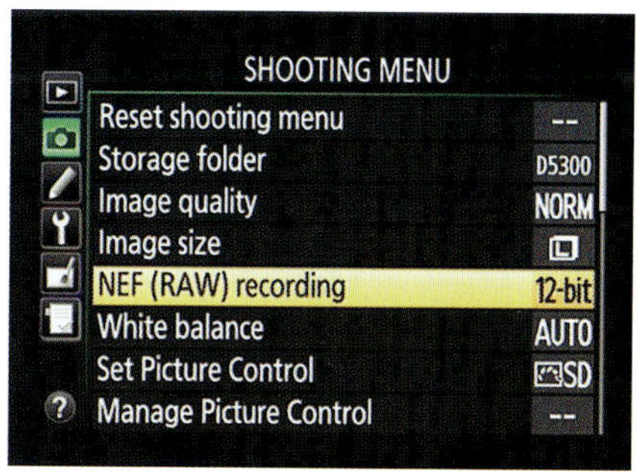

Figure 2-22: For Raw files, you can specify how many bits of color data you want to record.

TIP

Maintaining a pristine view

Often lost in discussions of digital photo defects — compression artifacts, pixelation, and noise — is the impact of plain-old dust and dirt on picture quality. But no matter what camera settings you use, you won't achieve great picture quality with a dirty lens. So clean the lens regularly, using one of the specialized cloths and cleaning solutions made for that purpose.

If you notice spots at the same position in all your images and cleaning the lens doesn't get rid of them, you have a dirty image sensor. The D5300 offers an internal sensor-cleaning mechanism that runs by default every time you turn the camera on or off. You also can perform a cleaning at any time via the Setup menu: Choose Clean Image Sensor, select Clean Now, and press OK. (Nikon recommends that you set the camera on a solid surface, base down, when you perform the cleaning.) Don't try to perform the cleaning several times in a row — if you do, the camera temporarily disables the function to protect itself.

The other option available from the Clean Image Sensor menu item, Clean At Startup/Shutdown, enables you to specify whether you want the camera to change from the default setting to clean only at startup, only at shutdown, or never. I suggest that you stick with the default.

Still having issues even after running the automated cleaner? If so, a manual sensor cleaning is necessary. I don't recommend that you tackle this job yourself unless you're experienced at the task; you can easily damage the sensor if you aren't careful. Instead, find a camera store that offers this service. (The store may perform the service for free if you bought the camera there.)

If you want to clean the sensor yourself, first make sure that the battery is fully charged. Then visit the Setup menu and select Lock Mirror Up for Cleaning, which moves the camera's mirror out of the way so that you can access the sensor. (The menu item is dimmed when the battery is low.) And please: Use the utmost caution to avoid winding up with a $1,000 paperweight.

Adding Flash

Another basic picture-taking option to consider is whether you want to add flash to illuminate your subject. With the D5300, you can use the built-in flash or attach an external flash head to the hot shoe.

REMEMBER

However, flash options depend on the exposure mode, as follows:

- **Flash disabled:** Flash isn't available in Auto Flash Off mode and the following Scene modes: Landscape, Sports, Beach/Snow, Night Landscape, Sunset, Dusk/Dawn, Candlelight, Blossom, and Autumn Colors. All Effects modes except Color Sketch and Toy Camera Effect also disable flash.
- **Minimal flash control:** In Auto mode as well as in the Portrait, Child, Close-Up, Night Portrait, Party/Indoor, Pet Portrait, and Food Scene modes, you can enable or disable flash, and you may be able to choose

from a couple different flash modes, such as Red-Eye Reduction mode. You also get some flash flexibility in the Color Sketch and Toy Camera Effect modes.

- **Advanced flash control:** In P, S, A, and M modes, you can enable or disable flash, choose from a variety of flash modes, and even control flash power.

The rest of this chapter explains how to enable flash, adjust the Flash mode, and take advantage of other flash options.

Enabling and disabling flash

In certain exposure modes, flash is set by default to fire automatically if the camera thinks that the ambient light is insufficient; in other modes, you have to manually enable the flash. Here's the breakdown:

- **Auto mode; all Scene modes that permit flash *except* Food mode; and the Color Sketch and Toy Camera Effect mode:** Flash is set to Auto by default. After you press the shutter button, the camera assesses the available light and automatically pops up the built-in flash if it finds that light lacking.

  If you don't want to use flash, you may be able to disable it via the Flash mode setting. See the next section for how-tos.

- **P, S, A, and M modes and the Food Scene mode:** There's no such thing as automatic flash in these modes. Instead, if you want to use the built-in flash, press the Flash button on the side of the camera, labeled in Figure 2-23. Don't want flash? Just press down gently on the top of the flash to close the unit.

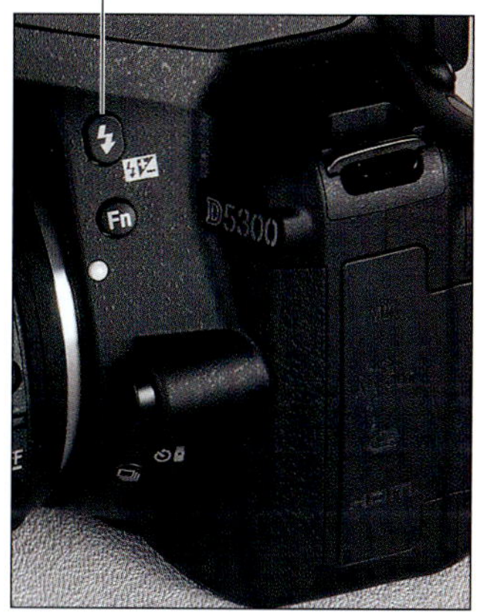

Figure 2-23: In P, S, A, and M modes (and the Food Scene mode), raise the built-in flash by pressing the Flash button.

- The camera does give you a little flash input, though: You see a blinking question mark or a flash symbol, or both, in the displays if the camera thinks you need flash. Press the Zoom Out button (the one with the question mark above it), and a message appears recommending that you use flash.

Choosing a Flash mode

The *Flash mode* determines how and when the flash fires. The next section introduces the various options; following that, you can find details on how to adjust the setting.

Sorting through your Flash mode options

Your camera offers the following flash modes, represented in the Information and Live View displays by the symbols you see in the margins here. (Skip to Figure 2-27 to see where to find the symbols in the Information and Live View displays.)

- **Auto:** The camera decides whether the flash fires. This mode isn't available in the P, S, A, M modes or the Food Scene mode.
- **Flash Off:** In Auto exposure mode or the Scene and Effects modes that permit flash, choose this Flash mode to prevent the flash from firing. (In the P, S, A, and M modes and the Food Scene mode, simply close the flash unit if you don't want to use flash.)
- **Fill Flash:** You can think of this mode, available in P, S, A, M and Food Scene modes, as normal flash. You may also hear this mode called *force* flash because the flash fires no matter the amount of available light.

  Although most people think of flash as an indoor lighting option, adding flash can improve outdoor photos, too. After all, your main light source — the sun — is overhead, so although the top of the subject may be adequately lit, the front typically needs additional illumination. As an example, Figure 2-24 shows a floral image taken both with and without a flash. The small pop of light provided by the built-in flash is also beneficial when shooting subjects that happen to be slightly shaded. For outdoor portraits, a flash is even more important to properly illuminate the face; the section on shooting portraits in Chapter 6 discusses that subject and offers a look at the difference flash can make.

  Shooting with flash in bright light involves a couple of complications, however; see the sidebar "Using flash outdoors," later in this chapter, for help.

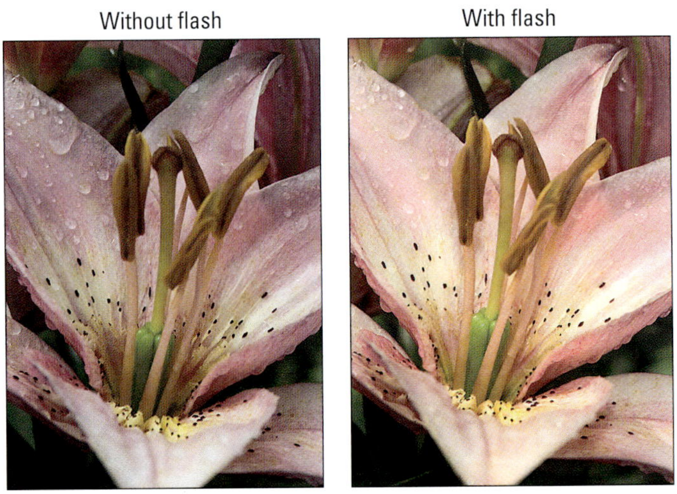

Figure 2-24: Adding flash resulted in better illumination and a slight warming effect.

- **Red-Eye Reduction:** *Red-eye* is caused when flash light bounces off a subject's retinas and is reflected back to the camera lens, making the subjects appear possessed by a demon. This flash mode is designed to reduce the chances of red-eye.

  When you use Red-Eye Reduction mode, the AF-assist lamp on the front of the camera lights briefly before the flash fires. The subject's pupils constrict in response to the light, allowing less flash light to enter the eye and cause that glowing red reflection. Be sure to warn your subjects to wait for the flash, or else they may step out of the frame or stop posing after they see the light from the AF-assist lamp.

  In Auto exposure mode as well as in certain other Scene and Effects modes that permit flash, Red-Eye Reduction flash is just a variation of the regular Auto flash setting. That is, if the camera sees the need for flash, it fires the flash with Red-Eye Reduction engaged. In this case, you see the word *Auto* next to the red-eye symbol. Additionally, a few Scene modes use a variation of red-eye reduction, combining that feature with a slow shutter speed. This flash mode displays the little eye icon plus the words *Auto Slow*. It's important to use a tripod and ask your subject to remain still during the exposure to avoid a blurry picture.

- **Slow-Sync and Rear-Sync:** In the flash modes listed so far, the flash and shutter are synchronized so that the flash fires at the exact moment the shutter opens.

  Technical types call this flash arrangement *front-curtain sync*, which refers to how the flash is synchronized with the opening of the shutter. Here's the deal: The camera uses a type of shutter involving two curtains that move across the frame. When you press the shutter button, the first curtain opens, allowing light to strike the image sensor. At the end of the exposure, the second curtain draws across the frame to once again shield the sensor from light. With front-curtain sync, the flash fires when the front curtain opens.

  Your camera also offers these four special sync modes:

  - *Slow-Sync:* This mode, available only in the P and A exposure modes, also uses front-curtain sync but allows a shutter speed slower than the 1/60 second minimum that's in force when you use Fill Flash and Red-Eye Reduction flash. Because of the longer exposure, the camera has time to absorb more ambient light, which has two benefits: Background areas that are beyond the reach of the flash appear brighter; and less flash power is needed, resulting in softer lighting.

The downside of the slow shutter speed is, well, the slow shutter speed. Any movement of your camera or subject during the exposure can blur the picture, and the slower the shutter speed, the greater the chances of camera or subject motion. A tripod is essential to a good outcome, as are subjects that can hold very, very still. I find that the best practical use for this mode is shooting nighttime still-life subjects like the one you see in Figure 2-25. However, if you're shooting a nighttime portrait and you have a subject that *can* maintain a motionless pose, slow-sync flash can produce softer, more flattering light.

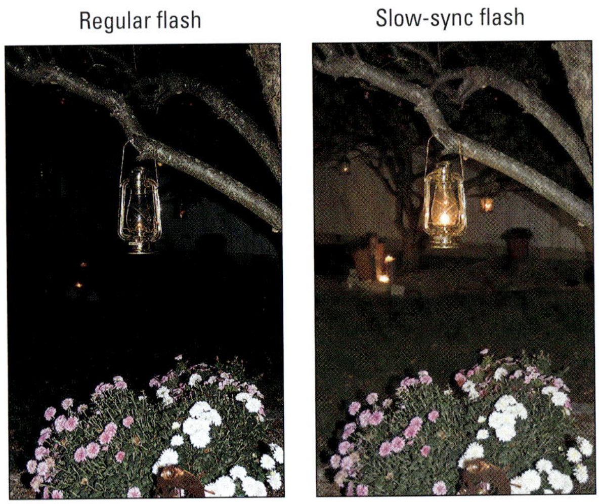

Figure 2-25: Slow-sync flash produces softer, more even lighting than normal flash in nighttime pictures.

Note that even though the official Slow-Sync mode appears only in the P and A exposure modes, you can get the same result in the M and S modes by simply using a slow shutter speed and the normal, Fill Flash mode. You can use a shutter speed as slow as 30 seconds when using flash in those modes. In fact, I prefer using those modes when I want the slow-sync look because I can directly control the shutter speed.

- *Rear-Curtain Sync:* In this mode, available only in shutter-priority (S) and manual (M) exposure modes, the flash fires at the end of the exposure, just before the shutter closes. The classic use of this mode is to combine the flash with a slow shutter speed to create trailing-light effects like the one you see in Figure 2-26. With Rear-Curtain Sync, the light trails extend behind the moving object (my hand, and the match, in this case), which makes visual sense. If instead you use slow-sync flash, the light trails appear in front of the moving object.

You can set the shutter speed as low as 30 seconds and as high as 1/200 second in this Flash mode.

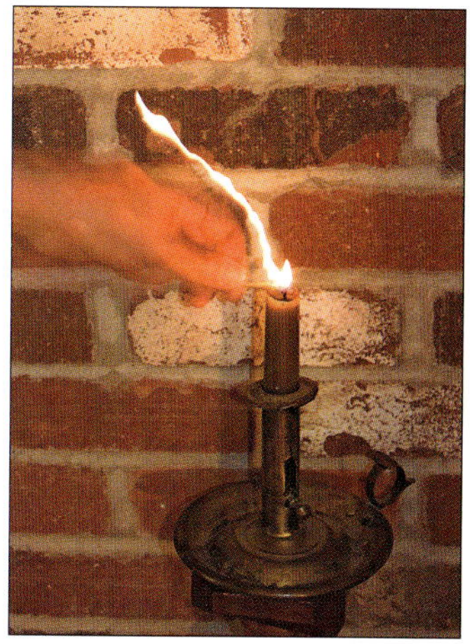

Figure 2-26: I used Rear-Curtain Sync Flash to create this candle-lighting image.

SLOW REAR

- *Slow-Rear:* Hey, not confusing enough for you yet? This mode enables you to produce the same motion trail effects as with Rear-Curtain Sync, but in the P and A exposure modes. The camera automatically chooses a slower shutter speed than normal after you set the f-stop, just as with regular Slow-Sync mode.
- *Slow-Sync with Red-Eye Reduction:* In P and A exposure modes, you can also combine a slow-sync flash with the red-eye reduction feature. The symbol that represents this mode is the normal red-eye eyeball combined with the word *Slow.*

TIP

In sync: Flash timing and shutter speed

To properly expose flash pictures, the camera has to synchronize the firing of the flash with the opening and closing of the shutter. For this reason, the range of available shutter speeds is limited when you use flash. The maximum shutter speed is 1/200 second; the minimum shutter speed varies, depending on the exposure mode:

- **Auto and all Scene modes except Night Portrait:** 1/60 second
- **Nighttime Portrait:** 1 second
- **Color Sketch and Toy Camera Effect modes:** 1/60 second
- **P, A:** 1/60 second (unless you use one of the Slow-Sync Flash modes, which permit a slower shutter speed)
- **S:** 30 seconds
- **M:** 30 seconds (for Fill Flash mode, you can exceed that limit if the shutter speed is set to Bulb)

Setting the Flash mode

You can view the current Flash mode in the Information and Live View displays, as shown in Figure 2-27. (In Live View mode, press the Info button to cycle through the various data-display modes to get to the one shown in the figure.) The lightning bolt with the eye shown in the figures represents the Red-Eye Reduction flash mode.

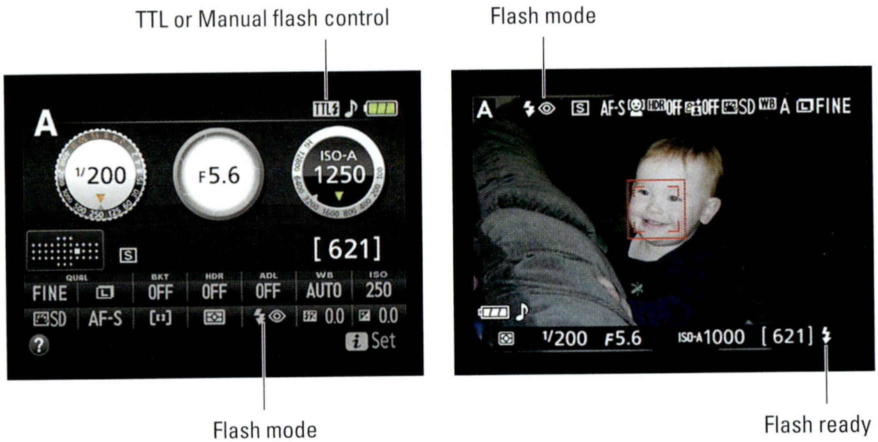

Figure 2-27: An icon representing the Flash mode appears in the displays.

In the viewfinder as well as in the lower-right corner of the Live View display, you see a single lightning bolt. This symbol simply tells you that the flash is ready to fire. (You can't view the Flash mode in the viewfinder.)

As for the TTL symbol, highlighted on the left in Figure 2-27, it represents the current setting of the Built-in Flash Cntrl (Control) option on the Custom Setting menu. TTL, which stands for *through the lens,* represents the normal flash metering operation: The camera measures the light coming through the lens and sets the flash output accordingly. Your other option is to set the flash output manually, as explained in the last section of this chapter. If you take that route, the letter *M* appears in place of *TTL.*

To change the Flash mode, you can go one of two ways:

- **Flash button + Command dial:** As soon as you press the button, the Flash mode option in the Information display becomes selected, as shown in Figure 2-28. The same thing happens in the Live View display, but the related symbol is at the top of the screen (refer to Figure 2-27). Either way, keep the Flash button pressed while rotating the Command dial to cycle through the available Flash modes.

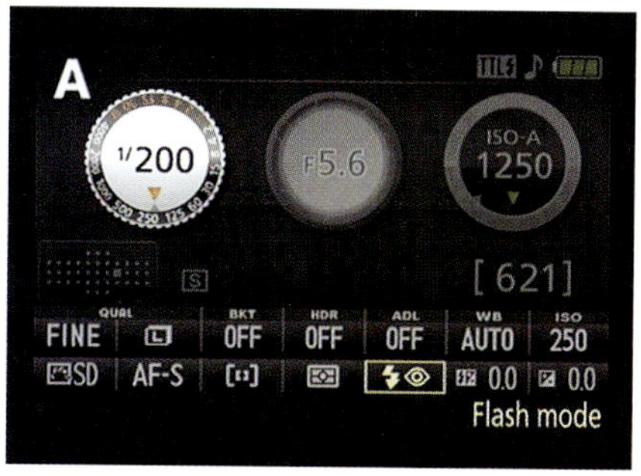

Figure 2-28: The fastest way to change the Flash mode is to hold down the Flash button and rotate the Command dial.

- ***i* button:** Press the button to activate the control strip in the Information and Live View displays. Highlight the Flash mode option, and press OK to display a screen listing the mode settings, as shown in Figure 2-29. Remember that the available Flash modes depend on the exposure mode.

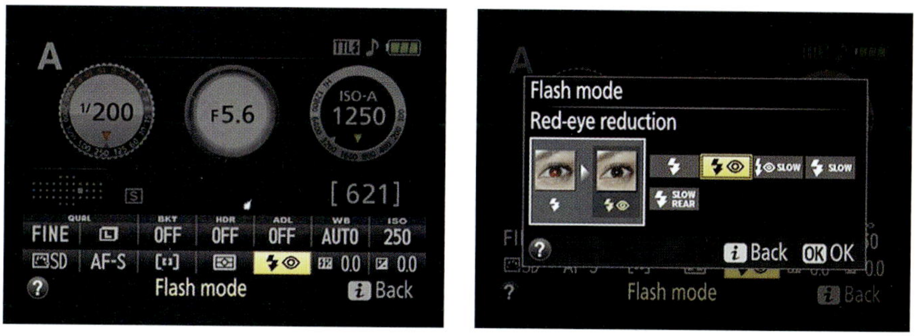

Figure 2-29: You also can adjust the Flash mode by using the normal control-strip method; press the *i* button to activate the control strip.

TIP

Using flash outdoors

Adding flash can often improve outdoor photos. But be aware of two "gotchas" when mixing flash and sunlight:

- **Colors may need tweaking.** When you combine multiple light sources, colors may appear warmer or cooler than neutral. For outdoor portraits, the warming effect is usually flattering, and I usually like the result with nature shots as well. But if you prefer a neutral color rendition, see the Chapter 5 section related to the White Balance control to find out how to address this issue. You can adjust white balance only in P, S, A, and M exposure modes.
- **Keep an eye on shutter speed.** Because of the way the camera needs to synchronize the firing of the flash with the opening of the shutter, the fastest shutter speed you can use with the built-in flash is 1/200 second. In bright sun, you may need to stop down the aperture significantly or lower the ISO, if possible, to avoid overexposing the image even at 1/200 second. As another option, you can place a neutral density filter over the lens; this accessory reduces the light that comes through the lens without affecting colors. Of course, if possible, you can simply move your subject into the shade.

On the flip side, the camera may select a shutter speed as slow as 1/60 second in the P and A modes, depending on the lighting conditions. If your subject is moving, it's a good idea to work in the S or M modes so that you control the shutter speed.

Adjusting the flash output (P, S, A, and M modes only)

TIP

In the P, S, A, or M exposure modes, you have some control over flash power, even if you stick with the default, TTL (through the lens) automatic flash metering. If you want a little more or less flash light than the camera thinks is appropriate, you can adjust the flash output by using *Flash Compensation.*

Flash Compensation settings are stated in terms of *exposure value (EV)* numbers. A setting of EV 0.0 indicates no flash adjustment; you can increase the flash power to EV +1.0 or decrease it to EV –3.0.

As an example of the benefit of this feature, look at the carousel images in Figure 2-30. The first image shows a flash-free shot. Clearly, I needed a flash to compensate for the fact that the horses were shadowed by the roof of the carousel. But at normal flash power, as shown in the middle image, the flash was too strong, creating glare in some spots and blowing out the highlights in the white mane. By dialing the flash power down to EV –0.7, I got a softer flash that straddled the line perfectly between no flash and too much flash.

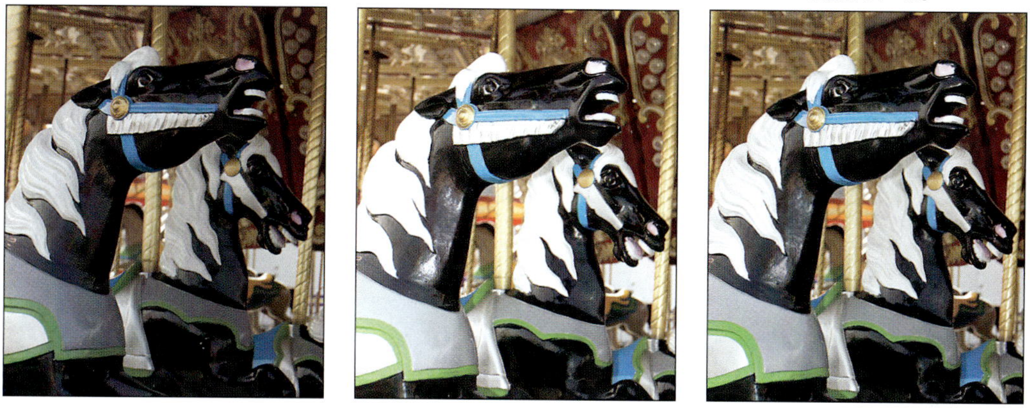

Figure 2-30: When normal flash output is too strong, dial in a lower Flash Compensation setting.

As for boosting the flash output, you may find it necessary on some occasions, but don't expect the built-in flash to work miracles even at a Flash Compensation of +1.0. The built-in flash has a maximum range of about 12 feet; it simply can't illuminate faraway objects. In other words, don't even try taking flash pictures of a darkened recital hall from your seat in the balcony — all you'll wind up doing is annoying everyone.

The current Flash Compensation setting appears in the Information display, as shown on the left in Figure 2-31. In the Live View display, you see only a symbol indicating that the feature is enabled, as shown on the right side of the figure. Note that if the feature is turned off (set to EV 0.0), the symbol doesn't appear in the Live View display.

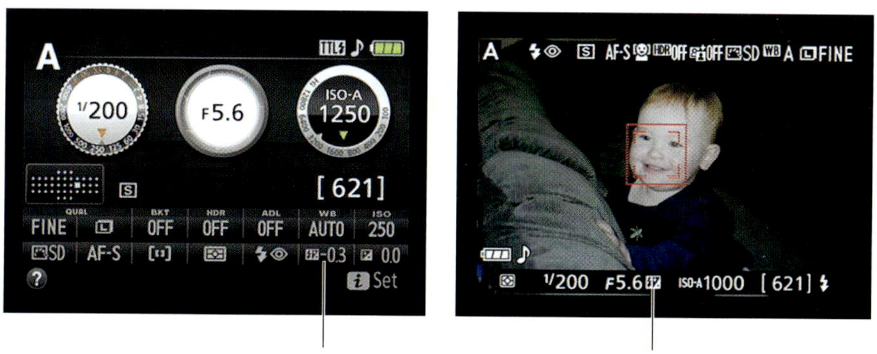

Figure 2-31: These symbols represent Flash Compensation.

To adjust the amount of Flash Compensation, use either of these tricks:

- **Use the two-button-plus-Command-dial maneuver.** First, press the Flash button to pop up the built-in flash. Then press and hold the Flash button and the Exposure Compensation button simultaneously. When you press the buttons, the Flash Compensation value becomes highlighted in the Information and Live View displays, as shown in Figure 2-32. In the viewfinder, the current setting takes the place of the usual Frames Remaining value. While keeping both buttons pressed, rotate the Command dial to adjust the setting. I find that any technique that involves coordinating this many fingers a little complex, but you may find it easier than I do.

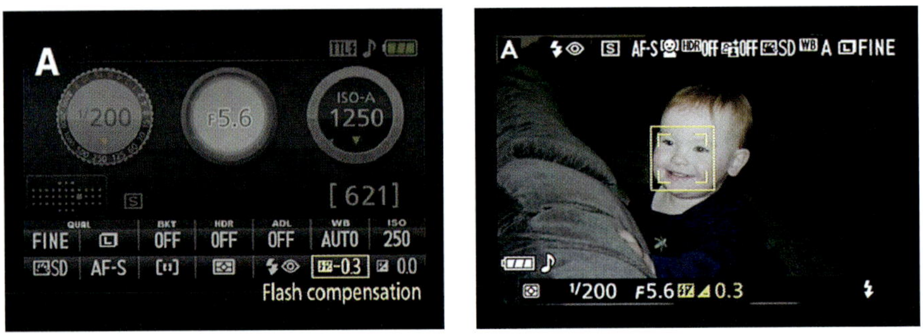

Figure 2-32: Rotate the Command dial while pressing the Flash and Exposure Compensation buttons to adjust the flash power.

- **Use the control strip.** Just press the *i* button to activate the control strip, and highlight the Flash Compensation setting, as shown on the left in Figure 2-33. Press OK to display a screen where you can set the compensation amount, as shown on the second screen of the figure.

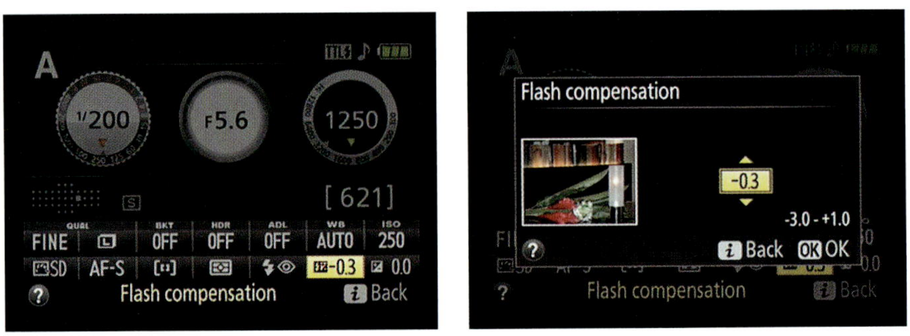

Figure 2-33: You also can adjust the setting by using the normal Information display control-strip method.

WARNING! Any flash-power adjustment remains in force until you reset the value, even if you turn off the camera. So be sure to check the setting before you next use the flash.

Controlling flash output manually

If you're experienced in the way of the flash, you can manually set flash output via the Flash Cntrl for Built-in Flash option, found in the Bracketing/ Flash section of the Custom Setting menu. The normal setting is TTL (for automatic, through-the-lens metering), but if you select Manual, as shown on the left in Figure 2-34, and then press the Multi Selector right, you can access the power settings, which range from Full to 1/32 power.

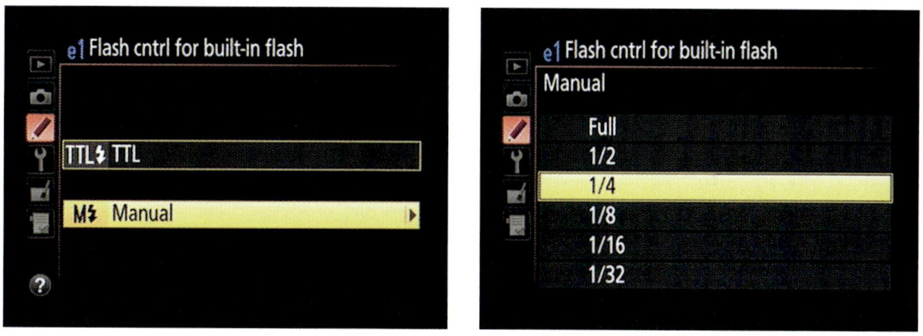

Figure 2-34: Using this option, you can control the flash output manually.

When flash is set to manual control, the TTL icon that normally appears in the upper-right corner of the Information display (refer to Figure 2-27) is replaced by the letter *M.* In the viewfinder, an icon that looks like the Shooting Info screen's Flash Compensation icon (a lightning bolt with a plus-minus sign) blinks.

Part II
Taking Creative Control

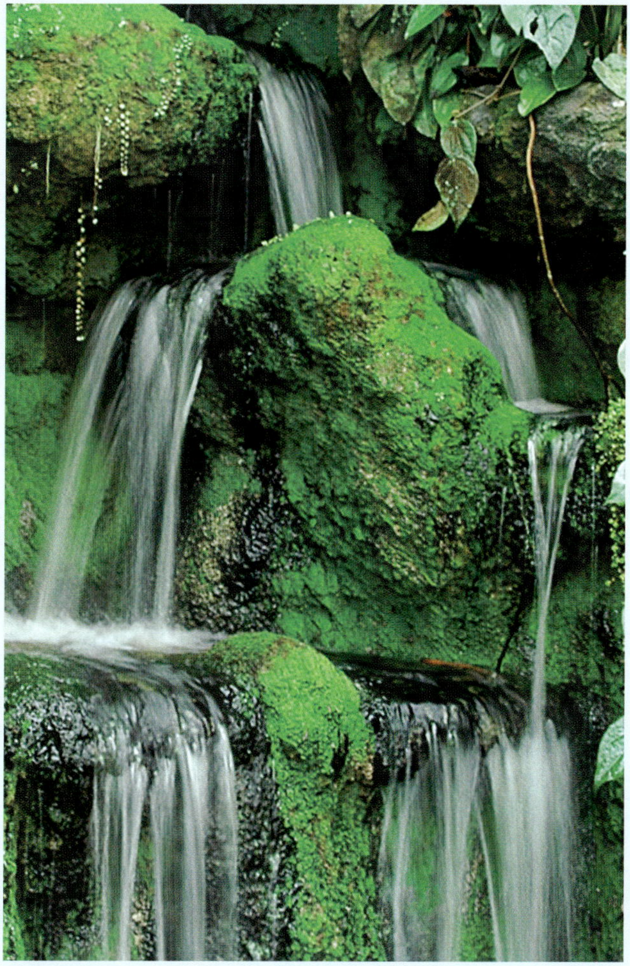

web extras

Look for tips about archiving your picture files at www.dummies.com/extras/nikon.

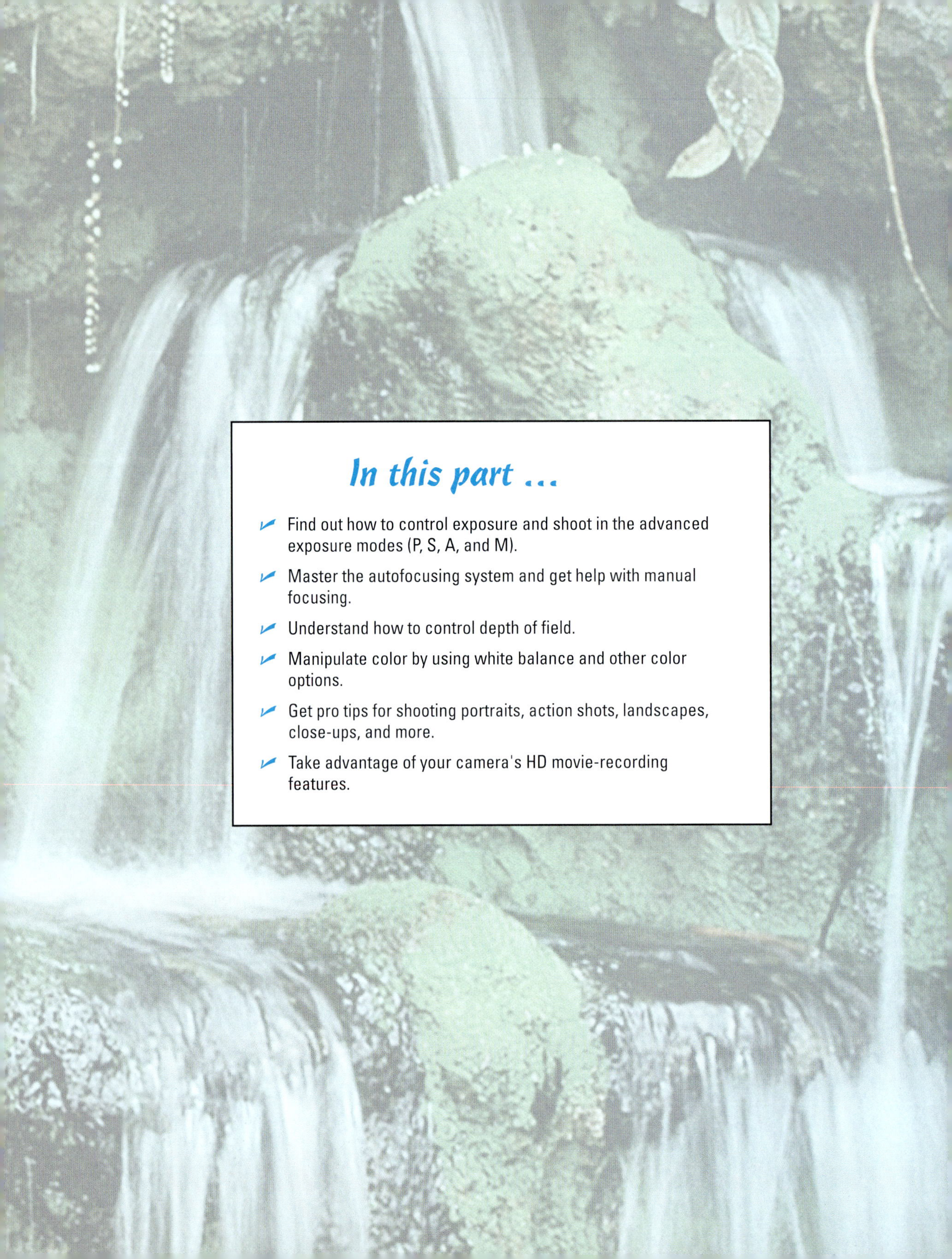

In this part ...

- Find out how to control exposure and shoot in the advanced exposure modes (P, S, A, and M).
- Master the autofocusing system and get help with manual focusing.
- Understand how to control depth of field.
- Manipulate color by using white balance and other color options.
- Get pro tips for shooting portraits, action shots, landscapes, close-ups, and more.
- Take advantage of your camera's HD movie-recording features.

3

Taking Charge of Exposure

In This Chapter

- Understanding the basics of exposure
- Choosing the right exposure mode: P, S, A, or M?
- Reading meters and other exposure cues
- Solving exposure problems
- Creating a safety net with automatic bracketing

Understanding exposure is one of the most intimidating challenges for a new photographer. Discussions of the topic are loaded with technical terms — *aperture, metering, shutter speed, ISO,* and the like. Add the fact that your camera offers many exposure controls, all sporting equally foreign names, and it's no wonder that most people throw up their hands and decide that their best option is to stick with the Auto exposure mode and let the camera take care of all exposure decisions.

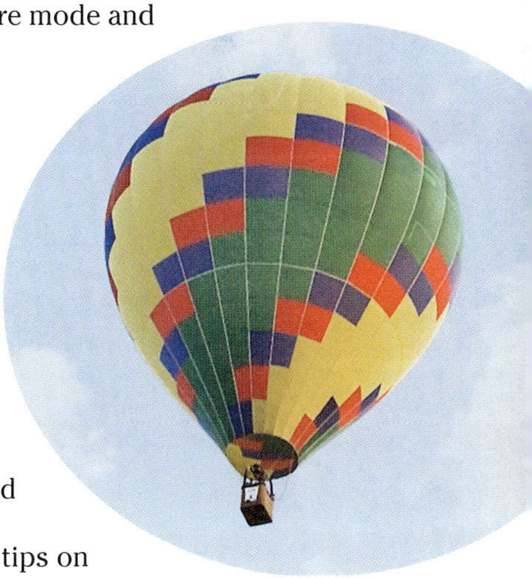

You can, of course, turn out good shots in Auto mode, and I fully relate to the confusion you may be feeling — I've been there. But I can also promise that when you take things nice and slow, digesting a piece of the exposure pie at a time, the topic is *not* as complicated as it seems on the surface. I guarantee that the payoff will be worth your time, too. You'll not only gain the know-how to solve just about any exposure problem but also discover ways to use exposure to put your creative stamp on a scene.

To that end, this chapter provides everything you need to know about controlling exposure, from a primer in exposure terminology (it's not as bad as it sounds) to tips on using the P, S, A, and M exposure modes, which are the only ones that offer access to all exposure features. ***Note:*** The one exposure-related topic not covered in this chapter is flash; I discuss flash in Chapter 2 because it's among the options you can access even in Auto mode and many of the other point-and-shoot modes. Also, this chapter deals with still photography; see Chapter 7 for information on movie-recording exposure issues.

Introducing the Exposure Trio: Aperture, Shutter Speed, and ISO

Any photograph is created by focusing light through a lens onto a light-sensitive recording medium. In a film camera, the film negative serves as that medium; in a digital camera, it's the image sensor, which is an array of light-responsive computer chips.

Between a digital camera's lens and sensor are two barriers — the aperture and shutter — which work in concert to control how much light makes its way to the sensor. In the digital world, the design and arrangement of the aperture, shutter, and sensor vary depending on the camera; Figure 3-1 offers an illustration of the basic concept.

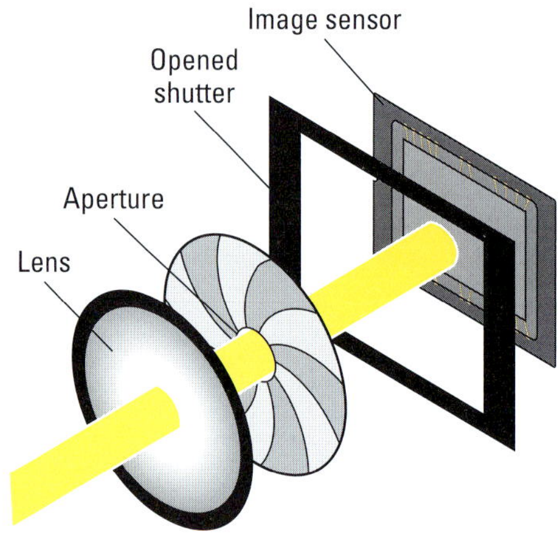

Figure 3-1: The aperture size and shutter speed determine how much light strikes the image sensor.

The aperture and shutter, along with a third feature — ISO — determine *exposure,* which is basically the picture's overall brightness and contrast. This three-part exposure formula works as follows:

- **Aperture (controls amount of light):** The *aperture* is an adjustable hole in a diaphragm inside the lens. You change the aperture size to control the size of the light beam that can enter the camera.

  Aperture settings are stated as *f-stop numbers,* or simply *f-stops,* and are expressed by the letter *f* followed by a number: f/2, f/5.6, f/16, and so on. The lower the f-stop number, the larger the aperture, and the more light is permitted into the camera, as illustrated by Figure 3-2. (If it seems backward to use a higher number for a smaller aperture, think of it this way: A higher value creates a bigger light barrier than a lower value.) The range of available aperture settings varies from lens to lens.

- **Shutter speed (controls duration of light):** The shutter works something like, er, the shutters on a window. The camera's shutter stays closed, preventing light from striking the image sensor (just as closed window shutters prevent sunlight from entering a room) until you press the shutter button. Then the shutter opens briefly to allow light that passes through the aperture to hit the sensor. The exception to this scenario is when you compose in Live View mode: When you enable Live View, the shutter opens and remains open so that the image can form on the sensor and be displayed on the monitor. When you press the shutter button, the shutter first closes and then reopens for the actual exposure.

Either way, the length of time that the shutter is open is the *shutter speed,* which is measured in seconds: 1/60 second, 1/250 second, 2 seconds, and so on.

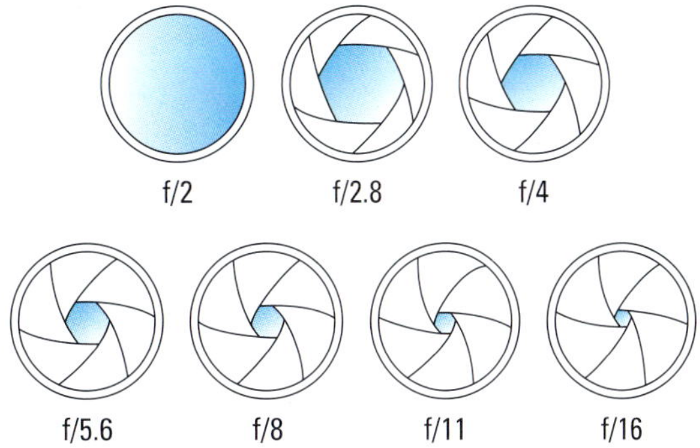

Figure 3-2: A lower f-stop number means a larger aperture, allowing more light into the camera.

- **ISO (controls light sensitivity):** *ISO,* which is a digital function rather than a mechanical structure on the camera, enables you to adjust how responsive the image sensor is to light.

  The term *ISO* is a holdover from film days, when an international standards organization rated each film stock according to light sensitivity: ISO 200, ISO 400, ISO 800, and so on. On a digital camera, the sensor itself doesn't actually get more or less sensitive when you change the ISO. Instead, the light "signal" that hits the sensor is either amplified or dampened through electronics wizardry, sort of like how raising the volume on a radio boosts the audio signal. The upshot is the same as changing to a more light-reactive film stock. Using a higher ISO means that less light is needed to produce the image, enabling you to use a smaller aperture, faster shutter speed, or both.

Distilled to its essence, the image-exposure formula is this simple:

- Together, aperture and shutter speed determine how much light strikes the image sensor.
- ISO determines how much the sensor reacts to that light and thus how much light is needed to expose the picture.

The tricky part of the equation is that aperture, shutter speed, and ISO settings affect pictures in ways that go beyond exposure:

- Aperture affects *depth of field,* or the distance over which focus remains acceptably sharp.
- Shutter speed determines whether moving objects appear blurry or sharply focused.
- ISO affects the amount of image *noise,* which is a defect that looks like specks of colored sand.

Understanding these side effects is critical to choosing the combination of aperture, shutter speed, and ISO that will work best for your subject, so the next three sections explore each issue. If you're already familiar with this stuff and just want to know how to adjust exposure settings, skip ahead to the section "Setting Aperture, Shutter Speed, and ISO."

Aperture affects depth of field

The aperture setting, or f-stop, affects *depth of field,* which is the distance over which focus appears acceptably sharp. With a shallow depth of field, your subject appears more sharply focused than faraway objects; with a large depth of field, the sharp-focus zone spreads over a greater distance.

As you reduce the aperture size by choosing a higher f-stop number — *stop down the aperture,* in photo lingo — you increase the depth of field. As an example, see Figure 3-3. For both shots, I established focus on the fountain statue. Notice that the background in the first image, taken at f/13, is sharper than in the right example, taken at f/5.6. Aperture is just one contributor to depth of field, however; the focal length of the lens and the distance between that lens and your subject also affect how much of the scene stays in focus. See Chapter 4 for the complete story.

f/13, 1/25 second, ISO 200 f/5.6, 1/125 second, ISO 200

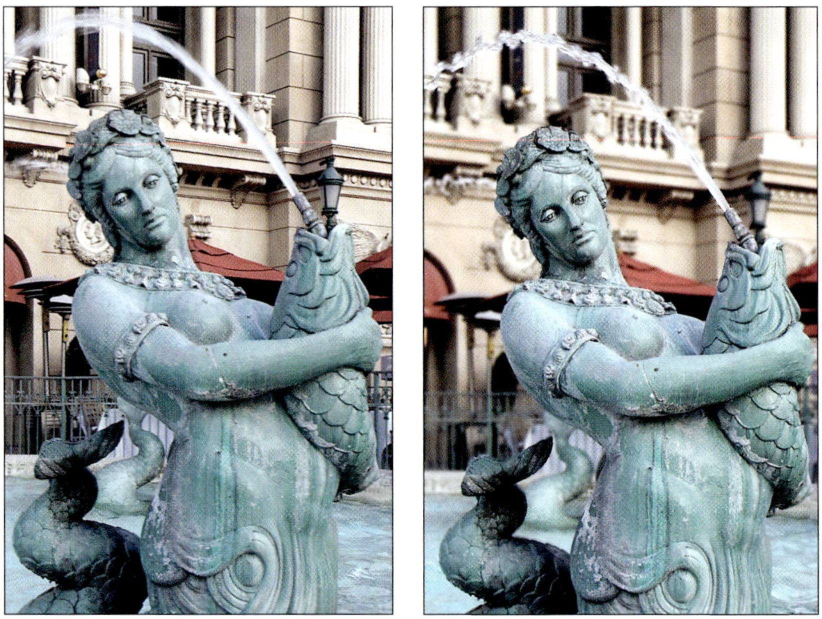

Figure 3-3: Widening the aperture (choosing a lower f-stop number) decreases depth of field.

TIP

One way to remember the relationship between f-stop and depth of field is to think of the *f* as standing for *focus.* A higher f-stop number produces a larger depth of field, so if you want to extend the zone of sharp focus to cover a greater distance from your subject, you set the aperture to a higher f-stop. Higher *f*-stop number, greater zone of sharp *f*ocus. (Please *don't* share this tip with photography elites, who will roll their eyes and inform you that the *f* in *f-stop* most certainly does *not* stand for focus but for the ratio between the aperture size and lens focal length — as if *that's* helpful to know if you're not an optical engineer. Chapter 1 explains focal length, which *is* helpful to know.)

Shutter speed affects motion blur

At a slow shutter speed, moving objects appear blurry; a fast shutter speed captures motion cleanly. This phenomenon has nothing to do with the actual focus point of the camera but rather on the movement occurring — and being recorded by the camera — while the shutter is open.

Compare the photos in Figure 3-3, for example. The static elements are perfectly focused in both images although the background in the left photo appears sharper because I shot that image using a higher f-stop, increasing the depth of field. But how the camera rendered the moving portion of the scene — the fountain water — was determined by shutter speed. At 1/25 second (left photo), the water blurs, giving it a misty look. At 1/125 second (right photo), the droplets appear more sharply focused, almost frozen in mid-air. How high a shutter speed you need to freeze action depends on the speed of your subject.

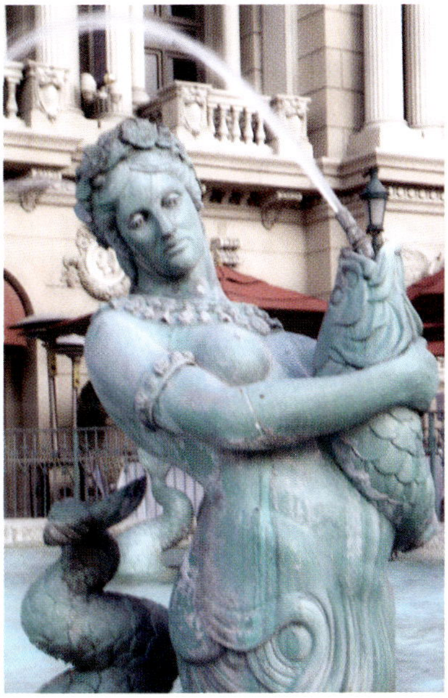

Figure 3-4: If both stationary and moving objects are blurry, camera shake is the usual cause.

WARNING!

If your picture suffers from overall blur, as in Figure 3-4, the camera itself moved during the exposure, which is always a danger when you handhold a camera. The slower the shutter speed, the longer the exposure time and the longer you have to hold the camera still to avoid the blur that's caused by camera shake. Use a tripod to avoid this issue.

TIP

Freezing action isn't the only way to use shutter speed to creative effect. When shooting waterfalls, for example, many photographers use a slow shutter speed to give the water even more of a blurry, romantic look than you see in my fountain example. With colorful subjects, a slow shutter can produce some cool abstract effects and create a heightened sense of motion. Chapter 6 offers examples of both effects.

Handholding the camera: How low can you go?

My students often ask how slow they can set the shutter speed and still handhold the camera rather than use a tripod. Unfortunately, there's no one-size-fits-all answer. The slow-shutter safety limit varies depending on a couple factors, including your physical abilities and your lens — the heavier the lens, the harder it is to hold steady. Camera shake also affects your picture more when you shoot with a lens that has a long focal length. You may be able to use a slower shutter speed with a 55mm lens than with a 200mm lens, for example.

A standard photography rule is to use the inverse of the lens focal length as the minimum handheld shutter speed. For example, with a 50mm lens, use a shutter speed no slower than 1/50 second. That rule was developed before the advent of today's modern lenses, though, which tend to be significantly lighter and smaller than older lenses, as do cameras themselves. For example, I have a very light, superzoom lens that I can handhold at speeds as low as 1/80 second even when I zoom to focal lengths way beyond 80mm. The best idea is to do your own tests to see where your handholding limit lies. See Chapter 8 to find out how to select the picture-playback mode that enables you to see the shutter speed you used for each picture.

Remember, too, that if your lens offers Vibration Reduction, turning on that feature can compensate for small amounts of camera shake. See the lens manual to find out whether your lens offers this feature and, if so, how to enable it.

ISO affects image noise

As ISO increases, making the image sensor more reactive to light, you increase the risk of producing noise. *Noise* is a defect that looks like sprinkles of sand and is similar in appearance to film *grain,* a defect that often mars pictures taken with high ISO film. Figure 3-5 offers an example.

Ideally, then, you should always use the lowest ISO setting on your camera to ensure top image quality. Sometimes, though, the lighting conditions don't permit you to do so and still use the aperture and shutter speeds you need. Take my rose image as an example. When I shot these pictures, I didn't have a tripod, so I needed a shutter speed fast enough to allow a sharp handheld image. I opened the aperture to f/6.3, which was the widest setting on the lens I was using, to allow as much light as possible into the camera. At ISO 100, I needed a shutter speed of 1/40 second to expose the picture, and that shutter speed wasn't fast enough for a successful handheld shot. You see the blurred result on the left in Figure 3-6. By raising the ISO to 200, I was able to use a shutter speed of 1/80 second, which enabled me to capture the flower cleanly, as shown on the right in the figure.

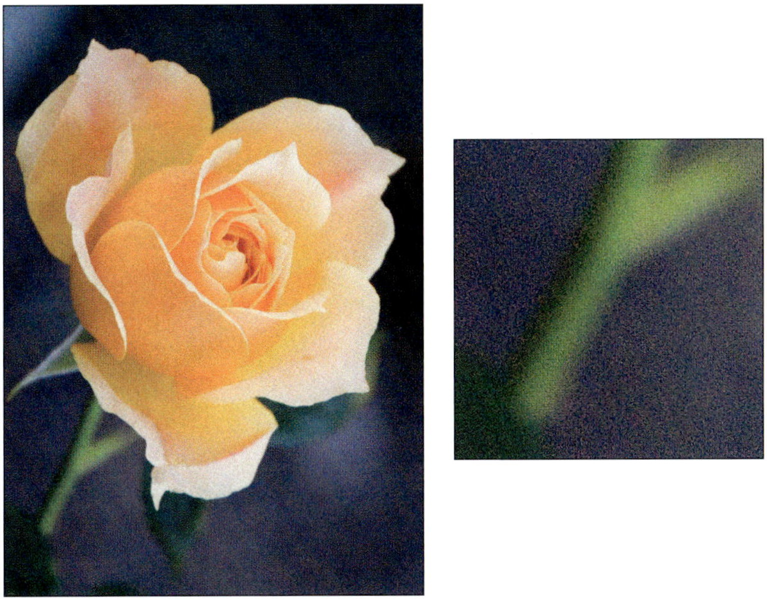

Figure 3-5: Caused by a very high ISO or long exposure time, noise becomes more visible as you enlarge the image.

ISO 100, 6.3, 1/40 second

ISO 200, 6.3, 1/80 second

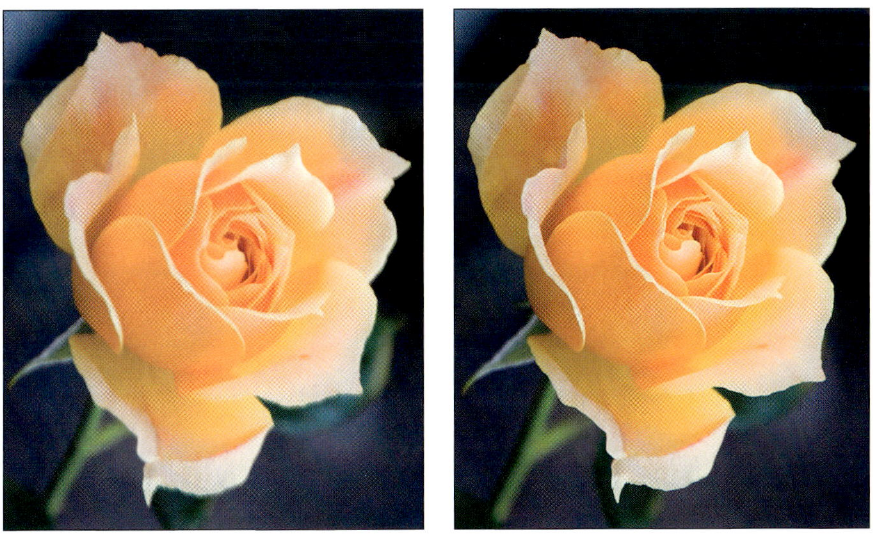

Figure 3-6: For this image, raising the ISO allowed me to bump up the shutter speed enough to capture a blur-free shot while handholding the camera.

Fortunately, you don't encounter serious noise on the D5300 until you really crank up the ISO. In fact, you may even be able to get away with a fairly high ISO if you keep the print or display size small. Some people probably wouldn't even notice the noise in the left image in Figure 3-5 unless they were looking for it, for example. But as with other image defects, noise becomes more apparent as you enlarge the photo, as shown on the right in that same figure. Noise is also easier to spot in shadow areas of the picture and in large areas of solid color.

How much noise is acceptable — and, therefore, how high of an ISO is safe — is your choice. Even a little noise isn't acceptable for pictures that require the highest quality, such as images for a product catalog or a travel shot that you want to blow up to poster size.

A high ISO isn't the only cause of noise: A long exposure time (slow shutter speed) can also produce the defect. So, how high you can raise the ISO before the image gets ugly varies, depending on shutter speed.

Your camera offers two features designed to combat both types of noise, but each has its pros and cons. See the sidebar "Dampening noise," later in this chapter, for a review of both options.

Doing the exposure balancing act

As you change any of the three exposure settings — aperture, shutter speed, and ISO — one or both of the other two must also shift to maintain the same image brightness. Say that you're shooting a soccer game and you notice that although the overall exposure looks great, the players appear slightly blurry at the current shutter speed. If you raise the shutter speed, you have to compensate with a larger aperture (to allow in more light during the shorter exposure) or a higher ISO setting (to make the camera more sensitive to the light) — or both.

Again, changing these settings impacts the image in ways beyond exposure:

- Aperture affects depth of field, with a higher f-stop number increasing the distance over which objects appear sharp.
- Shutter speed affects whether motion of the subject or camera results in a blurry photo. A faster shutter "freezes" action and also helps safeguard against all-over blur that can result from camera shake when you're handholding the camera.
- ISO affects the camera's sensitivity to light. A higher ISO makes the camera more responsive to light but also increases the chance of image noise.

When you boost that shutter speed to capture your soccer subjects, you have to decide whether you prefer the shorter depth of field that comes with a larger aperture or the increased risk of noise that accompanies a higher ISO.

Exposure stops: How many do you want to see?

In photo lingo, the word *stop* refers to an increment of exposure. To increase exposure by one stop means to adjust the aperture or shutter speed to allow twice as much light into the camera as the current settings permit. To reduce exposure a stop, you use settings that allow half as much light. Doubling or halving the ISO value also adjusts exposure by one stop.

By default, most exposure-related settings on your camera are based on one-third stop adjustments. If you prefer, you can tell the camera to present exposure adjustments in half-stop increments so that you don't have to cycle through as many settings each time you want to make a change. Make your preferences known through the EV Steps for Exposure Cntrl setting, found in the Exposure section of the Custom Setting menu and shown here. This setting affects the shutter speed, aperture, Exposure Compensation, Flash Compensation, and exposure bracketing settings. It also determines the increment used to indicate the amount of under- or overexposure in the meter.

Obviously, the default setting, 1/3 stop, provides the greatest degree of exposure fine-tuning, so I stick with that option. In this book, instructions assume that you're using the defaults as well.

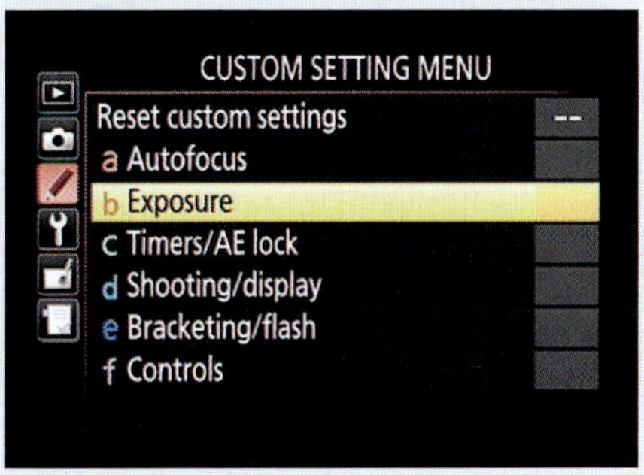

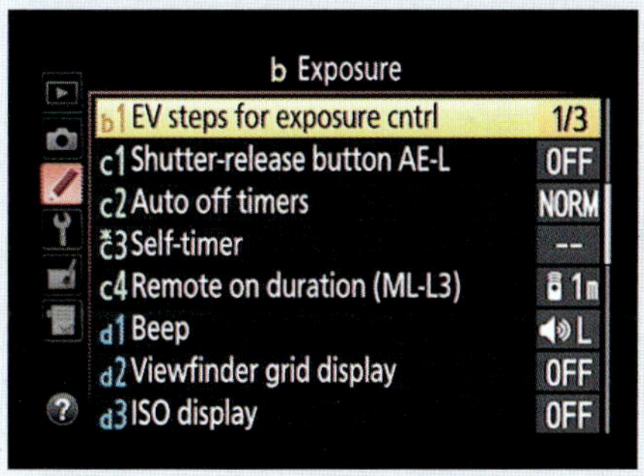

Everyone has their own approach to finding the right combination of aperture, shutter speed, and ISO, and you'll no doubt develop your own system as you become more familiar with these concepts. In the meantime, here's how I handle things:

- I use ISO 100, the lowest setting on the camera, unless the lighting conditions are so poor that I can't use the aperture and shutter speed I want without raising the ISO.
- If my subject is moving, I give shutter speed the next highest priority in my exposure decision. I might choose a fast shutter speed to ensure a blur-free photo or, on the flip side, select a slow shutter to intentionally blur that moving object, an effect that can create a heightened sense of motion.

- For nonmoving subjects, I make aperture a priority over shutter speed, setting the aperture according to the depth of field I have in mind. For portraits, for example, I use a large aperture — say, in the range of f/2.8 to f/5.6 — so that I get a short depth of field, creating a nice, soft background for my subject. For landscapes, I usually go the opposite direction, stopping down the aperture as much as possible to capture the subject at the greatest depth of field. (Again, remember that the range of f-stops you can choose depends on your lens.)

Keeping all this straight is a little overwhelming at first, but the more you work with your camera, the more the whole exposure equation will make sense to you. You can find tips for choosing exposure settings for specific types of pictures in Chapter 6; keep moving through this chapter for details on how to actually adjust aperture, shutter speed, and ISO.

Stepping Up to Advanced Exposure Modes (P, S, A, and M)

REMEMBER

In the fully automatic exposure modes — Auto, Auto Flash Off, Scene modes, and Effects modes — you have little control over exposure. You may be able to choose from one or two Flash modes, and you can adjust ISO in the Scene modes and in all Effects modes except Night Vision. But to gain full control over exposure, set the Mode dial to one of the advanced modes highlighted in Figure 3-7: P, S, A, or M. You also need to use these modes to take advantage of many other camera features, including some of its color and autofocus options.

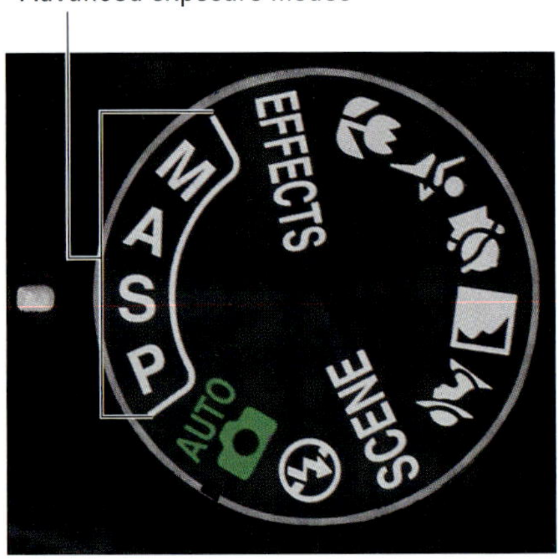

Figure 3-7: You can control exposure and certain other picture properties fully only in P, S, A, or M mode.

I introduce the P, S, A, and M modes in Chapter 2, but because they're critical to your control over exposure, I want to offer some additional information and pointers here. First, a recap of how the four modes differ:

- **P (programmed autoexposure):** The camera selects both aperture and shutter speed to deliver a good exposure at the current ISO setting. But you can choose from different combinations of the two for creative flexibility, which is why the official name of this mode is *flexible programmed autoexposure.*

- **S (shutter-priority autoexposure):** You set the shutter speed, and the camera chooses the aperture setting that produces a good exposure at that shutter speed and the current ISO setting.
- **A (aperture-priority autoexposure):** The opposite of shutter-priority autoexposure, this mode asks you to select the aperture setting. The camera then selects the appropriate shutter speed — again, based on the selected ISO setting.
- **M (manual exposure):** In this mode, you specify both shutter speed and aperture.

REMEMBER

To sum up, the first three modes are semiautomatic modes that are designed to offer exposure assistance while still providing you with some creative control. Note one important point about P, S, and A modes, however: In extreme lighting conditions, the camera may not be able to select settings that will produce a good exposure, and it doesn't stop you from taking a poorly exposed photo. You may be able to solve the problem by using features designed to modify autoexposure results, such as Exposure Compensation (explained later in this chapter) or by adding flash, but you get no guarantees.

Manual mode puts all exposure control in your hands. If you're a longtime photographer who comes from the days when manual exposure was the only game in town, you may prefer to stick with this mode. If it ain't broke, don't fix it, as they say. And in some ways, manual mode is simpler than the semiautomatic modes — if you're not happy with the exposure, you just change the aperture, shutter speed, or ISO setting and shoot again. You don't have to fiddle with features that enable you to modify your autoexposure results.

My choice is to use aperture-priority autoexposure when I'm shooting stationary subjects and want to control depth of field — aperture is my *priority* — and to switch to shutter-priority autoexposure when I'm shooting a moving subject and I'm most concerned with controlling shutter speed. Frankly, my brain is taxed enough by all the other issues involved in taking pictures — what my Release mode setting is, what resolution I need, where I'm going for lunch as soon as I make this shot work — that I appreciate having the camera do some of the exposure "lifting."

However, when I know exactly what aperture and shutter speed I want to use or I'm after an out-of-the-ordinary exposure, I use manual exposure. For example, sometimes when I'm doing a still life in my studio, I want to create a certain mood by underexposing a subject or even shooting it in silhouette. The camera will always fight you on that result in the P, S, and A modes because it so dearly wants to provide a good exposure. Rather than dial in all the autoexposure tweaks that could eventually force the result I want, I simply set the mode to M, adjust the shutter speed and aperture directly, and give the autoexposure system the afternoon off.

But even when you use the M exposure mode, you're never really flying without a net: The camera assists you by displaying the exposure meter, explained next.

Checking the Exposure Meter

Before explaining how to adjust aperture, shutter speed, and ISO, I want to introduce you to your camera's most important exposure guide: the *exposure meter*. The meter tells you whether the camera thinks your picture will be properly exposed at your chosen exposure settings.

However, if and when the meter appears depends on whether you shoot in the M, P, S, or A exposure mode:

- **M mode:** The meter is always present in the Information and Live View displays, as shown in Figure 3-8, and also appears in the viewfinder data display. You can see a close-up look at how the meter looks in the viewfinder in Figure 3-9.

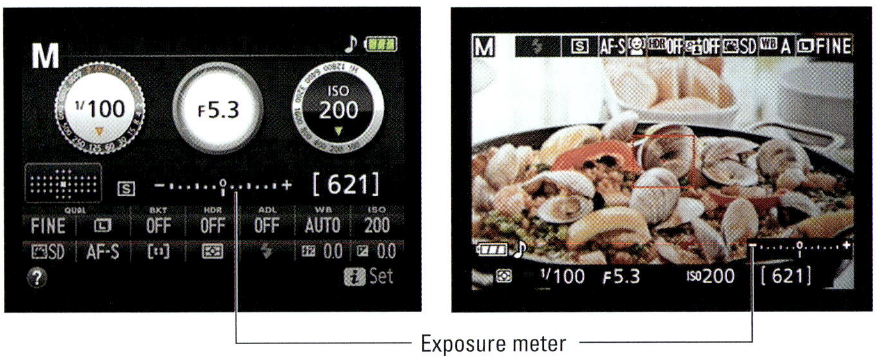

Figure 3-8: In M exposure mode, the exposure meter appears in the Information and Live View displays.

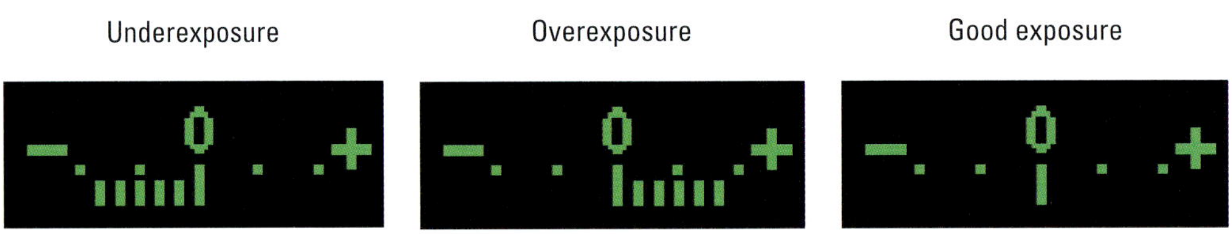

Figure 3-9: The bars under the meter indicate the amount of under- or overexposure.

- **P, S, and A modes:** The meter doesn't appear unless the camera anticipates an exposure problem — for example, if you're shooting in S (shutter-priority autoexposure) mode, and the camera can't select an f-stop that will properly expose the image at your chosen shutter speed and ISO.

Either way, here's what you need to know about using the meter:

- **Waking up the meter:** By default, the meter appears when you press the shutter button halfway and then turns off automatically after 8 seconds of inactivity to save battery power. To wake up the meter, just give the shutter button another half-press.

  You can adjust the meter's auto shutdown timing via the Auto Off Timers option, found in the Timers/AE Lock section of the Custom Setting menu. Chapter 11 has details, if you need help.

- **Reading the meter:** The minus-sign end of the meter represents underexposure; the plus sign, overexposure. If the little notches under the meter fall to the left of 0, as shown in the first example in Figure 3-9, the image will be underexposed. If the notches move to the right of 0, as shown in the second example, the image will be overexposed. When all notches except the center bar disappear, as in the third example in Figure 3-9, you're good to go.

  A couple of details to note:

  - *The markings on the meter indicate exposure stops.* The squares on either side of the 0 represent one full stop each. The small lines below, which appear only when the meter needs to indicate over- or underexposure, break each stop into thirds. So the middle readout in Figure 3-9, for example, indicates an overexposure of 1 and 2/3 stop. The left readout indicates the same amount of underexposure. (The third-stop display assumes that you haven't asked the camera to present exposure data in half-stop increments, in which case you see just one bar between each stop. Again, this feature is controlled by the EV Steps for Exposure Cntrl option, located in the Exposure section of the Custom Setting menu.)
  - *If a triangle appears at the end of the meter, the amount of over- or underexposure exceeds the two-stop range of the meter.* In other words, you have a serious exposure problem.
  - *You can reverse the meter orientation.* For photographers used to a camera that orients the meter with the positive (overexposure) side appearing on the left and the negative (underexposure) side on the right — the design that Nikon used for years — the D5300 offers the option to flip the meter to that orientation. This option also lies on the Custom Setting menu, on the Controls submenu. Look for the Reverse Indicators option, as shown in Figure 3-10. (The setting shown in the figure is the default.)

- **Understanding how exposure is calculated:** The information the meter reports is based on the *Metering mode,* which determines which part of the frame the camera considers when calculating exposure. At the default setting, exposure is based on the entire frame, but you can select two other Metering modes. See the next section for details.

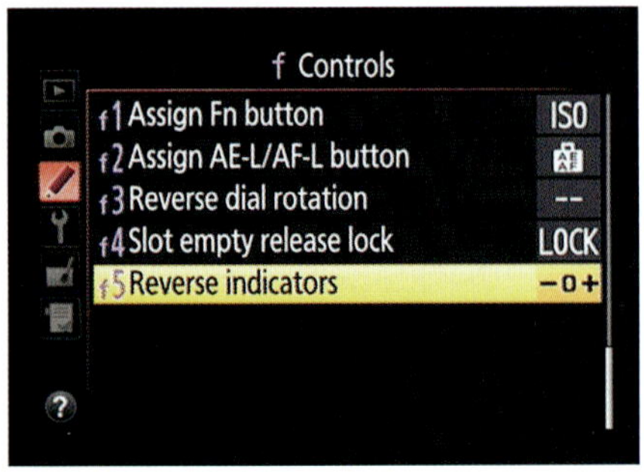

Figure 3-10: You can reverse the meter orientation.

There's one metering quirk to note with respect to Live View photography: In Live View mode, metering may be calculated differently for some scenes than when you use the viewfinder. The rationale is to produce an exposure that's close to what you see in the live preview, which gets darker or lighter as you change exposure settings in an attempt to simulate the exposure you'll get. However, I don't recommend that you trust the preview, because it can be deceiving depending on the ambient light in which you're viewing the monitor. In addition, when you apply Exposure Compensation, an option that produces a brighter or darker image in the P, S, and A modes, the monitor can't adjust itself to accommodate the full range of Exposure Compensation settings. Long story short: The meter is a more accurate indication of exposure than the live preview.

Finally, keep in mind that the meter's suggestion on exposure may not always be the one you want to follow. For example, you may want to shoot a backlit subject in silhouette, in which case you *want* that subject to be underexposed. In other words, the meter is a guide, not a dictator.

Choosing an Exposure Metering Mode

To interpret what the exposure meter tells you, you need to be aware of the current *Metering mode,* which determines which part of the frame the camera analyzes to calculate exposure. The Metering mode affects the meter reading in M mode as well as the exposure settings that the camera chooses in the fully automatic shooting modes as well as in the P, S, and A modes.

The Information display and Live View screen both contain a symbol representing the current metering mode; look in the areas labeled in Figure 3-11. You can choose from three modes, described in the following list and represented in the displays by the icons shown in the margins:

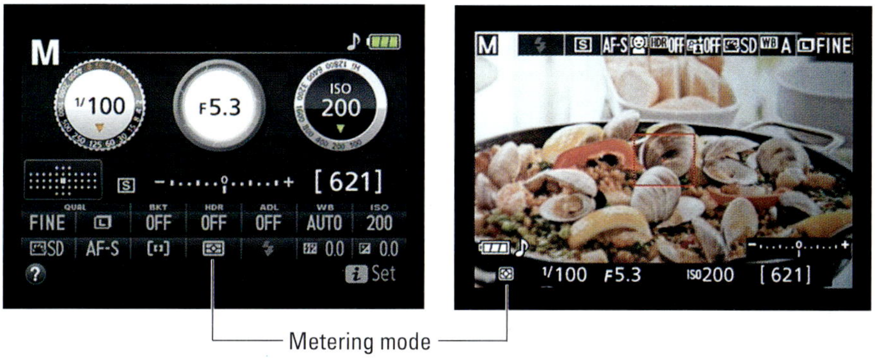

Figure 3-11: This symbol represents the Matrix metering mode.

- **Matrix:** The camera analyzes the entire frame and then selects an exposure that's designed to produce a balanced exposure.

  Your camera manual refers to this mode as 3D Color Matrix II, which is the label that Nikon created to describe the specific technology used in this mode.

- **Center-weighted:** The camera bases exposure on the entire frame but puts extra emphasis — or *weight* — on the center of the frame. Specifically, the camera assigns 75 percent of the metering weight to an 8mm circle in the center of the frame.

- **Spot:** In this mode, the camera bases exposure entirely on a circular area that's about 3.5mm in diameter, or about 2.5 percent of the frame. The location used for this pinpoint metering depends on an autofocusing option called the AF-area mode. Detailed in Chapter 4, this option determines which of the camera's focus points the autofocusing system uses to establish focus. Here's how the setting affects exposure:

  - *If you choose the Auto Area mode,* in which the camera chooses the focus point for you, exposure is based on the center focus point.

  - *If you use any of the other AF-area modes,* which enable you to select a specific focus point, the camera bases exposure on that point.

WARNING!

Because of this autofocus/autoexposure relationship, it's best to switch to one of the AF-area modes that allow focus-point selection when you want to use spot metering. In Auto Area mode, exposure may be incorrect if you compose your shot so that the subject isn't at the center of the frame.

As an example of how Metering mode affects exposure, Figure 3-12 shows the same image captured in each mode. In the matrix example, the bright background caused the camera to select an exposure that left the statue quite dark. Switching to center-weighted metering helped somewhat but didn't quite bring the statue out of the shadows. Spot metering produced the best result as far as the statue goes, although the resulting increase in exposure left the sky a little washed out.

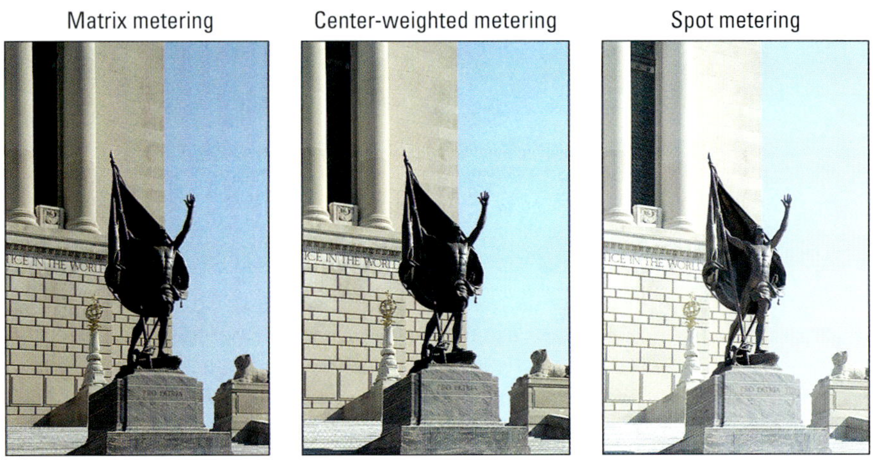

Figure 3-12: The Metering mode determines which area of the frame the camera considers when calculating exposure.

Matrix metering is the default setting, and you can change the Metering mode only in the P, S, A, and M exposure modes. The only way to adjust the setting is via the Information display or Live View control strip, as shown in Figure 3-13. Remember: You activate the strip by pressing the ***i*** button.

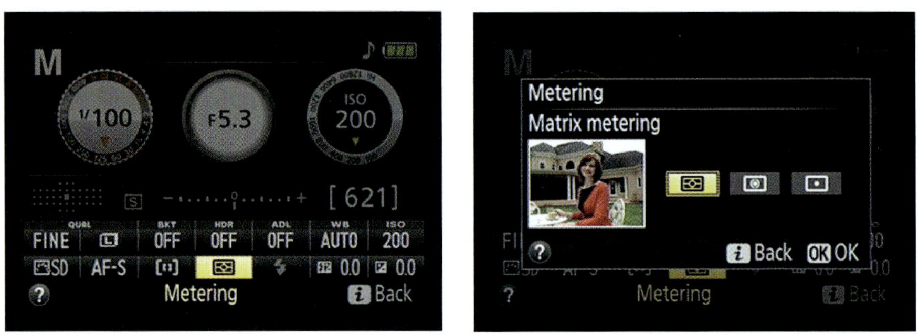

Figure 3-13: Press the ***i*** button to activate the control strip and access the Metering mode setting.

TIP

In theory, the best practice is to check the Metering mode before you shoot and choose the one that best matches your exposure goals. But that's a bit of a pain, not just in terms of having to adjust yet one more capture setting but also in terms of having to *remember* to adjust one more capture setting. Here's my advice: Until you're really comfortable with all the other controls on your camera, just stick with the default setting, which is matrix metering. That mode produces good results in most situations, and after all, you can see in the monitor whether you disagree with how the camera metered or exposed the image and simply reshoot after adjusting the exposure settings to your liking. This option, in my mind, makes the whole Metering mode issue a lot less critical than it is when you shoot with film.

The one exception might be when you're shooting a series of images in which a significant contrast in lighting exists between subject and background. Then, switching to center-weighted metering or spot metering may save you the time spent having to adjust the exposure for each image.

Setting Aperture, Shutter Speed, and ISO

The next sections detail how to view and adjust these critical exposure settings. For a review of how each setting affects your pictures, check out the first part of this chapter.

Adjusting aperture and shutter speed

You can view the current aperture (f-stop) and shutter speed in the Information display and Live View display, as well as in the viewfinder, as shown in Figures 3-14 and 3-15. (If you don't see this data in Live View mode, press the Info button to cycle through the various display options until your screen looks similar to the one in the figure.)

REMEMBER

In the viewfinder, shutter speeds are presented as whole numbers, even if the shutter speed is set to a fraction of a second. For example, the number 100 indicates a shutter speed of 1/100 second. When the shutter speed slows to 1 second or more, quote marks appear after the number — 1" indicates a shutter speed of one second, 4" means four seconds, and so on.

To select aperture and shutter speed, start by pressing the shutter button halfway to kick the exposure system into gear. You can then release the button. The next step depends on the exposure mode, as follows:

- **P (programmed autoexposure):** The camera displays its recommended f-stop and shutter speed when you press the shutter button halfway. But you can rotate the Command dial to select a different combination of settings. The number of possible combinations depends on the aperture settings the camera can select, which depends on your lens.

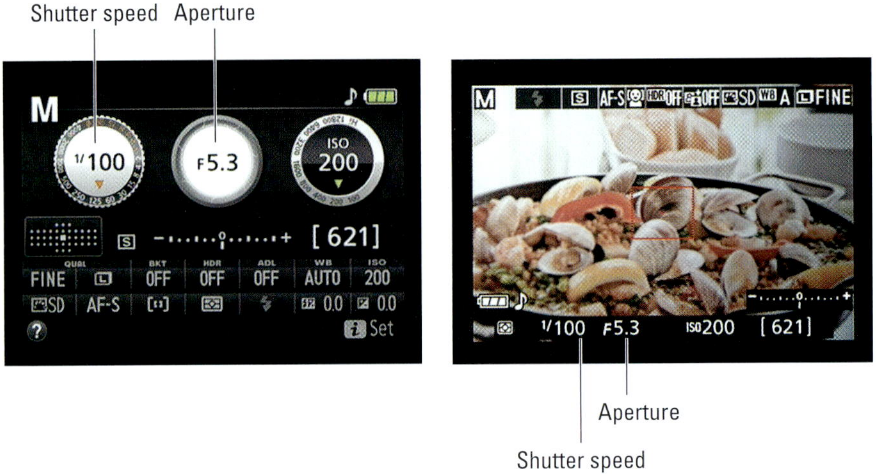

Figure 3-14: You can view the current f-stop and shutter speed on the Information display and Live View screen.

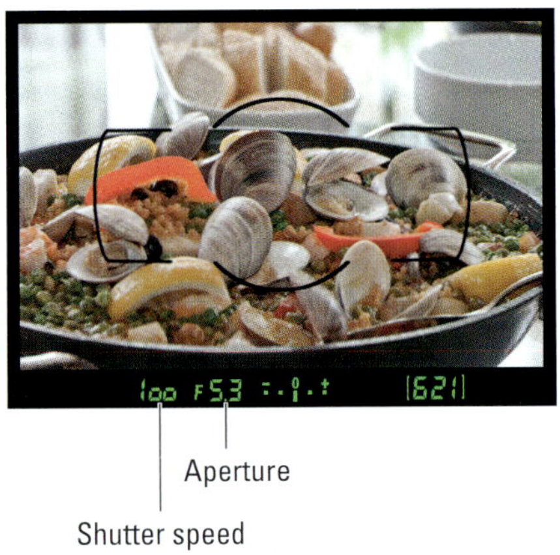

Figure 3-15: The settings also appear in the viewfinder.

An asterisk (*) appears next to the P symbol in the upper-left corner of the Information and Live View displays if you adjust the aperture/shutter speed settings. You see a tiny P* symbol at the left end of the viewfinder display as well. To get back to the initial combo of shutter speed and aperture, rotate the Command dial until the asterisk disappears from the displays and the P* viewfinder symbol turns off.

- **S (shutter-priority autoexposure):** Rotate the Command dial to set the shutter speed. As you do, the camera automatically adjusts the aperture as needed to maintain proper exposure.

  Available shutter speeds range from 30 seconds to 1/4000 second *except* when flash is enabled. When you use flash, the top shutter speed is 1/200 second; minimum shutter speeds vary depending on the exposure mode. (See Chapter 2 for flash details.) This limitation is due to the way the camera must time the flash with the opening of the shutter.

field — so even though you're
an eye on the f-stop, too, if depth
Also note that in extreme lighting
be able to adjust the aperture enough to
e current shutter speed. So you may need
speed or ISO.

autoexposure): Rotate the Command dial to adjust
. The camera automatically selects the appropriate
ed needed to expose the image at your chosen aperture.

he range of available f-stop settings depends on your lens. For zoom lenses, the range typically also changes as you zoom in and out. For example, a lens may offer a maximum aperture of f/3.5 when set to its widest angle (shortest focal length) but limit you to f/5.6 when you zoom in to a longer focal length. Check your lens manual for details on the minimum and maximum aperture settings.

TIP

The aperture symbol that surrounds the f-stop value in the Information display is designed to remind you what the f-stop setting does: The center of the graphic grows or shrinks as you change the f-stop value, indicating that the setting is opening or closing the aperture. Note that this graphic disappears if you switch from the default Information display style (called Graphic) to a simpler display (Classic). You adjust this setting via the Info Display Format option on the Setup menu; Chapter 11 has details.

WARNING!

When you raise the f-stop value, be careful that the shutter speed doesn't drop so low that you risk camera shake if you handhold the camera. And if your scene contains moving objects, make sure that the shutter speed the camera selects is fast enough to stop action (or slow enough to blur it, if that's your creative goal). These same warnings apply when you use P mode.

- **M (manual exposure):** Set aperture and shutter speed like so:
  - *To adjust shutter speed:* Rotate the Command dial.

TIP

In Manual mode, you can access two shutter speed settings not available in the other modes: Rotate the dial one notch past the slowest speed (30 seconds) to access the *Bulb* setting, which keeps the shutter open as long as the shutter button is pressed. If you use the ML-L3 wireless remote control unit, rotate the dial one more time to display the *Time* setting. When you select the Time setting, press the remote's shutter button once to begin the exposure and a second time to end it; maximum exposure time is 30 minutes. If you set the shutter speed to either of these options and then change the Mode dial to S, an alert appears in the Information and Live View displays to let you know that you can't use those options in S mode; you must shift back to M mode to take advantage of them.

- *To adjust aperture:* Press the Exposure Compensation button (on top of the camera) while rotating the Command dial. Notice the little aperture-like symbol that lies next to the button? That's your reminder of the button's role in setting the f-stop in M mode.

In P, S, or A mode, the settings that the camera selects are based on what it thinks is the proper exposure. If you don't agree, you can switch the camera to manual exposure mode and dial in the aperture and shutter speed that deliver the exposure you want. Or, if you want to stay in P, S, or A mode, you can tweak exposure using the features explained in the section "Solving Exposure Problems," later in this chapter.

Controlling ISO

REMEMBER

The ISO setting adjusts the camera's sensitivity to light. A higher ISO enables you to use a faster shutter speed or a smaller aperture (higher f-stop number) because less light is needed to expose the image. But a higher ISO also increases the possibility of noise (refer to Figure 3-5).

You can't adjust ISO in Auto and Auto Flash Off exposure modes; the camera sets the ISO automatically. In any other exposure mode except Night Vision Effects mode, you can choose ISO values ranging from 100 to 12800, plus three Hi settings: Hi 0.3, 0.7, and 1, with Hi 1 taking the ISO all the way up to 25600. You also have the option of sticking with Auto ISO and letting the camera select the ISO it feels is appropriate for your chosen aperture and shutter speed.

To see the ISO setting, look in the Information and Live View displays, in the areas labeled in Figure 3-16. The viewfinder reports the ISO value only when the option is set to Auto. The value appears on the right end of the viewfinder, just to the left of the Shots Remaining value. Otherwise, the ISO area of the viewfinder is empty.

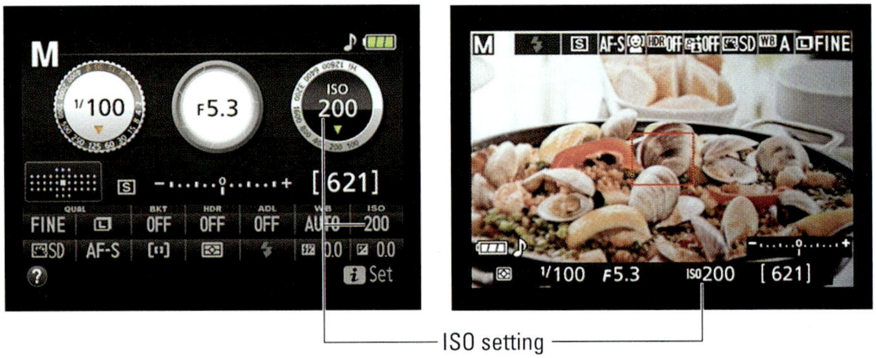

Figure 3-16: The ISO setting appears in the Information and Live View displays.

If you want to view the ISO setting in the viewfinder, you can tell the camera to display that number in the area normally reserved for the Shots Remaining value. Make the change via the ISO Display option, found in the Shooting/Display section of the Custom Setting menu. Choose On to replace the Shots Remaining value with the ISO value. You can then refer to the Information and Live View displays to check the Shots Remaining value. (All figures and instructions in this book assume that you stick with the default arrangement.)

To adjust ISO, you have these options:

- **Fn (Function) button:** By default, pressing the Fn button (left front side of the camera) highlights the ISO setting in the displays. Hold the button while rotating the Command dial to change the setting.
- ***i* button:** You also can adjust the setting via the control strip, as illustrated in Figure 3-17.

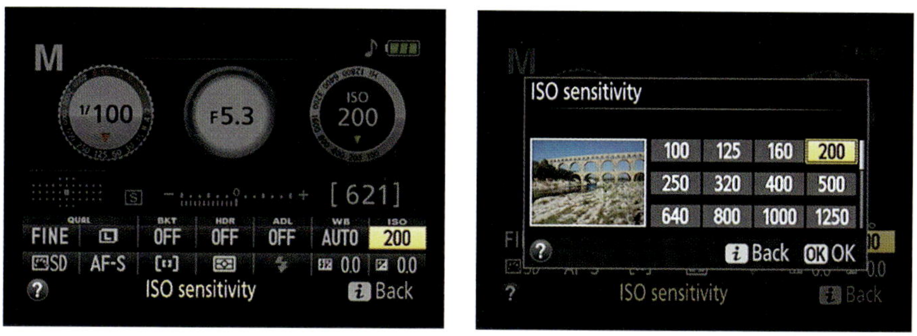

Figure 3-17: In the control strip, look for the ISO setting here.

- **Shooting menu:** Finally, you can change the setting via the ISO Sensitivity Settings option on the Shooting menu, shown in Figure 3-18. The second screen in the figure shows options available in the P, S, A, and M modes; you can access only the top option (ISO Sensitivity) in the other exposure modes. Either way, that's the option that sets the ISO level.

So what's up with the special menu options provided for the P, S, A, and M modes? Well, in those modes, Auto ISO doesn't appear as an option when you select an ISO setting. But by way of the Shooting menu options, you can enable Auto ISO as a backup. Here's how it works: You dial in a specific ISO setting — say, ISO 100. If the camera decides that it can't properly expose the image at that ISO given the current aperture and shutter speed, it automatically adjusts ISO as necessary.

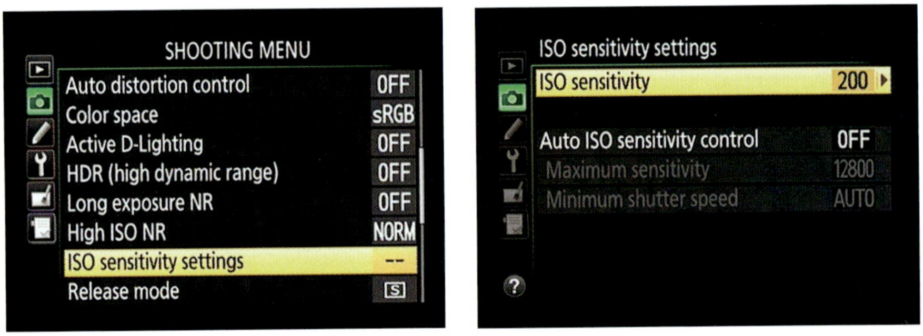

Figure 3-18: You can access advanced ISO options from the Shooting menu.

To enable this option, select ISO Sensitivity Settings on the Shooting menu, as shown on the left in Figure 3-18, and press OK. On the next screen, turn the Auto ISO Sensitivity Control option to On, as shown in Figure 3-19.

Next, use these two menu options to tell the camera when it should step in and offer ISO assistance:

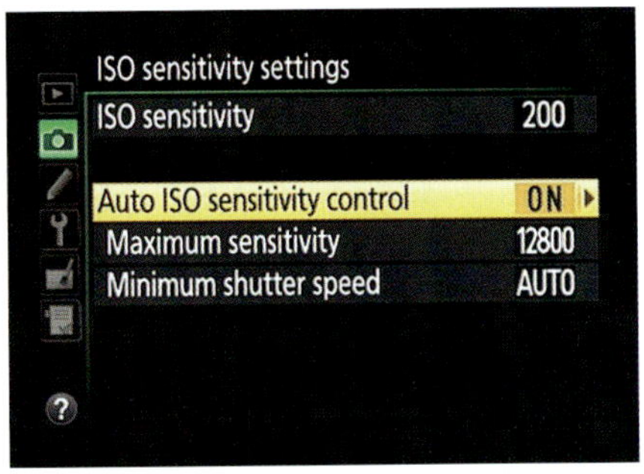

Figure 3-19: In the P, S, A, and M modes, use these options to set up automatic ISO override.

- **Maximum Sensitivity:** This option sets the highest ISO that the camera can use when it overrides the selected setting — a great feature because it enables you to decide how much noise potential you're willing to accept in order to get a good exposure. For example, the value in Figure 3-19 is set to ISO 12800. So even if the picture can't be properly exposed at ISO 12800, the camera won't go any higher than that limit.
- **Minimum Shutter Speed:** Set the minimum shutter speed at which the ISO override engages when you use the P and A exposure modes.

  TIP

  If you set this option to Auto, the camera selects the minimum shutter speed setting based on the focal length of your lens — the idea is that with a longer lens, you need a faster shutter speed to avoid the blur that camera shake can cause when you handhold the camera. After selecting Auto, press the Multi Selector right to access a screen that lets you assign a faster or slower shutter speed to this setting. However, ultimately, exposure trumps camera shake issues: If the camera can't expose the picture at what it thinks is a safe shutter speed for your lens focal length, it uses a slower speed.

  When the camera is about to override your ISO setting, it alerts you by blinking the ISO Auto label in the viewfinder and in the Live View display. The message "ISO-A" blinks in the ISO graphic in the Information display as well. When you view your pictures in the monitor, the ISO value appears in red if you use certain playback display modes. (Chapter 8 has details.)

TIP: To disable Auto ISO override, set the Auto ISO Sensitivity Control option to Off.

Dampening noise

High ISO settings and long exposure times can result in *noise,* a defect that gives pictures a speckled look. To help solve the problem, your camera offers two noise-removal filters: *Long Exposure Noise Reduction,* which dampens the type of noise that occurs during long exposures; and *High ISO Noise Reduction,* designed to reduce the appearance of ISO-related noise. You enable both filters from the Shooting menu, as shown in the figures here.

If you turn on Long Exposure Noise Reduction, the camera applies the filter to pictures taken at shutter speeds of longer than 1 second. For High ISO Noise Reduction, you can choose from four settings. The High, Normal, and Low settings let you control the strength of the noise-removal effect. At the fourth setting, Off, the camera actually still applies a tiny amount of noise removal "as required." In other words, you can't really disable this function altogether. Nikon does promise that the amount of noise reduction at the Off setting is less than at the Low setting, so that's something.

Why would you want to turn off noise reduction anyway? Because enabling these features has a few disadvantages. First, the filters are applied after you take the picture, as the camera processes the image data. While the Long Exposure Noise Reduction filter is being applied, the message "Job Nr" appears in the viewfinder. The time needed to apply this filter can significantly slow your shooting speed — in fact, it can double the time the camera needs to record the file to the memory card.

Second, although filters that go after long-exposure noise work fairly well, those that attack high ISO noise work primarily by applying a slight blur to the image. Don't expect this process to totally eliminate noise, and do expect some resulting image softness. You may be able to get better results by using the blur tools or noise-removal filters found in many photo editors, because you can blur just the parts of the image where noise is most noticeable — usually in areas of flat color or little detail, such as skies.

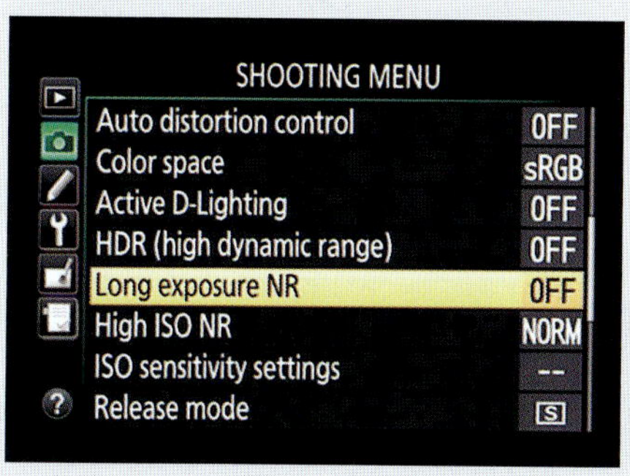

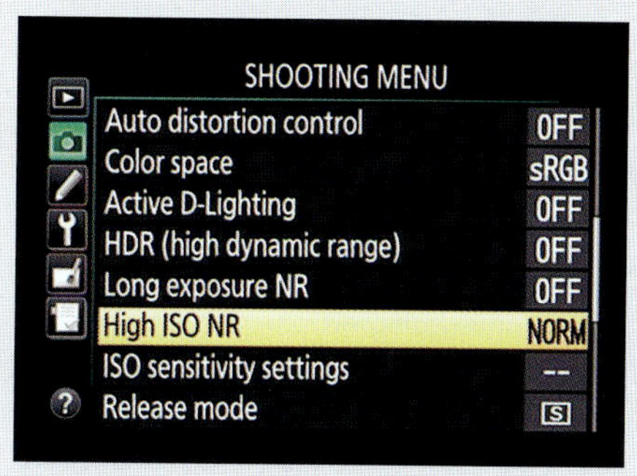

Solving Exposure Problems

Along with controls over aperture, shutter speed, and ISO, your camera offers a collection of tools designed to solve tricky exposure problems.

If the problem is underexposure due to a lack of ambient light, your camera's built-in flash is at the top of the list of exposure aids to consider. Chapter 2 explains how to get good flash results. But you also have several other exposure-correction features at your disposal, whether your subject appears under- or overexposed. The next several sections introduce you to these features. Also check out Chapter 10, which shows you how to tweak exposure of existing photos by applying tools found on the Retouch menu.

Applying Exposure Compensation

In the P, S, and A exposure modes, you have some input over exposure: In P mode, you can rotate the Command dial to choose from different combinations of aperture and shutter speed; in S mode, you can dial in the shutter speed; and in A mode, you can select the aperture setting. But because these are semiautomatic modes, the camera ultimately controls the final exposure. If your picture turns out too bright or too dark in P mode, you can't simply choose a different f-stop/shutter speed combo because they all deliver the same exposure — which is to say, the exposure that the camera has in mind. And changing the shutter speed in S mode or adjusting the f-stop in A mode won't help either because as soon as you change the setting that you're controlling, the camera automatically adjusts the other setting to produce the same exposure it initially delivered.

Not to worry: You actually do have final say over exposure in P, S, and A modes. The secret is Exposure Compensation, a feature that tells the camera to produce a brighter or darker exposure on your next shot, whether or not you change the aperture or shutter speed (or both, in P mode).

As an example, take a look at the first image in Figure 3-20. The initial exposure selected by the camera left the balloon too dark; I used Exposure Compensation to produce the brighter image on the right.

How the camera arrives at the brighter or darker image depends on the exposure mode: In A mode, the camera adjusts the shutter speed but leaves your selected f-stop in force. In S mode, the camera adjusts the f-stop and keeps its hands off the shutter speed control. In P mode, the camera decides whether to adjust aperture, shutter speed, or both. In all three modes, the camera may also adjust ISO if you enable Auto ISO Sensitivity Control. Keep in mind, though, that the camera can adjust f-stop only so much, according to the aperture range of your lens. And the range of shutter speeds, too, is limited by the camera itself. So there's no guarantee that the camera can actually deliver a better exposure when you dial in Exposure Compensation. If you reach the end of the f-stop or shutter speed range, you either have to adjust ISO or compromise on your selected f-stop or shutter speed.

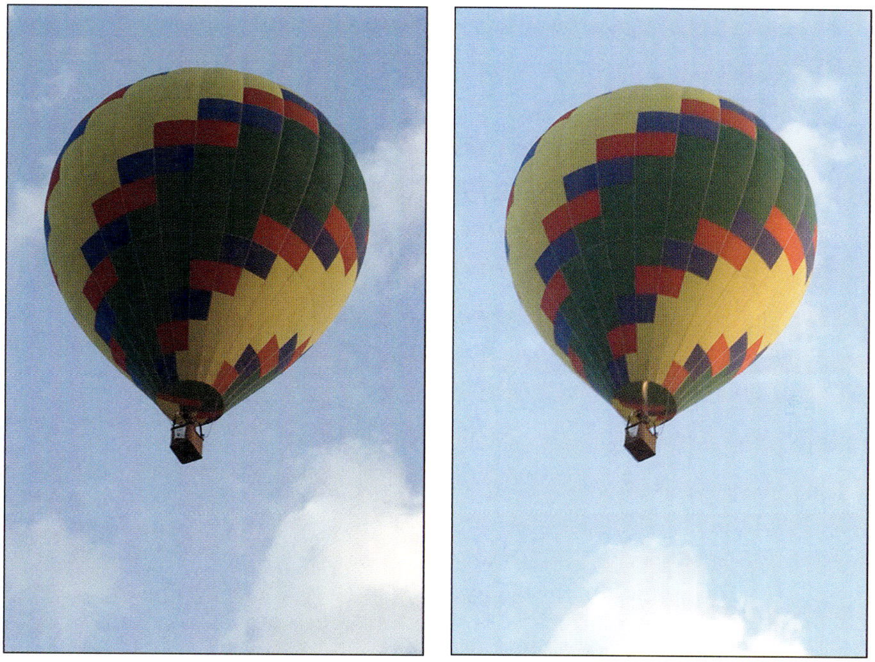

Figure 3-20: For a brighter exposure, raise the Exposure Compensation value.

With that background out of the way, here are the details about this feature:

- **Exposure Compensation settings are stated in terms of EV numbers, as in EV +2.0.** Possible values range from EV +5.0 to EV –5.0. (*EV* stands for *exposure value.*) Each full number on the EV scale represents an exposure shift of one stop. A setting of EV 0.0 results in no exposure adjustment. For a brighter image, raise the Exposure Compensation value; for a darker image, lower the value. For my balloon image, I set the value to EV +1.0.
- **Where and how you check the current setting depends on the display, as follows:**
  - *Information display:* This one's straightforward: The setting appears in the area labeled on the left in Figure 3-21. In addition, the meter shows the amount of compensation being applied. In Figure 3-21, for example, the meter indicator appears one stop toward the positive end of the meter, reflecting the EV +1.0 setting.
  - *Live View display:* If Exposure Compensation is turned on, you see the plus/minus symbol labeled on the right in the figure; otherwise, that area of the display appears empty.

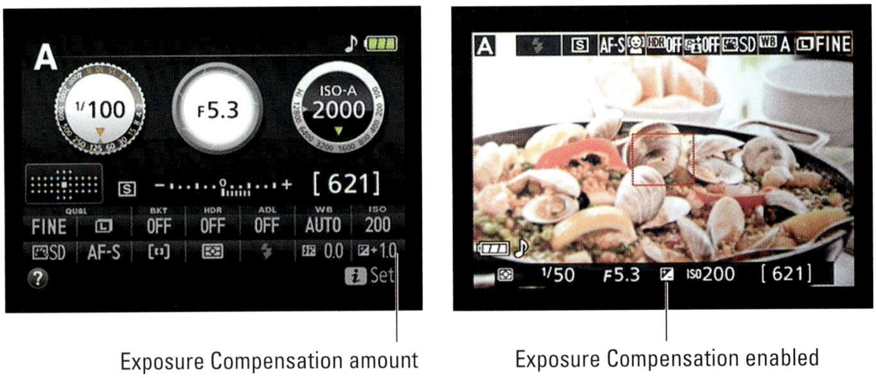

Figure 3-21: These indicators tell you whether Exposure Compensation is enabled.

To view the selected adjustment amount in Live View mode, press the Exposure Compensation button. While the button is pressed, the EV value appears next to the plus/minus symbol.

- *Viewfinder:* The viewfinder also displays the plus/minus symbol only, but again, you can press the Exposure Compensation button to temporarily view the EV setting. Or just look at the exposure meter: As in the Information display, the exposure meter tells you how much exposure shift is in force.

- **You can change the Exposure Compensation setting in two ways:**
  - *Press the Exposure Compensation button while rotating the Command dial.* Pressing the button automatically activates the setting, as shown in Figure 3-22, and you can just spin the Command dial to enter the amount of adjustment you want to apply. (Although the figure shows the Information display, this technique also works in Live View mode.)

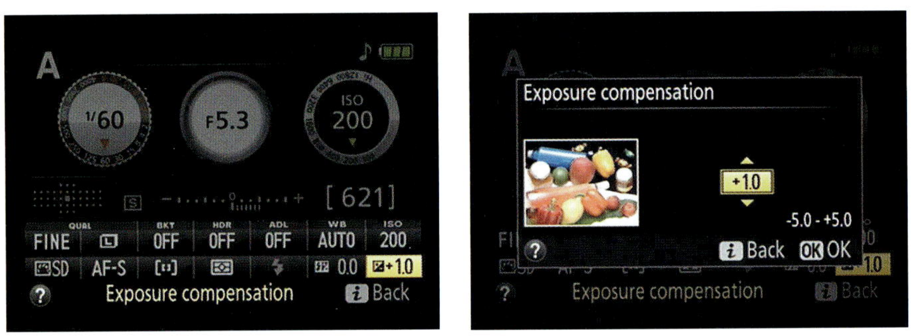

Figure 3-22: Press the Exposure Compensation button and rotate the Command dial to adjust the setting.

- *Use the control strip.* You know the drill: Press the ***i*** button to activate the strip, highlight the Exposure Compensation value, and then press OK to display the screen where you can set the amount of adjustment.

- **As you adjust the setting in Live View mode, the monitor brightness updates to show you how the change will affect exposure.** However — and this is a biggie, so stop texting and pay attention — the preview can only show an adjustment up to +/– EV 3.0, even though you can set the adjustment as high as +/– EV 5.0.

- **Your Exposure Compensation setting remains in force until you change it, even if you power off the camera.** So make a habit of checking the setting before each shoot, or always set the value back to EV 0.0 after taking the last shot for which you want to apply compensation.

- **When you use flash, the Exposure Compensation setting affects both background brightness and flash power.** But you can further modify the flash power through a related option, Flash Compensation. You can find out more about that feature at the end of Chapter 2.

- **Exposure Compensation affects the meter in M exposure mode.** Although the camera doesn't change your selected exposure settings in M (manual) exposure mode if Exposure Compensation is enabled, the exposure *meter* is affected: It indicates whether your shot will be properly exposed based on the Exposure Compensation setting. So if you don't realize that Exposure Compensation is enabled, you may mistakenly adjust your exposure settings when they're actually on target. This is yet another reason why it's best to always reset the Exposure Compensation setting back to EV 0.0 after you're done using the feature.

- **You also can apply Exposure Compensation in Night Vision Effects mode and during movie recording.** See Chapter 10 for help using Effects mode; Chapter 7 covers movie features. Note that in Night Vision mode, the Exposure Compensation value *is* reset to EV 0.0 when you turn off the camera or choose a different exposure mode.

Expanding tonal range

A scene like the one in Figure 3-23 presents the classic photographer's challenge: Choosing exposure settings that capture the darkest parts of the subject appropriately causes the brightest areas to be overexposed. And if you instead *expose for the highlights* — that is, set the exposure settings to capture the brightest regions properly — darker areas are underexposed.

Active D-Lighting off　　　　Active D-Lighting on

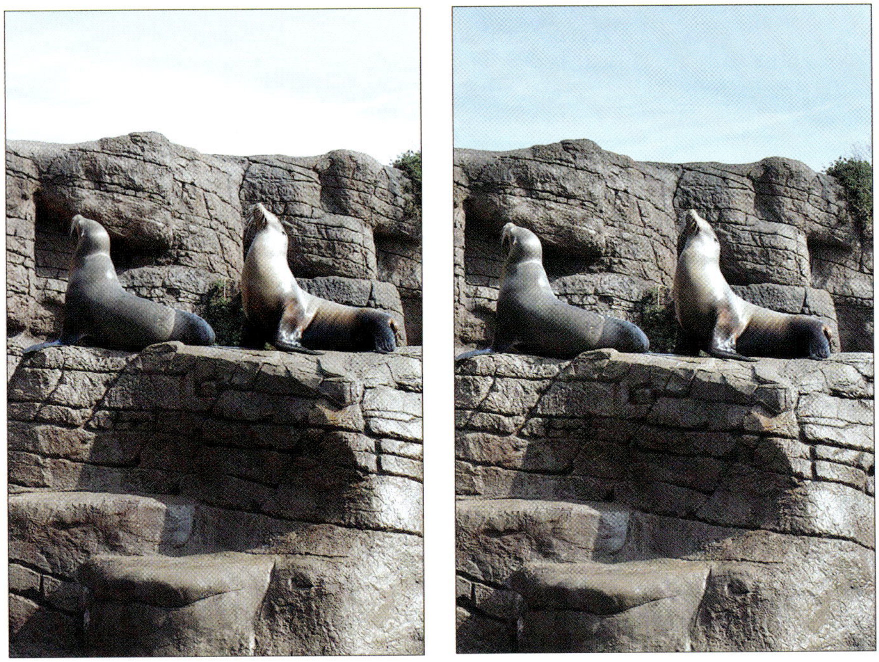

Figure 3-23: Active D-Lighting captured the shadows without blowing out the highlights.

In the past, you had to choose between favoring highlights or shadows. But with the D5300, you can expand *tonal range* — the range of brightness values in an image — through two features: Active D-Lighting and HDR (high dynamic range). The next two sections explain both options.

Applying Active D-Lighting

One way to cope with a high-contrast scene like the one in Figure 3-23 is to turn on Active D-Lighting. The *D* is a reference to *dynamic range,* the term used to describe the range of brightness values that an imaging device can capture. By turning on this feature, you enable the camera to produce an image with a slightly greater dynamic range than usual.

Specifically, Active D-Lighting gives you a better chance of keeping highlights intact while better exposing the darkest areas. In my seal scene, Active D-Lighting produced a brighter rendition of the darkest parts of the rocks and the seals, for example, yet the color in the sky didn't get blown out, as it did when I captured the image with Active D-Lighting turned off. The highlights in the seal and in the rocks in the lower-right corner of the image also are toned down a tad in the Active D-Lighting version.

Active D-Lighting does its thing in two stages. First, it selects exposure settings that result in a slightly darker exposure than normal, which helps to retain highlight details. After you snap the photo, the camera brightens the darkest areas of the image to rescue shadow detail.

Symbols representing the current Active D-Lighting setting appear in the Information and Live View displays, in the areas labeled in Figure 3-24. The symbol that you see in the figures represents the Auto setting, which tells the camera to select the amount of exposure adjustment. I used this setting for my seal image.

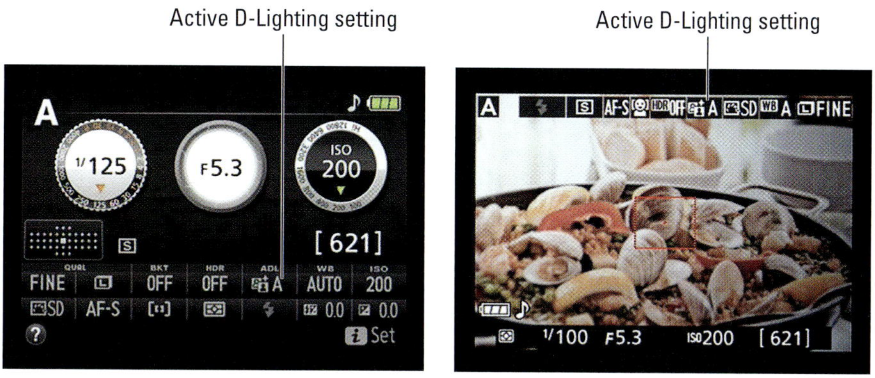

Figure 3-24: These symbols represent the Auto Active D-Lighting setting.

In Auto, Auto Flash Off, Scene, and Effects exposure modes, you're stuck with Auto Active D-Lighting; you can't disable the feature or vary the extent of the adjustment. In the P, S, A, and M modes, Auto is the default Active D-Lighting setting, but you can choose from five other settings: H* (extra high), H (high), N (normal), L (low), and Off.

TIP

I usually keep this option set to Off so that I can decide for myself whether I want any adjustment instead of having the camera apply it to every shot. Even with a high-contrast scene that's designed for the Active D-Lighting feature, you may decide that you prefer the "contrasty" look that results from disabling the option.

To select the setting you want to use, you can take two paths:

- **Control strip:** Press the ***i*** button to activate the control strip, and then use the Multi Selector to highlight the Active D-Lighting option, as shown on the left in Figure 3-25. Press OK to get to the screen shown on the right, where you can specify the adjustment level.

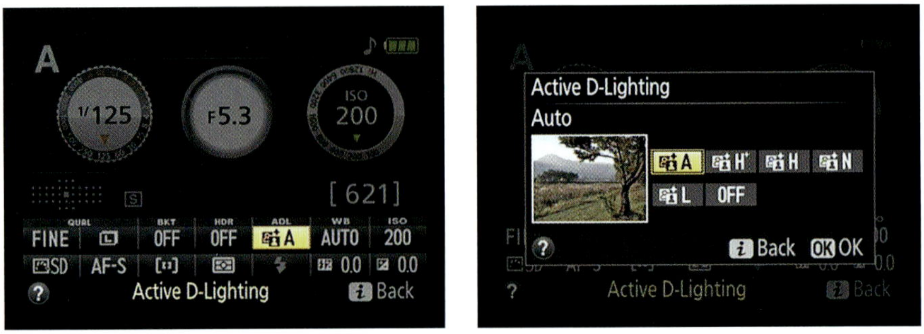

Figure 3-25: Press the *i* button to activate the control strip and adjust the Active D-Lighting setting.

- **Shooting menu:** You also can change the setting via the Shooting menu, as shown in Figure 3-26.

TIP

A few pointers about using Active D-Lighting:

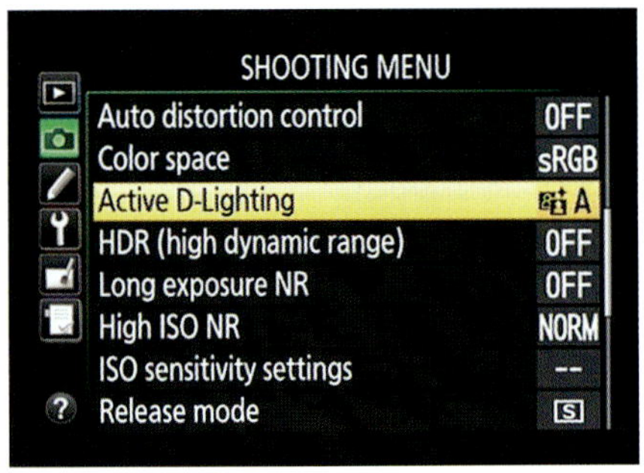

Figure 3-26: Or select the setting via the Shooting menu.

- You get the best Active D-Lighting results in matrix metering mode.
- Active D-Lighting doesn't work when the ISO Sensitivity is set to Hi 0.3 or above.
- Although Nikon doesn't recommend that you use Active D-Lighting in the M exposure mode, it's worth taking a test shot anyway if you can't get the results you like with the feature turned off. In M mode, the camera doesn't change the shutter speed or f-stop to achieve the darker exposure it needs for Active D-Lighting to work; instead, the meter readout guides you to select the right settings unless you have automatic ISO override enabled. In that case, the camera may instead adjust ISO to manipulate the exposure.
- If you're not sure whether the picture will benefit from Active D-Lighting, try Active D-Lighting bracketing, which automatically records the scene once with the feature disabled and once at a level you select. See the last section in this chapter for details.

TIP

If you opt out of Active D-Lighting, remember that the camera's Retouch menu offers a D-Lighting filter that applies a similar adjustment to existing pictures. See Chapter 10 for help.

Exploring high dynamic range (HDR) photography

In the past few years, many digital photographers have been experimenting with a technology called HDR photography. HDR stands for *high dynamic range* — again, dynamic range refers to the spectrum of brightness values that a camera or another imaging device can record.

The idea behind HDR is to capture the same shot multiple times, using different exposure settings for each image. You then use special imaging software, called *tone mapping software,* to combine the exposures in a way that uses specific brightness values from each shot. By using this process, you get a shot that contains a much higher dynamic range than the camera can capture in a single image.

TIP

The D5300 offers a feature that provides automated HDR photography. When you enable this option, the camera records two images, each at different exposure settings, and then does the tone-mapping manipulation for you to produce a single HDR image. This feature is available only in the P, S, A, and M exposure modes.

So how is HDR different from Active D-Lighting — other than the fact that it records two photos instead of manipulating a single capture? Well, with the HDR feature, you can request an exposure shift that results in up to three stops difference between the two photos. That enables you to create an image that has a broader dynamic range than you can get with Active D-Lighting.

Figure 3-27 shows an example of the type of results you can expect. In this scene, half of the area is in bright sunshine, and the other is in shadow. For the top-left photo in the figure, I exposed for the highlights, which left the right side of the scene too dark. For the top-right image, I set exposure for the shaded area, which blew out the highlights in the sunny areas. With the HDR feature, I was able to produce the bottom image in the figure. The shadows aren't completely eliminated, and some parts of the rose bush on the left side of the shot are a little brighter than I want, but on the whole, the camera balanced out the exposure fairly well.

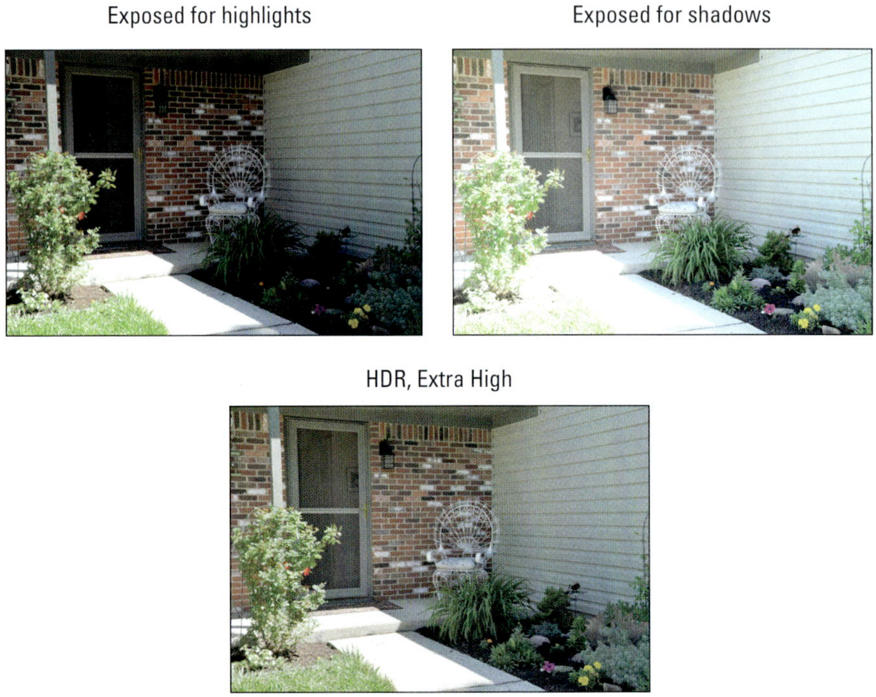

Figure 3-27: The HDR option enables you to produce an image with an even greater tonal range than Active D-Lighting.

Before you try the HDR feature, note these important points:

- Although the camera shoots two frames, you wind up with just a single HDR photo. You can't play back or access the original two shots.
- Because the camera is recording and merging two photos, the feature works well only on stationary subjects. If the subject is moving, it appears as two translucent forms in different areas in the merged frame.
- Use a tripod to make sure that you don't move the camera between shots. Otherwise, the merged shots may not align properly.
- You can't use the HDR feature if you set the Image Quality option to Raw (NEF). It works only for photos captured in the JPEG format. (Set the Image Quality option to Fine, Normal, or Basic.)
- When HDR is turned on, you can't use flash or the Continuous Release mode settings.

- You can choose from four levels of HDR exposure shift: Low, Normal, High, or Extra High. Choose Extra High for the 3-stop exposure maximum. I used this setting to produce the image in Figure 3-27. If you select Auto, the camera chooses what it considers the best adjustment.
- One clunky aspect of this tool: The camera disables HDR after your first two frames are captured and merged. That makes experimenting cumbersome because you have to continuously enable the feature each time you want to try different exposure settings or simply shoot another HDR frame. Annoying, to say the least.

I should also explain that if you want to produce the more-extreme type of HDR imagery that you see in photography magazines, you need to go beyond the two-frame, three-stop limitations of the in-camera HDR feature. To give you a point of comparison, Figure 3-28 shows an example I created by blending five frames with a variation of five stops between frames. The first two images show you the brightest and darkest exposures; the last image shows the HDR composite.

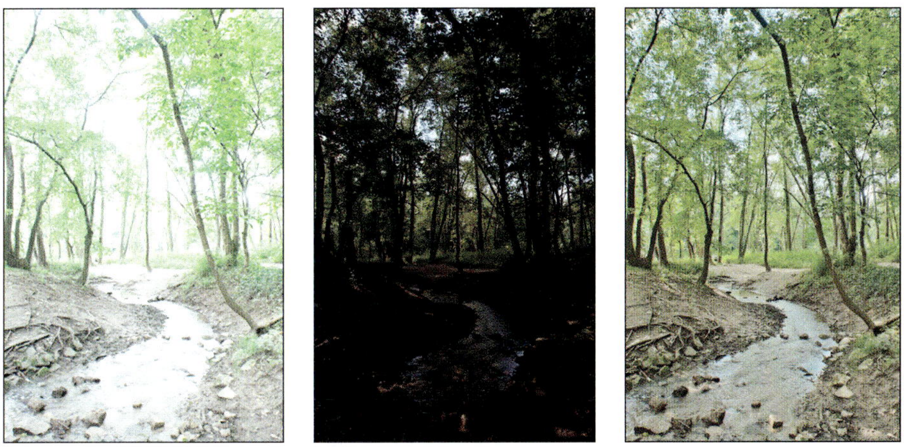

Figure 3-28: Using HDR software tools, I merged the brightest and darkest exposures (left and middle) along with several intermediate exposures, to produce the composite image (right).

On the other hand, the effect created by the camera's HDR tool looks more realistic than the one in Figure 3-29 because the tonal range isn't stretched to such an extent. When applied to its extreme limits, HDR produces something of a graphic-novel look. My example is pretty tame; some people might not even realize that any digital trickery has been involved. To me, it has the look of a hand-tinted photo.

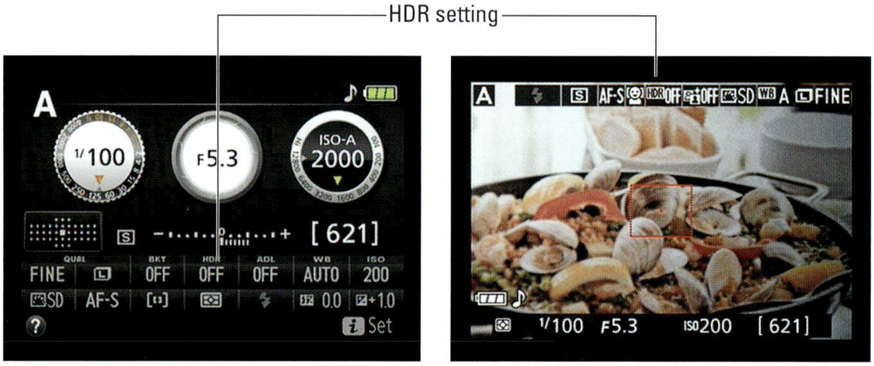

Figure 3-29: These symbols indicate whether HDR is enabled.

And of course, even though the in-camera HDR tool may not be enough to produce the surreal HDR look that's all the rage these days, you can still use your D5300 for HDR work — you just have to adjust the exposure settings yourself between shots and then merge the frames using your own HDR software. You should also shoot the images in the Raw format because HDR tone-mapping tools work best on Raw images, which contain more bits of picture data than JPEG files.

All that said, the HDR feature is worth investigating when you're confronted with a high-contrast scene and you want to see how much you can broaden the dynamic range. Just take one shot with the feature enabled and a second with it turned off, and then compare the results to see which setting works best.

Both the Information and Live View displays include a symbol that tells you whether HDR is enabled; look in the areas labeled in Figure 3-29. To adjust the setting, use these options:

- **Control strip:** The fastest way to enable HDR and choose the level of exposure shift is via the control strip, as illustrated in Figure 3-30.
- **Shooting menu:** You also can set up your HDR shot via the Shooting menu, as shown in Figure 3-31.

REMEMBER

Either way, frame your subject a little loosely; the camera may need to trim away the edges of the frame in order to perfectly align the two shots in the HDR image. When you press the shutter button, the camera records two frames in quick succession and then creates the merged HDR image. The message "Job Hdr" appears in the viewfinder as this digital manipulation is being accomplished.

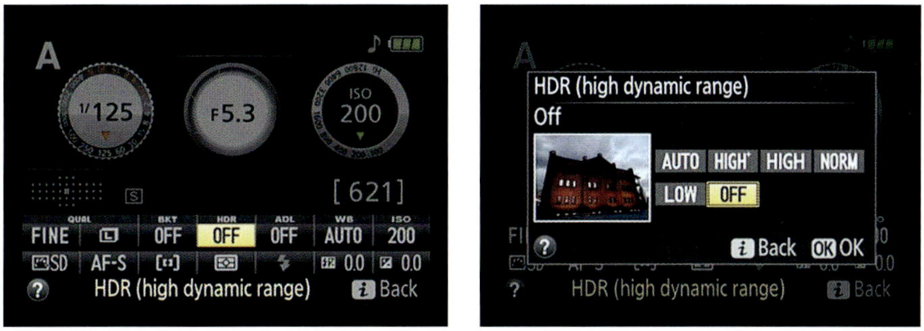

Figure 3-30: The fastest way to enable the HDR feature is via the control strip.

Using autoexposure lock

To help ensure a proper exposure, your camera continually meters the light until the moment you depress the shutter button fully. In autoexposure modes, it also keeps adjusting exposure settings as needed to maintain a good exposure.

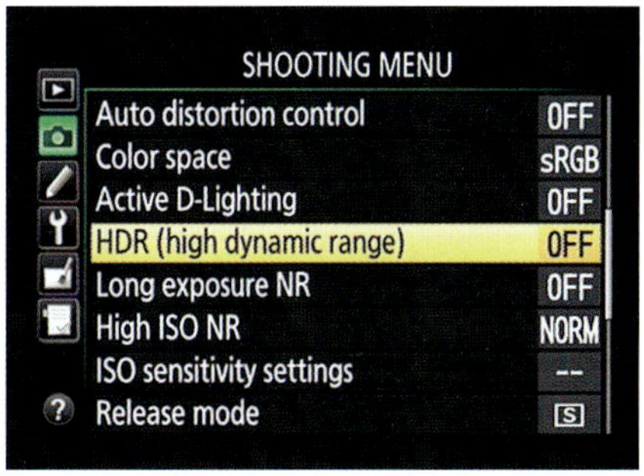

Figure 3-31: You also can enable HDR via the Shooting menu.

For most situations, this approach works great, resulting in the right settings for the light that's striking your subject at the moment you capture the image. But on occasion, you may want to lock in a certain combination of exposure settings. For example, perhaps you want your subject to appear at the far edge of the frame. If you were to use the normal shooting technique, you'd place the subject under a focus point, press the shutter button halfway to lock focus and set the initial exposure, and then reframe to your desired composition to take the shot. The problem is that exposure is then recalculated based on the new framing, which can leave your subject under- or overexposed.

The easiest way to lock in exposure settings is to switch to M (manual) exposure mode and use the f-stop, shutter speed, and ISO settings that work best for your subject. But if you prefer to stay with an autoexposure mode, you can press the AE-L/AF-L button to lock exposure before you reframe. This feature is known as *autoexposure lock,* or AE Lock for short. You can take advantage of AE Lock in any autoexposure mode except Auto or Auto Flash Off.

A few fine points about using this feature:

- **While AE Lock is in force, the letters AE-L appear in the displays.** Look for this indicator at the left end of the viewfinder; next to the Metering mode icon at the bottom of the Live View display; and just beneath the shutter speed setting in the Information display.
- **By default, focus is also locked when you press the button if you're using autofocusing.** You can change this behavior by customizing the AE-L/AF-L button function, as outlined in Chapter 11.
- **For the best results, pair this feature with the Spot Metering mode and autofocus settings that enable to you select a single focus point.** Then, if you frame your subject under that focus point, exposure is set and locked based on your subject. You can find out how to use Spot metering earlier in this chapter; see Chapter 4 for help with autofocus settings.
- **Be sure to keep holding the AE-L/AF-L button until you release the shutter button.** And if you want to use the same focus and exposure settings for your next shot, just keep the AE-L/AF-L button pressed.

Bracketing Exposures

Many photographers use *exposure bracketing* to ensure that at least one shot of a subject is properly exposed. *Bracketing* simply means to shoot the same subject multiple times, slightly varying the exposure settings for each image.

In the P, S, A, and M exposure modes, your camera offers *automatic bracketing.* When you enable this feature, your only job is to press the shutter button to record the shots; the camera automatically adjusts the exposure settings between each image. This feature is especially helpful in situations where you don't have time to review images and adjust exposure settings between shots. The D5300, however, takes things one step further than most cameras that offer automatic bracketing, enabling you to bracket not just basic exposure but also Active D-Lighting or white balance.

REMEMBER

The camera records a three-shot series of bracketed images when you use the autoexposure and white-balance bracketing options. For Active D-Lighting, you get only two shots in the series: one with the feature turned off and one at the setting currently in force for the Active D-Lighting option. (See "Applying Active D-Lighting," earlier in this chapter, for details on changing that setting.)

Chapter 5 explains how to use the white-balance bracketing option. To try your hand at exposure or Active D-Lighting bracketing, follow these steps:

1. **Set your camera to the P, S, A, or M exposure mode.**

   You can't take advantage of the feature in any other mode.

2. **Display the Custom Setting menu, highlight Bracketing/Flash, and press OK.**

3. **Select Auto Bracketing Set, as shown on the left in Figure 3-32, and press OK.**

   You see the options shown on the right in the figure. This screen is where you tell the camera whether you want to bracket the exposure (AE), white balance (WB), or Active D-Lighting (ADL). Note that even though the first option is called AE (for autoexposure), it enables you to bracket exposure in M (manual exposure) mode just the same.

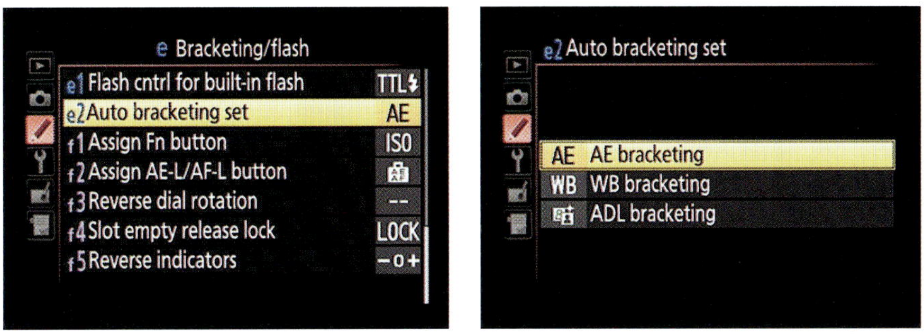

Figure 3-32: Before enabling auto bracketing, select the feature you want the camera to adjust between shots.

4. **Select the desired bracketing option and press OK.**

5. **Press the *i* button to display the control strip, where you can specify the bracketing increment.**

   Highlight the BKT setting, as shown on the left in Figure 3-33, and press OK to display the second screen in the figure. The available settings depend on the feature you're bracketing, as follows:

   - *For exposure bracketing,* the settings control the amount of exposure shift between frames. The settings are based on Exposure Compensation values. For example, if you choose 0.7 for an autoexposure bracketing set, the camera makes three exposures: one with exposure values as metered by the camera, one exposure with EV +0.7, and one exposure with EV –0.7 Your choices are from 0.3 EV to 2.0 EV. Choosing Off disables bracketing.

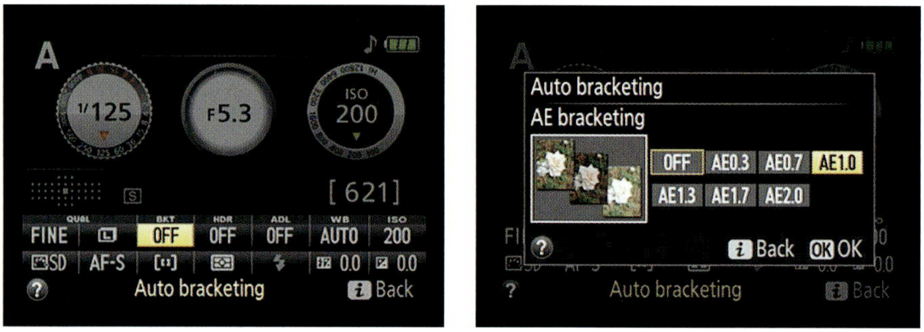

Figure 3-33: Set the bracketing amount from the Information display control strip.

- *For Active D-Lighting bracketing,* you get only two options: ADL and Off. Select ADL. (This option is a little weird — if you select Off, you just disable bracketing.)

6. **Press OK to return to the control strip; then press the *i* button again to exit the strip.**
7. **Shoot your first bracketed series.**

   Remember: For autoexposure bracketing, a series consists of three shots; for Active D-Lighting, two shots.

   When bracketing is enabled, the Information and Live View displays offer a *bracketing indicator,* as shown in Figure 3-34. That's a technical way of saying, "Little bars appear under the meter, each one representing one shot in your bracketed series." The indicator updates after each picture to show you how many more shots are left in the series. For example, the middle bar represents your first shot; after you take your first picture, it disappears. You then see one or two bars — and thus, one or two shots left to shoot — depending on whether you're bracketing exposure or Active D-Lighting. A label on top of the meter reminds you which feature you're bracketing — AE-BKT (autoexposure) bracketing, in the figure.
8. **To disable bracketing, repeat Step 5 and select Off from the second screen shown in Figure 3-33.**

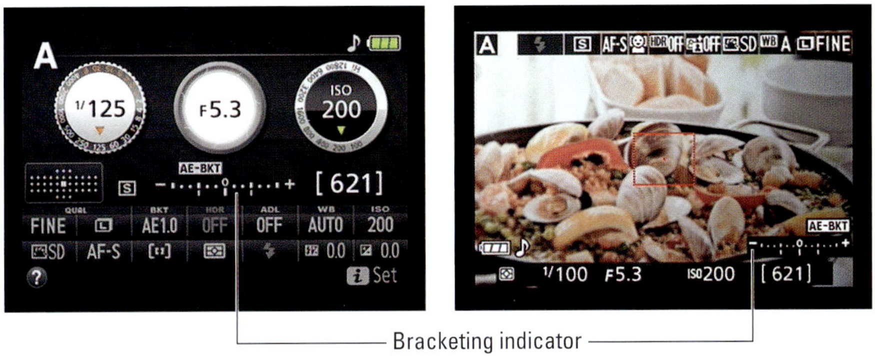

Figure 3-34: The bars under the meter tell you which frame of the bracketed series you're about to shoot.

If you set the Release Mode to Continuous Low or Continuous High, you can save yourself some button pressing: In those two Release modes, the camera records the entire bracketed series with one push of the shutter button. To change the Release mode, press the Release mode button or select Release Mode from the Shooting menu. Remember, though, that you can't use flash in either Release mode. See Chapter 2 for more details about the Release mode setting.

4

Controlling Focus and Depth of Field

In This Chapter

- Understanding autofocusing options
- Choosing a specific autofocusing point
- Tracking focus when shooting moving subjects
- Taking advantage of manual-focusing aids
- Manipulating depth of field

To many people, the word *focus* has just one interpretation when applied to a photograph: Either the subject is in focus or it's blurry. But an artful photographer knows that there's more to focus than simply getting a sharp image of a subject. You also need to consider *depth of field,* or the distance over which other objects in the scene appear sharply focused. This chapter explains how to manipulate both aspects of a an image.

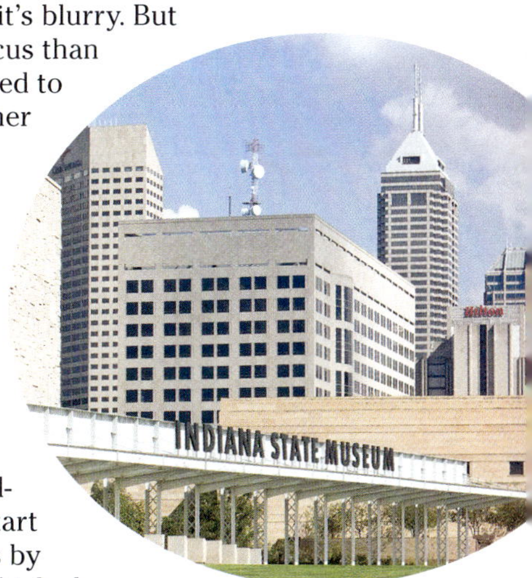

The chapter begins with details of the focusing options available for viewfinder photography; following that, you can get help with focusing during Live View photography and movie recording. Just a word of warning: The two focusing systems are quite different, and mastering them takes time and practice. So don't think that you're not up for the challenge if everything doesn't sink in right away. If you start feeling overwhelmed, take a break and simplify things by following the steps laid out at the end of Chapter 1, which show you how to take a picture using the default autofocus settings and the Auto exposure mode. Then return another day to study the advanced focusing options discussed here.

Things get much easier (and more fun) at the end of the chapter, where I explain how to control depth of field. Thankfully, the concepts related to that subject apply no matter whether you're using the viewfinder, taking advantage of Live View photography, or shooting movies.

Exploring Standard Focusing Options (Viewfinder Photography)

In case you're the type who doesn't read chapter introductions (I bring this up only because I'm that type), I want to reiterate that the D5300 uses different focusing technologies depending on whether you're using the viewfinder or taking advantage of Live View. This part of the chapter deals with viewfinder photography. For help with the other half of the focusing equation, skip to the section "Focusing During Live View and Movie Shooting."

Mastering the D5300 focus system

Assuming that your lens supports autofocusing with the D5300, the first step in taking advantage of autofocusing is to set the lens focus method to auto. On most lenses, you find a switch with two settings: A (or AF) for autofocusing and M (or MF) for Manual focusing, as shown in Figure 4-1. Some lenses, though, sport a switch with a dual setting, such as AF/M, which enables you to use autofocusing initially but then fine-tune focusing by turning the lens focusing ring. On this type of lens, you select the M (or MF) setting for manual-only focusing.

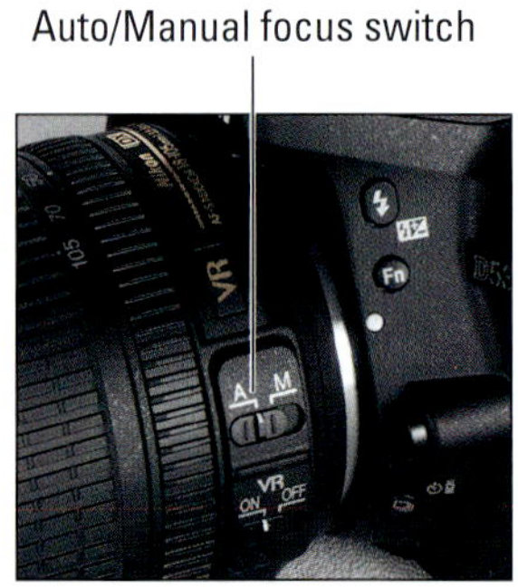

Figure 4-1: On this lens, as on many Nikon lenses, you set the switch to A for autofocusing and to M for manual focusing.

REMEMBER

As for the camera, these settings determine focusing behavior:

- **Focus mode:** For autofocusing, you can set the camera to lock focus when you press the shutter button halfway; to adjust focus continually up to the moment you depress the button fully to take the picture; or to decide for you which option is best. You also get a setting that disables autofocusing so that you can focus manually.
- **AF-area mode:** This setting determines which focus points the camera uses to establish focus. You can tell the camera to select a point for you or to base focus on a point that you select.

You can view the current settings in the Information display, as shown in Figure 4-2. The symbols in the figure represent AF-A for the Focus mode and Auto Area for the AF-Area mode, which are the default settings for all exposure modes except for a few of the Scene modes. At these settings, the camera decides whether to lock focus when you press the shutter button halfway and also selects the focus point for you.

The next several sections explain these settings, offer advice on which combination of settings work best for different subjects, and provide step-by-step focusing recipes for shooting stationary subjects and moving subjects.

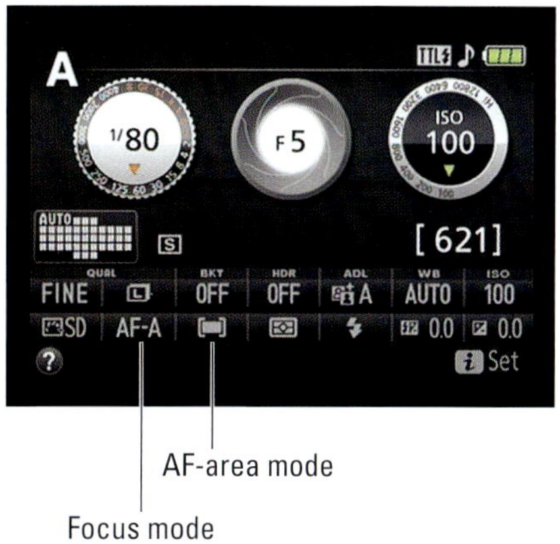

Figure 4-2: The Focus mode and AF-area mode settings appear here.

Just a note before you dig in: When you use the Night Vision Effects mode, you can use autofocusing only in Live View mode. If you use the viewfinder, you're limited to manual focusing.

Changing the Focus mode setting

First up on your list of focus settings to investigate is the Focus mode. You get three settings for tweaking autofocusing behavior and one option for manual focusing.

Choose the Focus mode via the Information display control strip, as illustrated in Figure 4-3. Remember: To activate the control strip, just press the ***i*** button.

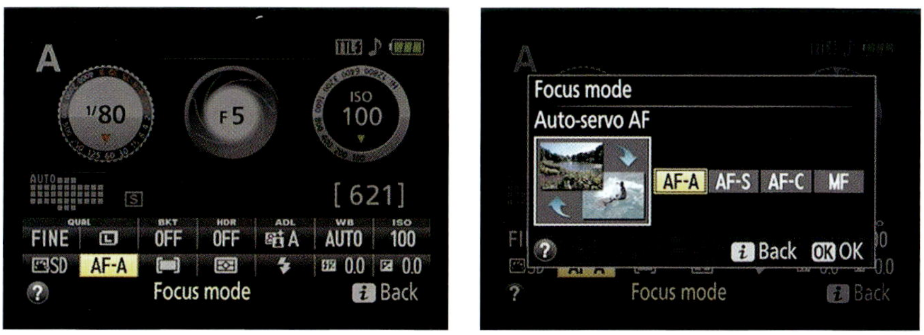

Figure 4-3: You can access all four Focus mode settings only in the P, S, A, and M exposure modes.

When the camera is in the P, S, A, or M exposure mode, you can choose from four options, which work as detailed in the following list; in other exposure modes, you can choose only the last two options (AF-A and MF). The exception, again, is the Night Vision Effects mode, which limits you to manual focusing when you use the viewfinder.

- **AF-S (single-servo autofocus):** Designed for shooting stationary subjects, this setting tells the camera to lock focus when you depress the shutter button halfway.

  In this mode, the camera won't release the shutter to take a picture until focus is achieved. If you can't get the camera to lock onto your focusing target, switching to manual focusing is the easiest solution. Also be sure that you're not too close to your subject; if you exceed the minimum focusing distance of the lens, you can't focus manually, either.

- **AF-C (continuous-servo autofocus):** Geared to photographing moving subjects, this mode causes the camera to adjust focus continuously while the shutter button is pressed halfway.

  By default, AF-C mode prevents you from taking a picture until focus is achieved, just like AF-S mode. But you can tell the camera to capture the shot at the instant you fully depress the shutter button, regardless of whether focus is set. Make the call via the AF-C Priority Selection option, found in the Autofocus section of the Custom Setting menu and shown in Figure 4-4. Focus is the default setting; choose Release to allow shutter release before focus is set.

  For the most part, I stick with Focus. Yes, I may miss a few shots waiting for the focus to occur, but if they're going to be out of focus, who cares? But when my subject is moving at a really rapid pace, I do unlock the shutter release. Although I may wind up with lots of wasted shots, I also increase the odds that I'll capture that split-second "highlight reel" moment. If the subject is slightly out of focus, I can probably retouch it enough to make it passable, especially if the picture content is truly special.

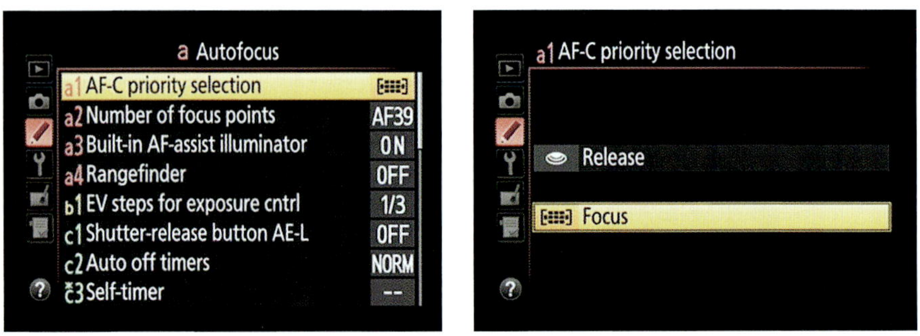

Figure 4-4: This setting controls whether you can take a picture before focus is achieved in the AF-C Focus mode.

- **AF-A (auto-servo autofocus):** This mode, which is the default, gives the camera control over whether focus is locked when you press the shutter button halfway or continuously adjusted until you snap the picture. The camera makes the decision based on whether it detects motion in front of the lens. Either way, shutter release is prevented if the camera can't focus.

AF-A mode works pretty well but can get confused sometimes. If your subject is motionless but other people are moving in the background, the camera may mistakenly switch to continuous autofocus. By the same token, if the subject is moving only slightly, the camera may not make the switch. So my advice is to choose AF-S or AF-C instead.

- **MF (manual focus):** Choose this setting to focus manually instead of using autofocus.

  On Nikon AF-S lenses, including the 18–105mm lens featured in this book and the 18–140mm lens available in a bundle with the camera body, simply setting the switch on the lens to M automatically sets the Focus mode to MF. However, the opposite isn't true: Choosing MF as the Focus mode does not free the lens focusing ring so that you can set focus manually; you must set the lens switch to the M position. For other lenses, check the lens instruction manual for focusing details.

Choosing an AF-area mode: One focus point or many?

The D5300 has 39 available autofocus points, which are located within the frame region indicated by the autofocus brackets in the viewfinder. Figure 4-5 shows you the approximate location of the individual points. (You don't actually see the points in the viewfinder; when you press the shutter button halfway, one or more points lights up, depending on your autofocusing settings.)

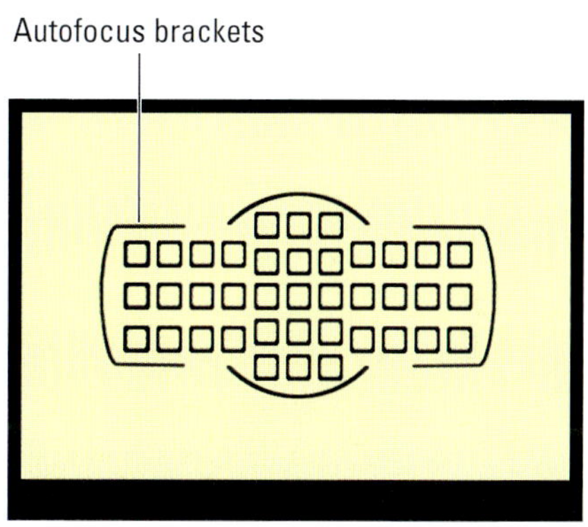

Figure 4-5: The camera's 39 autofocus points are located within the portion of the frame surrounded by the AF-area brackets.

The AF-area mode tells the camera which autofocus points to consider when establishing focus. You have these choices:

- **Single Point:** This mode is designed to quickly and easily lock focus on a still subject. You select a single focus point, and the camera bases focus on that point only. This option is best paired with the single-servo (AF-S) Focus mode, which is also geared to still subjects.
- **Dynamic Area:** Dynamic Area autofocusing is designed for capturing moving subjects. You select an initial focus point, but if your subject moves away from that point before you snap the picture, the camera looks to surrounding points for focusing information.

  To use Dynamic Area autofocusing, you must set the Focus mode to AF-C or AF-A. In fact, the Dynamic Area options don't even appear when the Focus mode is set to AF-S.

You can choose from three Dynamic Area settings:

- *9-point Dynamic Area:* Rather than look at all 39 autofocus points, the camera takes focusing cues from your selected point plus the 8 surrounding points. If you choose the center focus point, for example, the points shown on the left in Figure 4-6 are active. This setting is ideal when you have a moment or two to compose your shot and your subject is moving in a predictable way, making it easy to reframe as needed to keep the subject within the 9-point area.

  This setting provides the fastest Dynamic Area autofocusing because the camera has to analyze the fewest number of autofocusing points.

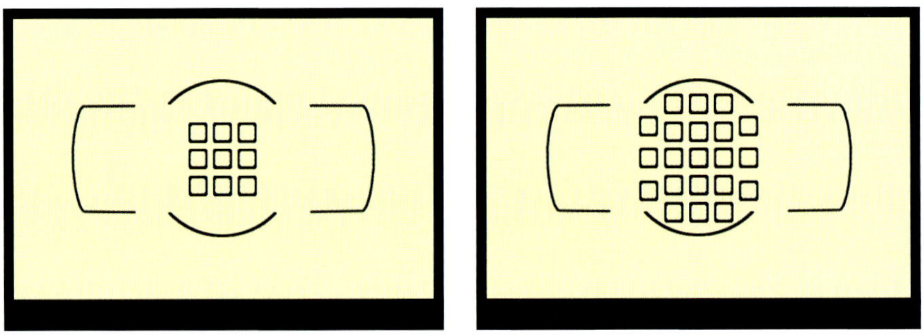

Figure 4-6: The camera considers these autofocus points when you select the center focus point and use the 9-point (left) and 21-point (right) Dynamic Area modes.

- *21-point Dynamic Area:* This mode uses your selected point plus the 20 surrounding points. The right screen in Figure 4-6 shows you which points are active if you select the center point. Obviously, this setting enables your subject to move a little farther afield from your selected focus point and still remain in the target zone. So it works better than 9-point mode when you can't quite predict the path your subject will take.
- *39-point Dynamic Area:* The camera makes use of the full complement of autofocus points. This mode is designed for subjects that are moving so rapidly that it's hard to keep them within the framing area of the 21-point or 9-point setting — a flock of birds, for example. The drawback to this setting is focusing time: With all 39 points on deck, the camera has to work a little harder to find a focus target.

- **3D Tracking:** This one is a variation of 39-point Dynamic Area autofocusing. As in that mode, you start by selecting a single focus point and then press the shutter button halfway to set focus. But the goal of the 3D Tracking mode is to maintain focus on your subject if you recompose the shot after you press the shutter button halfway to lock focus.

The problem with 3D Tracking is that the camera detects your subject by analyzing the colors of the object under your selected focus point. So if not much difference exists between the subject and its background, the camera can get fooled. And if your subject moves out of the frame, you must release the shutter button and reset focus by pressing it halfway again.

REMEMBER

As with Dynamic Area mode, if you want to use 3D Tracking autofocus, you must set the Focus mode to AF-C or AF-A.

- **Auto Area:** At this setting, the camera automatically chooses which of the 39 focus points to use, usually locking on the object closest to the camera.

  Although Auto Area mode requires the least input from you, it's typically the slowest option because of the technology it uses. First, the camera analyzes all 39 focus points. Then it consults an internal database to try to match the information reported by those points to a huge collection of reference photographs. From that analysis, it makes an educated guess about which focus points are most appropriate for your scene. Although it's amazingly fast considering what's happening in the camera's brain, it's slower than the other AF-area options.

  Frankly, I don't use Auto Area mode very often unless I'm handing the camera over to someone who's inexperienced and who wouldn't know how to use the other two modes. And with a camera that costs as much as the D5300, I can think of only a few people whom I'd even trust to hand it over *to.* ("Oh, I'm sorry, but I'm borrowing this from my boss and I *swore* I wouldn't let anyone else use it.") So I keep things nice and simple and stick with Single Point for still subjects and with one of the Dynamic Area modes for moving subjects.

You can select from the full complement of AF-area mode settings in all exposure modes *except* the Miniature and Night Vision Effects modes. Miniature mode always uses Single-Point mode, and autofocusing is off-limits altogether in Night Vision mode.

Here's how to dial in the AF-area setting you want to use and specify a focus point:

TIP

- **Selecting the AF-area mode setting:** Get the job done via the Information display control strip, as shown in Figure 4-7.

  When you return to the Information display, notice the graphic labeled *Autofocus points symbol* in Figure 4-8. This symbol gives you information about which focus points are active. A solid gray square indicates the selected focus point. A fuzzy gray square indicates that the point is active, meaning that if the camera can't establish focus based on the selected point, it may consider the other active points. Any other points are inactive. In the figure, the symbol reflects the 9-point Dynamic Area setting, with the center point selected, for example.

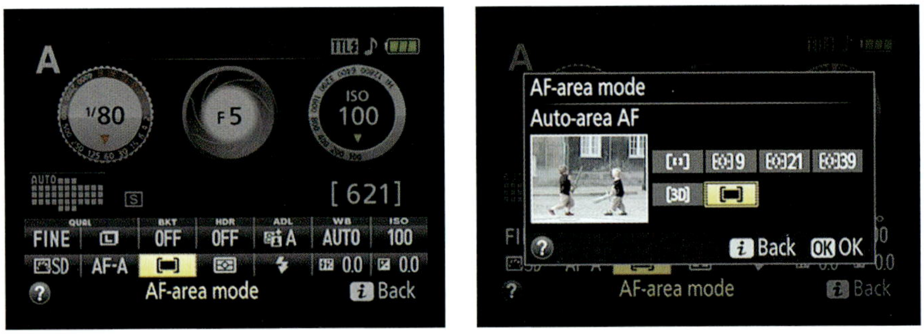

Figure 4-7: Select the AF-area mode setting via the Information display control strip.

- **Selecting a single focus point:** To choose a focus point in the Single Area, Dynamic Area, or 3D Tracking modes, look through the viewfinder and press the shutter button halfway and release it. The currently selected point flashes red and then turns black. For example, in Figure 4-9, the point directly over the top of the clock tower is selected. Use the Multi Selector to cycle through the available focus points until the one you want to use flashes red and then turns black.

  TIP: You can quickly select the center focus point by pressing OK.

Autofocus points symbol

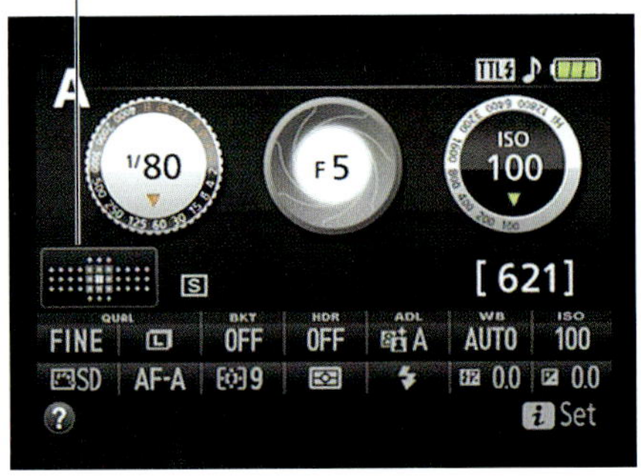

Figure 4-8: This symbol gives you more information about which autofocus points are active in the current AF-area mode.

A few additional tips:

Selected focus point

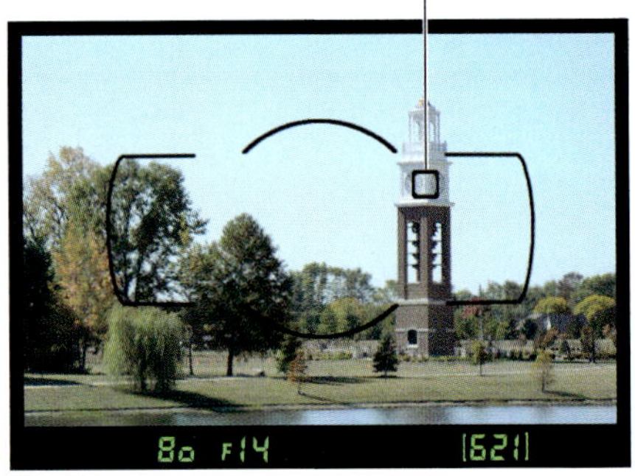

Figure 4-9: Use the Multi Selector to select the focus point that's over your subject.

- **You can reduce the number of focus points available for selection from 39 to 11.** Why would you do this? Because it enables you to choose a focus point more quickly — you don't have to keep pressing the Multi Selector zillions of times to get to the one you want to use. Make the change via the Number of Focus Points option, found in the Autofocus section of the Custom Setting menu, as shown on the left in Figure 4-10. The right half of the figure shows you which autofocus points you can select at the reduced setting.

If you change the setting to 11, the Information display symbol that represents the active autofocus points (refer to Figure 4-8) changes to show the reduced number of selectable points.

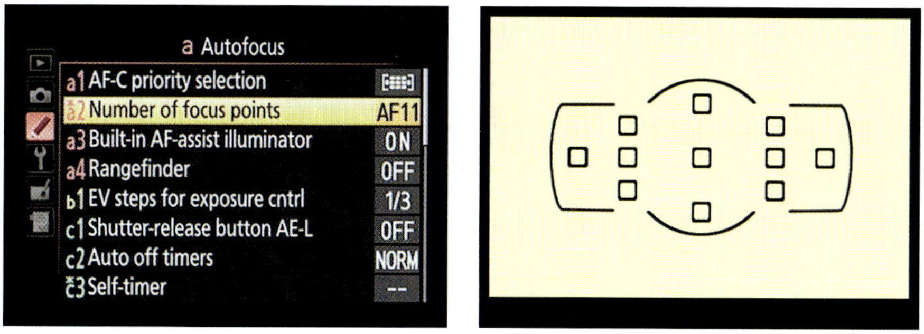

Figure 4-10: You can limit the number of focus points available for selection to the 11 shown here.

- **The nine autofocus points at the center of the frame are more capable than others.** These points use *cross-type sensors,* which evaluate focus by analyzing both horizontal and vertical lines in the scene. The other points assess only horizontal lines. Cross-type sensors typically work better, especially in dim lighting, so if you're having trouble getting the camera to focus, select one of these focus points.
- **When you use spot metering, the camera bases exposure on the selected focus point.** The point you choose affects the way the camera calculates flash exposure as well. See Chapter 3 for details on spot metering; see Chapter 2 for help with flash photography.
- **In any exposure mode except P, S, A, or M, the camera resets the AF-area mode to the default setting if you change exposure modes.** So this setting is one that you need to check before every shoot if you aren't using the P, S, A, or M modes.

Choosing the right autofocus combo

You get the best autofocus results if you pair your chosen Focus mode with the most appropriate AF-area mode, because the two settings work in tandem. Here are the combinations I suggest:

- **For still subjects: AF-S and Single Point.** You select a focus point, and the camera locks focus on that point when you press the shutter button halfway. (It helps to remember the *s* factor: For *s*till subjects, *S*ingle Point and AF-S.)
- **For moving subjects: AF-C and 39-point Dynamic Area.** You still begin by selecting a focus point, but the camera adjusts focus as needed if your subject moves within the frame after you press the shutter

button halfway to establish focus. (Think *motion, dynamic, continuous.*) Remember to reframe as needed to keep your subject within the boundaries of the autofocus points, though. And if you want speedier autofocusing, consider switching to 21-point or 9-point Dynamic Area mode — just remember that you need to keep your subject within that smaller portion of the frame for the focus adjustment to work properly.

The next two sections spell out the steps you use to set focus with both autofocus pairings.

Autofocusing with still subjects: AF-S + Single Point

For stationary subjects, the fastest, most precise autofocus option is to pair the AF-S (single-servo) Focus mode with the Single Point AF-area mode, as shown in Figure 4-11.

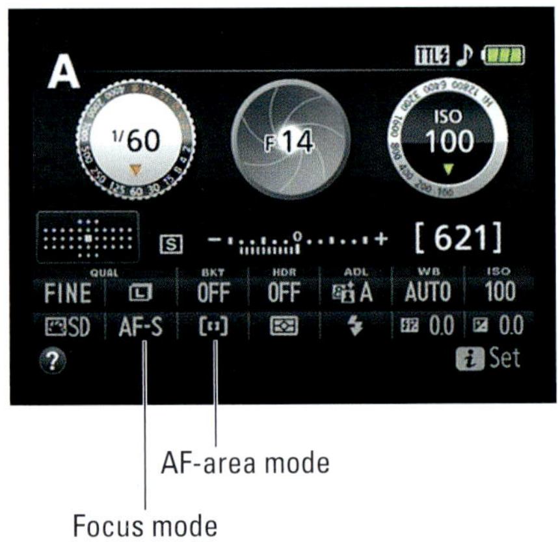

Figure 4-11: Select these autofocus settings for stationary subjects.

After selecting these options (via the Information display control strip), follow these steps to focus:

1. **Looking through the viewfinder, use the Multi Selector to position the focus point over your subject.**

   The focus point is represented by a black rectangle within the AF-area brackets. You can get a look at one in Figure 4-12.

   If the focus point doesn't respond, press the shutter button halfway and release it to wake up the camera. Then try again.

2. **Press the shutter button halfway to set focus.**

   When focus is achieved, the camera displays a green focus light in the viewfinder (refer to Figure 4-12). Unless you're using the Quiet Shutter release mode, you also hear a beep. (You can disable the sound through the Beep option found in the Shooting/Display section of the Custom Setting menu.)

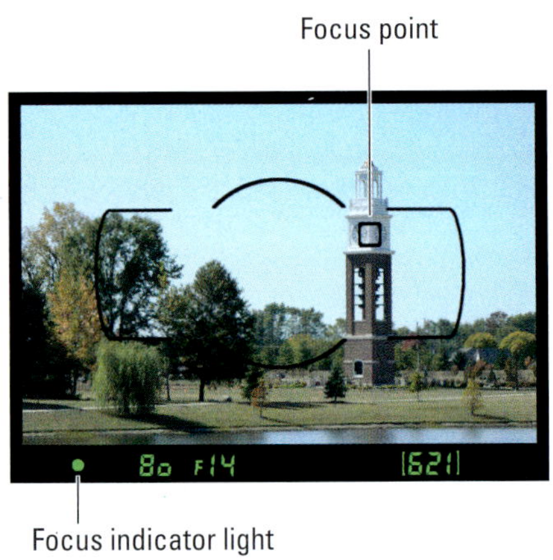

Figure 4-12: The camera won't take the picture until focus is achieved and the green focus indicator lights up.

Focus remains locked as long as you keep the shutter button pressed halfway. If you're using autoexposure (any exposure mode but M), the initial exposure settings are also chosen at the moment you press the shutter button halfway, but they're adjusted as needed up to the time you take the shot.

3. **Press the shutter button the rest of the way to take the shot.**

TIP

If needed, you can position your subject outside a focus point. Just compose the scene initially so that your subject is under a point, press the shutter button halfway to lock focus, and then reframe. However, if you're using autoexposure, you may want to lock focus and exposure together before you reframe, by pressing the AE-L/AF-L button. Otherwise, exposure is adjusted to match the new framing, which may not work well for your subject. See Chapter 3 for more details about autoexposure lock.

Focusing on moving subjects: AF-C + Dynamic Area

To autofocus on a moving subject, select AF-C for the Focus mode and choose one of the Dynamic Area options for the AF-area mode. The earlier section "Choosing an AF-area mode: One focus point or many?" provides information to help you decide whether to use the 9-, 21-, or 39-point Dynamic Area setting.

The focusing process is the same as just outlined, with a couple exceptions:

- **When you press the shutter button halfway, the camera sets the initial focusing distance based on your selected autofocus point.** But if your subject moves from that point, the camera checks surrounding points for focus information.
- **Focus is adjusted as needed until you take the picture.** You see the green focus indicator light in the viewfinder, but it may flash on and off as focus is adjusted. The beep that you usually hear when using the AF-S Focus mode doesn't sound in AF-C mode, which is a Good Thing — otherwise, things could get pretty noisy because the beep would sound every time the camera adjusted focus.
- **Try to keep the subject under the selected focus point to increase the odds of good focus.** But as long as the subject falls within one of the other focus points (9, 21, or 39, depending on which Dynamic Area mode you selected), focus should be adjusted accordingly. Note that you don't see the focus point actually move in the viewfinder, but the focus tweak happens just the same. You can feel and hear the focus motor doing its thing, if you pay attention.
- **By default, the camera doesn't let you take the picture until focus is achieved.** To change this behavior, head for the AF-C Priority Selection option, found in the Autofocus section of the Custom Setting menu, and change the setting to Release.

REMEMBER

TIP

Shutter speed and blurry photos

A poorly focused photo isn't always caused by the issues discussed in this chapter. Any movement of the camera or subject can also cause blur. Both of these problems are related to shutter speed, an exposure control that I cover in Chapter 3. Be sure to also visit Chapter 6, which provides some additional tips for capturing moving objects without blur.

Getting comfortable with continuous autofocusing takes some time, so it's a good idea to practice before you need to photograph an important event. After you get the hang of the AF-C/Dynamic Area system, though, I think you'll really like it.

Using autofocus lock

When you set your camera's Focus mode to AF-C (continuous-servo autofocus), focusing is continually adjusted while you hold the shutter button halfway, so the focusing distance may change if the subject moves out of the active autofocus point or you reframe the shot before you take the picture. The same is true if you use AF-A mode (auto-servo autofocus) and the camera senses movement in front of the lens, in which case it operates as I just described. Either way, the upshot is that you can't control the exact focusing distance the camera ultimately uses.

Should you want to lock focus at a specific distance, you have the following options:

- **Focus manually.**
- **Change the Focus mode to AF-S (single-servo autofocus).** In this mode, focus is locked when you press and hold the shutter button halfway.
- **Lock focus with the AE-L/AF-L button.** First, set focus by pressing the shutter button halfway. When the focus is established at the distance you want, press and hold the AE-L/AF-L button. Focus remains set as long as you hold down the button.

  Keep in mind, though, that by default, pressing the AE-L/AF-L button also locks autoexposure. You can change this behavior, however, setting the button to lock just one or the other. Chapter 11 explains this option.

TIP

For my money, manual focusing is by far the easiest solution; the next section offers more advice on that topic.

Focusing manually

Some subjects confuse even the most sophisticated autofocusing systems, causing the camera's autofocus motor to spend a long time hunting for its focus point. Animals behind fences, reflective objects, water, and low-contrast subjects are just some of the autofocus troublemakers. Autofocus systems also struggle in dim lighting, although that difficulty is often offset by the AF-assist lamp, which shoots out a beam of light to help the camera find its focusing target.

When you encounter situations that cause an autofocus hang-up, you can try adjusting the autofocus options discussed earlier in this chapter. But often, it's easier and faster to switch to manual focusing. For the best results, follow these manual-focusing steps:

1. **Adjust the viewfinder to your eyesight.**

   If you don't adjust the viewfinder, scenes that are in focus may appear blurry and vice versa. If you haven't already done so, look through the viewfinder and rotate the little dial near its upper-right corner. As you do, the viewfinder data and the AF-area brackets become more or less sharp. (Press the shutter button halfway to wake up the meter if you don't see any data in the viewfinder.)

2. **Set the lens and camera to manual focusing.**

   First, move the focus-method switch on the lens to the manual position. The setting is usually marked M or MF.

   Next, you need to set the camera to manual focusing by setting the Focus mode to MF. (Get the job done via the Information display control strip.) Note, though, that you can skip this step if you're using the 18–140mm kit lens or certain other compatible lenses, because the camera automatically changes the Focus mode to MF as soon as you set the lens to manual focusing.

3. **Select a focus point.**

   Use the same technique as when selecting a point during autofocusing: Looking through the viewfinder, press the Multi Selector right, left, up, or down until the point you want to use flashes red.

   During autofocusing, the selected focus point tells the camera what part of the frame to use when establishing focus. And technically speaking, you don't *have* to choose a focus point for manual focusing — the camera focuses according to the position you set by turning the focusing ring. However, choosing a focus point is still a good idea, for two reasons: First, even though you're focusing manually, the camera provides some feedback to let you know whether focus is correct, and that feedback is based on the selected focus point. Second, if you use spot metering, an exposure option covered in Chapter 3, exposure is based on the selected focus point.

4. **Frame the shot so that your subject is under the selected focus point.**
5. **Press and hold the shutter button halfway to initiate exposure metering.**
6. **Rotate the focusing ring on the lens to bring the subject into focus.**

   When the camera thinks focus is set on the object under the focus point, the green focus lamp in the lower-left corner of the viewfinder lights, just as it does during autofocusing.

7. **Press the shutter button the rest of the way to take the shot.**

I know that when you first start working with an SLR-style camera, focusing manually is intimidating. But if you practice a little, you'll find that it's really no big deal and saves you the time and aggravation of trying to bend the autofocus system to your will when it has "issues."

TIP

In addition to the green focus lamp, your camera offers another manual focusing aid: You can swap out the viewfinder's exposure meter with a *rangefinder,* which uses a similar, meter-like display, as shown in Figure 4-13, to indicate whether focus is set on the object in the selected focus point. If bars appear to the left of the 0, as shown in the left example in Figure 4-13, focus is set in front of the subject; if the bars are to the right, as in the middle example, focus is slightly behind the subject. The more bars you see, the greater the focusing error. As you twist the focusing ring, the rangefinder updates to help you get focus on track. When you see a single bar on either side of the 0, you're good to go.

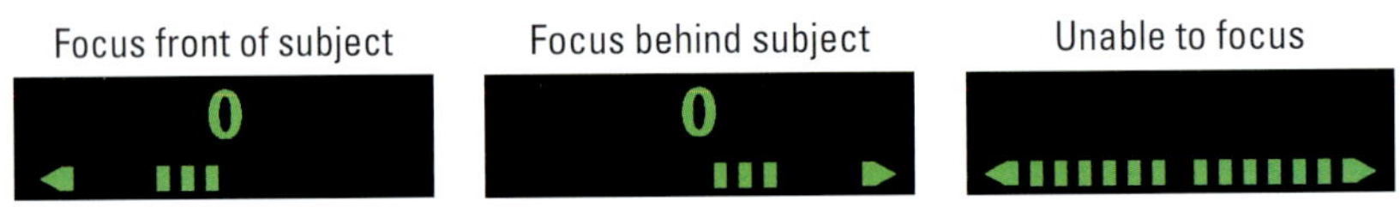

Figure 4-13: The rangefinder offers manual-focusing assistance.

Before I tell you how to activate this feature, I want to point out a couple things:

- You can use the rangefinder in any exposure mode except M (manual exposure). In M mode, the viewfinder always displays the exposure meter.
- In the other exposure modes, you can continue to view the exposure meter in the Information display, even with the rangefinder enabled.
- Your lens must offer a maximum aperture of f/5.6 or lower.

- With subjects that confuse the camera's autofocus system, the rangefinder may not work well either; it's based on the same system. If the system can't find the focusing target, you see the rangefinder display (refer to the right side of Figure 4-13).
- The rangefinder is automatically replaced by the normal exposure meter if you switch back to autofocusing, but reappears when you return to manual focus.

TIP

Personally, I leave the rangefinder off and just rely on the focus indicator light and my eyes to verify focus. I shoot in the S and A exposure modes frequently, and I find it a pain to monitor exposure in the Information display rather than in the viewfinder. But if you want to try the rangefinder, set the Mode dial to any setting but M and then head for Autofocus submenu of the Custom Setting menu. Change the Rangefinder option from Off to On, as shown in Figure 4-14, to enable the feature.

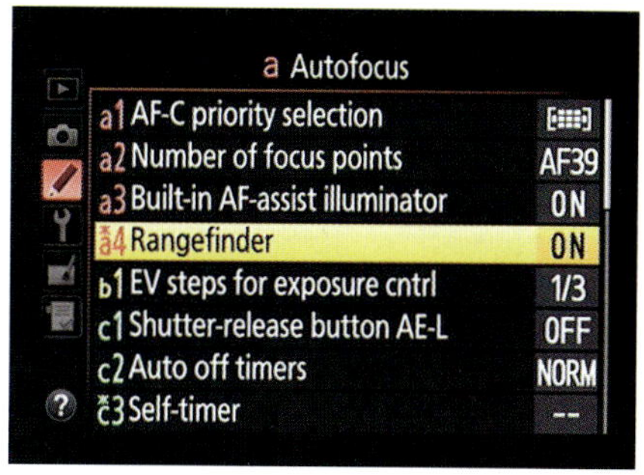

Figure 4-14: Enable the rangefinder via the Custom Setting menu.

Correcting lens distortion

When you shoot with a wide-angle lens, vertical structures sometimes appear to bend outward from the center of the image. This is known as *barrel distortion.* On the flip side of the coin, shooting with a telephoto lens can cause vertical structures to bow inward, which is known as *pincushion distortion.*

The Retouch menu offers a post-capture Distortion Control filter you can apply to try to correct both problems. But the D5300 also has an Auto Distortion Control feature that attempts to correct the image as you're shooting. It works with only certain types of lenses — specifically, those that Nikon classifies as type G, E, or D, excluding PC (perspective control), fisheye, and certain other lenses. To activate the option, just set the Auto Distortion Control on the Shooting Menu to On, as shown here.

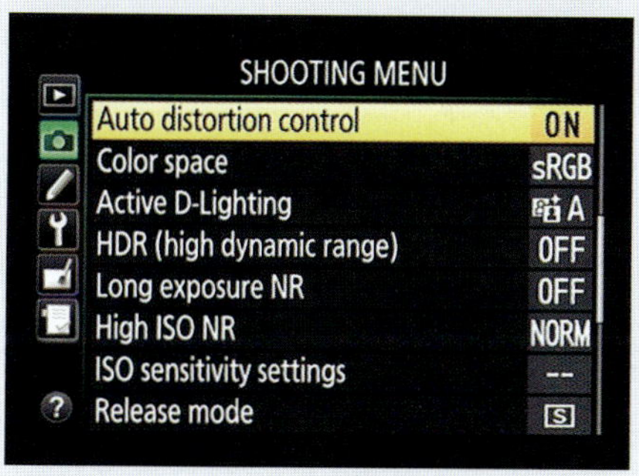

One caveat: Some of the area you see in the viewfinder may not be visible in your photo because the anti-distortion manipulation requires some cropping of the scene. So frame your subject a little loosely when you enable Auto Distortion Control. Also note that the feature isn't available for movie recording.

Focusing During Live View and Movie Shooting

As with viewfinder photography, you can opt for autofocusing or manual focusing during Live View and movie shooting, assuming that your lens supports autofocusing with the D5300. But focus options and techniques differ from those you use for viewfinder photography.

WARNING! The next several sections detail Live View and movie focusing. It's important to understand, however, that the camera typically takes longer to autofocus in Live View mode than it does during viewfinder photography — the difference is because of the type of autofocusing the camera must use when in Live View. For the fastest autofocusing response during still photography, take the camera out of Live View mode. Unfortunately, Live View is the only game in town for movie recording; you can't use the viewfinder to frame movie shots. You also need to use Live View if you want to use autofocusing in the Night Vision Effects mode; otherwise, you must focus manually.

Understanding Live View autofocusing

Whether you're shooting stills or movies, you control the camera's Live View focusing performance through the same two settings as for viewfinder photography: Focus mode and AF-area mode. Again, the settings are different from those available for viewfinder photography, though; the next two sections provide details.

REMEMBER You can view the current settings at the top of the screen when you use the default Live View display mode, Show Photo Information, as shown in Figure 4-15, as well as in Show Movie Information mode. (Just press the Info button to change the display mode.)

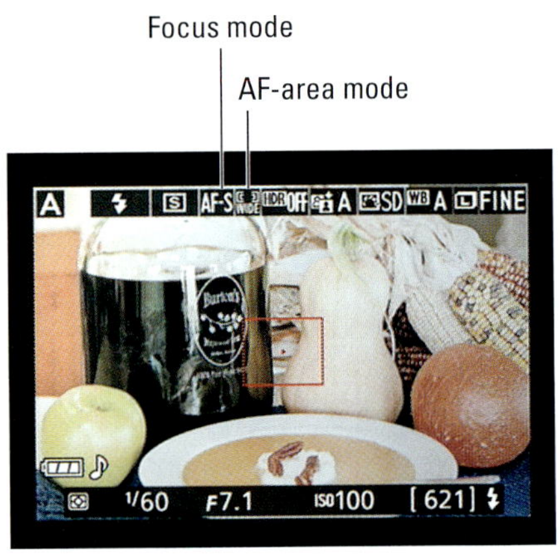

Figure 4-15: During Live View shooting, the Focus mode and AF-area mode settings appear here.

Choosing a Focus mode

By using the Focus mode setting, you specify whether you want the autofocus system to lock focus at the time you press the shutter button halfway or continue to adjust focus until you take the picture or throughout movie recording. Or you can tell the camera that you prefer to focus manually.

Here's how things work at each of the Focus mode settings:

- **AF-S (single-servo autofocus):** The camera locks focus when you press the shutter button halfway. This focus setting is one of the few that works the same during Live View shooting as it does during viewfinder photography. Generally speaking, AF-S works best for focusing on still subjects.
- **AF-F (full-time servo AF):** This option is available for all exposure modes except for the Effects modes Color Sketch, Toy Camera, and Miniature.

  The main purpose of AF-F is to enable continuous focus adjustment throughout a movie recording. To use this option, keep your finger *off* the shutter button. Just switch the camera to the AF-F mode, wait for it to find its focus point, and then press the movie-record button to start recording. Focus is adjusted as needed if your subject moves through the frame or you pan the camera. If you decide to lock focus, press and hold the shutter button halfway down. As soon as you release the button, continuous autofocusing begins again.

  WARNING! Unfortunately, there's a downside that makes AF-F less than ideal. If you shoot a movie with sound recording enabled and use the internal microphone, the microphone may pick up the sound of the autofocus motor as it adjusts focus. So if pristine audio is your goal, use AF-S mode and lock focus before you begin recording, or abandon autofocus altogether and focus manually. As another option, you can attach an external microphone to the camera and place it far enough away that it doesn't pick up the camera sounds.

  For still photography in AF-F mode, focus locks when you press the shutter button halfway, just as with AF-S mode. The only difference between the two modes is that AF-F mode finds a focusing target and keeps adjusting it until you press the shutter button halfway. You might find this option helpful when you're not sure where a moving subject will be when you want to snap the picture: As your subject moves or you pan the camera to keep the subject in the frame, autofocus is adjusted so that when the moment comes to take the shot, you just press the shutter button halfway, pause, and take the picture.
- **MF (manual focus):** Select this option to focus manually, by twisting the focusing ring on the lens.

  TIP With the 18–140mm kit lens and some other Nikon AF-S lenses, moving the switch on the lens to the manual-focusing position automatically selects the MF Focus mode setting. For other lenses, you need to select the Focus mode setting yourself.

To change the setting, press the ***i*** button to activate the control strip. Then highlight the Focus mode setting, as shown in Figure 4-16, and press OK to display the screen where you can select the option you want to use.

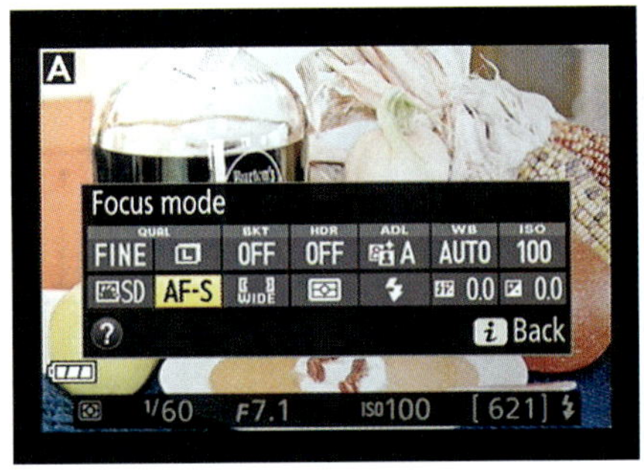

Figure 4-16: Press the ***i*** button to bring up the control strip and adjust the Focus mode setting.

Selecting the AF-area mode

Through the AF-area mode, you give the camera's autofocusing system instructions on what part of the frame contains your subject so that it can set the focusing distance correctly. For Live View photography and movie recording, the camera offers these settings:

- **Wide Area:** In this mode, you use the Multi Selector to move a rectangular focusing frame around the screen to specify a focusing spot. (Details on using this option and others are provided in the upcoming section "Stepping through the autofocusing process.")
- **Normal Area:** This mode works the same way as Wide Area autofocusing but uses a smaller focusing frame. The idea is to enable you to base focus on a very specific area. With such a small focusing frame, however, you can easily miss your focus target when handholding the camera. If you move the camera slightly as you're setting focus and the focusing frame shifts off your subject as a result, focus will be incorrect. For the best results, use a tripod in this mode.
- **Face Priority:** Designed for portrait shooting, this mode attempts to hunt down and focus on faces. Face Detection typically works only when your subjects are facing the camera, however. If the camera can't detect a face, you see a plain red focus frame, and things work as they do in Wide Area mode. In a group shot, the camera typically focuses on the closest face.
- **Subject Tracking:** This mode tracks a subject as it moves through the frame and is designed for focusing on a moving subject. But subject tracking isn't always as successful as you might hope. For a subject that occupies only a small part of the frame — say, a butterfly flitting through a garden — autofocus may lose its way. Ditto for subjects moving at a fast pace, subjects getting larger or smaller in the frame (when moving toward you and then away from you, for example), or scenes in which not much contrast exists between the subject and the background. Oh, and scenes in which there's a great deal of contrast can create problems, too. My take on this feature is that when the conditions are right, it works well, but otherwise the Wide Area setting gives you a better chance of keeping a moving subject in focus.

You can't adjust this option in Auto mode or Auto Flash Off mode. In those two modes, the camera insists on using Face Priority mode. Nor do you have control in the Miniature Effects mode, which always uses Wide Area focusing. Subject Tracking mode isn't available for the Night Vision, Toy, Color Sketch, and Selective Color Effects modes.

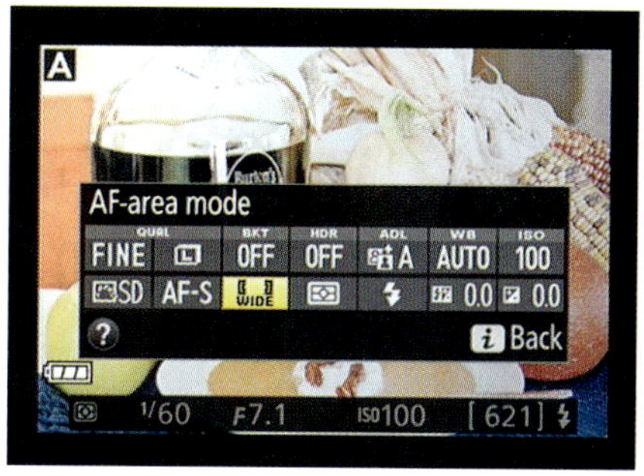

Figure 4-17: Access the AF-area mode via the control strip.

In other exposure modes, adjust the setting via the control strip. Highlight the AF-area mode icon, as shown in Figure 4-17, and press OK to display the screen where you can select the option you want to use.

Choosing the right Live View and movie focusing pairs

To recap, the way the camera sets focus during Live View and movie shooting depends on your Focus mode and AF-area mode settings. Until you get fully acquainted with the various combinations of Focus mode and AF-area mode settings and can make your own decisions about which pairings you like best, I recommend the following settings (assuming, of course, that the exposure mode you're using permits them):

- **For moving subjects:** Set the Focus mode to AF-F and the AF-area mode to Wide Area. You also can try the Subject Tracking AF-area mode, but see my comments in the preceding section regarding which subjects may not be well suited to that mode. Either way, remember that in AF-F mode, you don't press the shutter button halfway until you're ready to lock focus and take the picture — focusing begins immediately after you switch the autofocus mode to AF-F and continues *until* you press the shutter button halfway.

  For movie recording, keep your finger off the shutter button if you want the camera to continuously adjust focus during the recording. Just remember that if you use the camera's internal microphone, the sound of the autofocus motor may be audible in the movie. Attach an external microphone or record audio using a separate device to avoid this problem.

- **For stationary subjects:** Set the Focus mode to AF-S and the AF-area mode to Wide Area. Or, if you're shooting a portrait, give the Face Priority AF-area option a try.

  Press the shutter button halfway to initiate focusing; after the camera finds the focusing point, focus is locked. For movie recording, you can then release the shutter button. For still photography, keep your finger on the button — otherwise, focus will be reset when you press the button to take the picture.

- **For difficult-to-focus subjects:** If the camera has trouble finding the right focusing point when you use autofocus, don't spend too much time fiddling with the different autofocus settings. Just set the camera to manual focusing and set focus yourself. Remember that every lens has a minimum focusing distance, so if you can't focus automatically *or* manually, you may simply be too close to your subject.

Stepping through the autofocusing process

Having laid out all the whys and wherefores of the Live View autofocusing options, I offer the following summary of the steps involved in choosing the autofocus settings and then actually setting focus:

1. **Choose the Focus mode and AF-area mode.**

   You adjust both settings via the control strip that appears when you press the ***i*** button. Refer to Figures 4-16 and 4-17 if you need help locating the two options. Remember that the camera doesn't let you access all settings in certain exposure modes; see the preceding sections for details on which modes permit which settings.

   If you set the Focus mode to AF-F, the autofocus system perks up and starts hunting for a focus point immediately.

2. **Locate the focus frame in the Live View display.**

   The frame appearance depends on the AF-area mode:

   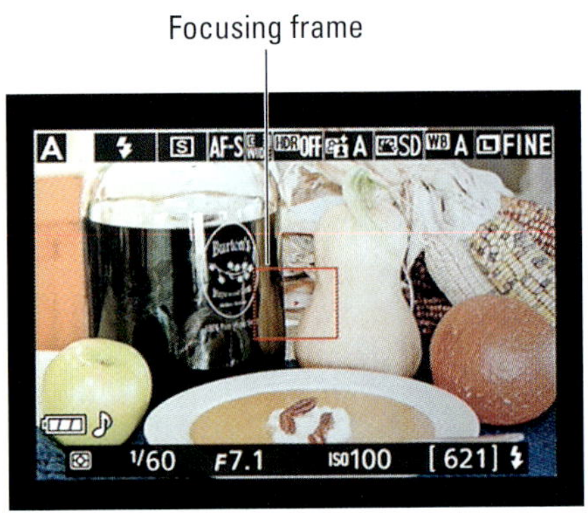

   Figure 4-18: The red box represents the focusing frame in Wide Area and Normal Area AF-Area mode.

   - *Wide Area and Normal Area:* You see a red rectangular frame, as shown in Figure 4-18. (The figure shows the frame at the size it appears in Wide Area mode; it's smaller in Normal Area mode.)
   - *Face Priority:* If the camera locates faces, you see a yellow focus frame around each one, as shown on the left in Figure 4-19. One frame sports corner brackets inside the frame — in the figure, it's the frame on the right. The brackets indicate the face that the camera will use to set focus — typically, the closest person.

     If you instead see a plain red frame, the camera can't detect a face and will set focus as it would if you were using Wide Area mode.
   - *Subject Tracking:* A focusing frame like the one shown on the right in Figure 4-19 appears.

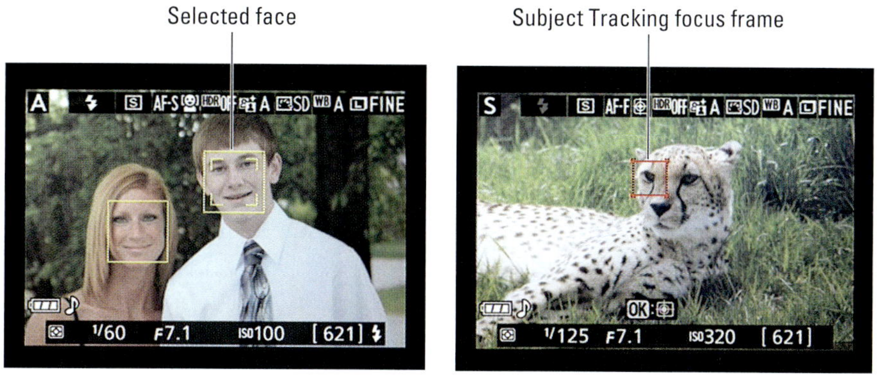

Figure 4-19: The focusing frame appears differently in Face Priority mode (left) and Subject Tracking mode (right).

In AF-F mode, the frame turns green when the object under the frame is in focus. The frame blinks any time focus is being reset.

3. **Press the Multi Selector up, down, right, or left to position the focusing frame over your subject.**

   For example, I moved the frame over the soup garnish in the left example in Figure 4-20.

   TIP

   A couple of tips for positioning the frame:

   - *In Face Priority mode,* use the Multi Selector to move the box with the double yellow border — which indicates the final focusing point — from face to face in a group portrait.
   - *In Wide Area and Normal Area modes,* press OK to quickly move the focus point to the center of the frame.

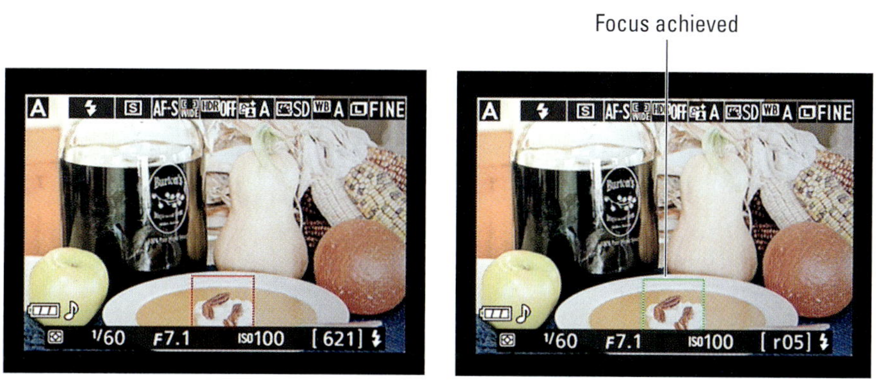

Figure 4-20: The focus frame turns green when focus is achieved.

4. **In Subject Tracking AF-Area mode, press OK to initiate focus tracking.**

   If your subject moves, the focus frame moves with it. To stop tracking, press OK again. (You may need to take this step if your subject leaves the frame — press OK to stop tracking, reframe, and then press OK to start tracking again.)

5. **In AF-S Focus mode, press the shutter button halfway to start autofocusing.**

6. **Wait for the focus frame to turn green (refer to the right screen in Figure 4-20).**

   The appearance of the frame depends on the AF-Area mode; the figure shows it as it looks in Wide Area mode.

   What happens next depends on the Focus mode:

   - *AF-S:* You also hear a little beep (assuming that you didn't disable the beep, which you can do via the Beep option, found in the Shooting/Display section of the Custom Setting menu). Focus is locked as long as you keep the shutter button pressed halfway.
   - *AF-F:* Focus is adjusted if the subject moves. The focus frame turns back to red (or yellow or white) if focus is lost; when the frame turns green and stops blinking, focus has been achieved again. You can lock focus by pressing the shutter button halfway. In most cases, the camera resets focus on your subject when you press the button, even if the focus frame is already green.

7. **(Optional) Press the Zoom In button to magnify the display to double-check focus.**

   Each press gives you a closer look at the subject. A small thumbnail appears in the lower-right corner of the screen, with the yellow highlight box indicating the area that's being magnified, as shown in Figure 4-21. Press the Multi Selector to scroll the display if needed.

   To reduce the magnification level, press the Zoom Out button. If you're not using Subject Tracking mode, you can also press OK to quickly return to normal magnification.

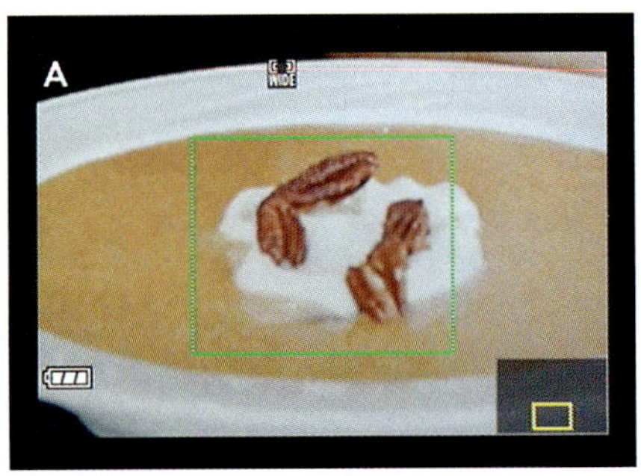

Figure 4-21: Press the Zoom In button to magnify the display and double-check focus.

Manual focusing during Live View and movie shooting

For manual focusing with the 18–140mm kit lens or a similarly featured Nikon lens (including the 18–105mm lens featured in this book), just set the A/M switch to M. The camera automatically changes the Focus mode setting to MF (manual focus). For other lenses, refer to the lens instruction manual to find out how to set the lens to manual focusing. Then rotate the lens focusing ring to bring the scene into focus. But note a few quirks:

- Even with manual focusing, you still see the focusing frame; its appearance depends on the current AF-area mode setting. In Face Priority mode, the frame automatically jumps into place over a face if it detects one. And if you press OK when Subject Tracking mode is enabled, the camera tries to track the subject under the frame until you press OK again. I find these two behaviors irritating, so I always set the AF-area mode to Wide Area or Normal Area for manual focusing.
- The focusing frame doesn't turn green to indicate successful focusing as it does with autofocusing.
- You can press the Zoom In button to check focus in manual mode just as you can during autofocusing. Refer to Step 7 in the preceding section for details. Press the Zoom Out button to reduce the magnification level.

Manipulating Depth of Field

Getting familiar with the concept of depth of field is one of the biggest steps you can take to becoming a better photographer. I introduce you to depth of field in Chapter 3, but here's a quick recap:

- *Depth of field* refers to the distance over which objects in a photograph appear acceptably sharp.
- With a shallow, or small, depth of field, distant objects appear more softly focused than the main subject (assuming that you set focus on the main subject, of course).
- With a large depth of field, the zone of sharp focus extends to include objects at a distance from your subject.

Which arrangement works best depends on your creative vision and your subject. In portraits, for example, a classic technique is to use a short depth of field, as I did for the photo on the left in Figure 4-22. This approach increases emphasis on the subject while diminishing the impact of the background. But for the photo shown on the right, I wanted to emphasize that the foreground figures were in St. Peter's Square, so I used a large depth of field, which kept the background buildings sharply focused and gave them equal weight in the scene.

Shallow depth of field　　Large depth of field

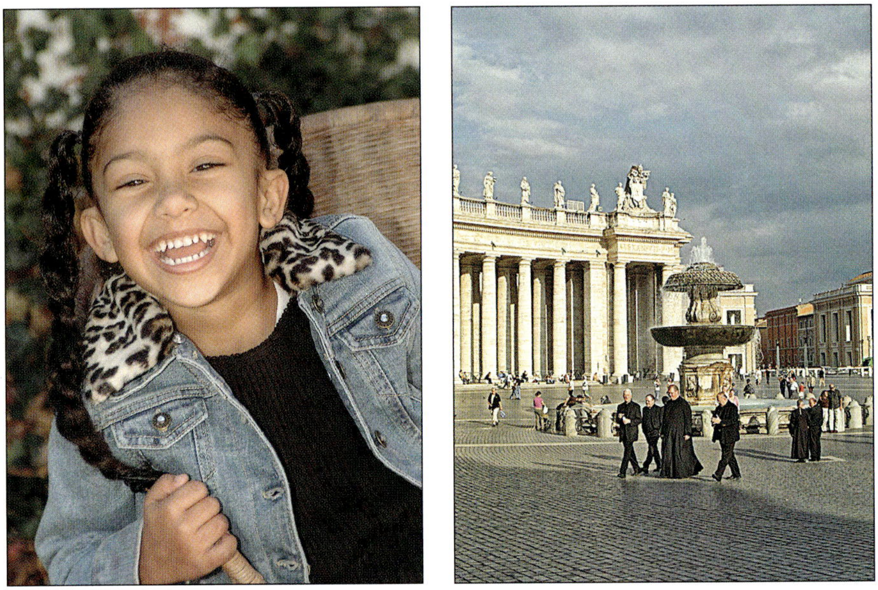

Figure 4-22: A shallow depth of field blurs the background (left); a large depth of field keeps both foreground and background in focus (right).

Depth of field depends on the aperture setting, lens focal length, and distance from the subject, as follows:

- **Aperture setting (f-stop):** The aperture is one of three main exposure settings, all explained fully in Chapter 3. Depth of field increases as you stop down the aperture (by choosing a higher f-stop number). For shallow depth of field, open the aperture (by choosing a lower f-stop number). Figure 3-23 offers an example; in the f/22 version on the left, focus is sharp all the way through the frame; in the f/2.8 version on the right, focus softens as the distance from the flag increases. I snapped both images using the same focal length and camera-to-subject distance, setting focus on the flag.
- **Lens focal length:** In lay terms, *focal length* determines what the lens "sees." As you increase focal length, measured in millimeters, the angle of view narrows, objects appear larger in the frame, and — the important point for this discussion — depth of field decreases. Additionally, the spatial relationship of objects changes as you adjust focal length. As an example, Figure 4-24 compares the same scene shot at a focal length of 127 mm and 183 mm. I used the same aperture and camera-to-subject distance for each shot, setting focus on the parrot.

Aperture: f/22; focal length: 93mm　　　Aperture: f/2.8; focal length: 93mm

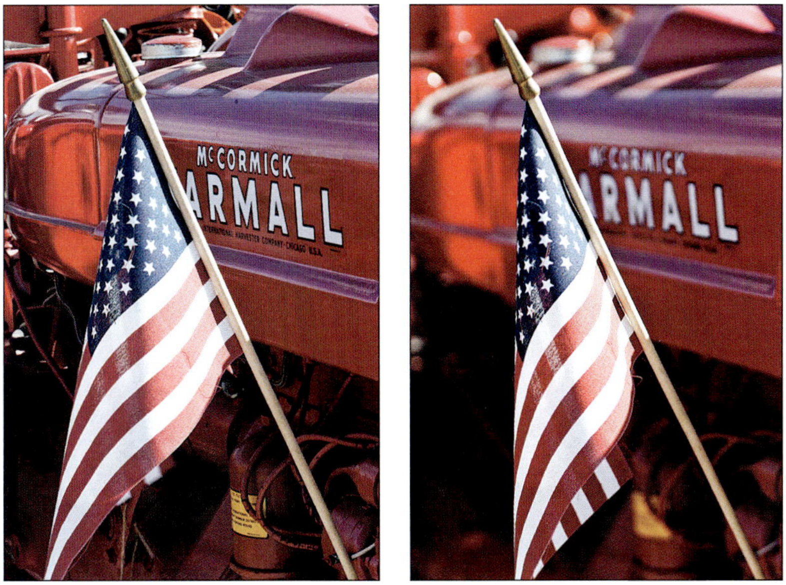

Figure 4-23: A lower f-stop number (wider aperture) decreases depth of field.

Whether you have any focal length flexibility depends on your lens: If you have a zoom lens, you can adjust the focal length by zooming in or out. If you have a prime lens — that is, not a zoom lens — the focal length is fixed, so scratch this means of manipulating depth of field.

For more details about focal length, flip to Chapter 1 and explore the sidebar related to that topic.

- **Camera-to-subject distance:** As you move the lens closer to your subject, depth of field decreases. This statement assumes that you don't zoom in or out to reframe the picture, thereby changing the focal length. If you do, depth of field is affected by both the camera position and focal length.

REMEMBER

Together, these three factors determine the maximum and minimum depth of field that you can achieve, as follows:

- **To produce the shallowest depth of field:** Open the aperture as wide as possible (the lowest f-stop number), zoom in to the maximum focal length of your lens, and get as close as possible to your subject.
- **To produce maximum depth of field:** Stop down the aperture to the highest possible f-stop number, zoom out to the shortest focal length (widest angle) your lens offers, and move farther from your subject.

Aperture: f/5.6; focal length; 127mm

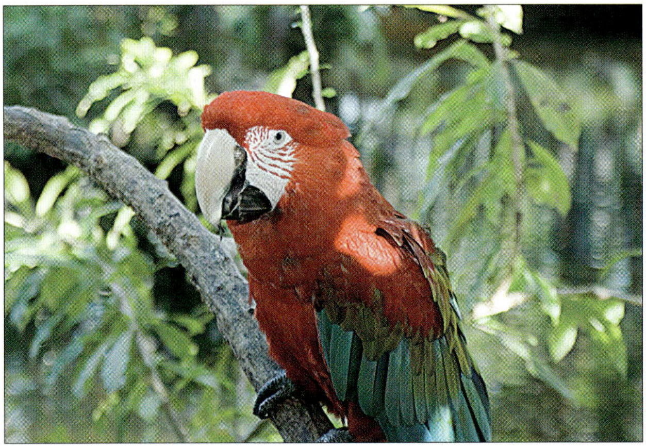

Aperture: f/5.6; focal length: 183mm

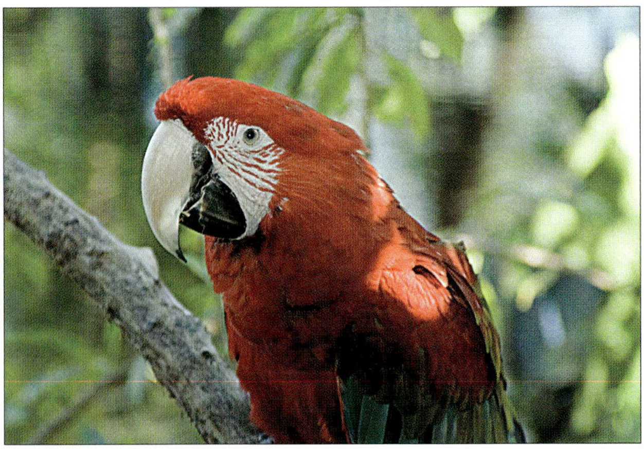

Figure 4-24: Zooming to a longer focal length also reduces depth of field.

A couple of final tips related to depth of field:

- **Aperture-priority autoexposure mode (A) enables you to easily control depth of field while enjoying exposure assistance from the camera.** In this mode, you rotate the Command dial to set the f-stop, and the camera selects the appropriate shutter speed to produce a good exposure. The range of available aperture settings depends on your lens.
- **For greater background blurring, move the subject farther from the background.** The extent to which background focus shifts as you adjust depth of field also is affected by the distance between the subject and the background.

WARNING!

- In Live View mode, depth of field doesn't change in the preview as you change the f-stop setting. The camera can't display the effect of aperture on depth of field properly because the aperture doesn't actually open or close until you take the photo. However, you can gauge the depth of field produced by the focal length and subject-to-camera distance in the preview.

5

Mastering Color Controls

In This Chapter

- Exploring white balance and its effect on color
- Creating custom White Balance settings
- Bracketing white balance
- Setting the Color Space (sRGB versus Adobe RGB)
- Experimenting with Picture Controls

Compared with understanding certain aspects of digital photography — resolution, aperture, shutter speed, and so on — making sense of your camera's color options is easy-breezy. First, color problems aren't all that common, and when they are, they're usually simple to fix with a quick shift of your camera's White Balance setting. And getting a grip on color requires learning only a couple of new terms, an unusual state of affairs for an endeavor that often seems more like high-tech science than art.

This chapter explains the aforementioned White Balance control along with other features that enable you to fine-tune the way your camera renders colors, whether you're shooting photos or recording movies. See Chapter 10 for some color adjustments you can make to existing pictures via the Retouch menu.

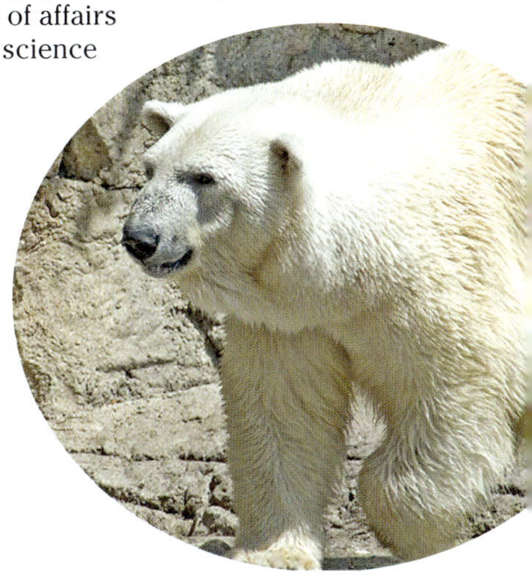

Understanding the White Balance Setting

Every light source emits a particular color cast. The old-fashioned fluorescent lights found in most public restrooms, for example, put out a bluish-greenish light, which is why we all look sickly when we view our reflections in the mirrors in those restrooms. And if you think that your beloved looks especially attractive by candlelight, you aren't imagining it: Candlelight casts a warm, yellow-red glow that is flattering to the skin.

Science-y types measure the color of light, officially known as *color temperature,* on the Kelvin scale, which is named after its creator. You can see the Kelvin scale in Figure 5-1.

When photographers talk about "warm light" and "cool light," though, they aren't referring to the position on the Kelvin scale — or at least not in the way most people think of temperatures, with a higher number meaning hotter. Instead, the terms describe the visual appearance of the light. Warm light, produced by candles and incandescent lights, falls in the red-yellow spectrum at the bottom of the Kelvin scale; cool light, in the blue spectrum, appears in the upper part of the Kelvin scale.

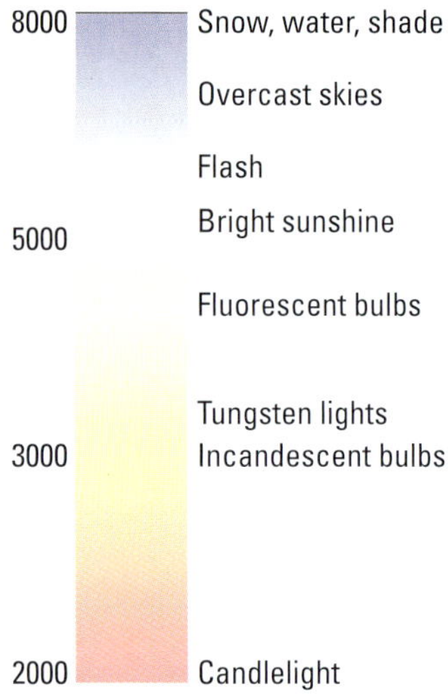

Figure 5-1: Each light source emits a specific color.

At any rate, most people don't notice these fluctuating colors of light, because human eyes automatically compensate for them. Except in extreme lighting conditions, we perceive a white tablecloth as white no matter whether it's lit by candlelight, fluorescent light, or daylight.

Similarly, a digital camera compensates for different colors of light through white balancing. Simply put, *white balancing* neutralizes light so that whites are always white, which in turn ensures that other colors are rendered accurately. If the camera senses warm light, it shifts colors slightly to the cool side of the color spectrum; in cool light, the camera shifts colors in the opposite direction.

The good news is that, as with your eyes, your camera's Auto White Balance setting tackles this process well in most situations, which means that you can usually ignore it and concentrate on other aspects of the picture. But if the scene is lit by two or more light sources that cast different colors, the white balance sensor can get confused, producing an unwanted color cast like the one you see in the left image in Figure 5-2.

I shot this image in my home studio — which is a fancy name for "guest bedroom" — using tungsten photo lights, which produce light with a color temperature similar to incandescent bulbs. The problem is that windows in the studio permit strong daylight to filter through. In Auto White Balance mode, the camera reacted to that daylight — which has a cool color cast — and applied too much warming, giving my original image a yellow tint. No problem: I switched the White Balance mode from Auto to the Incandescent setting. The image on the right in Figure 5-2 shows the corrected colors.

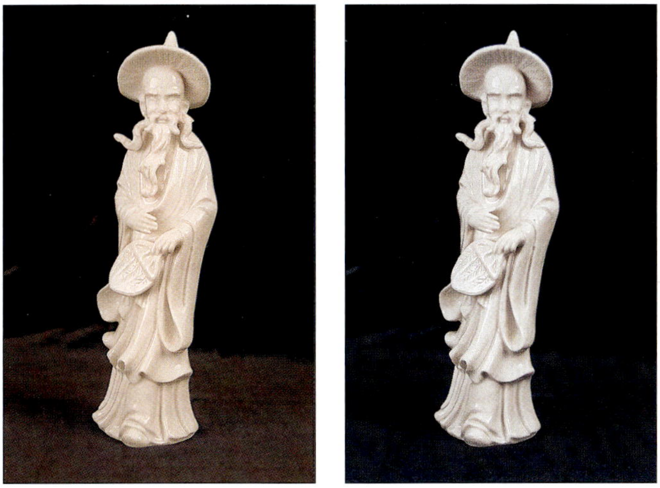

Figure 5-2: Multiple light sources resulted in a yellow color cast in Auto White Balance mode (left); switching to the Incandescent setting solved the problem (right).

There's one problem with white balancing as it's implemented on your D5300, though: You can't make this kind of manual White Balance selection if you shoot in the fully automatic exposure modes. So if you spy color problems in your camera monitor, switch to P, S, A, or M exposure mode.

The next section explains how to make a simple white balance correction; following that, you can explore advanced options.

Changing the White Balance setting

You can view the current White Balance setting in the Information and Live View displays, as shown in Figure 5-3. The icons in the figures represent the Auto setting; settings other than Auto are represented by the icons you see in Table 5-1.

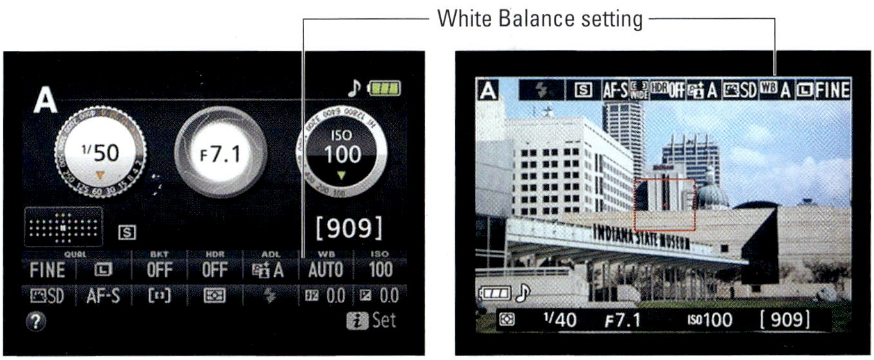

Figure 5-3: A symbol representing the current White Balance setting appears in the displays.

Table 5-1	Manual White Balance Settings
Symbol	*Light Source*
	Incandescent
	Fluorescent
	Direct sunlight
	Flash
	Cloudy
	Shade
PRE	Preset

In Live View mode, colors in the preview are rendered according to the current White Balance setting. If you're unsure of which setting to use, just experiment: After you adjust the setting, the preview updates to show you the effect on photo colors.

You can adjust the White Balance setting in two ways:

- **Control strip:** Activate the strip by pressing the ***i*** button. After highlighting the White Balance option, as shown on the left in Figure 5-4, press OK to access the available settings, as shown on the right.
- **Shooting menu:** You also can access the setting from the Shooting menu, as shown in Figure 5-5.

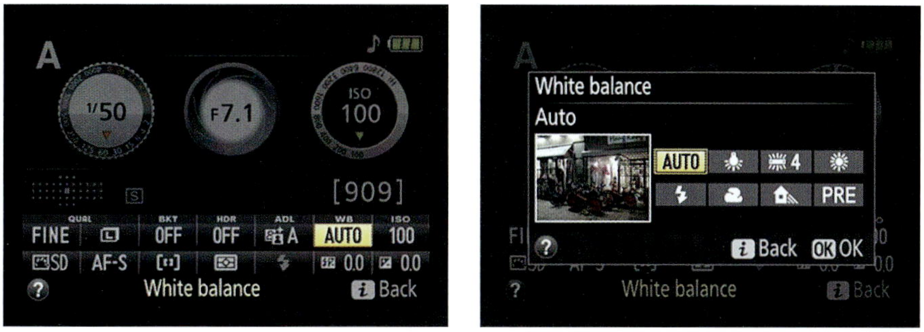

Figure 5-4: Select a White Balance setting by using the control strip.

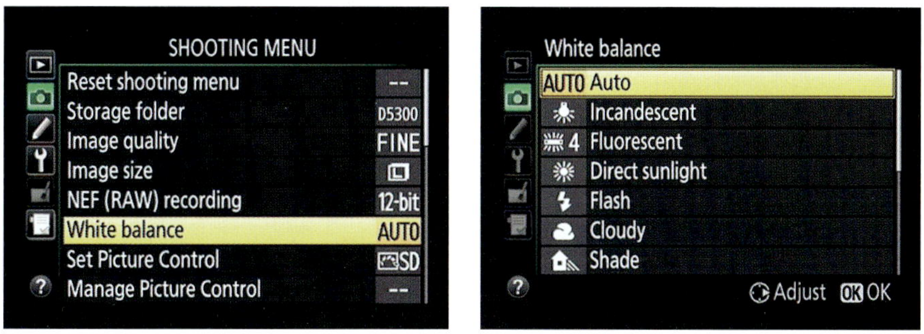

Figure 5-5: To uncover more White Balance options, open the Shooting menu.

When you go the menu route, you can access the following advanced white balance features:

- **Fine-tune the settings.** If you choose any setting but Fluorescent, pressing the Multi Selector right takes you to a screen where you can fine-tune the setting, a process I explain in the next section.
- **Select a specific type of fluorescent bulb.** When you choose Fluorescent from the menu, as shown on the left in Figure 5-6, pressing the Multi Selector right displays the second screen in the figure, where you can select a specific type of bulb. Select the option that most closely matches your bulbs and then press OK. Or, to go to the fine-tuning screen, press the Multi Selector right.
- **Create a custom white balance preset.** Selecting the PRE option as the White Balance setting enables you to create and store a precise, customized White Balance setting, as explained in the upcoming section "Creating white balance presets." This feature provides the fastest way to achieve accurate colors when the scene is lit by multiple light sources that have differing color temperatures.

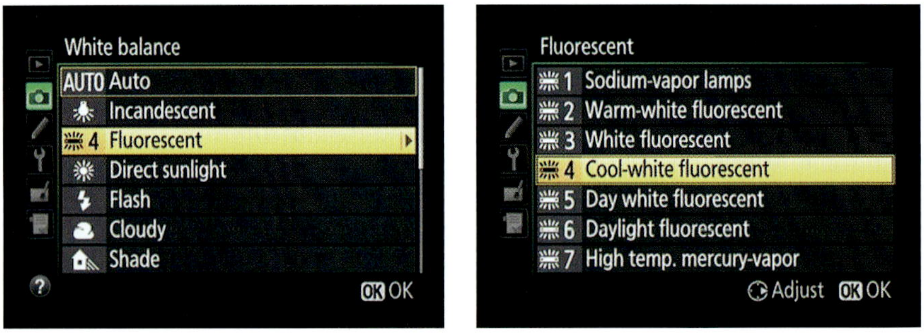

Figure 5-6: If you adjust the White Balance setting from the Shooting menu, you can select a specific type of fluorescent bulb.

WARNING!

The selected White Balance setting remains in force for the P, S, A, and M exposure modes until you change it. Get in the habit of checking the setting before every shoot to make sure that you don't need to modify it. Otherwise, your pictures may take on an unwanted color cast due to an incorrect setting for the new lighting conditions.

Fine-tuning White Balance settings

You can fine-tune any White Balance setting except a custom preset that you create by using the PRE option. Make the adjustment as spelled out in these steps:

1. **Display the Shooting menu, highlight White Balance, and press OK.**
2. **Highlight the White Balance setting you want to adjust, as shown on the left in Figure 5-7, and press the Multi Selector right.**

   You're taken to a screen where you can do your fine-tuning (refer to the right side of Figure 5-7).

   REMEMBER

   If you select Fluorescent, you first go to a screen where you select a specific type of bulb, as covered in the preceding section. After you highlight your choice, press the Multi Selector right again to get to the fine-tuning screen.
3. **Fine-tune the setting by using the Multi Selector to move the white balance shift marker in the color grid.**

   The grid is set up around two color pairs: Green and Magenta, represented by G and M; and Blue and Amber, represented by B and A. By pressing the Multi Selector, you can move the adjustment marker (refer to the little black box labeled in Figure 5-7) around the grid.

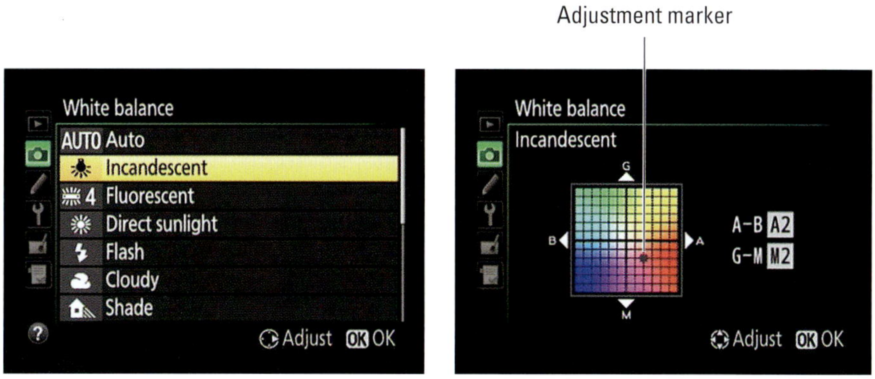

Figure 5-7: Press the Multi Selector right to get to the fine-tuning screen.

As you move the marker, the A–B and G–M boxes on the right side of the screen show you the current amount of color shift. A value of 0 indicates the default amount of color compensation applied by the selected White Balance setting. In Figure 5-7, for example, I moved the marker two levels toward amber and two levels toward magenta to specify that I wanted colors to be a tad warmer.

4. **Press OK to complete the adjustment.**

After you fine-tune a White Balance setting, an asterisk appears next to the icon representing the setting on the Shooting menu, as shown in Figure 5-8. You see an asterisk next to the White Balance setting in the Information and Live View displays as well.

Creating white balance presets

If none of the standard White Balance settings does the trick and you don't want to fool with fine-tuning them, take advantage of the PRE (Preset Manual) feature. This option enables you to do two things:

- Base white balance on a direct measurement of the actual lighting conditions.
- Match white balance to an existing photo.

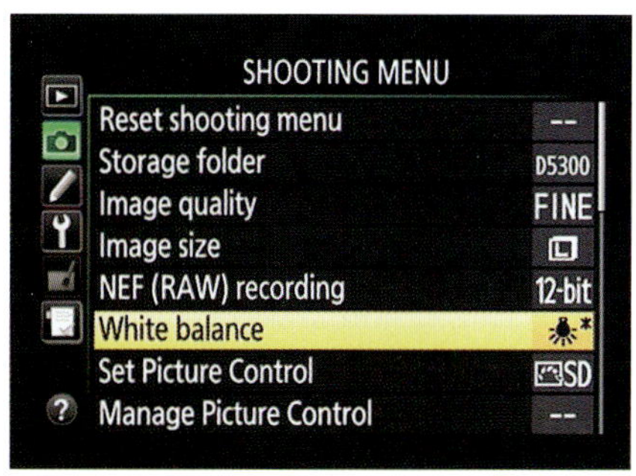

Figure 5-8: The asterisk indicates that you applied a fine-tuning adjustment to the White Balance setting.

Although you can create a preset using either method, you can store only one preset at a time. For example, if you create a preset based on lighting conditions on Monday and then decide on Tuesday to create a different one based on a photo, the light-based preset goes kaput.

The next two sections provide step-by-step instructions for creating both types of presets.

Setting white balance with direct measurement

To use this technique, you need a piece of card stock that's either neutral gray or absolute white — not eggshell white, sand white, or any other close-but-not-perfect white. (You can buy reference cards, made just for this purpose, in many camera stores for less than $20.)

Position the reference card so that it receives the same lighting you'll use for the photo. Then take these steps:

1. **Set the camera to the P, S, A, or M exposure mode.**

   If the exposure meter reports that the image will be under- or overexposed at the current exposure settings, make the necessary adjustments now. (Chapter 3 tells you how.) Otherwise, the camera can't create your preset.

2. **Frame your shot so that the reference card fills the viewfinder.**

   You must use the viewfinder to take the reference shot; you can't create a preset in Live View mode.

3. **From the Shooting menu, select White Balance, press OK, and select the PRE Preset Manual White Balance setting, as shown on the left in Figure 5-9.**

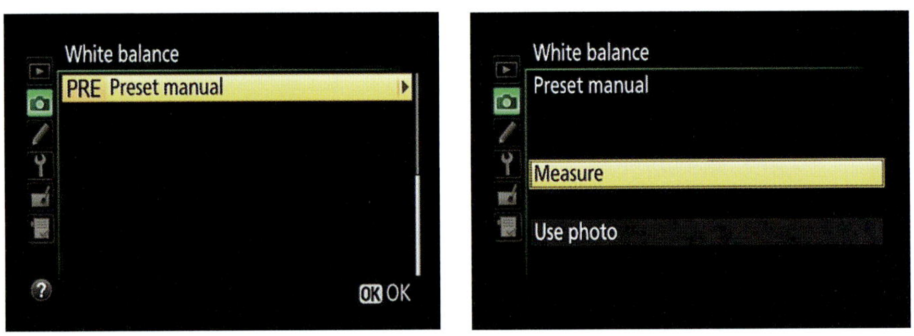

Figure 5-9: Select these options to set white balance by measuring a white or gray card.

4. **Press the Multi Selector right, select Measure (as shown on the right in the figure), and press OK.**

   A warning appears, asking you whether you want to overwrite existing data.

5. **Select Yes and press OK.**

   You see a message telling you to take your picture. You have about 6 seconds to do so. (The letters *PRE* flash in the viewfinder and Information display to let you know the camera is ready to record your white balance reference image.)

6. **Take the reference shot.**

   TIP: Your camera may have a hard time autofocusing because the reference card doesn't contain any contrast. To solve the problem, use manual focusing.

   If the camera is successful at recording the white balance data, the letters *Gd* flash in the viewfinder and the message "Data Acquired" appears in the Information display. If the camera can't set the custom white balance, you instead see the message *No Gd* in the viewfinder, and a message in the Information display urges you to try again. Try adjusting the lighting before doing so.

TIP: You also can create a direct-measurement preset via the Information display control strip: After setting the White Balance option to PRE, press the OK button for a couple seconds until the letters *PRE* start to flash. Then take your reference shot.

After you complete the process, the camera automatically sets the White Balance option to PRE so that you can begin using your preset. Your custom setting is stored in the camera until you override the setting with a new preset. Whenever you want to use the preset again, just choose PRE as the White Balance setting.

Matching white balance to an existing photo

Suppose that you're the marketing manager for a small business and one of your jobs is to shoot portraits of the company bigwigs for the annual report. You build a small studio just for that purpose, complete with a couple of photography lights and a nice, conservative beige backdrop. Of course, the bigwigs can't all show up to get their pictures taken in the same month, let alone on the same day. But you have to make sure that the colors in that beige backdrop remain consistent for each shot, no matter how much time passes between photo sessions. This scenario is one possible use for a feature that enables you to create a White Balance preset based on an existing photo.

Two words of caution:

- Basing white balance on an existing photo works well only in strictly controlled lighting situations, where the color temperature of the lights is consistent from day to day. Otherwise, the White Balance setting that produces color accuracy when you shoot Big Boss Number One may add an ugly color cast to the one you snap of Big Boss Number Two.
- If you previously created a preset using the direct measurement option, you wipe out that preset when you base a preset on an existing photo.

With those caveats out of the way, follow these steps to create a preset based on a photo:

1. **Copy the picture that you want to use as the reference photo to your camera memory card, if it isn't already stored there.**

   You can copy the picture to the card using a card reader and whatever method you usually use to transfer files from one drive to another. Assuming that you're using the default folder names, copy the file to the 100D5300 folder, inside the main DCIM folder.

2. **Open the Shooting menu, highlight White Balance, and press OK.**
3. **Select PRE Preset Manual and press the Multi Selector right.**

   The screen shown on the left in Figure 5-10 appears.

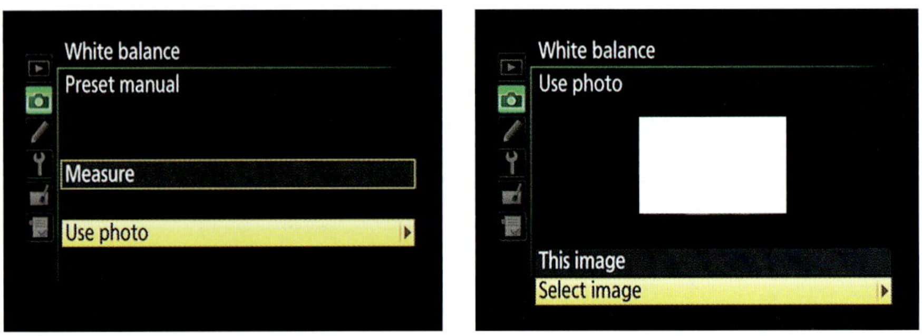

Figure 5-10: You can create a white balance preset based on a photo.

4. **Highlight Use Photo and press the Multi Selector right.**

   The options shown on the right in Figure 5-10 appear. If you haven't yet used the photo option to store a preset, you see an empty white box in the middle of the screen, as shown in the figure. If you previously selected a photo to use as a preset reference, the thumbnail for that image appears instead.

5. **Select the photo you want to use.**

   If the photo is already displayed on the screen, highlight This Image and press OK. Otherwise, highlight Select Image and press the Multi Selector right to access screens that let you scroll through your pictures. Highlight your choice and press OK to return to the screen shown on the right in Figure 5-10. Your selected photo appears on the screen.

6. **Highlight This Image and press OK to set the preset white balance based on the selected photo.**

Whenever you want to base white balance on your selected photo, just set the White Balance setting to the PRE option.

Bracketing white balance

Chapter 3 introduces you to automatic exposure bracketing, which records the same image at different exposure settings or Active D-Lighting settings. You also can bracket white balance, creating a series of three images recorded at different white balance settings.

REMEMBER

Note the following details about this feature:

- **Bracketing is available only in the P, S, A, and M exposure modes.** Chapter 3 tells you how to use these exposure modes, if you haven't yet discovered them.
- **You must set the Image Quality option to one of the JPEG options (Fine, Normal, or Basic).** Why is the Raw (NEF) setting off limits? Because with Raw, white balance and other color settings aren't established until you process your images. So there's no reason to waste time bracketing white balance when you shoot Raw — you just adjust colors as you see fit during the Raw conversion process. (Chapter 9 shows you how to use the in-camera Raw converter.)
- **You can apply white balance bracketing only along the blue-to-amber axis of the color grid.** You can't shift colors along the green-to-magenta axis, as you can when tweaking a specific White Balance setting.
- **A single press of the shutter button creates all three images.** The camera captures the first photo at the selected White Balance setting and then creates two copies, one shifted toward amber and one toward blue.
- **You can shift colors from one to three steps between frames.** As an example of the maximum color shift you can achieve, refer to Figure 5-11, which I created using a three-step shift. As you can see, even at that "max" setting, the differences between the shots are subtle.

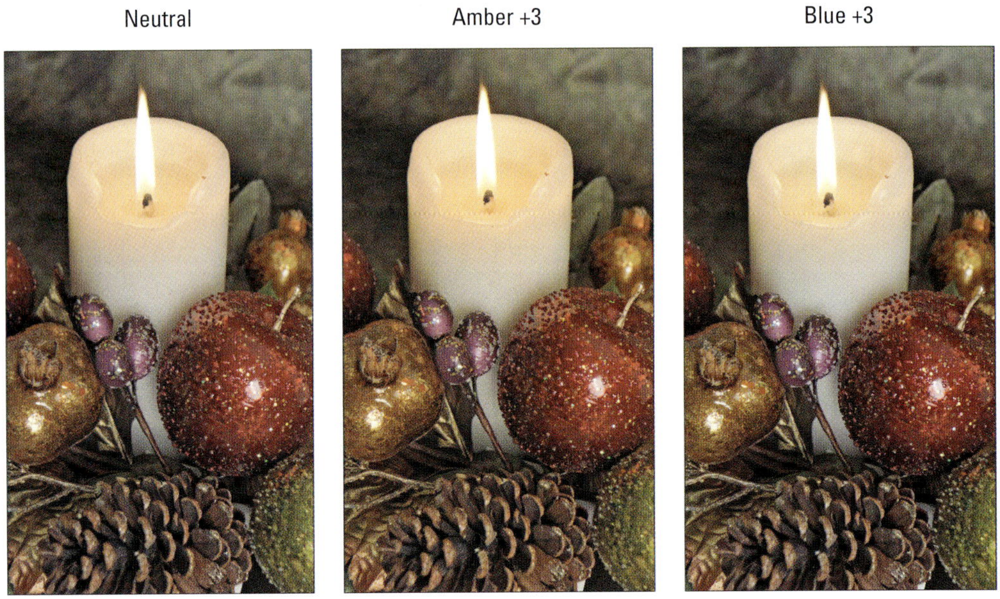

Figure 5-11: I created three color variations by using White Balance bracketing.

To use White Balance bracketing, take these steps:

1. **Set the Auto Bracketing Set option on the Custom Setting menu to White Balance, as shown in Figure 5-12.**

   Look for the option in the Bracketing/Flash section of the Custom Setting menu.

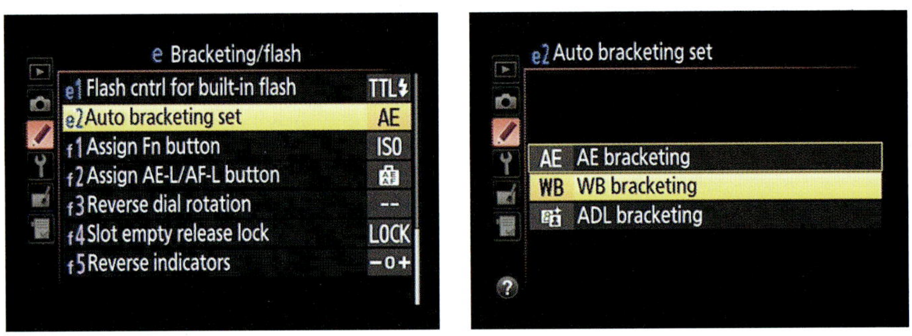

Figure 5-12: Tell the camera you want to bracket white balance by way of this Custom Setting menu option.

2. **Enable bracketing and set the bracketing shift amount via the control strip, as shown in Figure 5-13.**

   As always, just press the ***i*** button to display the control strip.

   After you enable bracketing, the Information display shows bracketing indicators, as shown in Figure 5-14, reminding you that white balance bracketing is in force. The same indicator appears in the lower-right corner of the Live View display.

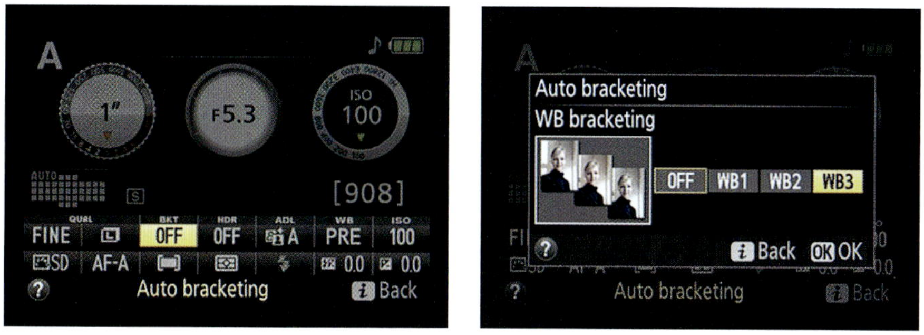

Figure 5-13: Enable bracketing and set the amount of color shift from the control strip.

3. **To record the bracketed series, press the shutter button once.**

   The camera captures the first image at the current White Balance setting and then spends a few seconds creating two bracketed copies.

4. **When you finish taking your bracketed shots, return to the control strip and turn off bracketing.**

   This step is important because the bracketing setting remains in effect even after you shut off the camera, and it's all too easy to overlook the fact that the feature is enabled when you head out for your next shoot.

White Balance bracketing indicator

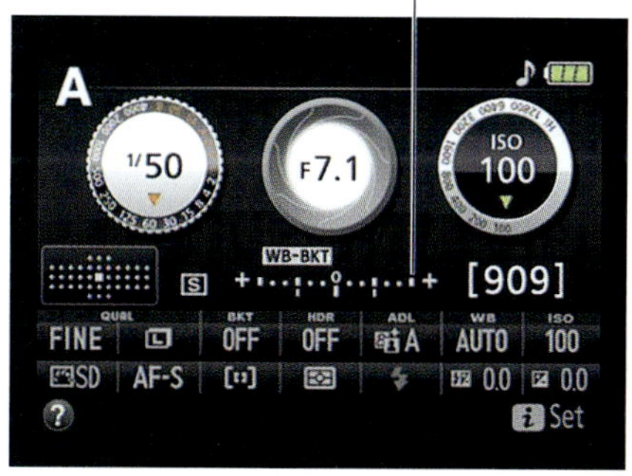

Figure 5-14: These markings remind you that white balance bracketing is enabled.

If you view your photos in a playback mode that displays color data, the White Balance readout indicates which shots were shifted along the color axis. For the amber version, you see the letter *A;* for the blue version, *B.* Next to the letter, the value 1, 2, or 3 indicates the increment of color shift. For the neutral shot, the readout displays 0, 0. Chapter 8 shows you how to view this type of data during playback.

Choosing a color space: sRGB versus Adobe RGB

By default, your camera captures images using the *sRGB color space,* which refers to an industry-standard spectrum of colors. (The *s* is for *standard,* and the *RGB* is for *r*ed, *g*reen, *b*lue, which are the primary colors in the digital color world.) This color space was created to help ensure color consistency as an image moves from camera (or scanner) to monitor and printer; the idea was to create a spectrum of colors that all devices can reproduce.

Because sRGB excludes some colors that *can* be reproduced in print and onscreen, at least by some devices, your camera also enables you to shoot in the Adobe RGB color space, which contains a larger spectrum of colors. You make the switch via the Color Space option on the Shooting menu.

Although using a larger color spectrum sounds like a no-brainer, choosing Adobe RGB isn't necessarily the right choice. Consider these factors when making your decision:

- Some colors in the Adobe RGB spectrum can't be reproduced in print; the printer substitutes the closest printable color, if necessary.
- If you print and share your photos without making any adjustments in your photo editor, sRGB is a better choice because most printers and web browsers are designed around that color space.
- Finally, to retain the original Adobe RGB colors when you work with your photos, your editing software must support that color space — not all programs do. You also must be willing to study the topic of digital color a little because you need to use specific software and printing settings to avoid mucking up the color works.

One final tip with regard to this option: The picture filename indicates which color space you used. Filenames of Adobe RGB images start with an underscore, as in _DSC0627.jpg. For pictures captured in sRGB, the underscore appears in the middle of the filename, as in DSC_0627.jpg.

Taking a Quick Look at Picture Controls

When you capture photos using the JPEG Image Quality settings (Fine, Normal, or Basic), colors are also affected by the Picture Control setting. This option affects other picture characteristics that the camera tweaks when you shoot in the JPEG format, including contrast and sharpening.

Sharpening is a software process that boosts contrast in a special way to create the illusion of slightly sharper focus. Let me emphasize, "slightly sharper focus." Sharpening produces a subtle *tweak;* it's not a fix for poor focus.

In the P, S, A, and M exposure modes, you can choose from the following Picture Controls, represented on the menus and in the displays by the two-letter codes labeled in Figure 5-15. In other exposure modes, the camera selects the Picture Control setting.

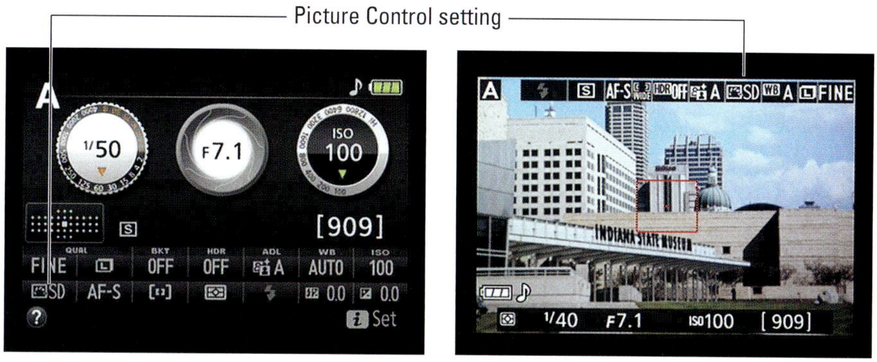

Figure 5-15: This two-letter code represents the Picture Control setting.

- **Standard (SD):** The default setting, this option captures the image "normally" — that is, using the characteristics that Nikon offers up as suitable for the majority of subjects.
- **Neutral (NL):** At this setting, the camera doesn't enhance color, contrast, and sharpening as much as in the other modes. The setting is designed for people who want to precisely manipulate these picture characteristics in a photo editor. By not overworking colors, sharpening, and so on when producing your original file, the camera delivers an original that gives you more latitude in the digital darkroom.
- **Vivid (VI):** In this mode, the camera amps up color saturation, contrast, and sharpening.
- **Monochrome (MC):** This setting produces black-and-white photos. However, in the digital world, they're called *grayscale images* because a true black-and-white image contains only black and white, with no shades of gray.

  TIP

  I'm not keen on creating grayscale images this way. I prefer to shoot in full color and then do my own grayscale conversion in my photo editor. That technique just gives you more control over the look of your black-and-white photos. Assuming that you work with a decent photo editor, you can control what original tones are emphasized in your grayscale version, for example. Additionally, keep in mind that you can always convert a color image to grayscale, but you can't go in the other direction. You can create a black-and-white copy of your color image directly in the camera, in fact; Chapter 10 shows you how.

- **Portrait (PT):** This mode tweaks colors and sharpening in a way that is designed to produce nice skin texture and pleasing skin tones. (If you shoot in the Portrait or Night Portrait Scene modes, the camera selects this Picture Control for you.)
- **Landscape (LS):** This mode emphasizes blues and greens. As you might expect, it's the mode used by the Landscape Scene mode.

The extent to which Picture Controls affect an image depends on the subject, but Figure 5-16 gives you a general idea of what to expect. As you can see, the differences are subtle, with the exception of the Monochrome setting.

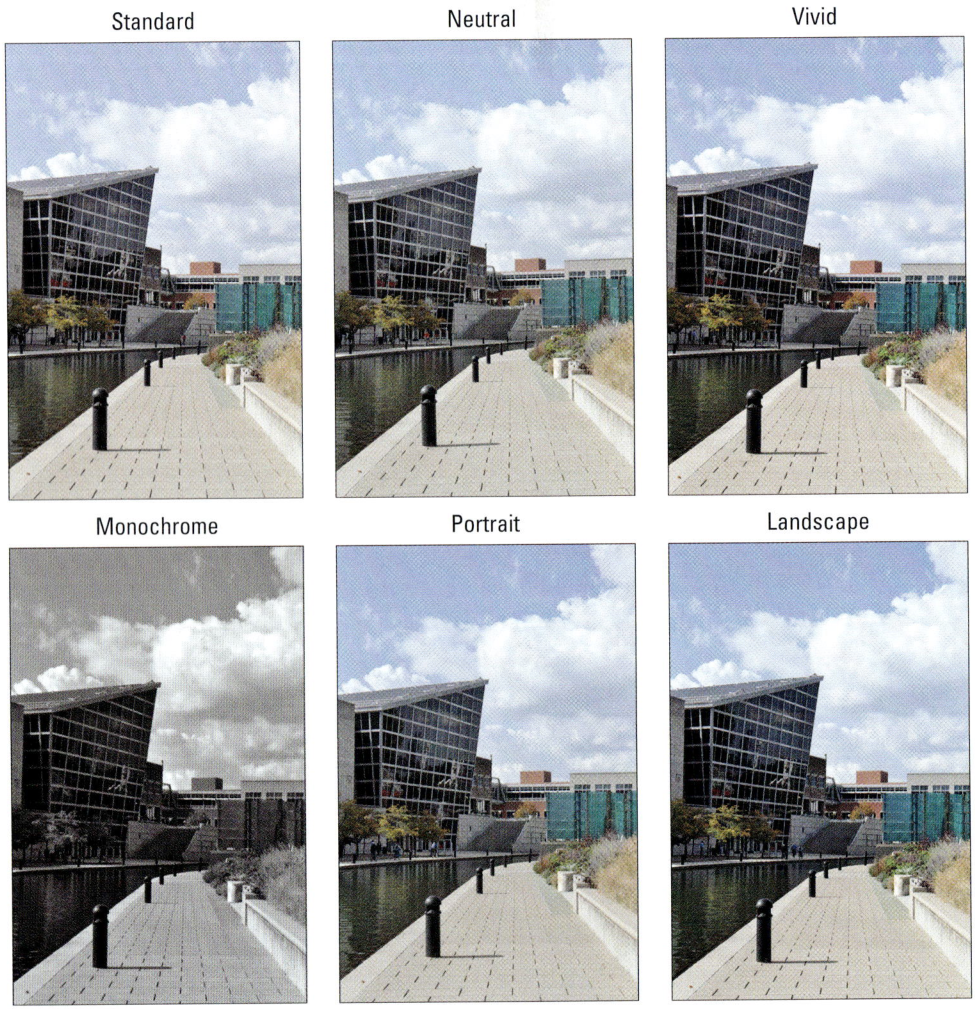

Figure 5-16: Picture controls apply preset adjustments to color, sharpening, and contrast to images you shoot in the JPEG file format.

Select the Picture Control setting via the control strip, as shown in Figure 5-17, or the Shooting menu, as shown in Figure 5-18. Using the control strip is faster — just press the ***i*** button to bring up the strip — but the menu offers a few options you can't get to from the strip.

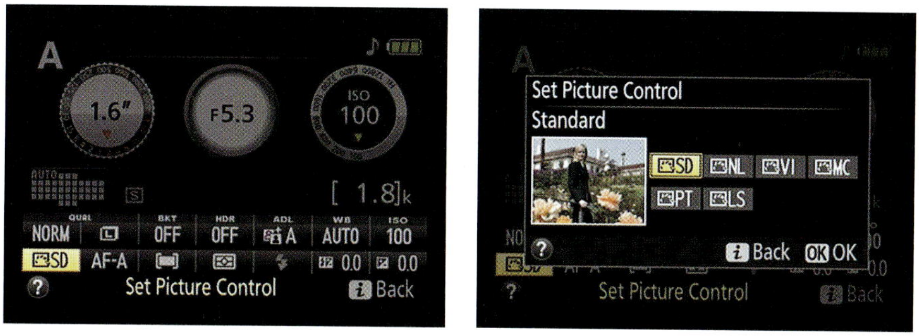

Figure 5-17: The fastest way to select a Picture Control is by using the control strip.

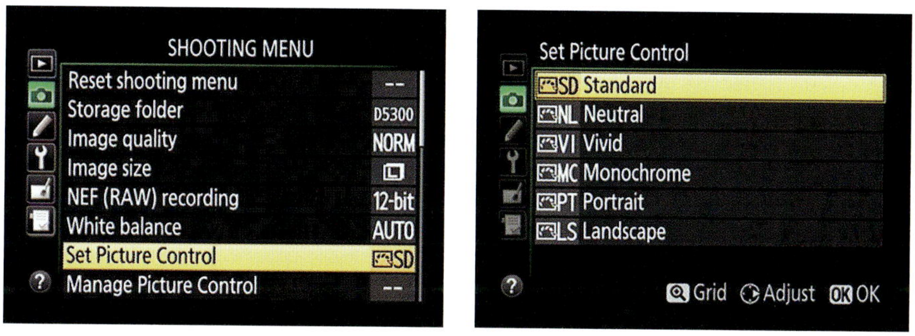

Figure 5-18: But the Shooting menu provides access to settings that let you tweak the results of each Picture Control.

TIP

While you're new to the camera, I recommend sticking with the default Picture Control setting, for two reasons. First, you have more important settings to worry about — aperture, shutter speed, autofocus, and all the rest. Why add one more setting to the list, especially when the impact of changing it is minimal?

Second, if you really want to mess with the characteristics that the Picture Control setting affects, you're better off shooting in the Raw (NEF) format and then making those adjustments as you process your Raw images. The camera tags the Raw file with whatever Picture Control is active when you take the shot, and that tag is used to render the image during playback mode. But the image adjustments are in no way set in stone, or even in sand — you can manipulate your photo at will during the image-processing stage.

For example, when you use the camera's built-in Raw processor, a feature I explain in Chapter 9, you can experiment with different Picture Control settings to see how each one affects the image. You have the same option when you use the free Nikon software, Nikon ViewNX, to process images. That program's Raw converter, as well as those found in Adobe Photoshop and other third-party programs, offer other ways to fine-tune color, contrast, and sharpness as well.

However, in the interest of full disclosure, I should alert you to a feature that may make Picture Controls a little more useful to some people: You can modify any Picture Control to more closely render a scene the way you envision it. For example, if you like the bold colors of Landscape mode but don't think that the effect goes far enough, you can adjust the setting to amp up colors even more.

To reserve page space in this book for functions that will be the most useful to the most readers, I opted not to provide full details about customizing Picture Controls. But the following steps provide a quick overview of the process so that if you encounter the menu screens that contain the related options, you'll have some idea of what you're seeing:

1. **Set the Mode dial to P, S, A, or M.**

   Again, these are the only exposure modes that enable you to select or modify a Picture Control setting.

2. **Display the Shooting menu, choose Set Picture Control, and press OK.**
3. **Highlight the Picture Control you want to modify.**

   For example, I highlighted the Landscape setting on the left in Figure 5-19.

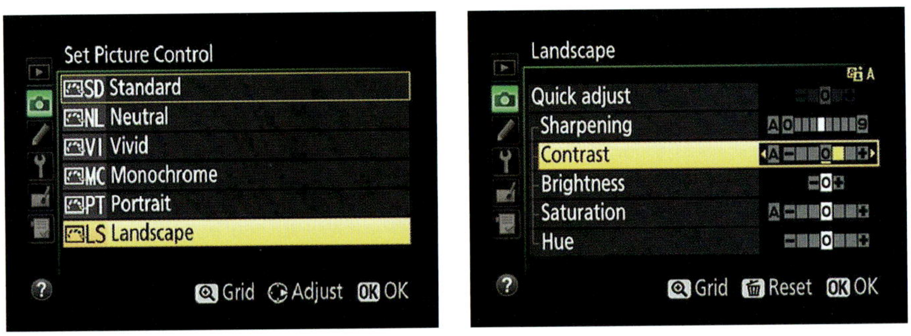

Figure 5-19: After selecting a Picture Control, press right to display options for adjusting its effect on your pictures.

4. **Press the Multi Selector right.**

   You see the screen shown on the right in Figure 5-19, containing sliders that you use to modify the Picture Control. Which options you can adjust depend on the Picture Control.

5. **Highlight a picture characteristic and then press the Multi Selector right or left to adjust the setting.**

   A few pointers:

   - Some Picture Controls offer the Quick Adjust setting, which enables you to easily increase or decrease the overall effect of the Picture Control. A positive value produces a more exaggerated effect; set the slider to 0 to return to the default setting.
   - After you highlight an option, the yellow line on the slider bar indicates the current setting for the option. The little line under the slider bar represents the default setting. For example, on the right screen in Figure 5-19, the bar under the zero indicates the default setting; the yellow box just to the right of the zero shows the new setting.
   - To display a grid that lets you see how the adjusted Picture Control compares with the original and with other Picture Controls in terms of color saturation and contrast, as shown in Figure 5-20, press and hold the Zoom In button. (I vote this screen most likely to confound new camera users who stumble across it.) The letter representing the default setting appears gray; the one representing the adjusted setting, yellow, as labeled in the figure.

     Note that the Standard and Portrait settings are identical in terms of contrast and saturation, so the P for Portrait doesn't appear on the grid unless you selected that Picture Control initially.

     You can't change settings via the grid — it's for informational purposes only. However, if you display the grid from the first Set Picture Control menu (refer to the left screen in Figure 5-19), you can press the Multi Selector up or down to select a different Picture Control. You then press right to access the adjustment screen.
   - Reset all options to their defaults by pressing the Delete button.

6. **Press OK to wrap up.**

   As when you fine-tune a White Balance setting, an asterisk appears next to the edited Picture Control on the menu and Information display to remind you that you have adjusted it.

Again, these steps are intended only as a starting point for playing with Picture Controls. Complete details are found in the electronic version of the camera manual, stored on one of the CDs that shipped with your camera. You can read the manual in Adobe Acrobat or any other program that can open PDF files. The paper manual contains only basic operating instructions, and Picture Controls didn't make the cut.

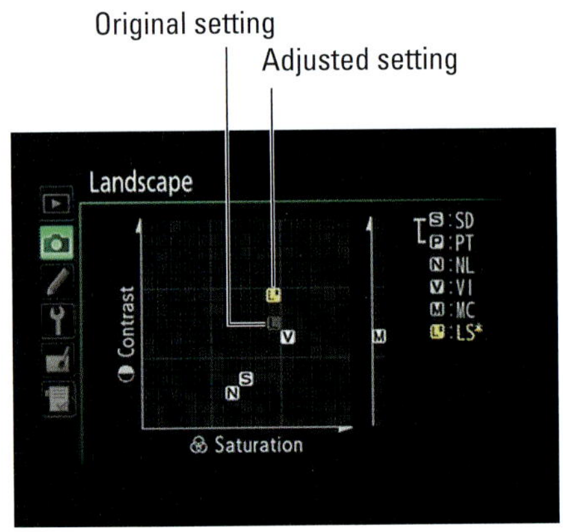

Figure 5-20: Press the Zoom In button to display a grid that ranks each Picture Control according to its level of saturation and contrast.

6

Putting It All Together

In This Chapter

- Reviewing the best all-around picture-taking settings
- Adjusting the camera for portrait photography
- Discovering the keys to super action shots
- Dialing in the right settings to capture landscapes and other scenic vistas
- Capturing close-up views of your subject
- Shooting fireworks and other tricky subjects

Earlier chapters of this book break down each and every picture-taking feature on your camera, describing in detail how the various controls affect exposure, picture quality, focus, color, and the like. This chapter pulls together all that information to help you set up your camera for specific types of photography.

Keep in mind, though, that there are no hard-and-fast rules for the "right way" to shoot a portrait, a landscape, or whatever. So feel free to wander off on your own, tweaking this exposure setting or adjusting that focus control, to discover your own creative vision. Experimentation is part of the fun of photography, after all — and thanks to your camera monitor and the Delete button, it's an easy, completely free proposition.

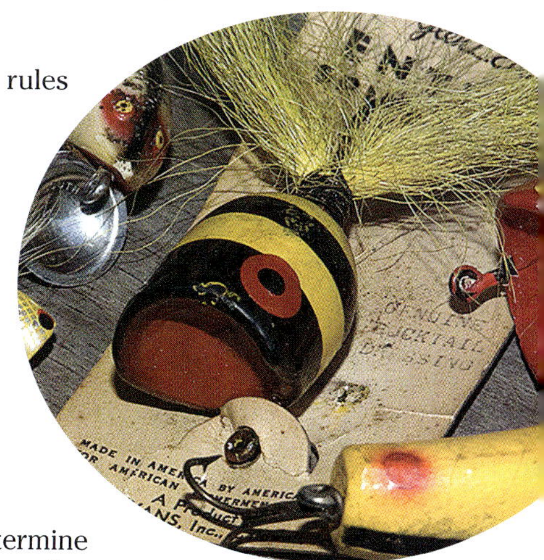

Recapping Basic Picture Settings

Your subject, creative goals, and lighting conditions determine which settings you should use for certain picture-taking options, such as aperture and shutter speed. I offer my take on those options throughout this chapter. But for many basic options, I recommend the same settings for almost every shooting scenario. Table 6-1 shows you those recommendations and also lists the chapter where you can find details about each setting.

Table 6-1 All-Purpose Picture-Taking Settings

Option	*Recommended Setting*	*See This Chapter*
Active D-Lighting	Off	3
AF-area mode	Still subjects, Single Point; moving subjects, 9-, 21-, or 39-point Dynamic Area	4
Exposure mode	P, S, A, or M	3
Focus mode	For autofocusing on still subjects, AF-S; moving subjects, AF-C	4
Image Quality	JPEG Fine or Raw (NEF)	2
Image Size	Large or medium	2
ISO Sensitivity	100	3
Metering	Matrix	3
Release mode	Action photos: Continuous Low or High; all others: Single Frame	2
White Balance	Auto	5

REMEMBER

One key point: The instructions in this chapter assume that you set the exposure mode to P, S, A, or M, as indicated in the table. These modes, detailed in Chapter 3, are the only ones that give you access to the entire cadre of camera features. In most cases, I recommend using S (shutter-priority autoexposure) when controlling motion blur is important, and A (aperture-priority autoexposure) when controlling depth of field is important. These two modes let you concentrate on one side of the exposure equation and let the camera handle the other. Of course, if you're comfortable making both the aperture and shutter speed decisions, you may prefer to work in M (manual) exposure mode instead. P (programmed autoexposure) is my last choice because it makes choosing a specific aperture or shutter speed more cumbersome.

Additionally, this chapter discusses choices for viewfinder photography. Although most picture settings work the same way during Live View photography as they do for viewfinder photography, the focusing process is quite different. For help with Live View focusing, visit Chapter 4.

Shooting Still Portraits

By *still portrait,* I mean that your subject isn't moving. For subjects who aren't keen on sitting still, skip to the next section and use the techniques given for action photography instead. Assuming that you do have a subject willing to pose, the classic portraiture approach is to keep the subject sharply focused while throwing the background into soft focus. This artistic choice emphasizes the subject and helps diminish the impact of any distracting background objects. The following steps show you how to achieve this look:

1. **Set the Mode dial to A (aperture-priority autoexposure) and select a low f-stop value.**

   A low f-stop setting opens the aperture, which not only allows more light to enter the camera but also shortens *depth of field,* or the distance over which focus appears sharp. So dialing in a low f-stop value is the first step in softening a portrait background. However, for a group portrait, don't go too low or else the depth of field may not be enough to keep everyone in the sharp-focus zone. Take test shots and inspect the results at different f-stops to find the right setting.

   TIP

   I recommend using aperture-priority mode when depth of field is a concern, because you can control the f-stop while relying on the camera to select the shutter speed. Just rotate the Command dial to select an f-stop. (You need to pay attention to shutter speed as well, however, to make sure that it's not so slow that movement of the subject or camera will blur the image.)

   You can monitor the current f-stop and shutter speed in the Information display and viewfinder, as shown in Figure 6-1.

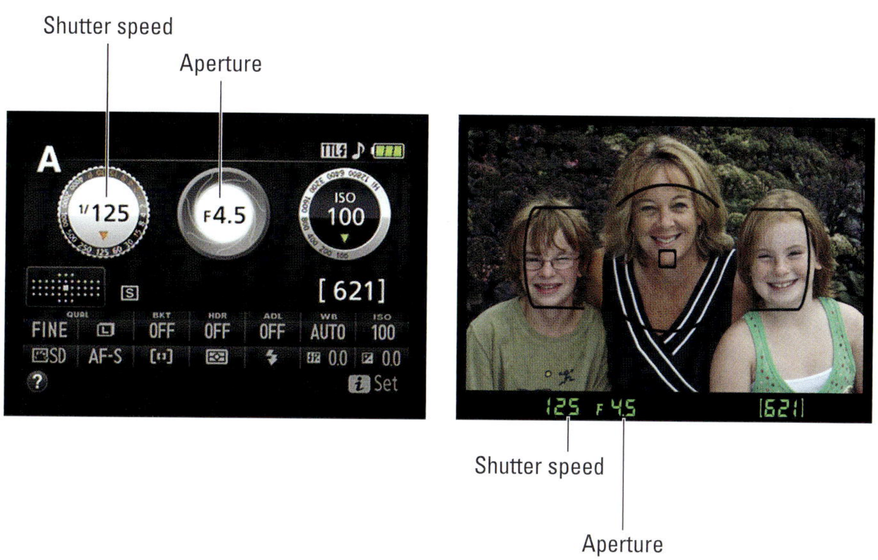

Figure 6-1: You can monitor aperture (f-stop) and shutter speed settings in the displays.

2. **To further soften the background, zoom in, get closer, and put more distance between the subject and background.**

   Zooming in to a longer focal length also reduces depth of field, as does moving physically closer to your subject. And the greater the distance between the subject and background, the more the background blurs. (A good rule is to place the subject at least an arm's length away from the background.)

   Avoid using a lens with a short focal length (a wide-angle lens) for portraits. They can cause features to appear distorted — sort of like how people look when you view them through the security peephole in a door. A lens with a focal length of 85–120mm is ideal for a classic head-and-shoulders portrait.

3. **Check composition.**

   Just two quick pointers on this topic:

   - *Consider the background.* Scan the entire frame, looking for background objects that may distract the eye from the subject. If necessary, reposition the subject against a more flattering backdrop.
   - *Frame the subject loosely to allow for later cropping to a variety of frame sizes.* Your camera produces images that have an aspect ratio of 3:2. That means your portrait perfectly fits a 4 x 6 print size but will require cropping to print at any other proportion, such as 5 x 7 or 8 x 10.

4. **For indoor portraits, shoot flash-free, if possible.**

   Shooting by available light rather than by flash produces softer illumination and avoids the problem of red-eye. To get enough light to go flash-free, turn on room lights or, during daylight, pose your subject next to a sunny window, as I did for the image in Figure 6-2.

   In the A exposure mode, simply keeping the built-in flash unit closed disables the flash. If flash is unavoidable, see my list of flash tips at the end of this step list to get better results.

5. **For outdoor portraits, use a flash if possible.**

   Even in daylight, a flash adds a beneficial pop of light to subjects' faces, as illustrated in Figure 6-3. A flash is especially important when the background is brighter than the subjects, as in this example.

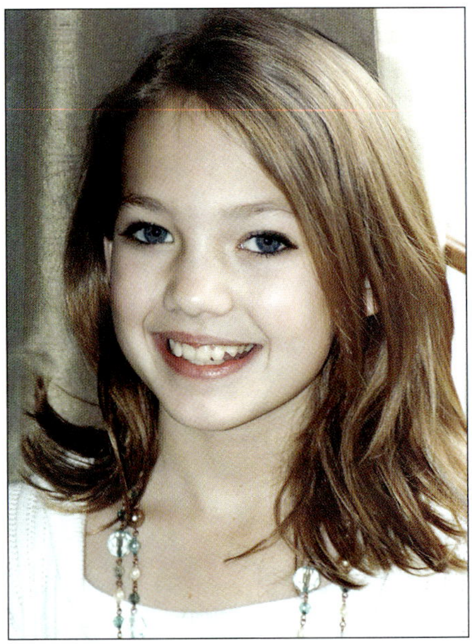

Figure 6-2: For more pleasing indoor portraits, shoot by available light instead of using flash.

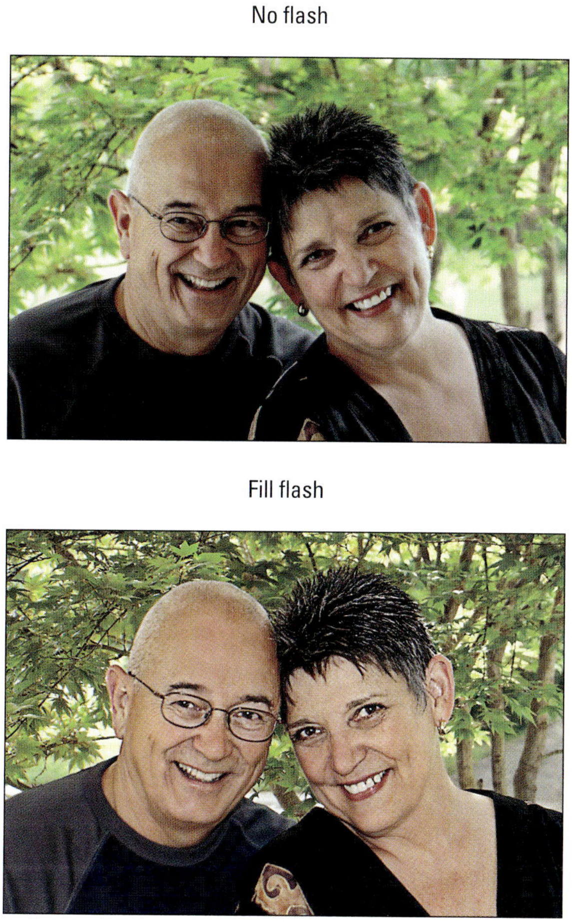

Figure 6-3: To properly illuminate the face in outdoor portraits, use flash.

In the A exposure mode, press the Flash button on the side of the camera to raise the built-in flash. For daytime portraits, set the Flash mode to Fill Flash. (That's the regular, basic Flash mode.) For nighttime images, try red-eye reduction or slow-sync flash; again, see the flash tips at the end of these steps to use either mode most effectively.

WARNING!

By default, the top shutter speed for flash photography is 1/200 second, so in bright light, you may need to stop down the aperture to avoid overexposing the photo, as I did for the bottom image in Figure 6-3. Doing so, of course, brings the background into sharper focus, so if that creates an issue, move the subject into a shaded area instead.

6. **Press and hold the shutter button halfway to initiate exposure metering and autofocusing.**

   If the camera has trouble finding the correct focusing distance, set your lens to manual focus mode and then twist the focusing ring to set focus. See Chapter 4 for help with focusing.

7. **Press the shutter button the rest of the way to capture the image.**

TIP

When flash is unavoidable, try these tricks to produce better results:

- **Indoors, turn on as many room lights as possible.** With more ambient light, you reduce the flash power that's needed to expose the picture. Adding light also causes the pupils to constrict, further reducing the chances of red-eye. As an added benefit, the smaller pupil allows more of the subject's iris to be visible in the portrait, so you see more eye color.
- **Try using a Flash mode that enables red-eye reduction or slow-sync flash.** If you choose the first option, warn your subject to expect both a preliminary light from the AF-assist lamp, which constricts pupils, and the flash. And remember that slow-sync flash modes use a slower-than-normal shutter speed, which produces softer lighting and brighter backgrounds than normal flash. (Chapter 2 explains the various Flash modes.)

  Take a look at Figure 6-4 for an example of how using slow-sync flash can improve an indoor portrait. When I used regular flash, the shutter speed was 1/60 second. At that speed, the camera has little time to soak up any ambient light. As a result, the scene is lit primarily by the flash. That caused two problems: The strong flash created some glare on the subject's skin, and the window panes and frame are much more prominent because of the contrast between them and the darker bushes outside the window. Although it was daylight when I took the picture, the skies were overcast, so at 1/60 second, the exterior appears dark.

  In the slow-sync example, shot at 1/4 second, the exposure time was long enough to permit the ambient light to brighten the exteriors to the point that the window frame almost blends into the background. And because much less flash power was needed to expose the subject, the lighting is much more flattering. In this case, the bright background also helps to set the subject apart because of her dark hair and shirt. If the subject had been a pale blonde, this setup wouldn't have worked as well. Again, too, note the warming effect that can occur when you use Auto White Balance and shoot in a combination of flash and daylight.

  WARNING!

  Using a slower-than-normal shutter speed increases the risk of blur due to camera shake, so use a tripod or otherwise steady the camera. Remind your subjects to stay absolutely still, too, because they'll appear blurry if they move during the exposure. I was fortunate to have both a tripod and a cooperative subject for my examples, but I probably wouldn't opt for slow-sync for portraits of young children or pets.

Regular fill flash, 1/60 second

Slow-sync flash, 1/4 second

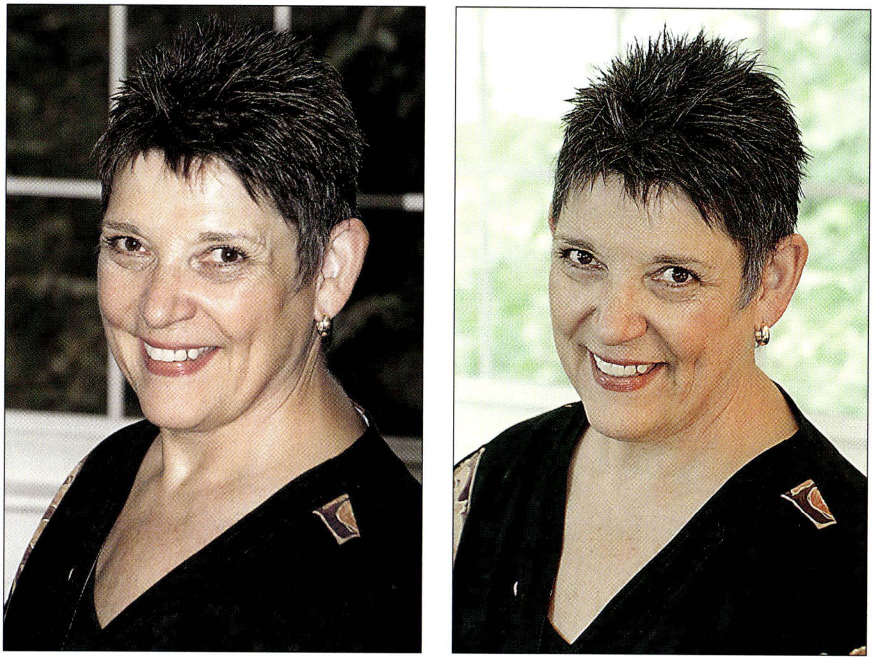

Figure 6-4: Slow-sync flash produces softer, more even lighting and brighter backgrounds.

- **For professional results, use an external flash with a rotating flash head.** Aim the flash head upward so that the flash light bounces off the ceiling and falls softly down onto the subject. External flashes can be pricey, but the results make the purchase worthwhile if you shoot lots of portraits. Compare the two portraits in Figure 6-5 for an illustration. In the first example, using the built-in flash resulted in strong shadowing behind the subject and harsh, concentrated light. To produce the better result on the right, I used a Nikon Speedlight external flash and bounced the light off the ceiling. I also moved the subject a few feet farther in front of the background to create more background blur.

  WARNING!

  Make sure that the ceiling or other surface you use to bounce the light is white; otherwise, the flash light will pick up the color of the surface and influence the color of your subject.

- **Invest in a flash diffuser to further soften the light.** A *diffuser* is simply a piece of translucent plastic or fabric that you place over the flash to soften and spread the light — much like how sheer curtains diffuse window light. Diffusers come in lots of different designs, including models that fit over the built-in flash.

- **Pay attention to white balance if your subject is lit by both flash and ambient light.** If you set the White Balance setting to Auto, as I recommend in Table 6-1, enabling flash tells the camera to warm colors to compensate for the cool light of a flash. If your subject is also lit by other light sources, such as sunlight, the result may be colors that are slightly warmer or cooler (more blue) than neutral. A warming effect typically looks nice in portraits, giving the skin a subtle glow. If you aren't happy with the result, see Chapter 5 to find out how to fine-tune white balance.

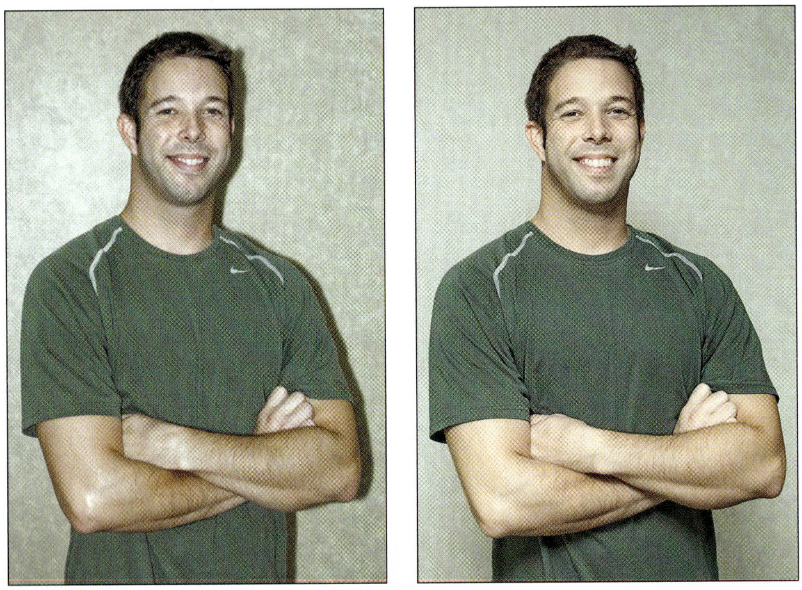

Figure 6-5: To eliminate harsh lighting and strong shadows (left), use bounce flash and move the subject farther from the background (right).

Capturing Action

Using a fast shutter speed is the key to capturing a blur-free shot of any moving subject, whether it's a flower in the breeze, a spinning Ferris wheel, or, as in the case of Figure 6-6, a racing cyclist.

Along with the basic capture settings outlined earlier, in Table 6-1, try the techniques in the following steps to photograph a subject in motion:

1. **Set the Mode dial to S (shutter-priority autoexposure).**

   In this mode, you control the shutter speed, and the camera takes care of choosing an aperture setting that will produce a good exposure.

2. **Rotate the Command dial to select the shutter speed.**

   Refer to Figure 6-1 to locate shutter speed in the Information display and viewfinder. After you select the shutter speed, the camera selects an aperture (f-stop) to match.

   What shutter speed should you choose? Well, it depends on the speed at which your subject is moving, so you need to experiment. But generally speaking, 1/320 second should be plenty for all but the fastest subjects (race cars, boats, and so on). For very slow subjects, you can even go as low as 1/250 or 1/125 second. My subject in Figure 6-6 zipped along at a pretty fast pace, so I set the shutter speed to 1/500 second. Remember, though, that when you increase shutter speed, the camera opens the aperture to maintain the same exposure. At low f-stop numbers, depth of field becomes shorter, so you have to be more careful to keep your subject within the sharp-focus zone as you compose and focus the shot.

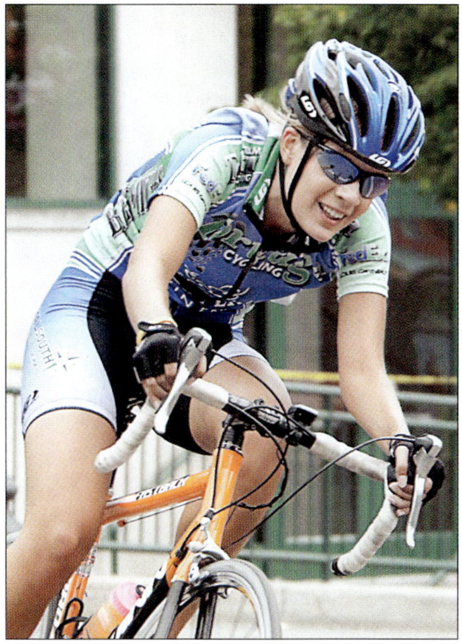

Figure 6-6: Use a high shutter speed to freeze motion.

   TIP: You also can take an entirely different approach to capturing action: Rather than choose a fast shutter speed, select a speed slow enough to blur the moving objects, which can create a heightened sense of motion and, in scenes that feature very colorful subjects, cool abstract images. I took this approach when shooting the carnival ride featured in Figure 6-7, for example. For the left image, I set the shutter speed to 1/30 second; for the right version, I slowed things down to 1/5 second. In both cases, I used a tripod, but because nearly everything in the frame was moving, the entirety of both photos is blurry — the 1/5 second version is simply more blurry because of the slower shutter.

3. **In dim lighting, raise the ISO setting, if necessary, to allow a fast shutter speed.**

   Unless you're shooting in bright daylight, you may not be able to use a fast shutter speed at a low ISO, even if the camera opens the aperture as far as possible. If auto ISO override is in force, ISO may go up automatically when you increase the shutter speed — Chapter 3 has details on that feature. Raising the ISO does increase the possibility of noise, so you have to decide whether a noisy shot is better than a blurry shot.

1/30 second 1/5 second

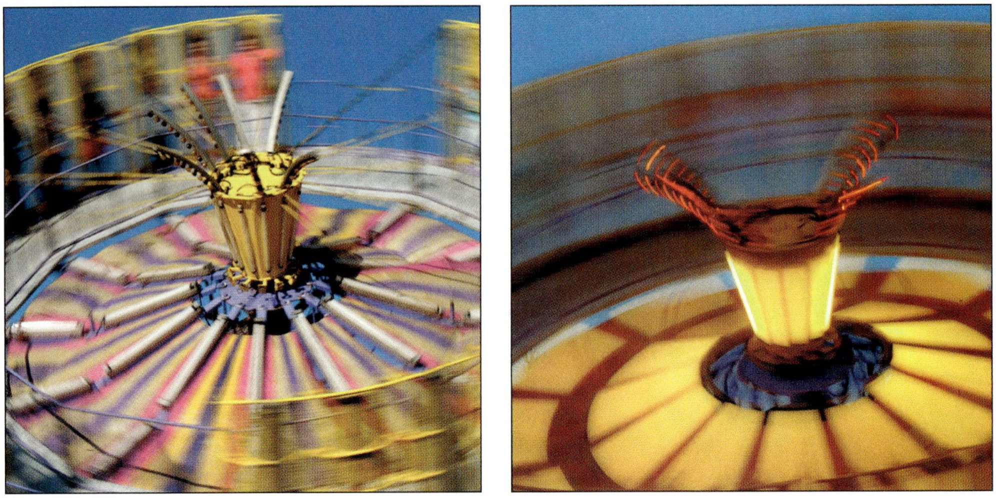

Figure 6-7: Using a shutter speed slow enough to blur moving objects can be a fun creative choice, too.

Why not add flash to brighten the scene? Well, adding flash is tricky for action shots, unfortunately. First, the flash needs time to recycle between shots, which slows the capture rate. Second, the built-in flash has limited range, so don't waste your time if your subject isn't close by. And third, remember that the fastest shutter speed you can use with flash is 1/200 second by default, which may not be high enough to capture a quickly moving subject without blur.

4. **For rapid-fire shooting, set the Release mode to Continuous Low or Continuous High.**

   In both modes, you can capture multiple images with a single press of the shutter button. Continuous Low captures up to 3 frames per second (fps), and Continuous High bumps the frame rate up to about 5 fps. As long as you hold down the button, the camera continues to record images. Here again, though, you need to go flash-free; otherwise, you get one shot per press of the shutter button, just as in Single Frame release mode.

5. **Select speed-oriented focusing options.**

   For fastest shooting, try manual focusing: It eliminates the time the camera needs to lock focus when you use autofocusing. If you use autofocus, select these two autofocus settings for best performance:

- Set the AF-area mode to one of the Dynamic Area settings. Chapter 4 has information to help you decide whether the 9-point, 21-point, or 39-point Dynamic Area setting is best for your subject.
- Set the Autofocus mode to AF-C (continuous-servo autofocus).

At these settings, the camera sets focus initially on your selected focus point but then looks to the surrounding points for focusing information if your subject moves away from the selected point. Focus is adjusted continuously until you take the shot. (Again, these instructions relate to viewfinder photography; for help with Live View focusing settings, see Chapter 4.)

6. **Compose the subject to allow for movement across the frame.**

   Frame your shot a little wider than you normally might so that you lessen the risk that your subject will move out of the frame before you record the image. You can always crop to a tighter composition later. (I used this approach for my cyclist image — the original shot includes a lot of background that I later cropped away.) It's also a good idea to leave more room in front of the subject than behind it. This makes it obvious that your subject is going somewhere.

Using these techniques should give you a better chance of capturing any fast-moving subject, but action-shooting strategies also are helpful for shooting candid portraits of kids and pets. Even if they aren't currently running, leaping, or otherwise cavorting, snapping a shot before they do move is often tough. So if an interaction catches your eye, set your camera into action mode and fire off a series of shots as fast as you can.

Capturing Scenic Vistas

Providing specific capture settings for landscape photography is tricky because there's no single best approach to capturing a beautiful stretch of countryside, a city skyline, or another vast subject. Most people prefer using a wide-angle lens, for example, to incorporate a large area of the landscape into the scene, but if you're far away from your subject, you may like the results you get from a telephoto or medium-angle lens. When shooting the scene in Figure 6-8, for example, I had to position myself across the street from the buildings, so I captured the shot using a focal length of 82mm. And consider depth of field: One person's idea of a super cityscape might be to keep all buildings in the scene sharply focused, but another photographer might prefer to shoot the same scene so that a foreground building is sharply focused while the others are less so, thus drawing the eye to that first building.

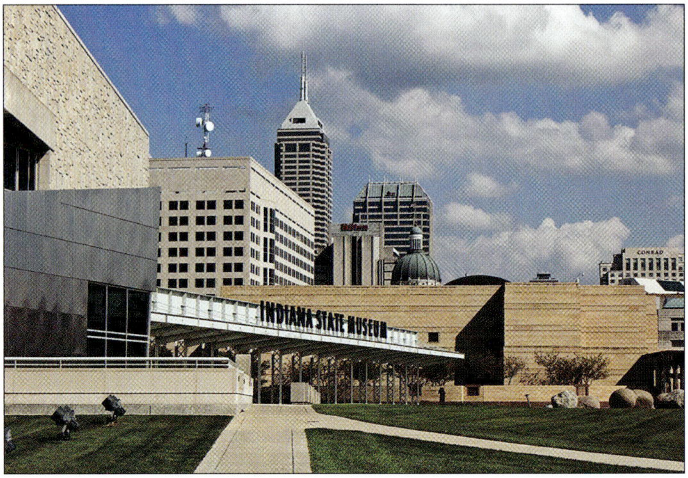

Figure 6-8: Use a high f-stop value to keep the foreground and background sharply focused.

I can, however, offer a few tips to help you photograph a landscape the way *you* see it:

- **Shoot in aperture-priority autoexposure mode (A) so that you can control depth of field.** If you want extreme depth of field so that both near and distant objects are sharply focused (refer to Figure 6-8), select a high f-stop value. I used an aperture of f/18 for this shot. For short depth of field, use a low value.
- **If the exposure requires a slow shutter speed, use a tripod to avoid blurring.** The downside to a high f-stop is that you may need a slower shutter speed to produce a good exposure. If the shutter speed drops below what you can comfortably handhold, use a tripod to avoid picture-blurring camera shake.
- **For dramatic waterfall shots, consider using a slow shutter to create that "misty" look.** The slow shutter blurs the water, giving it a soft, romantic appearance, as shown in Figure 6-9. Again, use a tripod to ensure that the rest of the scene doesn't also blur due to camera shake. Shutter speed for the image in Figure 6-9 was 1/5 second.

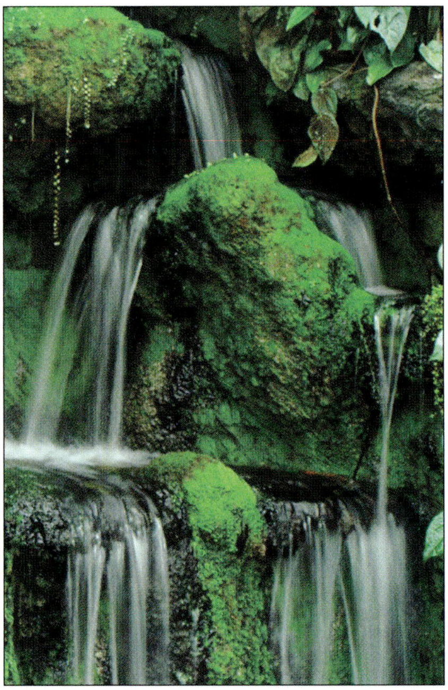

Figure 6-9: For misty waterfalls, use a slow shutter speed and a tripod.

TIP: In very bright light, you may overexpose the image at a very slow shutter, even if you stop the aperture all the way down and select the camera's lowest ISO setting. As a solution, consider investing in a *neutral density filter* for your lens. This type of filter works something like sunglasses for your camera: It simply reduces the amount of light that passes through the lens, without affecting image colors, so that you can use a slower shutter than would otherwise be possible.

- **At sunrise or sunset, base exposure on the sky.** The foreground will be dark, but you can usually brighten it in a photo editor, if needed. If you base exposure on the foreground, on the other hand, the sky will become so bright that all the color will be washed out — a problem you usually can't fix after the fact. You can also invest in a *graduated neutral-density filter,* which is clear on one side and dark on the other. You orient the filter so that the dark half falls over the sky and the clear side falls over the dimly lit portion of the scene. This setup enables you to better expose the foreground without blowing out the sky colors.

  Also experiment with the Active D-Lighting and HDR features that I cover in Chapter 3; both are designed to create images that contain a greater range of brightness values than is normally possible.

- **For cool nighttime city pics, experiment with slow shutter speeds.** Assuming that cars or other vehicles with their lights on are moving through the scene, the result is neon trails of light like those you see in the foreground of the image in Figure 6-10. Shutter speed for this image was about 10 seconds.

  TIP: Rather than change the shutter speed manually between each shot, try *Bulb* mode. Available only in M (manual) exposure mode, this option records an image for as long as you hold down the shutter button. So just take a series of images, holding down the button for different lengths of time for each shot. In Bulb mode, you also can exceed the standard maximum exposure time of 30 seconds.

- **For the best lighting, shoot during the *magic hours.*** That's the term photographers use for early morning and late afternoon, when the light cast by the sun is soft and warm, giving everything that beautiful, gently warmed look.

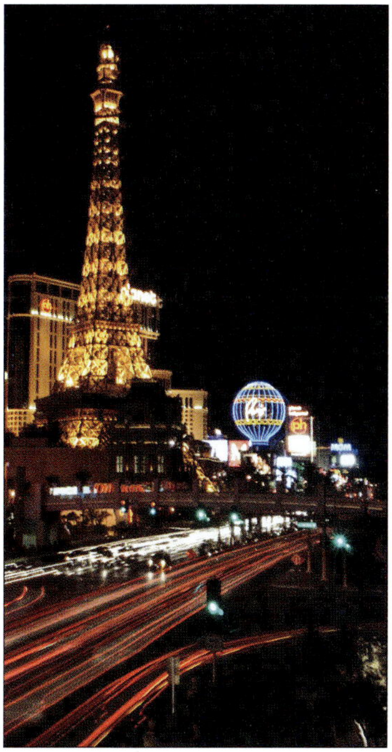

Figure 6-10: Using a slow shutter speed creates neon light trails in nighttime city street scenes.

TIP

Can't wait for the perfect light? Tweak your camera's White Balance setting, using the instructions laid out in Chapter 5, to simulate the color of magic-hour light.

- **In tricky light, bracket exposures.** *Bracketing* simply means to take the same picture at several different exposure settings to increase the odds that at least one of them will capture the scene the way you envision. Bracketing is especially a good idea in difficult lighting situations, such as sunrise and sunset. Chapter 3 shows you how to make bracketing easier by using automatic exposure bracketing.

Capturing Dynamic Close-Ups

For great close-up shots, try these techniques:

- **Check your lens manual to find out its minimum close-focusing distance.** How "up close and personal" you can get to your subject depends on your lens, not on the camera body.
- **Take control over depth of field by setting the camera mode to A (aperture-priority autoexposure) mode.** Whether you want a shallow, medium, or extreme depth of field depends on the point of your photo. In classic nature photography, for example, the artistic tradition is a very shallow depth of field, as shown in Figure 6-11, and requires an open aperture (low f-stop value). If you want the viewer to be able to clearly see all details throughout the frame — for example, you're shooting a product shot for a sales catalog — you need to go in the other direction, stopping down the aperture as far as possible.
- **Remember that depth of field decreases when you zoom in or move closer to your subject.** Go back to that product shot: If you need depth of field beyond what you can achieve with the aperture setting, you may need to back away, zoom out, or both. (You can always crop your image to show just the parts of the subject that you want to feature.)

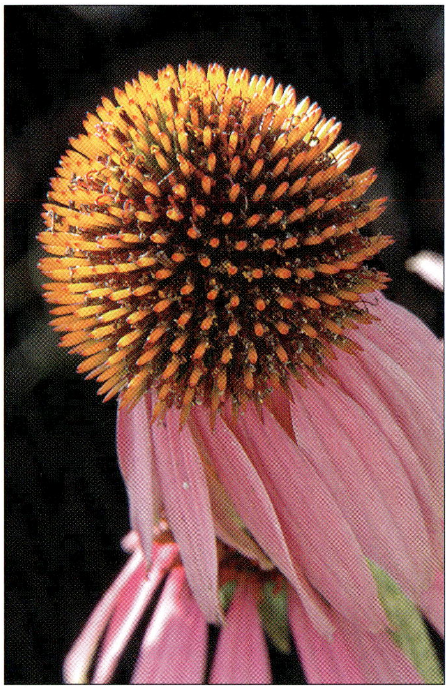

Figure 6-11: Shallow depth of field is a classic technique for close-up floral images.

- **When shooting flowers and other nature scenes outdoors, pay attention to shutter speed, too.** Even a slight breeze may cause your subject to move, causing blurring at slow shutter speeds.
- **Use flash for better outdoor lighting.** Just as with portraits, a tiny bit of flash typically improves close-ups when the sun is the primary light source. Again, though, keep in mind that the maximum shutter speed possible when you use the built-in flash is 1/200 second. So in very bright light, you may need to use a high f-stop setting to avoid overexposing the picture. You can also adjust the flash output via the Flash Compensation control. Chapter 2 offers details.
- **When shooting indoors, try not to use flash as the primary light source.** Because you're shooting at close range, the light from your flash may be too harsh even at a low Flash Compensation setting. If flash is inevitable, turn on as many room lights as possible to reduce the flash power that's needed — even a shop light from a hardware store can do in a pinch as a lighting source. (Remember that if you have multiple light sources, though, you may need to tweak the White Balance setting.)
- **To get really close to your subject, invest in a macro lens or a set of diopters.** A true macro lens, which enables you to get really, really close to your subjects, is an expensive proposition; prices range from a few hundred to a couple thousand dollars. If you enjoy capturing the tiny details in life, though, it's worth the investment.

  Nikon has a great guide to its macro lenses — officially titled *Micro-Nikkor Lenses* — at its `www.nikonusa.com` website, if you're ready to start shopping.

  For a less expensive way to go, you can spend about $40 for a set of *diopters,* which are sort of like reading glasses that you screw onto your existing lens. Diopters come in several strengths — +1, +2, +4, and so on — with a higher number indicating a greater magnifying power. I took this approach to capture the extreme close-up in Figure 6-12, attaching a +2 diopter to my lens. The downside of using a diopter, sadly, is that it typically produces images that are very soft around the edges, a problem that doesn't occur with a good macro lens.

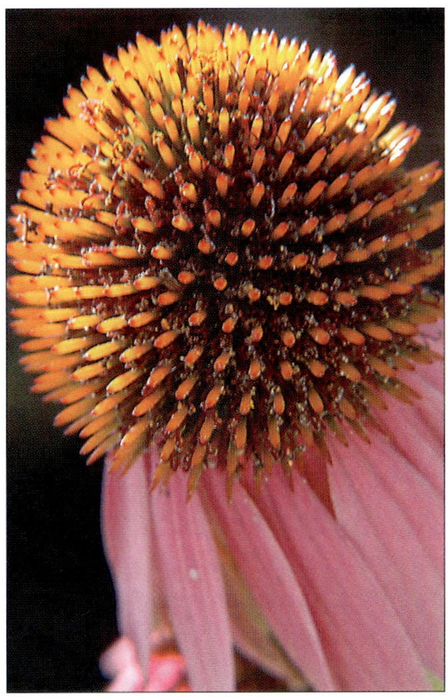

Figure 6-12: To extend your lens's close-focus capability, you can add magnifying diopters.

Coping with Special Situations

A few subjects and shooting situations pose some additional challenges not already covered in earlier sections. To close this chapter, here's a quick list of ideas for tackling a variety of common tough-shot photos:

- **Shooting fireworks:** First off, use a tripod; fireworks require a long exposure, and trying to handhold your camera simply won't work. If using a zoom lens, zoom out to the shortest focal length (widest angle). Switch to manual focusing and set focus at infinity (the farthest focus point possible on your lens). Set the exposure mode to manual, choose a relatively high f-stop setting — say, f/16 or so — and start at a shutter speed of 1 to 5 seconds. From there, it's simply a matter of experimenting with different shutter speeds. Also play with the timing of the shutter release, starting some exposures at the moment the fireworks are shot up, some at the moment they burst open, and so on. For the example featured in Figure 6-13, I used a shutter speed of about 5 seconds and began the exposure as the rocket was going up — that's what creates the "corkscrew" of light that rises up through the frame.

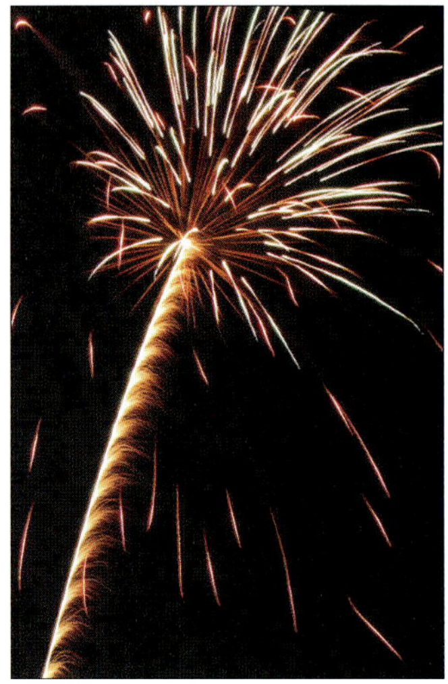

Figure 6-13: A shutter speed of 5 seconds captured this fireworks shot.

  TIP

  Be especially gentle when you press the shutter button — with a very slow shutter, you can easily create enough camera movement to blur the image. If you purchased the accessory remote control for your camera, this is a good situation in which to use it.

- **Shooting through glass:** To capture subjects that are behind glass, such as animals at a zoo, you can try a couple of tricks. First, set your camera to manual focusing — the glass barrier can give the autofocus mechanism fits. Disable the flash to avoid creating any unwanted reflections, too. Then, if you can get close enough, your best odds are to put the lens right up to the glass. (Be careful not to scratch your lens.) If you must stand farther away, try to position your lens at a 90-degree angle to the glass. I used this approach in Figure 6-14.

- **Shooting out a car window:** Set the camera to shutter-priority autoexposure or manual mode and dial in a fast shutter speed to compensate for the movement of the car. Also turn on Vibration Reduction, if your lens offers it. Oh, and keep a tight grip on your camera.

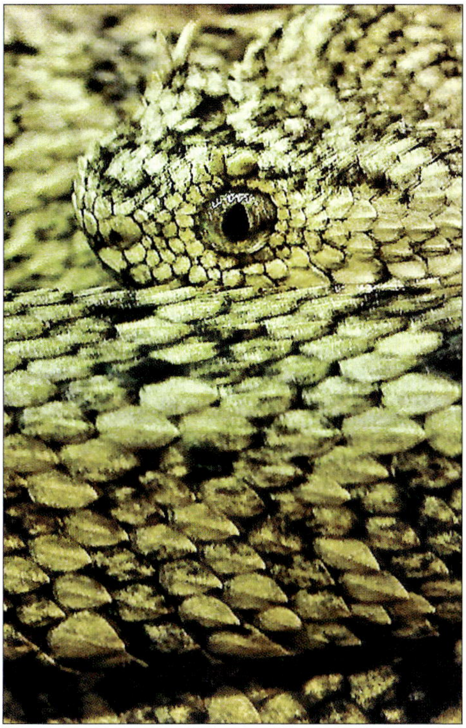

Figure 6-14: To photograph subjects that are behind glass, use manual focusing and disable flash.

- **Shooting in strong backlighting:** When the light behind your subject is very strong, the result is often an underexposed subject. You can try using flash to better expose the subject, assuming that you're shooting in an exposure mode that permits flash. The Active D-Lighting feature covered in Chapter 3 can also help brighten your subject without blowing out highlights. And don't forget that your camera has a built-in HDR (high dynamic range) mode, which blends two exposures to include more shadows and highlights in the scene. (Chapter 3 has examples.)

For another creative choice, you can purposely underexpose the subject to create a silhouette effect, as shown in Figure 6-15. Base the exposure on the brightest areas of the background so that the darker areas of the frame remain dark.

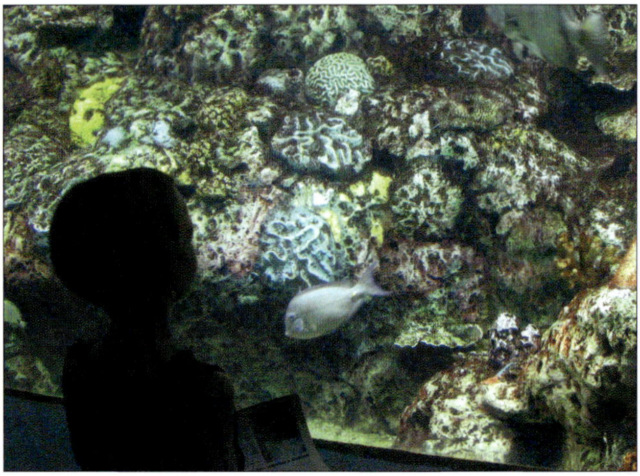

Figure 6-15: Experiment with shooting backlit subjects in silhouette.

7

Shooting, Viewing, and Trimming Movies

In This Chapter

- Recording your first movie using the default settings
- Understanding the frame rate, frame size, and movie quality options
- Adjusting audio-recording options
- Controlling exposure during movie recording
- Playing and trimming movies
- Taking a still photo during recording

In addition to being a stellar still-photography camera, your D5300 enables you to record HD (high-definition) movies. This chapter tells you everything you need to know to take advantage of the movie-recording options.

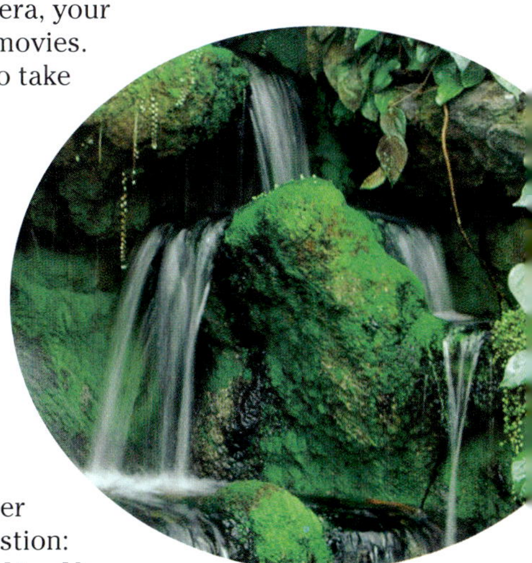

Check that: This chapter tells you *almost* everything about movie recording. What's missing here is detailed information about focusing, which works the same way for movie shooting as it does when you use Live View to shoot a still photo. Rather than cover the subject twice, I detail your focusing options in Chapter 4 and provide just a basic recap in these pages.

Also be sure to visit the end of Chapter 1, which lists precautions to take while Live View is engaged whether you're shooting stills or movies. (To answer your question: No, you can't use the viewfinder for movie recording; Live View is your only option.)

For even more insights into recording movies with a dSLR, hop online and check out Nikon Cinema, at `cinema.nikonusa.com`.

Shooting Movies Using the Default Settings

Video enthusiasts will appreciate the fact that the D5300 enables you to tweak a variety of movie-recording settings. But if you're not up to sorting through those options, just use the default settings. (You can restore the critical defaults by opening the Shooting menu and choosing Reset Shooting Menu.) At these settings, you get a full HD movie with sound enabled.

Movies are created in the MOV format, which means you can play them on your computer using most video-playback programs. You also can view movies in Nikon ViewNX 2, the free software provided with your camera. If you want to view your movies on a TV, see the end of Chapter 8 to find out how to connect your camera to your set.

The following steps show you how to record a movie using autofocusing. If you prefer manual focusing, just bypass the autofocusing instructions (again, you can find specifics on manual focusing during Live View in Chapter 4):

1. **Set the Mode dial on top of the camera to Auto.**

   In this mode, the camera takes care of most movie settings for you, including ones that affect exposure and color.

2. **Set the lens to autofocus mode.**

   Depending on your lens, you accomplish this by setting the lens switch to A, AF, or AF/M (auto with manual focus override). See your lens manual for help if you're unsure.

3. **Engage Live View by rotating the Live View switch, shown in Figure 7-1, toward the back of the camera.**

   The viewfinder goes dark, and your subject appears on the monitor.

4. **Press the Info button until the display is set to Show Movie Indicators view, as shown in Figure 7-2.**

   Later sections decode the various bits of data; for now, just pay attention to the available recording time readout, labeled in the figure. At the default settings, your movie can be 20 minutes long, but that number presumes that your memory card has enough space on it to hold the entire movie. The maximum file size for a movie is 4GB (gigabytes).

   If the upper-left corner of the screen displays the letters *REC* with a slash through

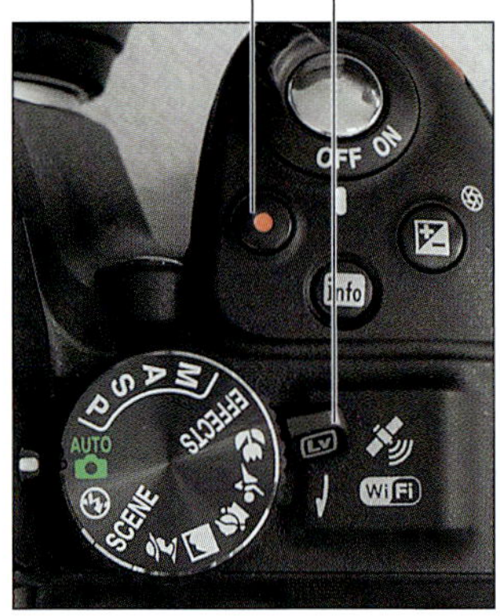

Figure 7-1: Your first step is to set the camera to Live View mode.

them, something is amiss: That's the camera's way of telling you that movie recording isn't possible. You see this symbol if no memory card is inserted or the card is full, for example.

5. **Set the Focus mode to AF-S or AF-F.**

   The right choice depends on two factors: whether you're shooting a moving subject or a stationary one and whether you require pristine audio. Here's what you need to know to make the call:

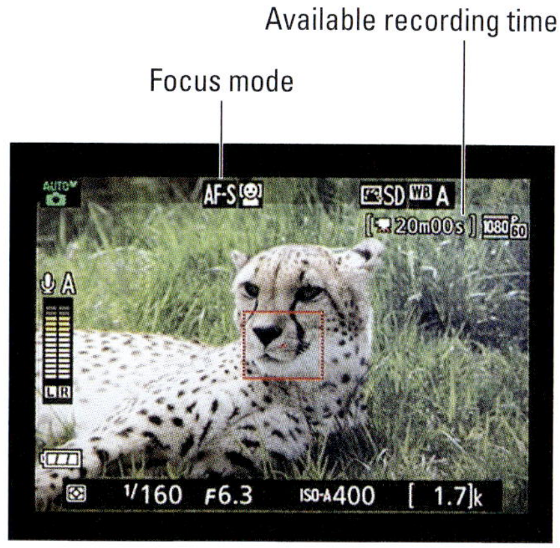

Figure 7-2: Press the Info button to cycle through the Live View display modes until you see these movie-recording symbols.

   - *AF-S:* The camera locks focus when you press the shutter button halfway. You then can lift your finger off the shutter button; for movies, focus remains set at the current distance throughout your recording unless you press the button halfway again to reset focus. Choose this option if you expect your subject to remain the same distance from the camera throughout the movie — for example, if you're recording a piano performance.
   - *AF-F:* This setting produces full-time, continuous autofocusing, with the camera adjusting focus as your subject moves or you pan the camera to follow the action. Focusing starts immediately after you set the Focus mode to AF-F, and if you want to lock focus, you press the shutter button halfway. When you release the button, continuous autofocusing resumes.

     Although this option is best for tracking moving subjects, the built-in microphone sometimes picks up the sound of the focusing motor. To avoid this issue, you can attach an external microphone and place it far enough from the camera body that it can't hear the focus motor. The only other solutions are to switch to AF-S mode and lock in focus before you begin recording or to use manual focusing.

You can see the current Focus mode setting at the top of the monitor, as shown in Figure 7-2. To change the setting, use the control strip shown in Figure 7-3. ***Remember:*** Press the ***i*** button to bring up the control strip.

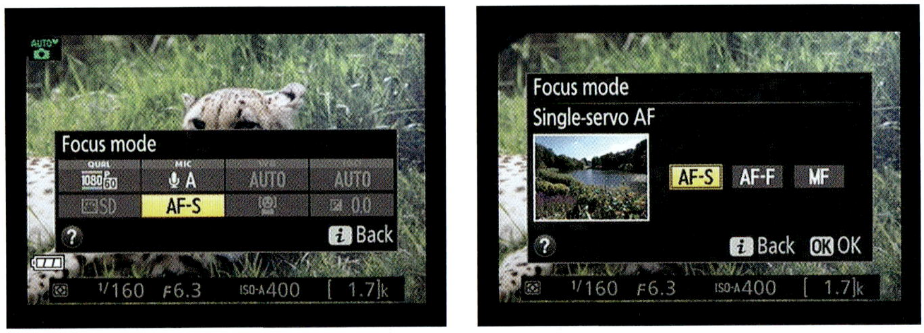

Figure 7-3: Set the Focus mode via the control strip.

6. **Compose your initial shot in the monitor.**

   The shaded areas at the top and bottom of the monitor indicate the boundaries of the default frame size, 1920 x 1080 pixels, which produces a 16:9 aspect ratio.

7. **If necessary, move the focusing frame over your subject.**

   By default, the camera uses the Face-Priority AF-area mode, which means that if your scene contains a human face, the focusing system automatically focuses on that portion of the frame. In this scenario, you see a yellow focus frame over the face. When the scene contains more than one face, you see multiple frames; the one with the interior corner markings indicates the face chosen as the focus point. You can use the Multi Selector to move the frame over a different face.

   If the camera doesn't detect a face, it instead uses the Wide Area AF-area mode, and the focus frame appears as a red rectangle, as shown in Figure 7-2. Again, use the Multi Selector to move the frame over your subject.

8. **Focus the shot.**

   Again, with AF-F focusing, you don't need to do anything; just wait for the focusing frame to turn green, indicating that initial focus is set. With AF-S focusing, press the shutter button halfway. The focusing frame turns green when focus is achieved, and you can then take your finger off the shutter button, if you want.

9. **To begin recording, press the red movie-record button on top of the camera (refer to Figure 7-1).**

   Most shooting data disappears from the screen, and a red Rec symbol flashes in the upper-left corner, as shown in Figure 7-4. As recording progresses, the area labeled *Time remaining* in the figure shows you how many more minutes of video you can record.

10. **To stop recording, press the movie-record button again.**

    Your movie is recorded to the memory card.

Two quick tips to add to these basics:

- **Declutter the display by pressing the Info button.** The display changes to the Hide Indicators display mode, shown in Figure 7-5. In this mode, four white horizontal marks appear to indicate the 16:9 movie-framing area; I labeled one of the marks in the figure. Press Info again to display a grid over the scene. Here's an important caveat, though: In these display modes, pressing the *i* button brings up the control strip for still photography. To view the movie version, you must use the Show Movie Indicators display.
- **You can stop recording and capture a still image in one fell swoop.** Just press and hold the shutter button until you hear the shutter release. The number found within the brackets in the lower-right corner of the screen indicates how many still photos you can fit in the empty card space if you stop recording. As each second of recording ticks by and card space is depleted, the value that indicates the number of remaining still shots drops. For another option, you can save a single frame of your movie as a still photo. The last section of this chapter tells you how.

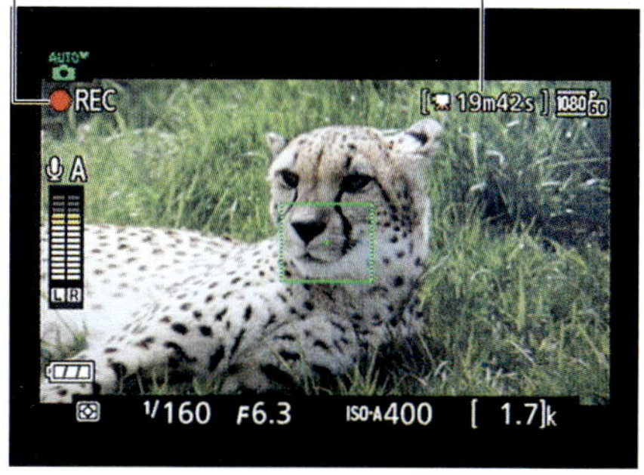

Figure 7-4: The red Rec symbol flashes while recording is in progress.

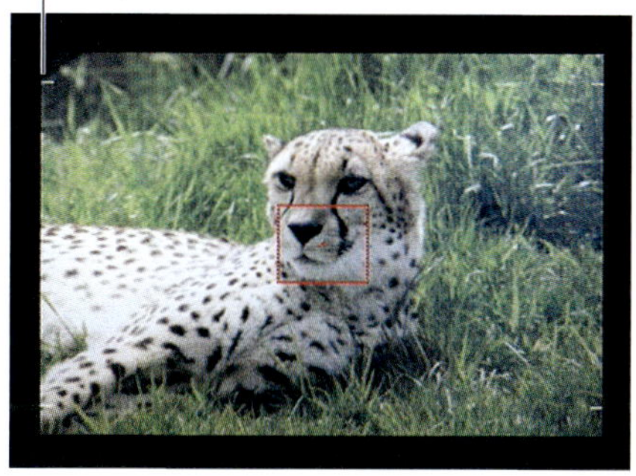

Figure 7-5: Press the Info button to hide most of the onscreen data.

Adjusting Video Settings

When you're ready to take more control over your movies, start by exploring the video settings detailed in the next three sections.

Choosing the video mode (NTSC or PAL)

The first option to consider is Video Mode, found on the Setup menu and shown in Figure 7-6. This setting determines whether movies adhere to the NTSC or PAL video standard. *NTSC* is used in North America; *PAL* is used in

Europe and certain other countries. (Don't worry about what NTSC and PAL mean — they're just acronyms for the names of the standards.)

Your camera should already be set to match the country in which it was purchased, but it never hurts to check, especially because your decision affects your choice of movie frame rates, explained next. In fact, when you try to change the Video Mode setting, the camera alerts you to this fact; just press OK to go forward.

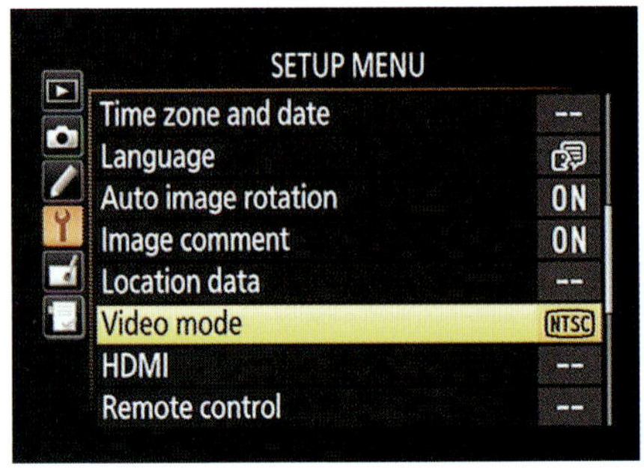

Figure 7-6: Set the video mode to the standard — NTSC or PAL — that's used in your country.

Understanding the Frame Size/Frame Rate options

This setting determines the *resolution,* or frame size, of your movie, as well as the number of frames per second (fps), both of which affect video quality.

One way to access the setting is via the Movie Settings option on the Shooting menu, as shown in Figure 7-7. After you select Frame Size/Frame Rate, press the Multi Selector right to display the options shown in Figure 7-8.

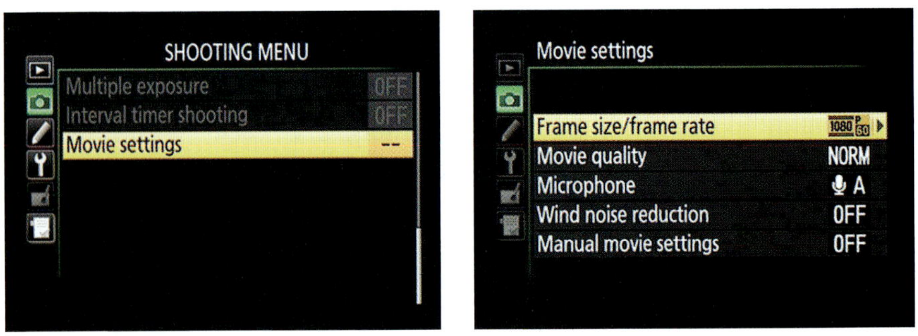

Figure 7-7: You can access the Frame Size/Frame Rate option via the Movie Settings option on the Shooting menu.

If you're a digital video expert, these options probably make perfect sense to you; take your pick and move on. If you're new to video, here's the information you need to decode the settings:

- **Frame size:** The first pair of values shown for each Frame Size/Frame Rate setting indicates the number of pixels used to create the movie frame. In the world of HDTV, 1920 x 1080 pixels is considered *Full HD,* whereas 1280 x 720 is known as *Standard HD* and produces slightly

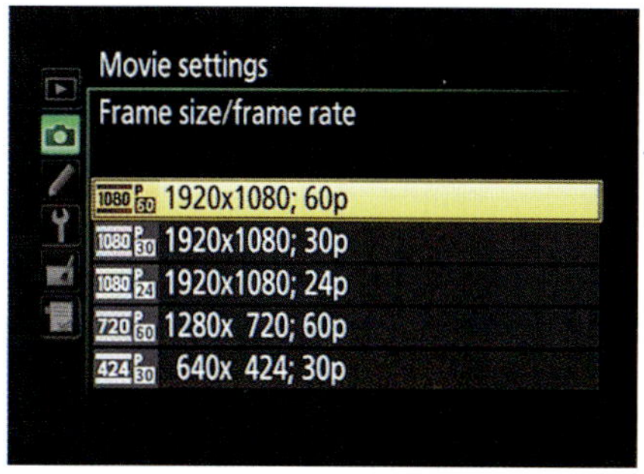

Figure 7-8: These options appear when NTSC is selected as the video mode.

lesser quality than Full HD (although I suspect few people can determine the difference). Both options result in a frame with a 16:9 aspect ratio.

Selecting the last option on the list steps the frame size down to 640 x 424 pixels, which translates to a regular definition (that is, not a high-def) movie. This setting also produces a movie that has an approximate aspect ratio of 3:2 rather than the HD 16:9 format. This smaller resolution can be useful for online videos.

- **Frame rate (fps):** The value immediately following the frame size indicates the *frame rate*. This value, measured in *frames per second* (fps), determines the smoothness of the playback.

  Your options here depend on whether you select NTSC or PAL as the video standard. Assuming NTSC as the video standard, the following frame rates are available:

  - *24:* This frame rate is the standard for motion pictures, giving your videos a softer, more movie-like look.
  - *30:* This setting is the standard for most network broadcast TV and produces a crisper picture than the 24 fps setting.
  - *60:* This option is often used for shooting video that will be played back in slow motion. With more frames per second, the video is smoother when you slow down the movie playback.

  For PAL video, you can choose from 24, 25 (the PAL television broadcast standard), or 50 fps.

TECHNICAL STUFF

- **p:** The *p* that follows all the settings refers to *progressive video*, which is one of two technologies used to record the lines of pixels that make up a digital video frame. The other technology is *interlaced video*. With interlaced video, a single frame is split into odd and even *fields*, or lines of pixels. The data from the odd lines is recorded first, followed rapidly by the data from the even lines — so rapidly, in fact, that the picture appears seamless during playback. With progressive video, all the lines are pulled out of the magic video hat in sequential order, in a single pass.

  Your camera offers only progressive video, but don't fret: Progressive, the newer technology, delivers smoother, cleaner footage than interlaced video when you're shooting fast motion or panning the camera. In other words, you can now forget about that *p* in the setting name until you want to impress your friends during the next discussion of digital video. Say, "Oh, your camera can do 60 fps only as interlaced video? Mine offers 60 fps progressive."

Two more notes about this setting:

- **Viewing the current setting:** See the little symbols appearing to the left of each setting in Figure 7-8? They're used in the monitor to indicate each setting, as shown in Figure 7-9. The first number specifies the vertical pixel count of the frame size; the *p* indicates progressive video, and the other number tells you the frame rate. Oh, that little star? It means that you selected High as the Movie Quality option, which I describe next. No star means that option is set to Normal.

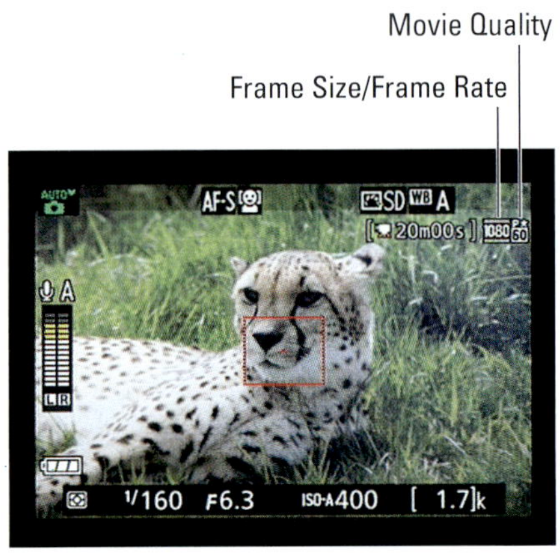

Figure 7-9: This data represents the current Frame Size/Frame Rate and Movie Quality settings.

- **Changing the setting via the control strip:** You also can adjust the Frame Size/Frame Rate option by using the control strip, as shown in Figure 7-10. In this case, the available Frame Size/Frame Rate settings are presented together with the Movie Quality option, enabling you to select both settings in one step. (Otherwise, you select the Quality setting separately via the Movie Settings menu option.)

  Together, these two settings affect the maximum length of the movie you can record. The gray box labeled *Maximum movie length* in Figure 7-10 updates to show you that length for the current combination of frame size/frame rate and movie quality. See the sidebar "Maximum recording times," later in this chapter, for a rundown of how many minutes of footage you can record at each combo.

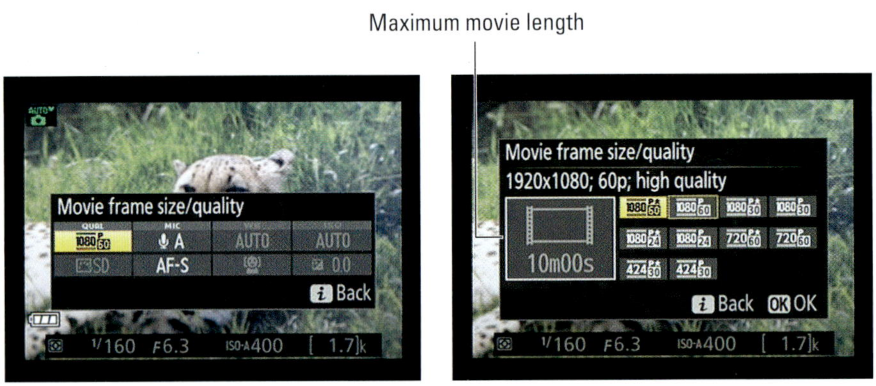

Figure 7-10: From the control strip, you select the Frame Size/Frame Rate and Movie Quality settings together.

Maximum recording times

The maximum recording time of a single video clip depends on the Frame Size/Frame Rate and Movie Quality options, as outlined here. Note that 60p, 30p, and 24p are the available Frame Size/Frame Rate settings when the Video Mode option is set to NTSC; when that option is set to PAL, available settings are 50, 25, and 24.

Frame Size	*FPS*	*Quality*	*Maximum Movie Length*
1920 x 1080	60, 50	High Normal	10 minutes 20 minutes
1920 x 1080	30, 25, 24	High Normal	20 minutes 29 minutes, 59 seconds
1280 x 720	60, 50	High Normal	20 minutes 29 minutes, 59 seconds
640 x 424	30, 25	High Normal	29 minutes, 59 seconds 29 minutes, 59 seconds

Selecting the Movie Quality option

Next up on the list of video settings to digest is the aforementioned Movie Quality option. This setting determines how much compression is applied to the video file, which in turn affects the *bit rate,* or how much data is used to represent 1 second of video, measured in Mbps (megabits per second). You get just two choices: High and Normal (the default). The High setting results in a higher bit rate, which means better quality and larger files. Choose Normal for a lower bit rate and smaller files.

Because bit rate affects the size of the video file, it also determines the maximum length of the video clip you can create each time you press the movie-record button. Again, the sidebar "Maximum recording times" tells you the record-time limits at each combination of Movie Quality and Frame Size/Frame Rate setting.

As with the Frame Size/Frame Rate setting, you can select the Movie Quality setting via the Movie Settings option on the Shooting menu, as shown in Figure 7-11. Or you can use the control strip to select both the Frame Size/ Frame Rate and Movie Quality setting together, as illustrated in Figure 7-10, in the preceding section.

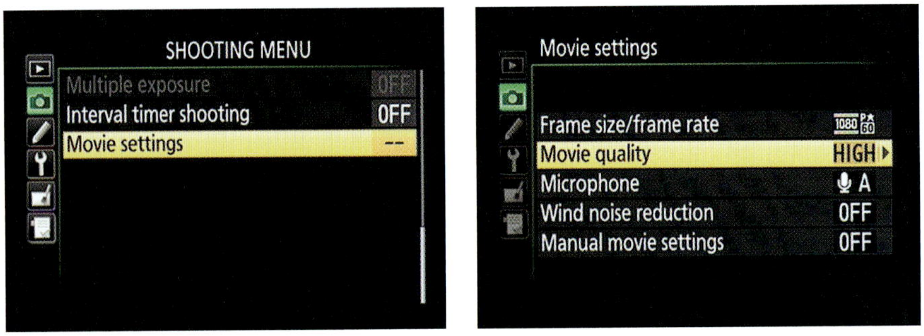

Figure 7-11: This option determines the movie bit rate, which affects playback quality and file size.

One last tip about this setting: In the Live View display, a star in the area labeled Movie Quality in Figure 7-9 indicates that the High bit rate is selected. No star means that the option is set to Normal.

Controlling Audio

You can record sound using the camera's built-in microphone, labeled on the left in Figure 7-12, or attach the optional Nikon ME-1 stereo microphone to the jack labeled on the right in the figure.

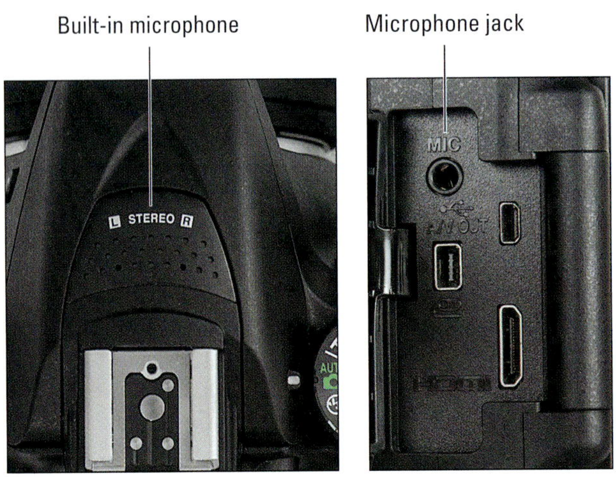

Figure 7-12: You can use the internal microphone (left) or plug in an external microphone (right).

If you use the built-in mic, you can adjust two audio settings, Microphone and Wind Noise Reduction, explained in the next two sections. For an external mic, only the Microphone setting applies.

Choosing the Microphone setting (volume control)

The most critical audio-recording control is the Microphone setting, which affects sound volume. You have three options:

- **Auto Sensitivity:** The camera automatically adjusts the volume according to the level of the ambient noise. This setting is the default.
- **Manual Sensitivity:** You specify the volume level, with settings ranging from 1 to 20.
- **Microphone Off:** Choose this setting to record a movie with no sound or when you're using an off-camera microphone and you don't want the camera itself to record audio.

Symbols representing the current setting appear in the display, as shown in Figure 7-13. The microphone symbol indicates that audio recording is enabled; the letter *A* next-door indicates the Auto Sensitivity option. If you set the camera to Manual Sensitivity, your selected volume level appears instead.

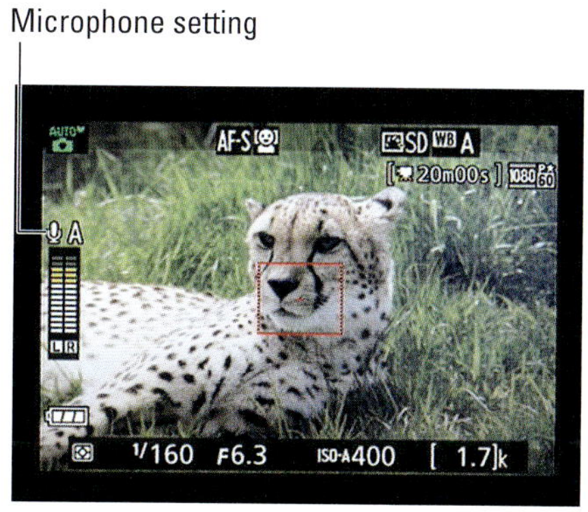

Figure 7-13: These symbols indicate the current Microphone setting and volume level.

Beneath those symbols, you see two vertical bars that indicate the volume level of the left and right audio channels that are recorded when you use a stereo microphone. (The built-in mic offers stereo recording.) For monaural recording, both bars reflect the same data.

Audio levels are measured in decibels (dB), and levels on the volume meter range from –40 (very, very soft) to 0 (as loud as can be measured digitally). Ideally, sound should peak consistently in the –12 range. The indicators on the meter turn yellow in this range, as shown in Figure 7-13. If the sound level is too high, the bar at the top of the meter turns red — a warning that audio may be distorted.

To adjust the Microphone setting, you can go two routes:

- **Shooting menu:** Choose Movie Settings from the menu and then select Microphone, as shown on the left in Figure 7-14. Press the Multi Selector right to display the second screen in the figure, where you can select the setting you want to use.

On the second screen, the two bars at the bottom are the horizontal version of the volume meter displayed on the Live View screen. For stereo sound, the top bar represents the left audio channel; the bottom bar, the right channel. Again, both bars show the same thing when you're not using a stereo microphone.

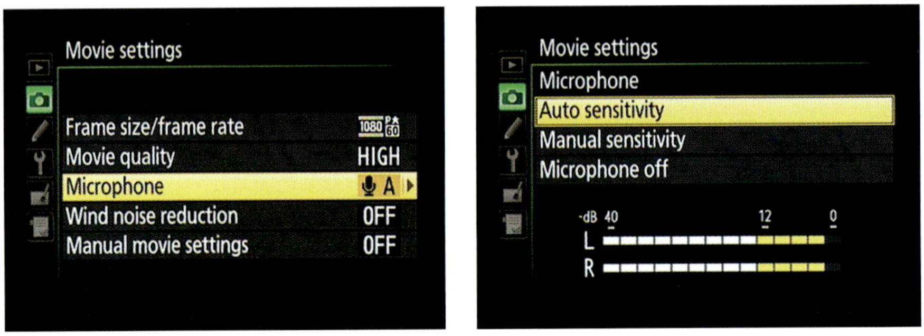

Figure 7-14: After opening the Shooting menu, select Movie Settings and then choose the Microphone option to access basic audio-recording options.

- **Control strip:** Press the ***i*** button to display the control strip, highlight the Microphone icon, as shown on the left in Figure 7-15, and press OK to display the second screen in the figure. Again, you see the volume meter plus symbols representing the Auto, Manual, and Off settings, as labeled in the figure. If you choose Manual, as shown in the figure, press the Multi Selector up and down to adjust the recording volume.

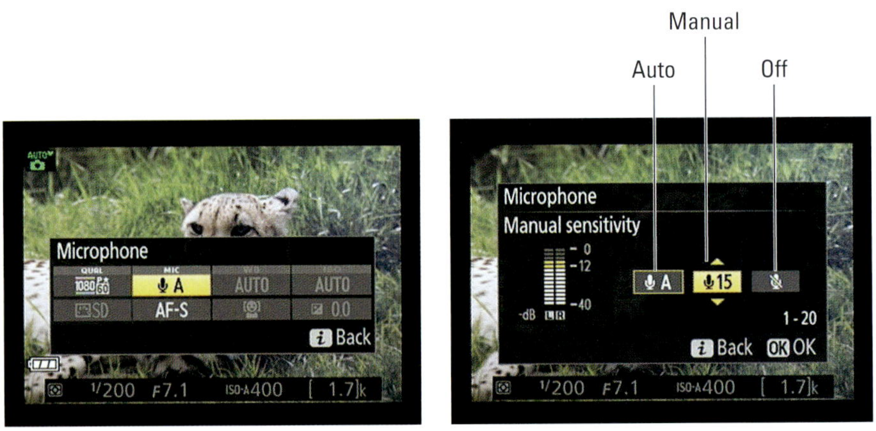

Figure 7-15: You also can adjust the Microphone setting from the control strip.

Either way, choose the Microphone setting *before* starting the recording; you can't change it while recording is in progress.

Reducing wind noise

Ever seen a newscaster out in the field, carrying a microphone that looks like it's covered with a big piece of foam? That foam thing is a wind filter. It's designed to lessen the sounds that the wind makes when it hits the microphone.

You can enable a digital version of the same thing via the Wind Noise Reduction option, accessed via the Movie Settings option on the Shooting menu, as shown in Figure 7-16. Essentially, the filter works by reducing the volume of noises that are similar to those made by wind. The problem is that some noises *not* made by wind can also be muffled when the filter is enabled. So when you're indoors or shooting on a still day, keep this option set to Off, as it is by default. Also note that when you use an external microphone, the Wind Filter feature has no effect.

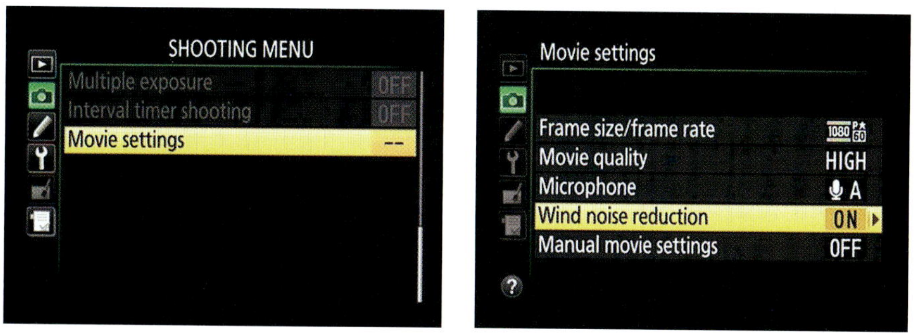

Figure 7-16: When using the built-in mic, enabling this feature can help diminish wind noise.

When the feature is enabled, the symbol labeled in Figure 7-17 appears at the bottom of the audio volume meter. The symbol disappears when the option is turned off.

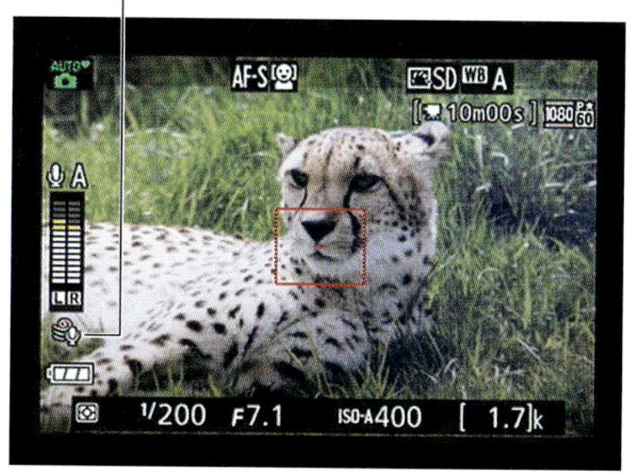

Figure 7-17: This symbol tells you that Wind Noise Reduction is turned on.

Exploring Other Recording Options

In addition to settings reviewed in the preceding sections, you can control a few other aspects of your cinematic effort. The following list runs through these options; Figure 7-18 labels the symbols that represent these settings in the display.

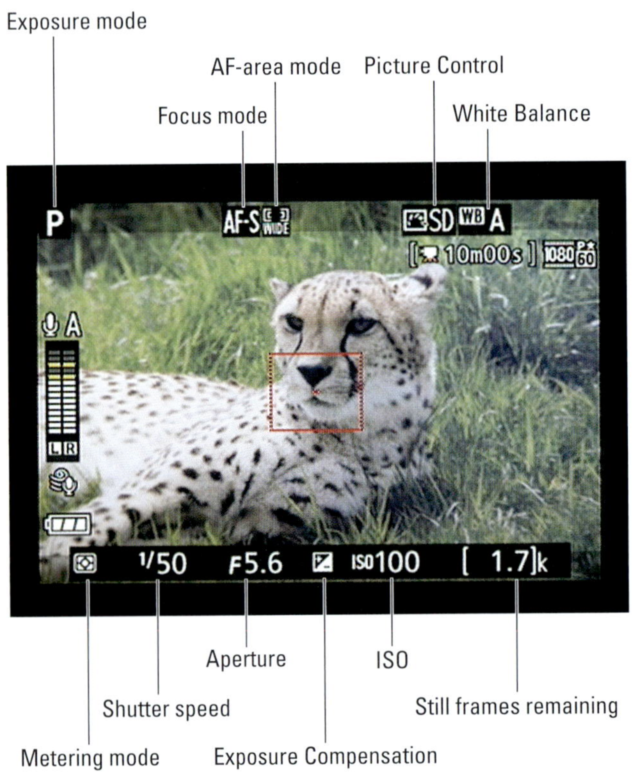

Figure 7-18: Here's your road map to other major settings you can monitor in the Show Movie Indicators display mode.

- **Exposure mode:** You can record movies in any exposure mode (Auto, Scene modes, Effects modes, P, M, and so on). As with still photography, your choice determines which camera settings you can access. (The Movie Settings menu options are available in all modes, however.)
- **Exposure settings:** The aperture (f-stop), shutter speed, ISO, Metering mode, and Exposure Compensation settings, all labeled in Figure 7-18, determine movie exposure. In the P, S, A, and M modes, as well as in Night Vision Effects mode, you have some control over all these options except Metering mode; the camera always uses Matrix metering for movie recording. See the next section for details on adjusting exposure. For all other exposure modes, the camera handles exposure automatically.

- **Focus options:** Your options are the same as for Live View still photography, detailed in Chapter 4. As a quick recap, you adjust autofocusing behavior through Focus mode and AF-area mode; look for the current settings in the spots labeled in Figure 7-18.
  - *Focus mode*: Choose AF-S to lock focus when you press the shutter button halfway; choose AF-F for continuous autofocusing. See the first section of this chapter for details about how each option works for movie recording. For manual focusing, choose MF.
  - *AF-area mode*: You can choose from Face Priority, Wide Area, Normal Area, or Subject Tracking. The default setting is Face Priority; if the camera doesn't detect a face in the frame, it automatically uses Wide Area focusing instead. With any of these modes, you start by using the Multi Selector to move the focusing frame over your subject. How things work from there depends on the specific mode; again, Chapter 4 provides step-by-step instructions.

  Adjust both settings via the control strip; press the ***i*** button to bring up the strip.
- **White Balance and Picture Control:** The colors in your movie are rendered according to the current White Balance and Picture Control settings, both detailed in Chapter 5. However, you have control over these options only when the Mode dial is set to P, S, A, or M. The current settings appear in the areas labeled in Figure 7-18; you can adjust both options either via the Shooting menu or the control strip.

  TIP: Want to record a black-and-white movie? Select Monochrome as the Picture Control. Instant *film noir.*

Manipulating Movie Exposure

Normally, the camera automatically adjusts exposure during movie recording. Exposure is calculated using Matrix (whole frame) metering, regardless of which Metering mode setting is selected. But in a few exposure modes, you can adjust exposure by changing the following settings:

- **Shutter speed and ISO:** Both options are set by the camera by default. But if you enable the Manual Movie Settings option on the Movie Settings menu, as shown in Figure 7-19, you can control both settings. (Look for the current settings in the areas labeled in Figure 7-18.) This path is one for experienced videographers, however. If you fit that category, here are a few things you need to know:
  - *Exposure mode*: You must set the Mode dial to M (manual exposure), and you must set the aperture (f-stop setting) as well as the shutter speed and ISO to dial in the correct exposure.

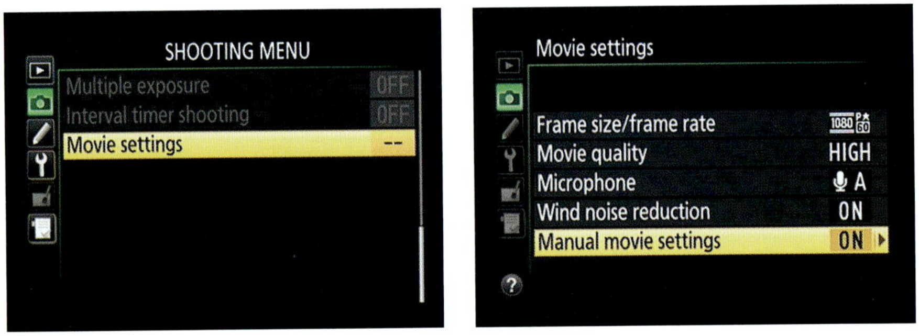

Figure 7-19: Enable this option to take control over movie exposure.

  To set the f-stop in M mode while the Manual Movie Settings option is enabled, you must exit Live View mode. Then press the Exposure Compensation button while rotating the Command dial. Rotate the Live View switch to return to Live View mode.

  - *Shutter speed:* You can select shutter speeds as high as 1/4000 second. The slowest shutter speed depends on your chosen frame rate. For 24p, 25p, and 30p, you can drop as low as 1/30 second; for 50p, 1/50 second; and for 60p, 1/60 second. To set the shutter speed in M mode, rotate the Command dial — you don't have to shift out of Live View mode for this one. (Again, which frame rates are available depends on whether the Video Mode option on the Setup menu is set to NTSC or PAL.)
  - *ISO:* You can set the ISO value as low as 100 or as high as Hi 1. Note that Auto ISO Sensitivity control doesn't work when the Manual Movie Settings option is enabled; the camera sticks with your selected setting regardless of the available light.

    To adjust ISO quickly, press the Fn button while rotating the Command dial. You can also select the ISO value via the ISO Sensitivity settings option on the Shooting menu.
  - *Camera override:* If you choose a shutter speed or ISO setting outside the stated ranges, the camera slaps your hand and chooses the closest in-range setting automatically.

- **Aperture (f-stop):** You can adjust the f-stop *before* (but not during) recording if you set the Mode dial to A (aperture-priority autoexposure) or M (manual exposure). This option enables you to control depth of field in your movies; Chapter 3 explains the aperture setting's role in depth of field.

  In A mode, rotate the Command dial to change the f-stop; again, in M mode, first exit Live View mode and then press and hold the Exposure Compensation button while rotating the dial. In either case, remember that the live preview doesn't indicate the depth of field that your f-stop setting will produce — the camera can't provide this feedback because the aperture doesn't actually open to your selected setting until you start recording.

- **Exposure Compensation:** Exposure Compensation, detailed in Chapter 3, enables you to override the camera's autoexposure decisions, asking for a brighter or darker picture. You can apply this adjustment for movies when the Mode dial is set to P, S, A, or M or you use Night Vision Effects mode. However, you're limited to an adjustment range of EV +3.0 to –3.0 rather than the usual five steps that are possible during normal photography. Note that the display shows the plus/minus symbol you see in Figure 7-18 only when Exposure Compensation is in force.

  To adjust the setting, press and hold the Exposure Compensation button while rotating the Command dial *unless* you're using Manual (M) exposure mode. In that mode, you must use the Information display control strip to apply Exposure Compensation. (Press the ***i*** button to access the control strip; the Exposure Compensation option is the setting in the lower-right corner of the strip.)

  REMEMBER

  Just to head off any possible confusion: For viewfinder photography, Exposure Compensation isn't needed in M exposure mode; if you want a brighter or darker exposure, you just change the aperture, shutter speed, or ISO Sensitivity settings. But because the camera doesn't give you control over shutter speed or ISO during movie recording — *unless you enable Manual Movie Settings* — you need some way to tell the camera that you want a brighter or darker picture in M mode, and Exposure Compensation is it.

- **Autoexposure lock:** In any exposure mode except Auto or Auto Flash Off, you can lock exposure at the current settings by pressing and holding the AE-L/AF-L button. Chapter 3 also tells you more about autoexposure lock.

Screening Your Movies

To play your movie, press the Playback button. In single-image playback mode, you can spot a movie file by looking for the little movie camera icon in the upper-left corner of the screen, as shown in Figure 7-20. You also can view other movie-related data, including the Frame Size, Frame Rate, and Movie Quality setting. (Remember: A star means that you set the Movie Quality option to High.) To start playback, press OK.

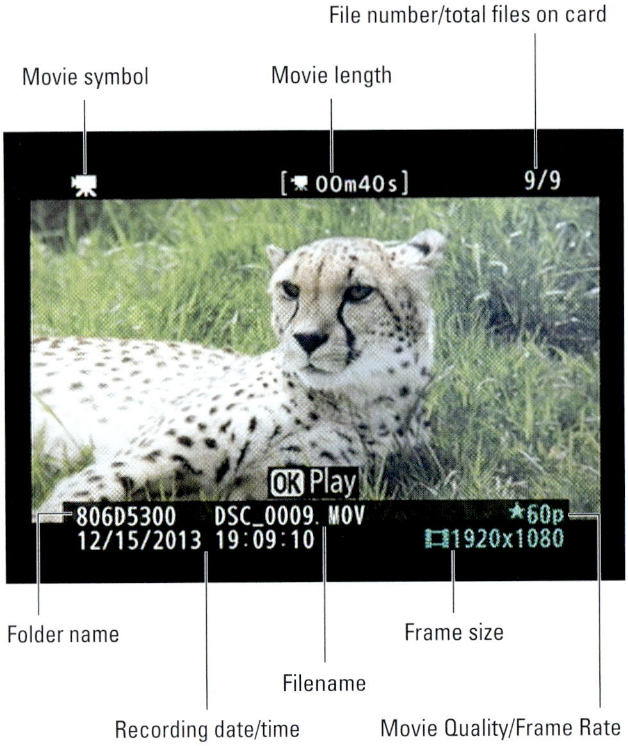

Figure 7-20: The movie camera symbol tells you you're looking at a movie file.

In the thumbnail and Calendar playback modes, both described in Chapter 8, you see little dots along the edges of image thumbnails to represent movie files. This time, press OK twice: once to shift to single-image view and again to start movie playback.

After playback begins, you see the data labeled in Figure 7-21. The progress bar and Time Elapsed value show you how much of the movie has played so far; you can also see the total movie length.

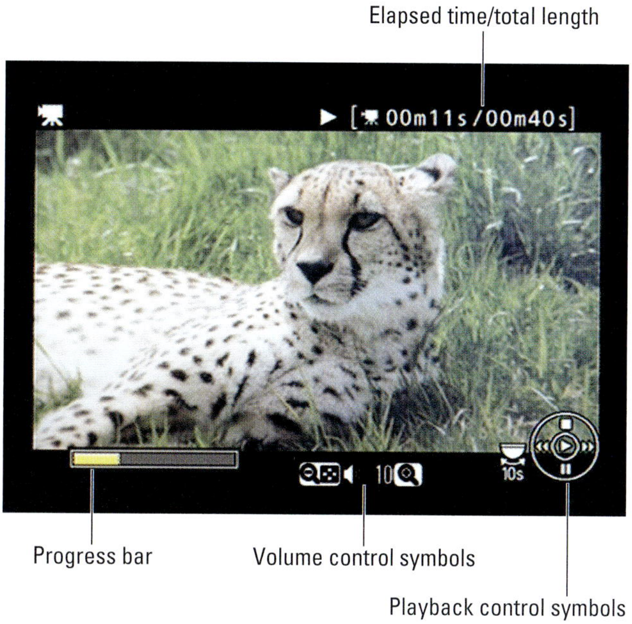

Figure 7-21: The icons at the bottom of the screen remind you which buttons to use to control playback.

The other symbols at the bottom of the screen are there to remind you that you can use various camera buttons to control playback, as follows:

- **Stop playback:** Press the Multi Selector up. The white circle labeled *Playback control symbols* in the figure (lower-right) represents the Multi Selector.
- **Pause/resume playback:** Press down to pause playback; press OK to resume playback.
- **Fast-forward/rewind:** Press the Multi Selector right or left to fast-forward or rewind the movie, respectively. Press again to double the fast-forward or rewind speed; keep pressing to increase the speed. Hold down the button to fast-forward or rewind all the way to the end or beginning of the movie.
- **Forward/rewind 10 seconds:** Rotate the Command dial to the right to jump 10 seconds forward through the movie; rotate to the left to jump back 10 seconds.

- **Advance frame by frame:** First press the Multi Selector down to pause playback. Then press the Multi Selector right to advance one frame; press left to go back one frame.
- **Adjust playback volume:** See the markings labeled *Volume control symbols* in Figure 7-21? They remind you that you can press the Zoom In button to increase volume and press the Zoom Out button to lower it. The number value tells you the current volume level (10, in the figure).

Trimming Movies

You can do some limited movie editing in camera. I emphasize: *limited* editing. You can trim frames from the start of a movie and clip off frames from the end, and that's it.

To eliminate frames from the start of a movie, take these steps:

1. **Display your movie in single-image view.**
2. **Press OK to begin playback.**
3. **When you reach the first frame you want to keep, press the Multi Selector down to pause the movie.**

   The onscreen display updates to show you the controls that appear on the left in Figure 7-22.

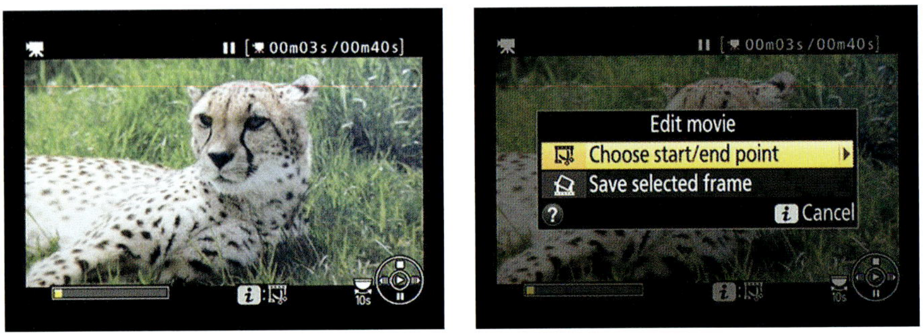

Figure 7-22: With the movie paused, press the *i* button to access the movie-editing screens.

4. **Press the *i* button.**

   You see the menu options shown on the right in Figure 7-22.
5. **Highlight Choose Start/End Point and press OK.**

   You see the options shown in Figure 7-23.
6. **Choose Start Point and press OK.**

You're returned to the playback screen.

7. **Press the Multi Selector up to lop off all frames that came before the current frame.**

   Now you see the options shown in Figure 7-24. To preview the movie, select Preview and press OK; after the preview plays, you're returned to the menu screen.

8. **To preserve your original movie and save the trimmed one as a new file, choose Save as New File and press OK.**

   Alternatively, you can opt to overwrite the existing file, but you can't get the original file back if you do.

   A message appears, telling you that the trimmed movie is being saved. During playback, edited files are indicated by a little scissors icon that appears in the upper-left corner of the screen, as shown in Figure 7-25.

To instead trim footage from the end of a film, follow the same steps but this time pause playback on the last frame you want to keep in Step 3. Then, in Step 6, select Choose End Point instead of Choose Start Point.

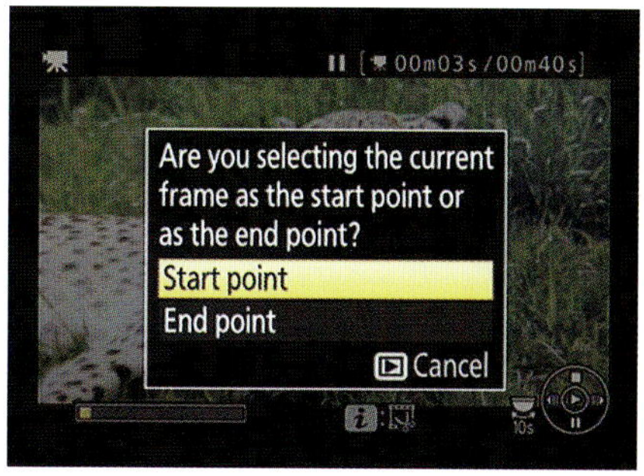

Figure 7-23: To trim frames from the beginning of a movie, select the Start Point option.

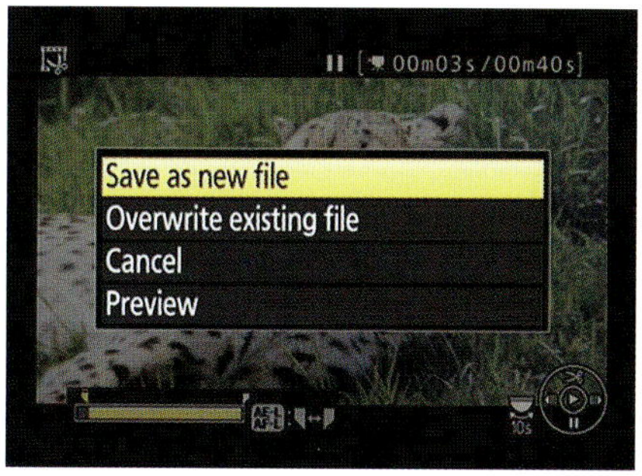

Figure 7-24: Choose Save as New File to avoid overwriting the original movie file.

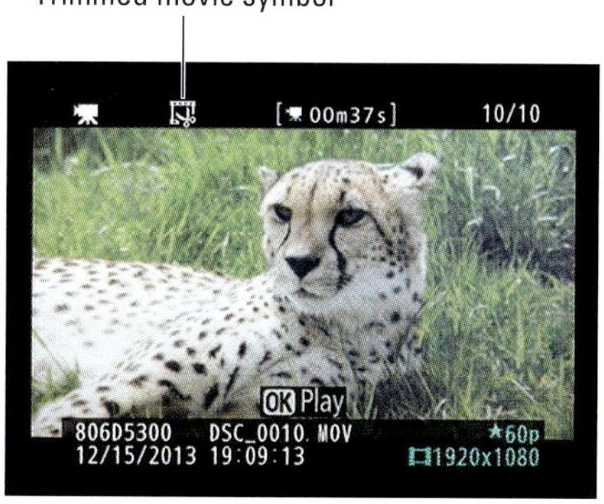

Figure 7-25: The scissors symbol tells you that you're looking at a trimmed movie.

Saving a Movie Frame As a Still Image

TIP

You can save a frame of the movie as a still photo. Here's how:

1. **Begin playing your movie.**
2. **When you reach the frame you want to capture, press the Multi Selector down to pause playback.**
3. **Press the *i* button to bring up the Edit Movie screen, as shown in Figure 7-26.**
4. **Choose Save Selected Frame, as shown in the figure, and press OK.**

   The frame appears on the monitor.
5. **Press the Multi Selector up.**
6. **On the confirmation screen that appears, select Yes and press OK.**

   Your frame is saved as a JPEG photo.

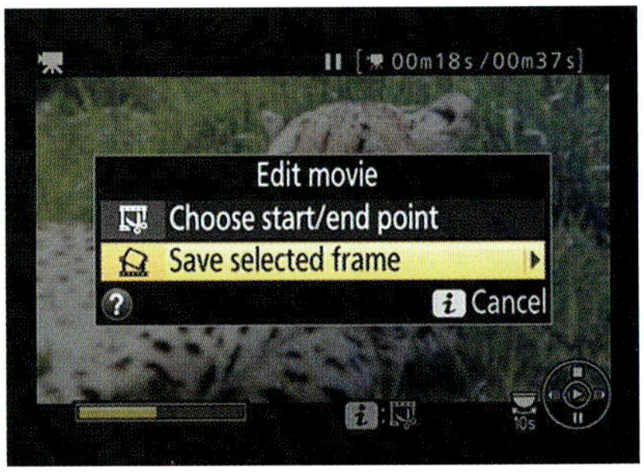

Figure 7-26: This option lets you save a single frame as a JPEG image.

Remember a few things about pictures you create this way:

- When you view the image, it's marked with a little scissors icon in the upper-left corner. (It looks just like the one labeled in Figure 7-25.)
- The resolution of the picture depends on the resolution of the movie: For example, if the movie resolution is 1920 x 1080, your picture resolution is 1920 x 1080.
- You can't apply editing features from the Retouch menu to the file, and neither can you view all the shooting data that's normally associated with a JPEG picture.

TIP

Before you begin movie playback, you also can press the *i* button to display a mini-menu that contains the Edit Movie option. Select that option to access the Edit Movie screen (the one shown in Figure 7-26). After choosing the editing function you want to use, press OK to start playback and proceed as outlined in the steps here and in the preceding section.

Part III

After the Shot

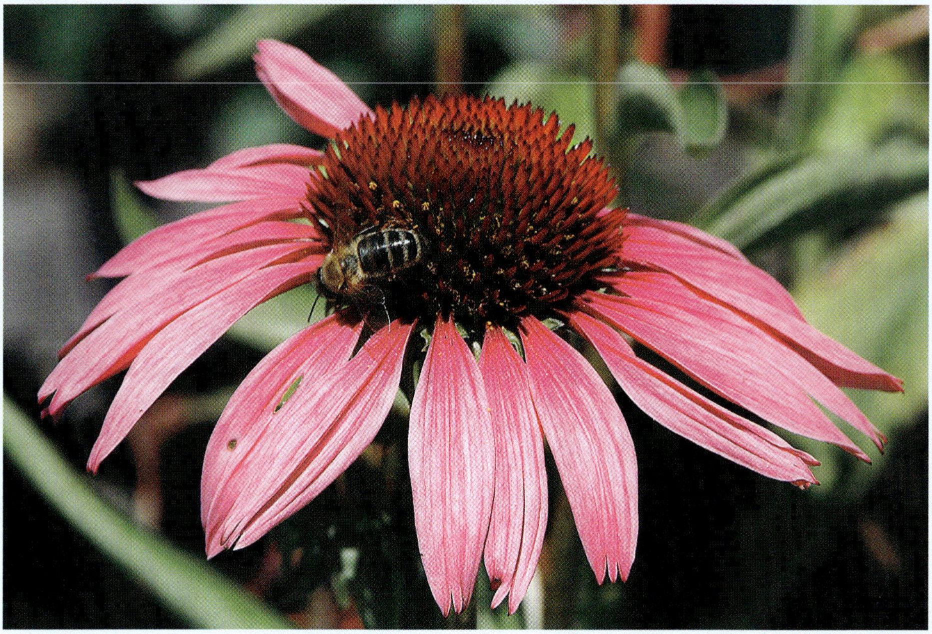

Discover five easy composition tricks you can use to shoot more captivating photos at www.dummies.com/extras/nikon.

In this part …

- Get the details on picture playback, including how to customize playback screens.
- Erase files you don't want and protect the ones you like from being accidentally deleted.
- Assign ratings to picture and movie files.
- Download files from the camera to the computer.
- Convert Raw (NEF) images using the in-camera converter and the one found in Nikon ViewNX 2.
- Prepare photos for online sharing.
- Transfer photos to a smartphone or other smart device via the built-in Wi-Fi feature.

8

Playback Mode: Viewing Your Photos

In This Chapter

- Exploring picture playback functions
- Deciphering the picture information displays
- Understanding histograms
- Creating an in-camera slide show
- Viewing pictures and movies on a television

Without question, my favorite thing about digital photography is being able to view my pictures the instant after I shoot them. No more guessing whether I captured the image or need to try again, as in the film days; no more wasting money on developing pictures that stink.

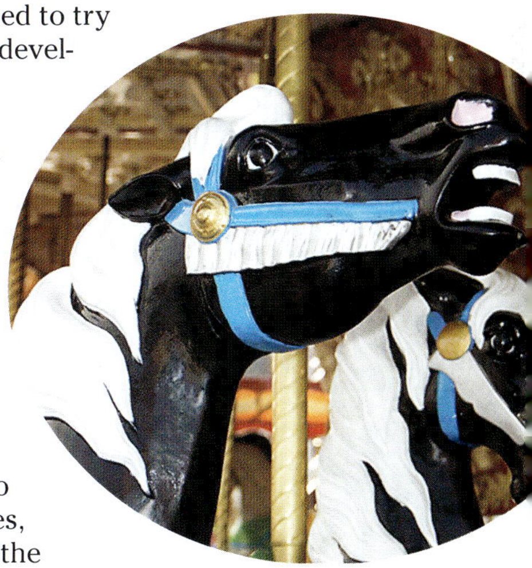

Seeing your pictures is just the start of the things you can do when you switch your camera to playback mode, though. You also can review settings you used to take the picture, display graphics that alert you to exposure problems, and magnify a photo to check details. This chapter introduces you to these playback features and also explains how to use the built-in slide-show feature and connect your camera to a television for playback.

Note: Some information in this chapter applies only to still photographs; if a feature also works for movie files, I spell that out. For the basics of movie playback, see the end of Chapter 7.

Adjusting Playback Timing Options

By default, the camera displays your photo for 4 seconds immediately after it finishes recording the picture data to the memory card. This feature is called Image Review.

To take a longer look, press the Playback button to set the camera to playback mode. Your photo then appears for 1 minute, after which the monitor goes to sleep if you don't press any buttons. (This auto shutdown is a Good Thing because the monitor is a major drain on the camera battery.)

If necessary, you can adjust the playback and Image Review duration from the Custom Settings menu. (Note that whatever setting you use for playback shutoff also affects the auto shutdown of menu displays.) To access the relevant settings, select the Timers/AE Lock menu option and then choose Auto Off Timers to display the screen you see on the left in Figure 8-1.

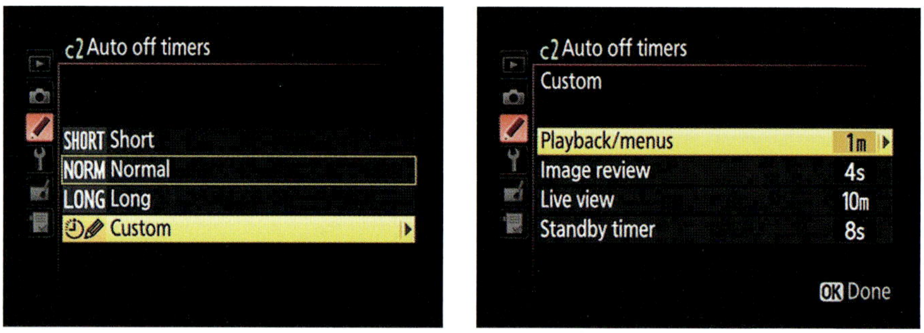

Figure 8-1: You can adjust the timing of auto shutdown during playback.

TIP

You're offered these three general settings: Short, Normal (the default), and Long. But these settings apply a set of timing options to the Live View display and exposure meter display as well as to the playback/menus and Image Review displays. I suggest that you select Custom, as shown on the left in the figure, and then press the Multi Selector right to display the screen shown on the right. You then can set the Playback/Menu timing and Image Review timing separately. (Chapter 11 goes into more detail about the automatic shutdown options.)

To turn off Image Review altogether, head for the Playback menu and set that option to Off, as shown in Figure 8-2.

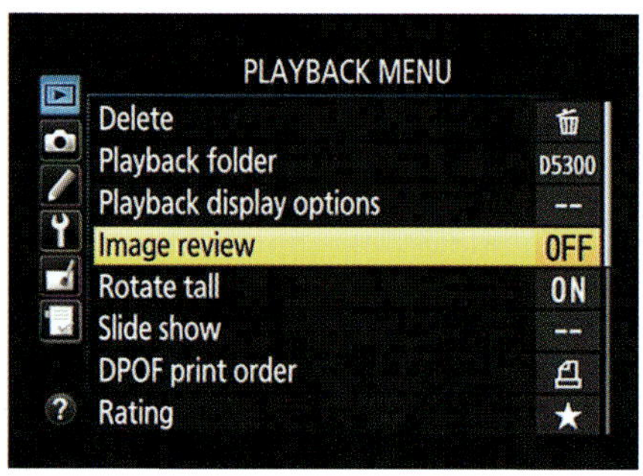

Figure 8-2: To disable instant review, set this option to Off.

Choosing Which Images to View

Your camera organizes pictures automatically into folders that are assigned generic names: 100D5300, 101D5300, and so on. You can see the name of the current folder by looking at the Storage Folder option on the Shooting menu. (The default folder name appears as simply *D5300* on the menu.) You also can create custom folders by using the process outlined in Chapter 11. Which folders' photos appear during playback depends on the Playback Folder option on the Playback menu, shown in Figure 8-3.

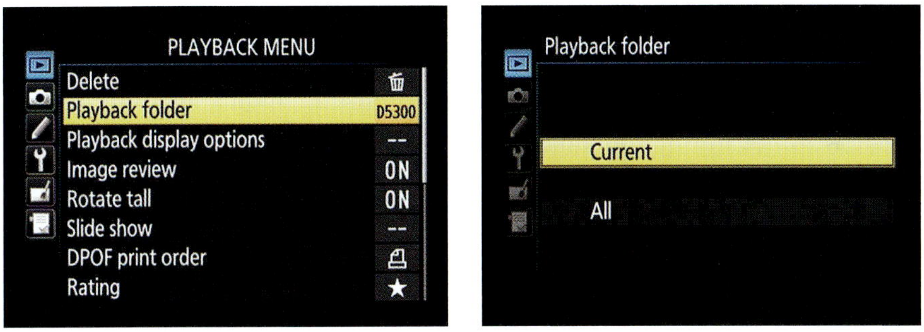

Figure 8-3: If your memory card contains multiple image folders, specify which folder you want to view.

You probably don't have to worry about this setting — all your photos likely are contained in one folder, and the camera selects that folder by default. But if you use a gargantuan memory card that contains zillions of images (and therefore may contain multiple folders), if you created custom folders, or if your card contains pictures taken on another Nikon camera, specify which folder you want to view by choosing one of the following options:

- **Current:** This setting is the default; the camera displays images contained in the folder selected as the Storage Folder option on the Shooting menu. Again, unless your card contains multiple folders, all your pictures are in that folder.
- **All:** This setting displays all pictures in all folders, as long as they're in an image format that the camera recognizes.

Viewing Images in Playback Mode

My guess is that you've already figured out the basics of picture playback. But you may not be familiar with all the tricks you can use when viewing your images, such as zooming in on an image for a close-up check or displaying multiple image thumbnails at a time. The next five sections introduce you to basic options; the later section "Viewing Picture Data" explains how to modify and understand the data that appears with photos during playback.

Displaying photos one at a time (full-frame playback)

For normal playback — that is, to see each photo one at a time, as shown in Figure 8-4 — take these steps:

1. **Press the Playback button, labeled in Figure 8-4.**

   The camera displays the last picture you took, along with some picture data, such as the filename of the photo and the date it was taken, as shown in the figure.

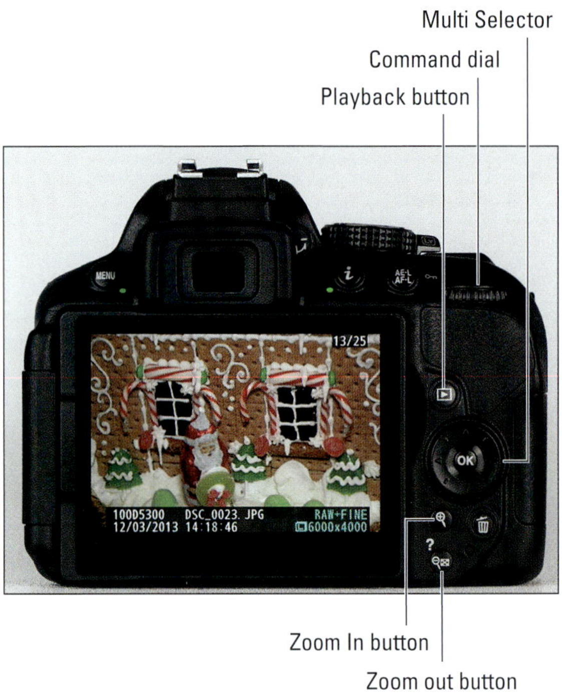

Figure 8-4: These buttons play the largest roles in picture playback.

2. **To scroll through your pictures, rotate the Command dial or press the Multi Selector right or left.**

   I labeled both controls in the figure.

   In this playback view, you can press the Zoom In button to magnify the display. Pressing the Zoom Out button reduces the display size. Again, refer to Figure 8-4 to see where these important playback buttons live. The upcoming section "Zooming in for a closer view" talks more about this feature.

3. **To return to picture-taking mode, press the Playback button again or press the shutter button halfway and then release it.**

Viewing multiple images at a time (thumbnails view)

Along with viewing images one at a time, you can display 4 or 9 thumbnails, as shown in Figure 8-5, or even a whopping 72 thumbnails.

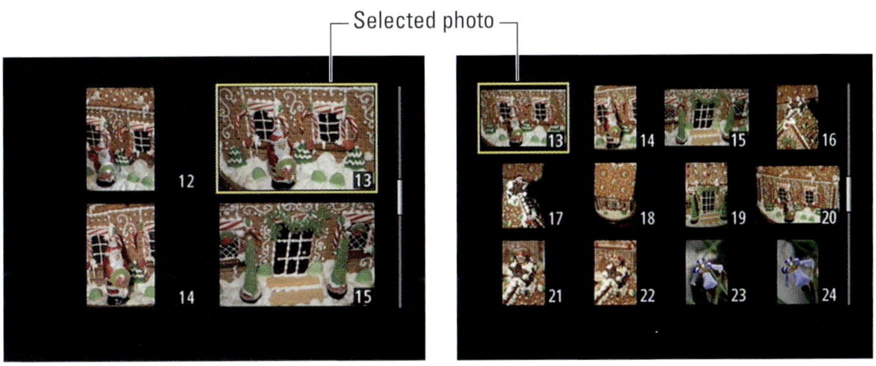

Figure 8-5: You can view multiple image thumbnails at a time.

Use these techniques to change to thumbnails view and navigate your photos:

- **Display thumbnails.** Press the Zoom Out button (refer to Figure 8-4) to cycle from single-picture view to 4-thumbnail view; press again to shift to 9-picture view; and press once more to bring up 72 itty-bitty thumbnails. One more press takes you to Calendar view, a nifty feature explained in the next section.

- **Display fewer thumbnails.** Pressing the Zoom In button (refer to Figure 8-4) takes you from Calendar view back to the standard thumbnails display or, if you're already in that display, reduces the number of thumbnails so that you can see each one at a larger size. Again, your first press takes you from 72 thumbnails to 9, your second press takes you to 4 thumbnails, and your third press returns you to single-image view.

  Notice the icons on these two buttons: The Zoom Out button sports a magnifying glass with a minus sign, the universal symbol for zoom out, plus a little grid that resembles a screen full of thumbnails. And the Zoom In button's magnifying glass has a plus sign, reminding you that you use this button to increase the image size.

- **Scroll the display.** Press the Multi Selector up and down to scroll to the next or previous screen of thumbnails.

- **Select an image.** To perform certain playback functions, such as deleting a photo or protecting it, you first need to select an image. A yellow box surrounds the selected image (refer to Figure 8-5). To select a different image, rotate the Command dial or use the Multi Selector to move the highlight box over the image.

- **Jump from any thumbnail display to full-frame view.** Rather than press the Zoom Out button multiple times, you can just press OK.

Displaying photos in Calendar view

In Calendar view, you see a little calendar on the screen, as shown on the left in Figure 8-6. By selecting a date on the calendar, you can quickly navigate to all pictures you shot on that day. A thumbnail-free date indicates that your memory card doesn't contain any photos from that day.

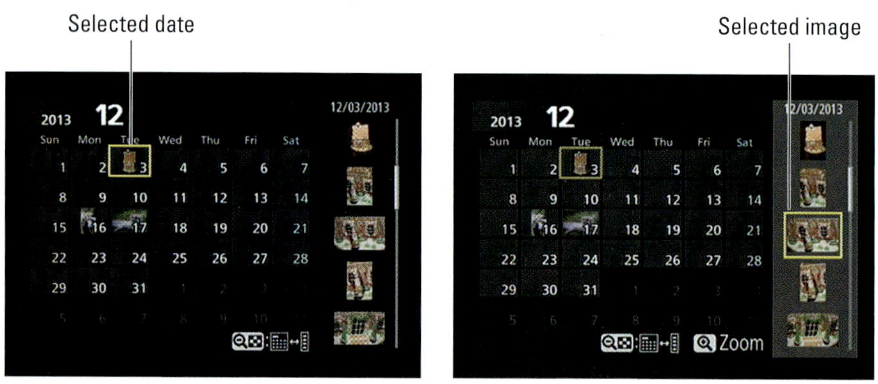

Figure 8-6: Calendar view makes it easy to view all photos shot on a particular day.

The key to navigating Calendar view is the Zoom Out button:

1. **Press the Zoom Out button as needed to cycle through the Thumbnail display modes until you reach Calendar view.**

   If you're viewing images in full-frame view, for example, you need to press the button four times to get to Calendar view.

2. **Using the Multi Selector or Command dial, move the yellow highlight box over a date that contains an image.**

   In Figure 8-6, the third day of December is selected. (The number of the month appears in the upper-left corner of the screen.) After you select a date, the right side of the screen displays thumbnails of pictures taken on that date. A highlight box outlines the selected photo.

3. **To view all thumbnails from the selected date, press the Zoom Out button again.**

   As a reminder of what button to press, the little icon underneath the calendar displays the symbols that appear on the Zoom Out button.

   After you press the button, the thumbnail strip becomes active (refer to the right side Figure 8-6), and you can scroll through the thumbnails by rotating the Command dial or pressing the Multi Selector up and down. A second highlight box appears in the thumbnail strip to indicate the selected image.

4. **To temporarily display a larger view of the selected thumbnail, hold down the Zoom In button.**

   Again, note the reminder icon in the lower-right corner of the screen; it shows the plus-sign magnifying glass that appears on the face of the Zoom In button.

   In the zoomed view, the image filename appears under the larger preview, as shown in Figure 8-7. When you release the Zoom In button, the large preview disappears, and the calendar comes back into view.

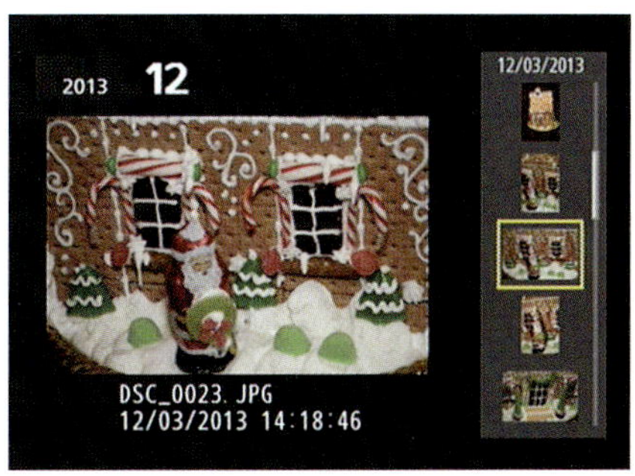

Figure 8-7: Highlight a photo in the thumbnail strip and press the Zoom In button to temporarily display it at a larger size.

5. **To jump from the thumbnail strip back to the calendar and select a different date, press the Zoom Out button again.**

   You can just keep pressing the button to jump between the calendar and the thumbnail strip as much as you want.

6. **To exit the thumbnail strip and return to single-image view, press OK.**

   If the calendar page is currently active instead of the thumbnail strip, press OK twice. Either way, the image that was highlighted in the strip appears onscreen.

Zooming in for a closer view

After displaying a photo in single-frame view, as shown on the left in Figure 8-8, you can magnify it to get a close-up look at important details, as shown on the right. Here's the scoop:

- **Zoom in.** Press the Zoom In button. You can magnify the image to a maximum of 13 to 33 times its original display size, depending on the picture resolution (Image Size). Just keep pressing the button until you reach the magnification you want.
- **Zoom out.** To zoom out to a reduced magnification, press the Zoom Out button.
- **View another part of the magnified picture.** When an image is magnified, a thumbnail showing the entire image appears briefly in the lower-right corner of the monitor (refer to the right side of Figure 8-8). The yellow outline in the thumbnail indicates the area that's consuming the rest of the monitor space. Use the Multi Selector to scroll the yellow box and display a different portion of the image. After a few seconds, the navigation thumbnail disappears; just press the Multi Selector in any direction to redisplay it.

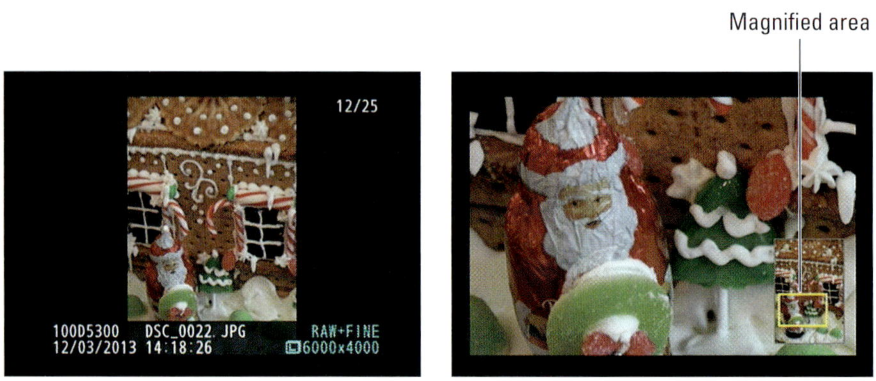

Figure 8-8: When viewing images in single-frame view (left), press the Zoom In button to magnify the picture (right).

- **Inspect faces.** Try this trick to inspect each face in a group shot: Press the Zoom In button once to magnify the image slightly. The picture-in-picture thumbnail then displays a white border around each detected face. (Typically, subjects must be facing the camera for faces to be detected.)

  Next, press the ***i*** button and then press the Multi Selector right or left to jump from face to face. Press OK to fill the frame with the selected face. Press the ***i*** button again to return to the normal playback zoom behavior.

- **View more images at the same magnification.** Here's another neat trick: While the display is zoomed, rotate the Command dial to display the same area of the next photo at the same magnification. So if you shot the same subject several times, you can easily check to see how a particular detail appears in each one.

- **Return to full-frame view.** When you're ready to return to the normal magnification level, you don't need to keep pressing the Zoom Out button until the view is all the way zoomed out. Instead, just press OK.

Enabling automatic picture rotation

When you take a picture, the camera can record the image *orientation* — whether you held the camera normally, creating a horizontally oriented image, or turned the camera on its side to shoot a vertically oriented photo. During playback, the camera can then read the orientation data and automatically rotate the image so that it appears in the upright position, as shown on the left in Figure 8-9. The image is also automatically rotated when you view it in Nikon ViewNX 2 and other photo programs that can interpret the data. If you disable rotation, vertically oriented pictures appear sideways, as shown on the right in Figure 8-9.

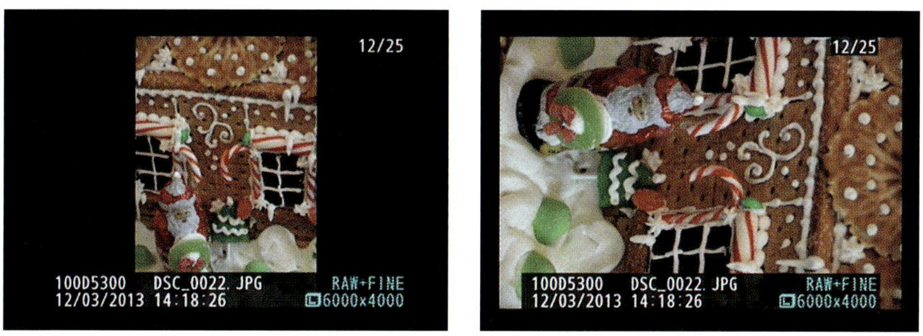

Figure 8-9: You can display vertically oriented pictures in their upright position (left) or sideways (right).

Photographers use the term *portrait orientation* to refer to vertically oriented pictures and *landscape orientation* to refer to horizontally oriented pictures. The terms stem from the traditional way that people and places are captured in paintings and photographs — portraits, vertically; landscapes, horizontally.

Set up your rotation preferences by using the following two menu options, both shown in Figure 8-10:

- **Auto Image Rotation:** This option, on the Setup menu, determines whether the orientation data is included in the picture file. The default setting is On.

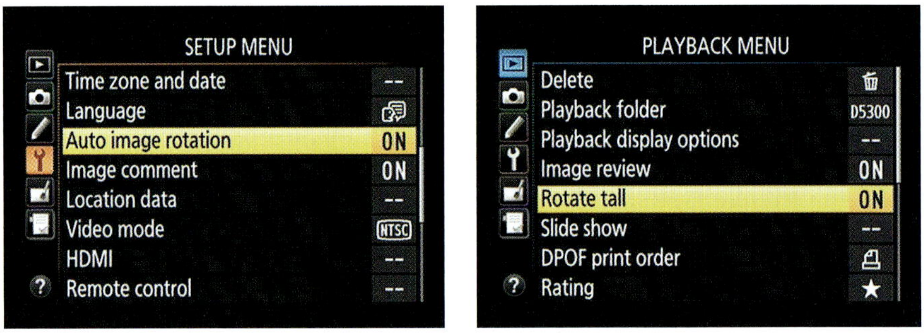

Figure 8-10: Visit the Setup menu (left) and Playback menu (right) to enable or disable image rotation.

- **Rotate Tall:** Found on the Playback menu, this option controls whether the camera pays attention to the orientation data. This one is also enabled by default.

Regardless of these settings, your pictures aren't rotated during the instant-review period. Nor are movie files rotated.

Viewing Picture Data

In single-picture view, you can choose from the six display modes shown in Figure 8-11. By default, however, only the File Information display is available.

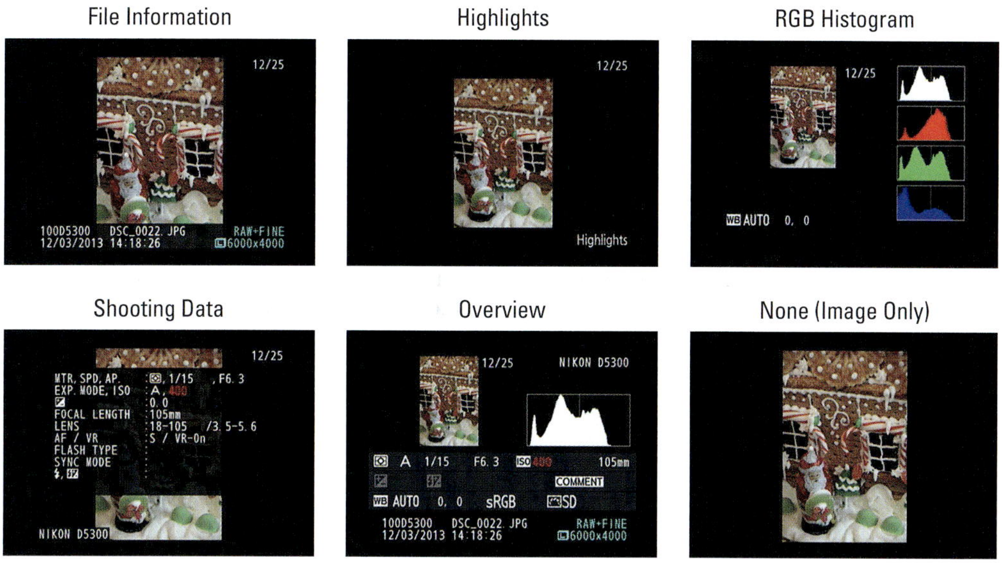

Figure 8-11: You can choose from six playback display modes.

To use any other display options, you must enable them from the Playback menu, by following these steps:

1. **Open the Playback menu and highlight Playback Display Options, as shown on the left in Figure 8-12.**

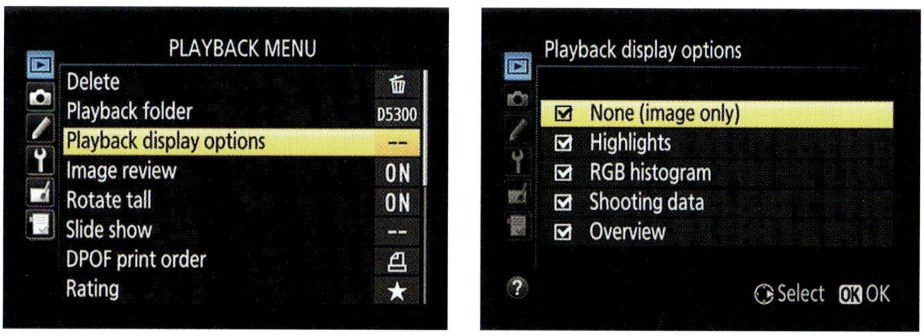

Figure 8-12: You must enable these display modes via the Playback menu.

2. **Press OK.**

   A menu listing all hidden display modes appears, as shown on the right in the figure. A check mark in the box next to a display mode means that the mode is enabled; by default, all modes are turned off.

3. **To toggle a display mode on, highlight it and then press the Multi Selector right.**

   A check mark appears in the box for that mode.

4. **After turning on the options you want to use, press OK.**

After enabling the additional display modes and returning to playback mode, press the Multi Selector up or down to cycle from one display to the next.

The next several sections explain exactly what details you can glean from each display mode, save for the image-only mode. I present them here in the order they appear if you cycle through the modes by pressing the Multi Selector down. You can spin through the modes in the other direction by pressing the Multi Selector up.

File Information mode

In the File Information display mode, the monitor displays the data shown in Figure 8-13. Here's the key to what information appears, starting at the top of the screen and working down:

- **File number/Total files:** The first value indicates the number of the currently displayed photo; the second tells you the total number of files in the same folder.
- **Folder name:** Folders are named automatically by the camera unless you create custom folders, a trick you can explore in Chapter 11. The first camera-created folder is 100D5300. Each folder can contain up to 9,999 images; when you exceed that limit, the camera creates a new folder and assigns the next folder number: 101D5300, 102D5300, and so on.
- **Filename:** The camera also automatically names your files. Filenames end with a 3-letter code that represents the file format, which is either JPG (for JPEG) or NEF (for Raw) for still photos. Chapter 2 discusses these formats. If you record a movie, the file extension is MOV; if you create a dust-off reference image file, an advanced feature designed for use with Nikon Capture NX 2, the camera instead uses the extension NDF. (Because this software must be purchased separately, I don't cover it in this book.)

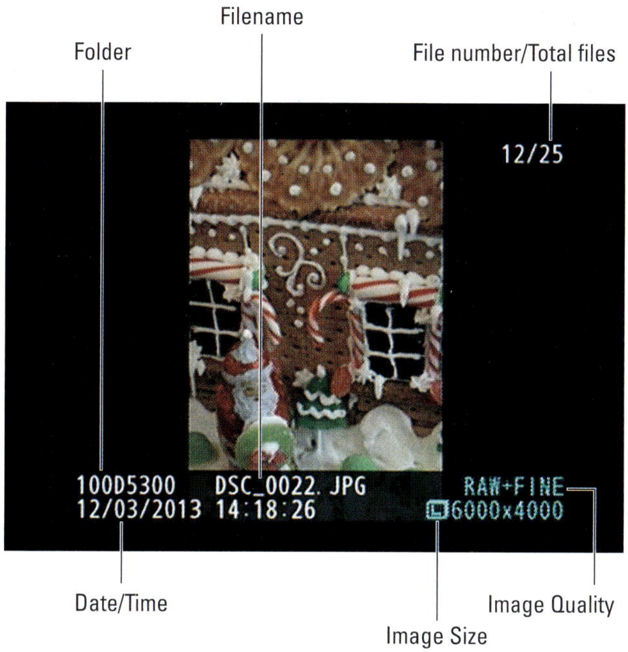

Figure 8-13: In File Information mode, you can view these bits of data.

The first four characters of filenames also vary. Here's what the possible codes indicate:

- *DSC_*: You captured the photo at the default Color Space setting, sRGB. You can investigate this option in Chapter 5.
- *_DSC*: If you change the Color Space setting to Adobe RGB, the underscore character comes first.
- *CSC_*: When you create an edited copy of a photo by using any of the Retouch menu features except Resize, the copy's filename begins with these characters. If the underscore precedes the letters, you captured the original in the Adobe RGB color space.
- *SSC_*: These letters indicate a lower-resolution copy of a photo that you created by using the Resize option on the Retouch menu; Chapter 9 details that option. If the Color Space was set to Adobe RGB at the time you created the copy, the filename begins with _SSC instead.

Each image is also assigned a 4-digit file number, starting with 0001. When you reach image 9999, the file numbering restarts at 0001, and the new images go into a new folder to prevent any possibility of overwriting the existing image files. For more information about file numbering, see the Chapter 1 section that discusses the File Number Sequence option, found on the Custom Setting menu.

- **Date and Time:** Just below the folder and filename info, you see the date and time that you took the picture. Of course, the accuracy of this data depends on whether you set the camera's date and time values correctly, which you do via the Time Zone and Date option on the Setup menu.
- **Image Quality:** Here you can see which Image Quality setting you used when taking the picture. Again, Chapter 2 has details, but the short story is this: Fine, Normal, and Basic are the three JPEG recording options, with Fine representing the highest JPEG quality. Raw refers to the Nikon Raw format, NEF (for Nikon Electronic Format). If you captured the picture in both formats, you see Raw+Fine (or Normal or Basic), as shown in the figure. Only one thumbnail appears to represent each file.
- **Image Size:** This value tells you the image resolution, or pixel count. See Chapter 2 to find out about resolution.

Figure 8-14 shows you some additional symbols that appear when you use certain after-the-shot camera features, as follows:

- **Protected symbol:** The key icon indicates that you used the file-protection feature to prevent the image or movie from being erased when you use the camera's Delete function. See the next chapter to find out more. (***Note:*** Formatting your memory card, a topic discussed in Chapter 1, *does* erase even protected pictures.) This area appears empty if you didn't apply protection.
- **Retouch symbol:** This icon appears on images that you created by applying one of the Retouch menu features to a picture. (The camera preserves the original and applies your alterations to a copy of the file.) For example, the image shown in Figure 8-14 is a cropped version

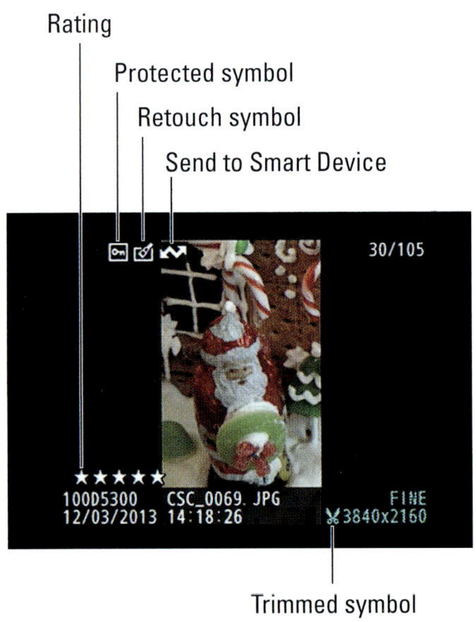

Figure 8-14: These symbols appear only if you use the related playback and retouching features.

of my original photo; I used the Trim feature to clip away some excess background. The Trim symbol appears at the bottom of the display, as shown in the figure, for cropped images. Chapter 10 explains this feature and other Retouch menu options. See Chapter 7 for help with the movie-editing function found on the menu; for edited movies, you see a little scissors icon instead of the Retouch symbol shown in the figure.

- **Send to Smart Device symbol:** After you tag a photo for Wi-Fi transfer to a smartphone or tablet, this symbol appears. Chapter 9 explains the Wi-Fi feature. (You can't transfer movies via Wi-Fi.)
- **Rating symbol:** Chapter 9 explains how you can rate a picture or movie, assigning it one to five stars or, if you're totally disgusted with the file, labeling it with a trash can so that you can easily locate it to delete it. The rating shown in Figure 8-14 indicates a five-star photo, for example. (I grade on a curve.)

Highlights (blinkies) mode

One of the most difficult problems to correct in a photo-editing program is known as *blown highlights* in some circles and *clipped highlights* in others. In plain English, both terms mean that *highlights* — the brightest areas of the image — are so overexposed that areas that should include a variety of light shades are instead totally white. For example, in a cloud image, pixels that should be light to very light gray become white due to overexposure, resulting in a loss of detail in those clouds.

REMEMBER

Highlights display mode alerts you to clipped highlights by blinking the affected pixels on and off. But just because you see the flashing alerts doesn't mean that you should adjust exposure — the decision depends on where the alerts occur and how the rest of the image is exposed. If your subject appears fine and the blinkies are in the background, don't worry about it. If you adjust exposure to get rid of the blown highlights, your subject will then be overexposed. In other words, sometimes you simply can't avoid a few clipped highlights when the scene includes a broad range of brightness values.

When you shift to Highlights display mode, you see the label *Highlights* at the bottom of the frame and the file number and total number of files in the upper-right corner, as shown in Figure 8-15. You also see the Protected, Retouch, Rating, and Send to Smart Device symbols (refer to Figure 8-14), if you used those features.

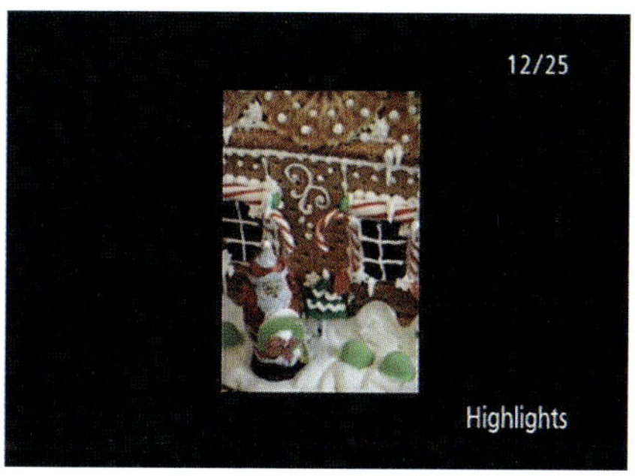

Figure 8-15: In Highlights mode, seriously overexposed pixels blink.

Like all playback display modes except File Information, Highlights mode is disabled by default. Follow the instructions in the "Viewing Picture Data" section, earlier in this chapter, to enable it.

RGB Histogram mode

Press the Multi Selector down to shift from Highlights mode to this mode, which displays your image as shown in Figure 8-16. Again, you can view your picture in this mode only if you enable it via the Display Mode option on the Playback menu. (See "Viewing Picture Data," earlier in this chapter, for help.)

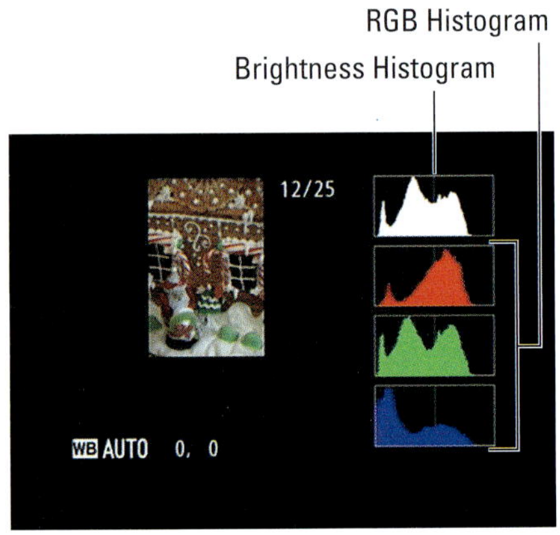

Figure 8-16: RGB Histogram mode presents exposure and color information in chart-like fashion.

Underneath the image thumbnail, you see just a few pieces of data. As with File Information mode, you see the Protected, Retouch, Rating, and Send to Smart Device icons if you used those features. (Refer to Figure 8-14.) Beneath that, you see the White Balance settings used for the shot. In the figure, the data shows that the picture was captured using the Auto White Balance with zero adjustment along the blue-to-amber axis and zero adjustment along the green-to-magenta axis. (Chapter 5 details White Balance options.) At the top of the display, you see the File number/Total files data, also part of the standard File Information display data.

The keys to this display mode, though, are those chart-like thingies called *histograms*. You get two types of histograms: The top one is a Brightness histogram; the three others are known collectively as an RGB (red, green, blue) histogram.

The next two sections explain what you can discern from the histograms. But first, here's a cool trick to remember: If you press the Zoom In button while in this display mode, you can zoom the thumbnail to a magnified view. The histograms then update to reflect only the magnified area of the photo. Use the Multi Selector to scroll the display to see other areas of the picture. To return to the regular view and once again see the whole-image histogram, press OK.

Reading a Brightness histogram

You can get an idea of image exposure by viewing your photo on the camera monitor and by looking at the blinkies in Highlight mode. But the Brightness histogram provides a way to gauge exposure that's a little more detailed.

A Brightness histogram indicates the distribution of shadows, highlights, and *midtones* (areas of medium brightness) in an image. Figure 8-17 shows you the histogram for the gingerbread-house photo featured in Figure 8-16.

The horizontal axis of the histogram represents the possible picture brightness values — the maximum *tonal range,* in photography-speak — from the darkest shadows on the left to the brightest highlights on the right. And the vertical axis shows you how many pixels fall at a particular brightness value. A spike indicates a heavy concentration of pixels at that brightness value.

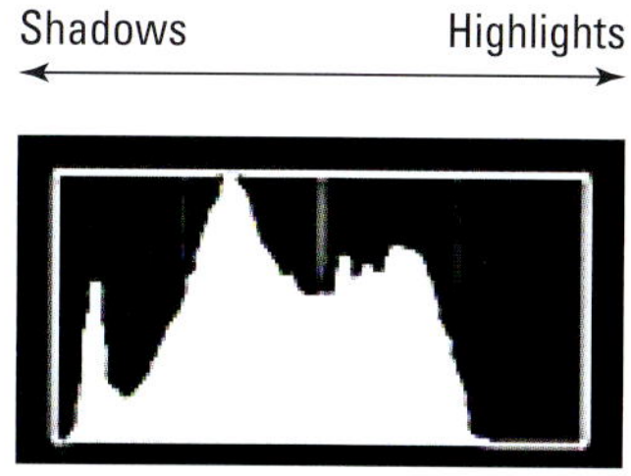

Figure 8-17: The Brightness histogram indicates tonal range, from shadows on the left to highlights on the right.

Keep in mind that there is no "perfect" histogram that you should try to achieve. Instead, interpret the histogram with respect to the distribution of shadows, highlights, and midtones that comprise your subject. You wouldn't expect to see lots of shadows, for example, in a photo of a polar bear walking on a snowy landscape. Pay attention, however, if you see a very high concentration of pixels at the far right or left end of the histogram, which can indicate a seriously overexposed or underexposed image, respectively.

When shooting subjects that contain a significant amount of white, such as the gingerbread house shown in my figures, I usually underexpose the photo just a hair. That way, I make sure that I don't blow out highlights. In such cases, the histogram may show no or few pixels at the right end of the scale (refer to Figure 8-17). Again, though, you have to read the histogram with an eye toward getting the exposure of the main subject correct. Had I increased exposure enough to get some pixel population on the highlights end of the histogram, I could easily have lost detail in Santa's beard, for example. (This is a good situation in which to use the autoexposure bracketing feature, explained at the end of Chapter 3; with that feature, you can easily capture the image at a few different exposure settings so that you have a safety net.)

Understanding RGB histograms

When you view your images in RGB Histogram display mode, you see two histograms: the Brightness histogram, covered in the preceding section, and an RGB histogram. Figure 8-18 shows you the RGB histogram for the gingerbread image.

To make sense of an RGB histogram, you first need to know that digital images are known as *RGB images* because they're created from three primary colors of light: red, green, and blue. Whereas the Brightness histogram reflects the brightness of all three color channels rolled into one, RGB histograms let you view the values for each channel.

When you look at the brightness data for a single channel, though, you glean information about color saturation rather than image brightness. (*Saturation* refers to the purity of a color; a fully saturated color contains no black or white.) I don't have space in this book to provide a full lesson in RGB color theory, but the short story is that when you mix red, green, and blue light, and each component is at maximum brightness, you create white. Zero brightness in all three channels creates black. If you have maximum red and no blue or green, though, you have fully saturated red. If you mix two channels at maximum brightness, you also create full saturation. For example, maximum red and blue produce fully saturated magenta. And, wherever colors are fully saturated, you can lose picture detail. For example, a rose petal that should have a range of tones from medium to dark red may instead be a flat blob of pure red.

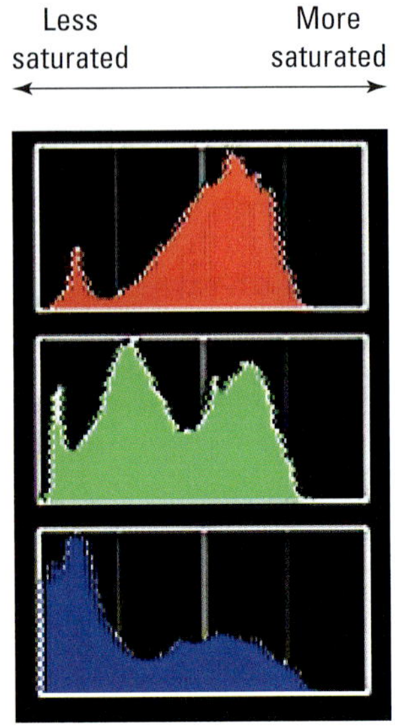

Figure 8-18: The RGB histogram can indicate problems with color saturation.

The upshot is that if all the pixels for one or two channels are slammed to the right end of the histogram, you may be losing picture detail because of overly saturated colors. If all three channels show a heavy pixel population at the right end of the histogram, you may have blown highlights — again, because the maximum levels of red, green, and blue create white. Either way, you may want to adjust the exposure settings and try again.

A savvy RGB histogram reader can also spot color balance issues by looking at the pixel values. But frankly, color balance problems are fairly easy to notice just by looking at the image on the camera monitor. See Chapter 5 to find out how to correct any color problems that you spot during picture playback.

Shooting Data display mode

REMEMBER

Before you can access Shooting Data mode, you must enable it via the Playback Display Options setting on the Playback menu. See the earlier section "Viewing Picture Data" for details. After turning on the option, press the Multi Selector down to shift from RGB Histogram mode to Shooting Data mode.

In this mode, you can view up to four screens of information, which you toggle among by pressing the Multi Selector up and down. The left image in Figure 8-19 shows you the first screen of data. On the right side of the figure, you see the fourth screen, which appears only if you enabled the built-in GPS (Global Positioning System) feature. This screen contains the latitude, longitude, and other GPS data recorded with the image. (Chapter 11 provides details about setting up GPS data recording.)

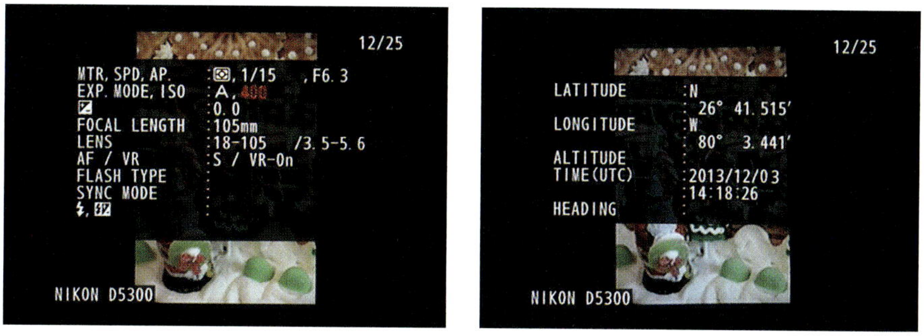

Figure 8-19: Here you see the first and fourth Shooting Data screens.

Most of the other data won't make sense until you explore Chapters 3 through 5, which explain the exposure, color, and focusing settings available on your camera. But I want to call your attention to a few facts now:

- The upper-left corner of the monitor shows the Protected, Retouch, and Send to Smart Device icons, if you used these features. If you assigned a rating to the file, the rating appears in the lower-left corner. Otherwise, these areas are empty, as in the figures. (Refer to Figure 8-14 to see each of these icons.)
- The current file number and total number of files appear in the upper-right corner of the display.
- The Comment item, which is the final item on the third screen, contains a value if you use the Image Comment feature on the Setup menu. I cover this option in Chapter 11 also.
- If the ISO value on Shooting Data Page 1 appears in red (refer to the left screen in Figure 8-19), the camera overrode the ISO Sensitivity setting that you selected in order to produce a good exposure. This shift occurs only if you enable automatic ISO adjustment in the P, S, A, and M exposure modes; see Chapter 3 for details.

Overview mode

In this mode, the playback screen contains a small image thumbnail along with scads of shooting data — although not quite as much as Shooting Data mode — plus a Brightness histogram. Figure 8-20 offers a look.

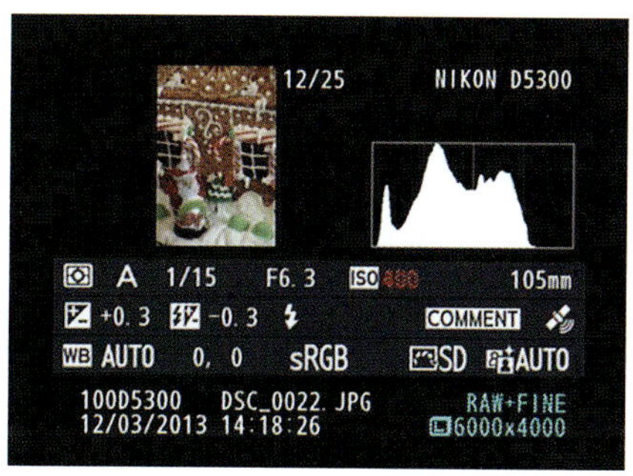

Figure 8-20: In Overview mode, you can view your picture along with the major camera settings you used to take the picture.

The earlier section "Reading a Brightness histogram" tells you what to make of that part of the screen. Just above the histogram, you see the

Protected, Retouch, and Send to Smart Device symbols, if you used those features, and the File number/Total files data appears at the upper-right corner of the image thumbnail. If you used the Rating feature (covered in Chapter 9), the rating appears under the thumbnail. (Again, refer to Figure 8-14 to see this miscellaneous symbols.)

To sort out the maze of other information, the following list breaks down the five rows that appear under the thumbnail and histogram. In the accompanying figures as well as in Figure 8-20, I include all possible data simply for the purpose of illustration; if any of the items don't appear on your screen, it simply means that the relevant feature wasn't enabled when you captured the shot. Also note that if you're looking at a movie file, the screen shows only the third row of data, minus the Active D-Lighting information, and the histogram represents the exposure of the first frame of the movie.

- **Row 1:** This row shows the exposure settings labeled in Figure 8-21, along with the focal length of the lens you used to take the shot. As in Shooting Data mode, the ISO value appears red if you enabled auto ISO override in the P, S, A, or M exposure modes and the camera adjusted the ISO for you.

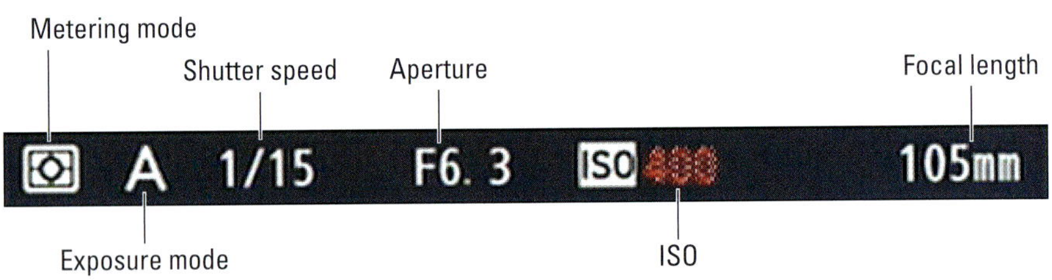

Figure 8-21: Here you can inspect major exposure settings along with the lens focal length.

- **Row 2:** This row contains a few additional exposure settings, labeled in Figure 8-22. On the right end of the row, the Comment and GPS labels appear if you took advantage of those options when recording the shot. (You must switch to Shooting Data mode to view the comment and GPS text.)

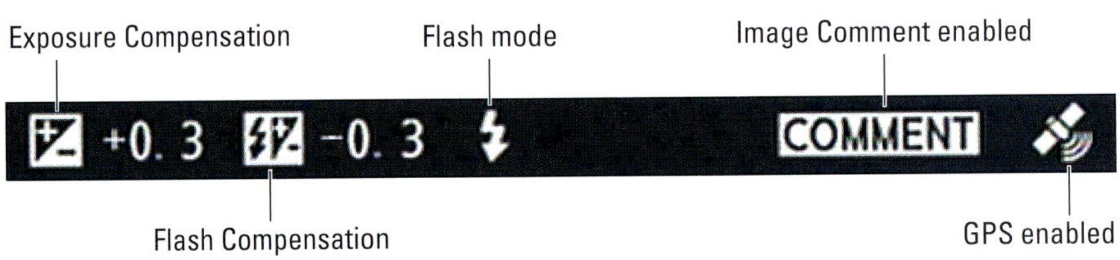

Figure 8-22: This row contains additional exposure information.

- **Row 3:** The first three items on this row, labeled in Figure 8-23, relate to the color options explored in Chapter 5. Again, the second White Balance value shows the amount of blue-to-amber fine-tuning adjustment; and the third, the amount of green-to-magenta adjustment (both values are 0 in the figure). The last item indicates the Active D-Lighting setting.

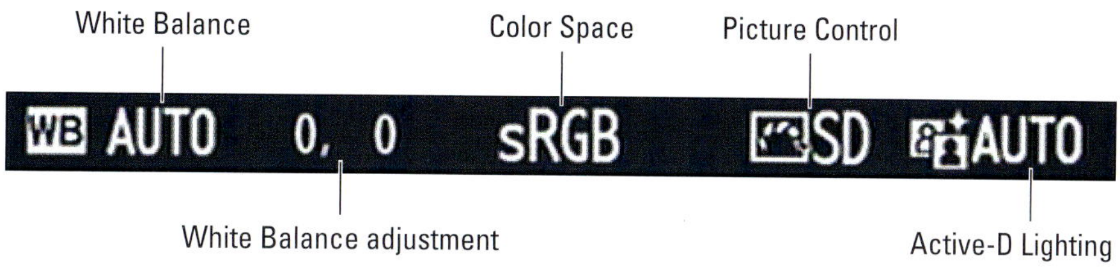

Figure 8-23: Look at this row for details about advanced color settings.

- **Rows 4 and 5:** The final two rows of data (refer to Figure 8-20) show the same information you get in File Information mode, explained earlier in this chapter.

Creating a Digital Slide Show

Many photo-editing programs offer a tool for creating digital slide shows that can be viewed on a computer or, if copied to a DVD, on a DVD player. You can even add music, captions, graphics, special effects, and the like to jazz up your presentations. But if you want to create a simple show — that is, one that just displays the photos and movies on the camera memory card one by one — you can create and run the show directly on your camera by using the Slide Show function on the Playback menu. And by connecting your camera to a television, as outlined in the next section, you can present your show to a whole roomful of people.

REMEMBER

One important point to note: The files the camera can access depend on the setting of the Playback Folder option on the Playback menu. If you haven't created any custom folders — a feature you can explore in Chapter 11 — you likely have only one folder on your card. If your memory card does contain multiple folders, see "Choosing Which Images to View," earlier in this chapter, for help with selecting the playback folder.

With that detail out of the way, follow these steps to present a slide show:

1. **Display the Playback menu and highlight Slide Show, as shown on the left in Figure 8-24.**

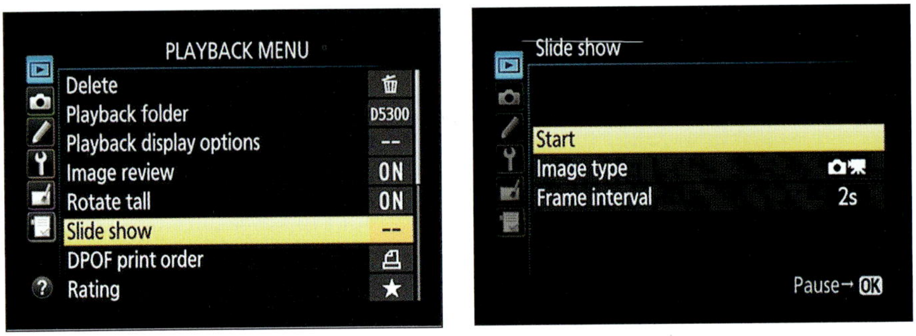

Figure 8-24: Choose Slide Show to set up automatic playback of your pictures and movies.

2. **Press OK to display the Slide Show setup screen (refer to the right side of Figure 8-24).**
3. **Highlight Image Type and press the Multi Selector right.**

   You're taken to the screen shown on the left in Figure 8-25, where you can choose what types of files to display in the show.

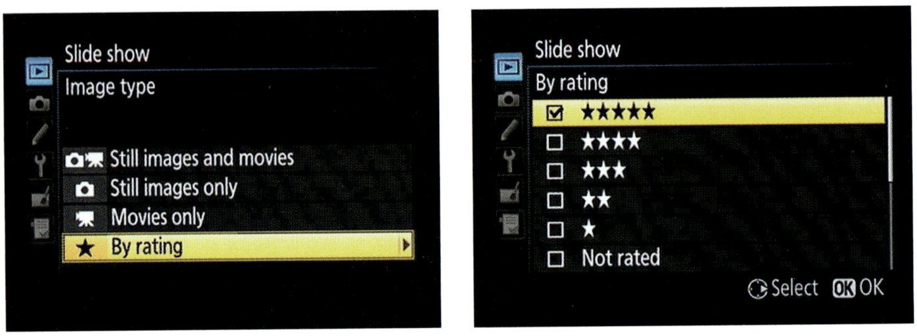

Figure 8-25: Choose the By Rating option to include only your pictures rated with five stars in the show.

4. **Select the type of files you want to include.**

   You have four options: Display both photographs and movies, photos only, movies only, or files that you assigned a specific rating. (The next chapter shows you how to rate photos.)

TIP

If you select By Rating, press the Multi Selector right to display the screen shown on the right in Figure 8-25. Here, you can specify the rating a picture or movie must have to make it into the show. For example, in the figure, I selected only the 5-star option. Highlight a rating and press the Multi Selector right to put a check in the box and include photos to which you assigned that rating.

After setting the Image Type, press OK to return to the Slide Show setup screen (refer to the second screen in Figure 8-24).

5. **Highlight Frame Interval and press the Multi Selector right.**

   On the next screen, you can specify how long you want each image to be displayed. You can set the interval to 2, 3, 5, or 10 seconds.

6. **Select the frame interval you want to use and press OK.**

   You return to the Slide Show setup screen.

7. **To start the show, highlight Start and press OK.**

When the show ends, you see a screen offering three options: You can choose to restart the show, adjust the frame interval, or exit to the Playback menu. Highlight your choice and press OK.

During the show, you can control playback as follows:

- **Pause the show.** Press OK. Again, you see three options onscreen. To restart playback, select Restart and press OK. You also can adjust the frame interval or exit to the Playback menu.
- **Exit the show.** You have three options:
  - *To return to regular playback,* press the Playback button.
  - *To return to the Playback menu,* press the Menu button.
  - *To return to picture-taking mode,* press the shutter button halfway.
- **Skip to the next/previous image manually.** Press the Multi Selector right or left.
- **Change the information displayed with the image.** Press the Multi Selector up or down to cycle through the display modes. See the earlier section "Viewing Picture Data" for help understanding the various modes.
- **Adjust the movie volume.** Press the Zoom In button to increase the volume; press the Zoom Out button to decrease it.

Viewing Your Photos on a Television

Your camera is equipped with a feature that allows you to play your pictures and movies on a television screen. In fact, you have three playback options:

- **Regular (standard definition) video playback:** Haven't made the leap yet to HDTV? No worries: You can set the camera to send a regular standard-definition audio and video signal to the TV. The cable you need is even provided in the camera box. Look for the cable that has yellow, red, and white plugs at one end.
- **HDMI playback:** If you have a high-definition television, you need to purchase an HDMI cable to connect the camera and television. You need a Type C mini-pin HD cable; prices start at about $20. Nikon doesn't make its own cable, so just look for a quality third-party version.

  By default, the camera decides the proper video resolution to send to the TV after you connect the two devices. But you have the option of setting a specific resolution as well. To do so, select HDMI from the Setup menu, press OK, and then choose Output Resolution, as shown in Figure 8-26. Press the Multi Selector right to access the available settings.

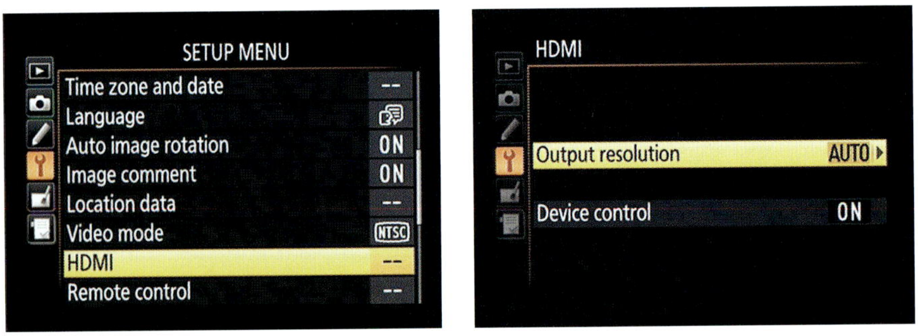

Figure 8-26: Select options for HD playback here.

- **For HDMI CEC TV sets:** If your television is compatible with HDMI CEC, your D5300 enables you to use the buttons on the TV's remote control to perform the functions of the OK button and Multi Selector during full-frame picture playback and slide shows. To make this feature work, you must enable it via the Setup menu. Again, start with the HDMI option, but this time, select Device Control and set the option to On.

You need to make one final preflight check before connecting the camera and television: Verify the status of the Video Mode setting on the Setup menu. You have two options: NTSC and PAL. Select the video mode used by your part of the world. (In the United States, Canada, and Mexico, NTSC is the standard.)

After you select the necessary Setup menu options, grab your video cable, turn off the camera, and open the little rubber door on the left side of the camera. There you find two connection ports: one for a standard audio/video (A/V) cable and one for the HDMI cable. Figure 8-27 labels the two ports.

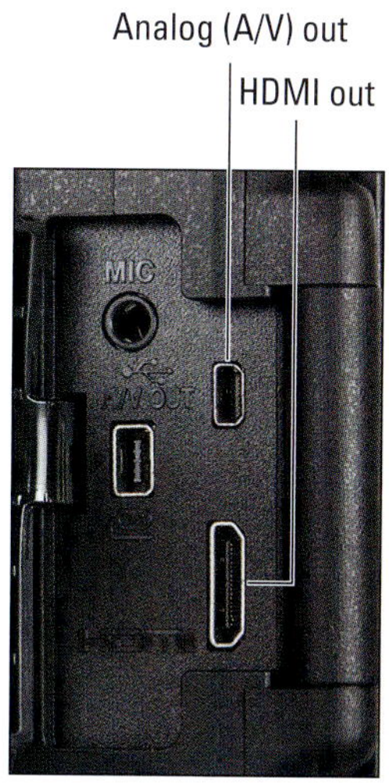

Figure 8-27: The video-out ports are under the little rubber door on the side of the camera.

The smaller plug on the A/V cable attaches to the camera. The yellow plug goes into your TV's video jack; the white one, to the left audio channel jack; and the red one, to the right audio channel jack. For HDMI playback, a single plug goes to the TV.

At this point, I need to point you to your TV manual to find out exactly which jacks to use to connect your camera. You also need to consult the manual to find out which channel to select for playback of signals from auxiliary input devices. Then just turn on your camera to send the signal to the TV set. If you don't have the latest and greatest HDMI CEC capability (or you lost your remote), control playback using the same techniques as you normally do to view pictures on your camera monitor. You can also run a slide show by following the steps outlined in the preceding section.

9

Working with Picture and Movie Files

In This Chapter

- Rating photos and movies
- Protecting files from accidental erasure
- Deleting unwanted files
- Downloading files to your computer
- Processing Raw files
- Shrinking files for online use
- Transferring files to a smartphone or tablet via Wi-Fi

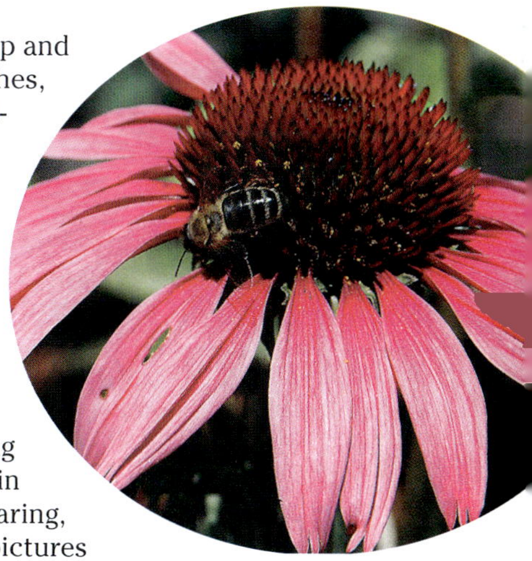

Every creative pursuit involves its share of cleanup and organizational tasks. Painters have to wash brushes, embroiderers have to separate strands of floss, woodcrafters have to haul out the wet/dry vac to suck up sawdust. Digital photography is no different: At some point, you have to stop shooting so that you can download and process your files.

This chapter explains these after-the-shot tasks. First up is a review of several in-camera file-management operations: rate files, delete unwanted files, and protect your best work from accidental erasure. Following that, you can get help with transferring files to your computer, processing files that you shot in the Raw (NEF) format, preparing images for online sharing, and using the camera's built-in Wi-Fi system to send pictures to a smartphone or tablet. Along the way, I also introduce you to Nikon's free photo software, Nikon ViewNX 2, which offers an easy way to handle many of these jobs.

Rating Photos and Movies

Using your camera's Rating feature, you can assign a rating to a picture or movie file: five stars for your best shots, one star for those you wish you could reshoot, and so on. You can even assign a "trash this" rating to flag images that you think you want to delete. *Note:* It's not polite to assign this rating to a photo that your significant other shot while borrowing your camera.

Rating pictures has several benefits. First, when you create a slide show, as outlined in Chapter 8, you can tell the camera to display only photos that have a certain rating. (If you want people to think you're an awesome photographer, don't include anything that has less than a four-star rating.) Second, assigning the Delete tag makes it easy to spot the rotten apples amid all your great photos and movies when you take the step of erasing files. Finally, if you use Nikon ViewNX 2 to view your files after downloading, you can sort pictures according to rating, making it easier to cull your photo collection and gather your best work for printing and sharing.

REMEMBER

Before showing you how to rate photos, I need to share one rule of the road: If you protect a photo using the feature described in the later section "Protecting Photos," you can't alter the file in any way — and that includes assigning a rating to it. See the aforementioned section to find out how to remove protected status from a file, if necessary.

Assuming that the file isn't protected, you can assign a rating in two ways:

- **Choose Rating from the Playback menu.** After selecting the Rating option, as shown on the left in Figure 9-1, press OK to display image thumbnails, as shown on the right. Press the Multi Selector right or left or use the Command dial to move the yellow highlight box over an image you want to rate, and then press the Multi Selector up or down to set a rating from 1 to 5; select the symbol that looks like a trash can to mark the picture as headed to the trash heap. A symbol representing the rating appears with the thumbnail, as labeled in the figure.

  For a closer view of a selected photo, press the Zoom In button. Release the button to return to thumbnails view.

  To rate another photo, move the highlight box over it and repeat the process. After rating your photos, press OK to exit to the Playback menu.

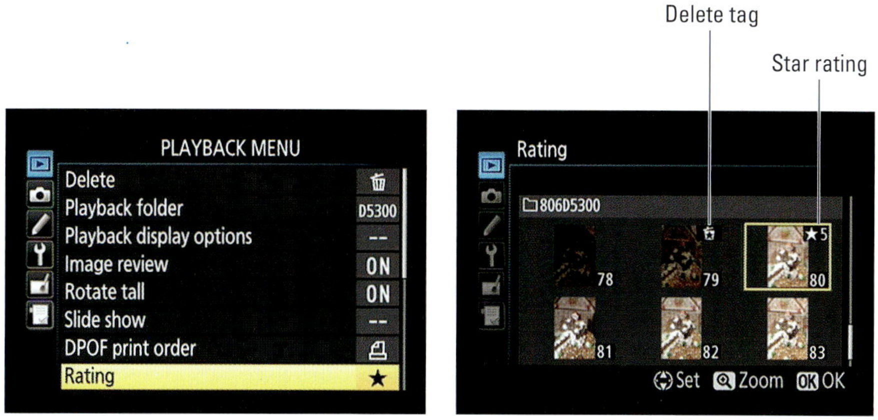

Figure 9-1: You can rate a batch of photos by choosing Rating from the Playback menu.

- **Set the camera to playback mode, display the photo, and press the *i* button.** The screen shown on the left in Figure 9-2 appears over your photo. Select Rating and press OK to view the photo, as shown on the right in the figure; then press the Multi Selector right or left to choose a star rating from 1 to 5. Select the far left dot, labeled *Delete rating* in the figure, to tag a picture for erasure. Press OK to complete the job.

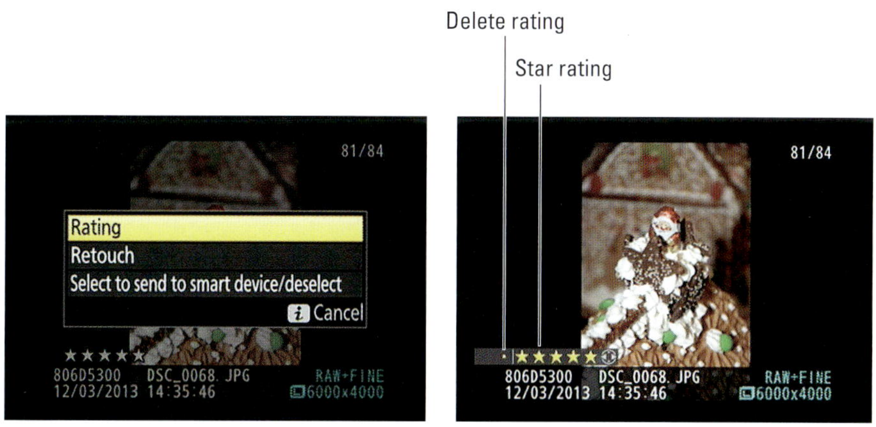

Figure 9-2: During playback, press the *i* button, select Rating, and then press the Multi Selector right or left to rate the photo.

During playback, you can view the rating. Figure 9-3 shows you where to find the rating in the default display mode (File Information mode). For more about playback display modes, see Chapter 8.

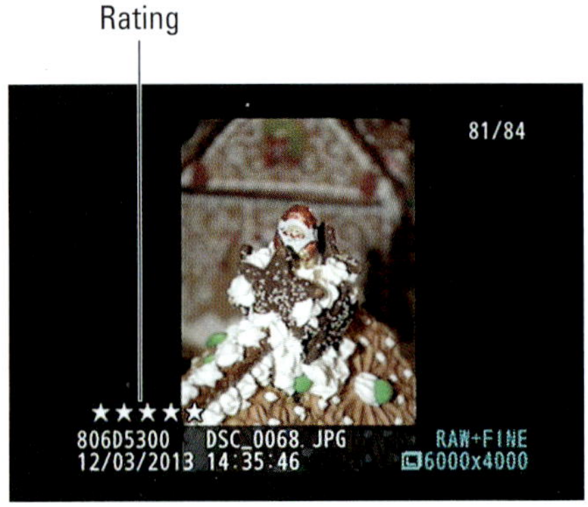

Figure 9-3: The current rating appears here in File Information playback mode.

Deleting Photos

You have three options for erasing pictures from a memory card when it's in your camera. The next few sections give you the lowdown.

One note before you begin: None of the Delete features erase pictures that you protect via the option that I outline in the upcoming section "Protecting Photos." To erase protected photos, you must first remove the file protection.

Deleting images one at a time

During picture playback, you can use the Delete button to erase photos and movie files. But the process varies depending on the current playback mode:

- In single-image view — that is, you're viewing each photo or movie one at a time — press the Delete button.
- In thumbnails view (displaying 4, 9, or 72 thumbnails), use the Multi Selector or Command dial to highlight the picture you want to erase, and then press Delete.
- In calendar view, highlight the date that contains the image. Then press the Zoom Out button to jump to the thumbnail list, highlight a specific image, and press Delete.

You then see a message asking whether you really want to erase the picture. If you do, press Delete again. To cancel the process, press the Playback button.

By default, the camera displays your photo briefly after the shot is recorded. (You enable or disable this feature via the Image Review option on the Playback menu.) During the instant review period, you can press the Delete button to trash the file immediately. But you have to be quick or else the camera returns to shooting mode.

Deleting all files

Open the Playback menu, select Delete (as shown on the left in Figure 9-4), and press OK to display the second screen in the figure. Then highlight All and press OK. The camera asks you to verify that you want to delete all your pictures and movies; select Yes and press OK.

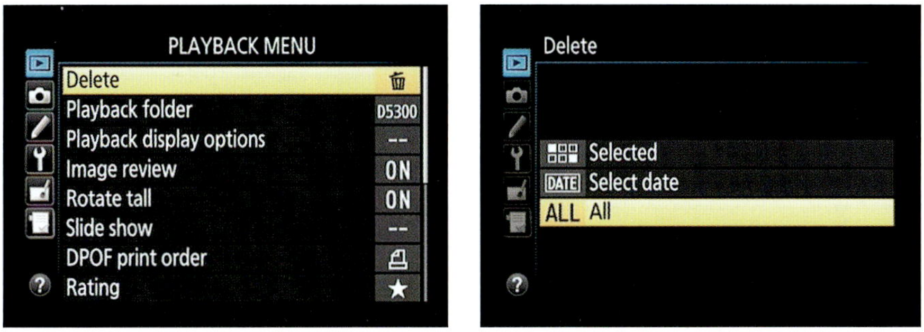

Figure 9-4: To delete all files on the memory card, use this Playback menu option.

If your memory card contains multiple folders, these steps delete only pictures in the folder that is currently selected via the Playback Folder option on the Playback menu. See the section "Choosing Which Images to View," in Chapter 8, for information.

Deleting a batch of selected photos

When you want to get rid of more than a few files — but not erase all pictures and movies on the card — don't waste time erasing each file, one at a time. Instead, you can tag multiple files for deletion and then take them all out to the trash at one time.

To start, display the Playback menu, highlight Delete, and then press OK. You then see the screen shown on the left in Figure 9-5, which offers two options for selecting specific files to erase:

- **Selected:** Use this option if the files you want to delete weren't all taken on the same day. Highlight Selected, as shown on the left in Figure 9-5, and press the Multi Selector right to display a screen of thumbnails, as shown on the right. Use the Multi Selector to place the yellow highlight box over the first file you want to delete and then press the Zoom Out button. A trash can appears in the upper-right corner of the thumbnail, as shown in the figure.

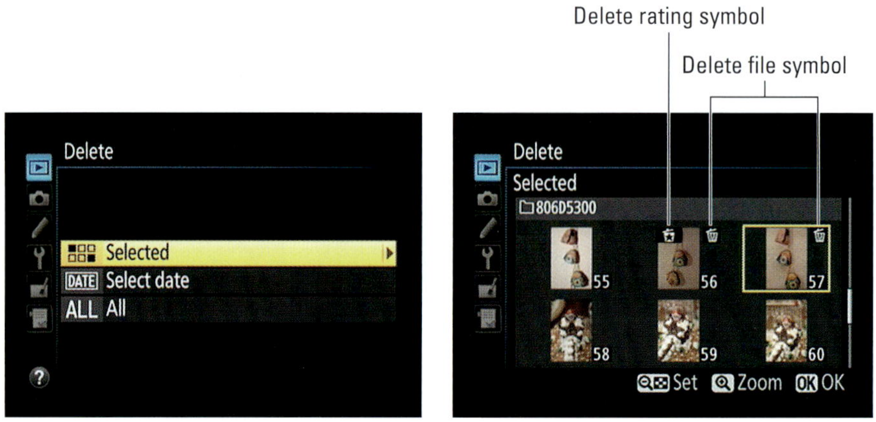

Figure 9-5: This Delete menu option offers a quick way to delete a batch of photos.

If you change your mind, press the Zoom Out button again to remove the Delete tag. To undo deletion for all selected photos, press the Playback button.

For a closer look at the selected image, press and hold the Zoom In button. When you release the button, the display returns to normal thumbnails view.

One important note: Images that you tag with the Delete rating, as explained in the first section of this chapter, are *not* officially marked for the trash heap. When you view your files, you see the Delete rating symbol, labeled on the right in Figure 9-5; when you select the photo via the Delete menu, you see the symbol marked Delete File in the figure. That's the symbol that triggers the camera to dump the file.

- **Select Date:** Use this option to quickly delete any record of that day you'd rather not remember. After choosing Select Date, as shown on the left in Figure 9-6, press the Multi Selector right to display a list of dates, as shown on the right. Next, highlight a date and press the Multi Selector right. A check mark appears in the box next to the date, tagging for deletion all images taken on that day. To remove the check mark, press the Multi Selector right again.

  Can't remember what photos are associated with the selected date? Try this:

  - To display thumbnails of all images taken on the selected date, press the Zoom Out button.
  - To temporarily view the selected thumbnail at full-size view, press the Zoom In button.
  - To return to the date list, press the Zoom Out button again.

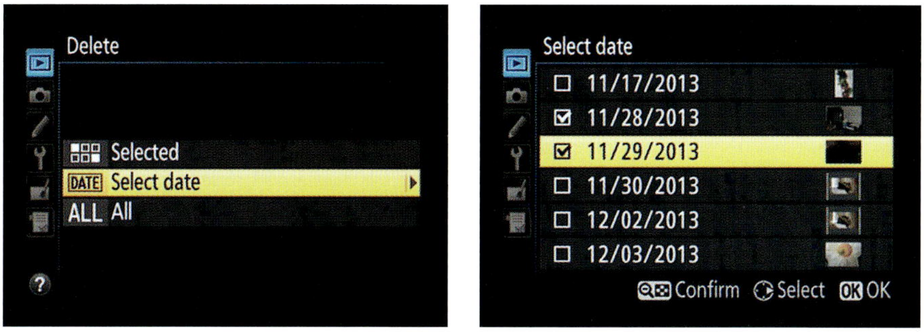

Figure 9-6: With the Select Date option, you can quickly erase all photos taken on a specific date.

After tagging files for deletion or specifying a date to delete, press OK to move forward. You see a confirmation screen; select Yes and press OK.

TIP

You have one alternative way to quickly erase all files shot on a specific date: In the Calendar display mode, highlight the date and then press the Delete button. You see the standard confirmation screen; press Delete again to wrap up. Visit Chapter 8 for the scoop on Calendar display mode.

Protecting Photos

You can protect picture and movie files from accidental erasure by giving them *protected* status. After you take this step, the camera doesn't allow you to delete the file from your memory card, whether you press the Delete button or use the Delete option on the Playback menu.

TIP

I also use the Protect feature when I want to keep a handful of pictures on the card but delete the rest. Rather than use the options I describe in the preceding section to select all the pictures I want to trash, I protect the handful I want to preserve. Then I set the Delete menu option to All and dump the rest. The protected pictures remain intact.

WARNING!

Formatting your memory card *does* erase even protected pictures. In addition, when you protect a picture, it shows up as a read-only file when you transfer it to your computer. Files that have the read-only status can't be altered until you unlock them in your photo software. (In Nikon ViewNX 2, select the image and then choose File⇨Protect Files⇨Unprotect.)

Remember, too, that locking the file prevents you from assigning a rating to it — so rate photos before giving them protected status. (Refer to the first section of this chapter for information about the Rating feature.)

To protect a file, take these steps:

1. **Display or select the picture or movie you want to protect.**
    - *In single-image view,* just display the photo or movie.
    - *In 4/9/72 Thumbnail mode,* use the Multi Selector or Command dial as needed to place the yellow highlight box over the file's thumbnail.
    - *In Calendar view,* highlight the file thumbnail in the strip of thumbnails that appears on the right side of the screen. (Press the Zoom Out button to jump between the calendar dates and the thumbnails.)
2. **Press the AE-L/AF-L button.**

    See the key symbol to the right of the button? That's your reminder that you use the button to lock a picture. A key symbol also appears with locked photos during playback, as shown in Figure 9-7.

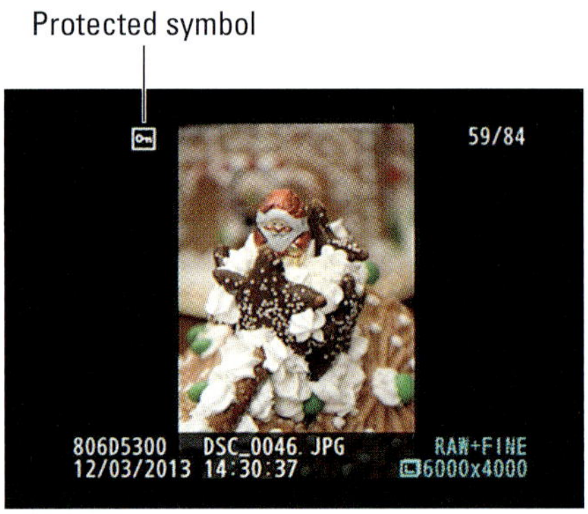

Figure 9-7: Press the AE-L/AF-L button to give an image protected status.

To remove protection, display or select the image and then press the AE-L/AF-L button again.

Taking a Look a Nikon's Free Photo Software (ViewNX 2)

When you're ready to move pictures and movies from your camera to your computer, you need some type of photo program to download, view, and manage the files. You may already have a favorite program, such as Apple's iPhoto or Adobe's Photoshop, Lightroom, or Photoshop Elements. If not, the program that Nikon provides, Nikon ViewNX 2, may be all you need. Along with features that enable you to download, view, and organize your photos, the program offers basic editing tools as well as a Raw-file converter. Figure 9-8 offers a look at the ViewNX 2 window as it appears when you use Image Viewer display mode, one of three options available from the View menu.

Nikon ViewNX 2 is provided on one of the CDs that ships with your camera and is also available for download from the Nikon website (in the United States, www.nikonusa.com). Just head for the support pages for the D5300,

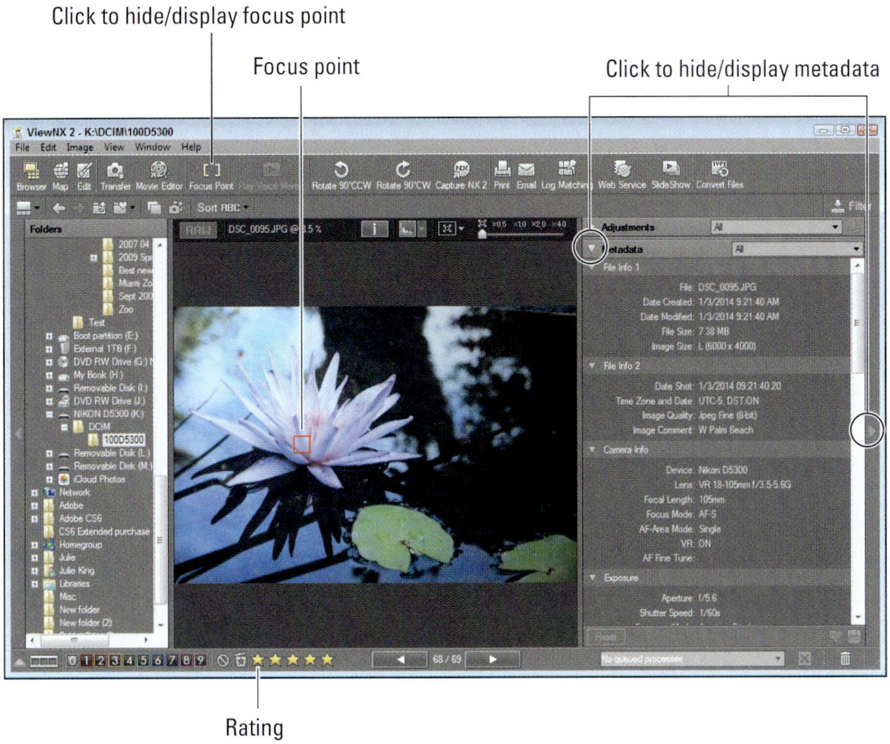

Figure 9-8: Nikon ViewNX 2, free with your camera, offers a photo organizer and some photo-editing functions.

where you'll find a link to camera software. Be sure to download the latest version: At the time I write this chapter, it's Version 2.3.8. Older versions of the software lack support for all D5300 file features.

I don't have room to provide a complete tutorial in using Nikon ViewNX 2, but upcoming sections show you how to use the program to download pictures to your computer, process Raw files, and shrink a high-resolution file to a size that's suitable for online sharing.

TIP

Before I dig into those file-handling features, I want to spotlight a few Nikon ViewNX 2 features that may make it worth your while to install the program even if you already have another program that you use regularly:

- **Viewing image metadata:** *Metadata* is hidden data that includes the camera settings you used to take the picture. If you added a descriptive label or GPS tracking data through the Image Comment and GPS features that I cover in Chapter 11, it's also stored as metadata.

  To display metadata, click an image thumbnail and then display the Metadata panel, located on the right side of the program window (refer to Figure 9-8). If the panel is hidden, choose Window➪Edit or click the triangle on the far right side of the window, and then click the triangle at the top of the panel. (I labeled both controls in the figure.) Many other photo programs also display metadata but sometimes can't reveal data that's very camera-specific.

- **Viewing the focus point:** Here's a trick that you can't do in other photo programs: Click the Focus Point button, labeled in Figure 9-8, to display a red rectangle that indicates which focus point (or points, in some cases) the camera used to establish focus, which can be helpful when you're trying to troubleshoot focus problems. You don't see the point if you used manual focusing, and it also may not appear if you used continuous autofocusing.
- **Viewing the assigned picture rating:** If you used the Rating feature described earlier in this chapter, the rating appears at the bottom of the screen (refer to Figure 9-8) and in the Tags section of the Metadata panel (not shown in the figure). You can change the rating or assign ratings to unrated photos in Nikon ViewNX 2 as well. To sort photos by rating, choose View➪Sort Thumbnails By➪Rating.
- **Viewing a GPS map:** If the file includes GPS data, you can display a map that pinpoints the shooting location, as shown in Figure 9-9. Just click the Map icon at the top of the program window, labeled in the figure.

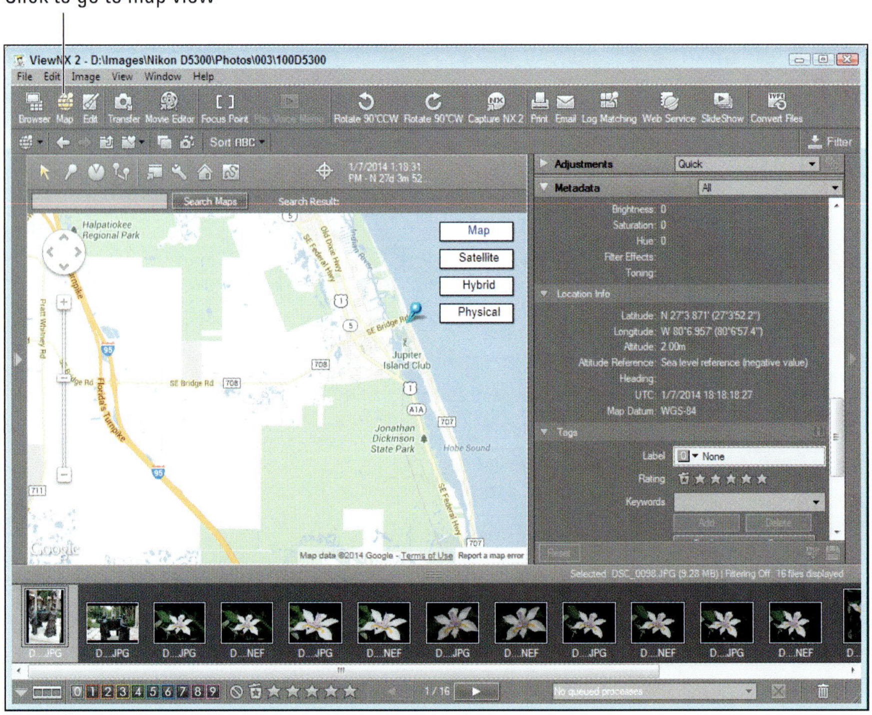

Figure 9-9: If a file contains GPS data, you can pinpoint its shooting location on a map.

For complete details on using these and other program features, select Help➪ViewNx 2 Help, which opens the built-in user manual.

Downloading Pictures to the Computer

You can move picture and movie files to your computer in two ways:

- **Connect the camera to the computer via a USB cable.** The cable you need is supplied in the camera box.
- **Use a memory card reader.** With a card reader, you simply pop the memory card out of your camera and into the card reader. Many computers and printers now have card readers, and you also can buy stand-alone readers for less than $30.

TIP

I recommend using a card reader because sending pictures directly from the camera requires that the camera be turned on during the download process, wasting battery power. However, I include information about cable transfer in the next section, in case you don't have a card reader. To use a card reader, skip ahead to "Starting the transfer process."

What about wireless transfer, you ask? Well, there is one way to do it: You can buy Eye-Fi memory cards, which have wireless connectivity built in. You can find out more about these cards and how to set them up to connect with your computer at the manufacturer's website, `www.eye.fi`. Also check the Eye-Fi details provided in the D5300 manual; look for the section related to the Eye-Fi Upload option on the Setup menu. (The menu item appears only when an Eye-Fi card is installed.) I don't cover these cards in this book.

As for the camera's Wi-Fi feature, it enables you only to connect to Android- and iOS-based phones, tablets, and other smart devices. You can't use it to download files to your computer using a standard wireless network. For details about using the Wi-Fi features, see the end of this chapter.

Connecting via USB

To link your camera to your computer via the provided USB cable, take these steps:

1. **Check the level of the camera battery.**

   WARNING!

   If the battery is low, charge it before continuing. Running out of battery power during downloading can cause problems, including lost picture data. Alternatively, if you purchased the optional AC adapter, use it to power the camera during downloading.

2. **Turn on the computer and give it time to finish its normal start-up routine.**
3. **Turn off the camera.**
4. **Insert the smaller of the two plugs on the USB cable into the USB port on the side of the camera.**

   Look under the rubber door on the left side of the camera for this port, labeled in Figure 9-10.
5. **Plug the other end of the cable into a USB port on the computer.**
6. **Turn on the camera.**

   What happens now depends on the photo software you have installed on your computer. The next section explains the possibilities and how to proceed with the transfer process.
7. **When the download is complete, turn off the camera and then disconnect it from the computer.**

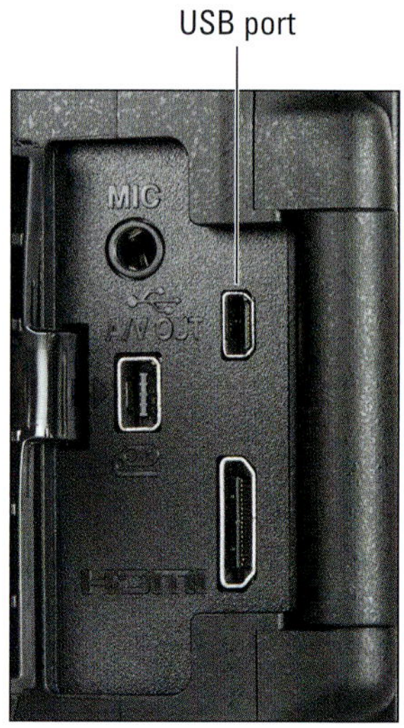

Figure 9-10: The port for connecting the USB cable is hidden under the rubber door on the left side of the camera.

Starting the transfer process

After you connect the camera to the computer or insert a memory card into a card reader, what happens next depends on the software installed on your computer. Here are the most common possibilities and how to move forward:

- **On a computer running Windows, a Windows message box similar to the one in Figure 9-11 appears.** The figure shows the dialog box as it appears in Windows 7. By default, clicking the Import Pictures and Videos icon starts the image transfer using the Windows picture-transfer utility, but you can click the Change Program link to choose Nikon ViewNX 2 or another program as your preferred transfer tool.

  In older versions of Windows, you may see a dialog box listing programs that can handle the transfer; if so, click the one you want to use.

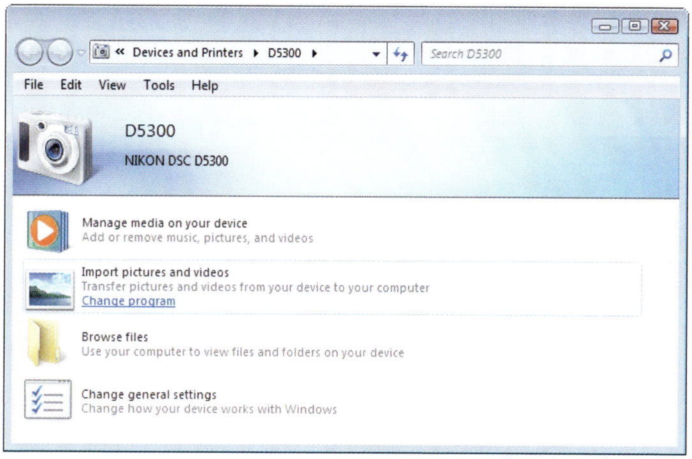

Figure 9-11: Windows 7 may display this initial boxful of transfer options.

- **An installed photo program automatically displays a photo-download wizard.** For example, the downloader associated with Nikon ViewNX 2, Adobe Lightroom, iPhoto, or another photo program may leap to the forefront. Usually, the downloader that appears is associated with the software that you most recently installed.

  If you don't want a program's downloader to launch whenever you insert a memory card or connect your camera, you can turn off that feature. Check the software manual to find out how to disable the auto launch.

- **Nothing happens.** Don't panic; assuming that your card reader or camera is properly connected, all is probably well. Someone simply may have disabled all the automatic downloaders on your system. Just launch your photo software and then transfer your pictures using whatever command starts that process.

  As another option, you can use Windows Explorer or the Mac Finder to drag and drop files from your memory card to your computer. You connect the card through a card reader, and the computer sees the card as just another drive on the system. Windows Explorer also shows the camera as a storage device when you cable the camera directly to the computer. So the process of transferring files is exactly the same as when you move any other file from a CD, DVD, or flash drive onto your computer. (With some versions of the Mac OS, including the most recent ones, the Finder doesn't recognize cameras in this way.)

In the next section, I provide details on using Nikon ViewNX 2 to download your files. If you use another program, the concepts are the same, but check the program manual to get the details. In most programs, you also can find lots of information by simply clicking open the Help menu.

Downloading using ViewNX 2

Built into ViewNX 2 is a downloading tool called Nikon Transfer 2. Follow these steps to use it to transfer pictures to your computer:

1. **Attach your camera to the computer or insert a memory card into your card reader.**

   Depending on what software you have installed on your system, you may see a dialog box asking you how to download your photos. If the window that appears is the Nikon Transfer 2 window, as shown in Figure 9-12, skip to Step 3. Similarly, if you see a Windows dialog box that contains the Nikon Transfer 2 option, click that option and skip to Step 3.

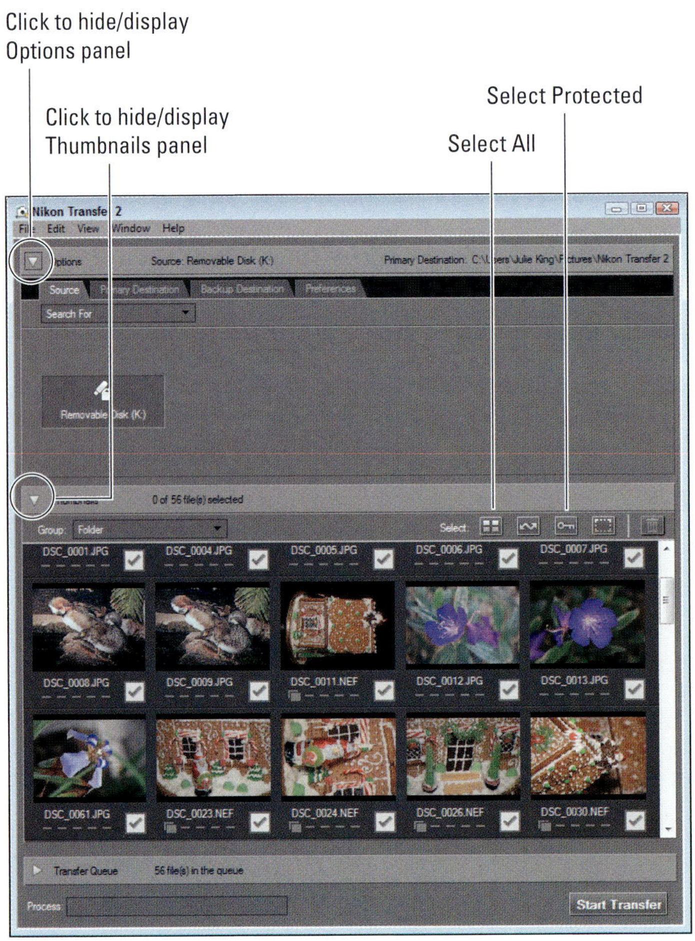

Figure 9-12: Select the check boxes of the images that you want to download.

If nothing happens, travel to Step 2, which shows you how to launch the Nikon Transfer 2 software if it didn't appear automatically.

2. **Launch Nikon Transfer 2 (if it isn't already open).**

   Open Nikon ViewNX 2 and then choose File⇨Launch Transfer or click the Transfer button at the top of the window. The window shown in Figure 9-12 appears. (If you use a Mac, the window decor is slightly different, but the main controls and features are the same.)

3. **Display the Source tab to view thumbnails of your pictures, as shown in the figure.**

   Don't see any tabs? Click the Options triangle (refer to Figure 9-12) to display them. Then click the Source tab. The icon representing your camera or memory card should be selected, as shown in the figure. If not, click the icon.

   Thumbnails of your files appear in the bottom half of the dialog box. If you don't see the thumbnails, click the Thumbnails triangle (refer to Figure 9-12) to open the thumbnails area.

4. **Select the files that you want to download.**

   Click a thumbnail to highlight it and then click the box in the lower-right corner of the thumbnail to select that image or movie for downloading. Here are a few tips to speed up this process:

   - *Select protected files only.* If you used the in-camera function to protect pictures, you can select just those images by clicking the Select Protected icon (refer to Figure 9-12).
   - *Select all files.* Click the Select All icon, also labeled in the figure.

5. **Click the Primary Destination tab to display options for handling the file transfer, as shown in Figure 9-13.**

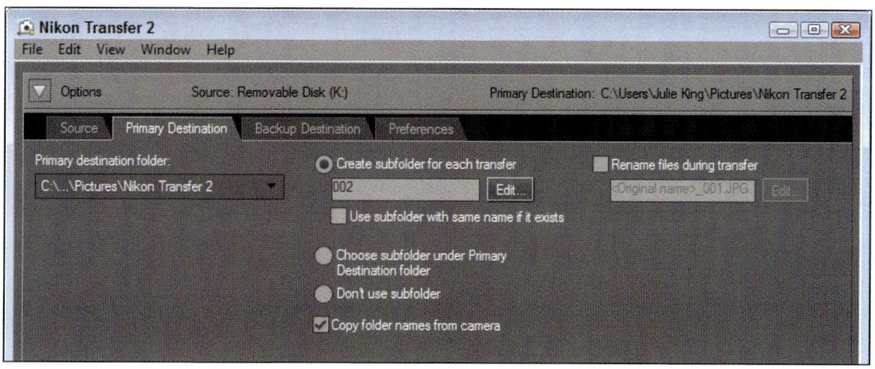

Figure 9-13: Specify the folder where you want to put the downloaded images.

Specify these options:

- *Primary Destination Folder:* Open this drop-down list and choose the folder on your computer's hard drive (or external drive) where you want to put the pictures.
- *Create Subfolder for Each Transfer:* By default, the program creates a new folder inside the storage folder you selected. Then it puts all the pictures from the current download session into that new subfolder. You can either use the numerical subfolder name that the program suggests or click the Edit button to set up your own naming system.
- *Use Subfolder with Same Name If It Exists:* If the folder shown in the Create Subfolder box already exists, select this check box to avoid overwriting existing photo files. The program automatically assigns new filenames to the downloaded photos if the folder contains images that have the same filenames as the downloading ones.
- *Choose Subfolder Under Primary Destination Folder:* If you don't want to create a new folder but put images into the existing subfolder under the primary folder, select this option. For example, if the primary folder is Pictures and the secondary folder is Nikon Transfer 2, your photos go into that Nikon Transfer 2 folder.
- *Don't Use Subfolder:* If you choose this option, pictures go into the primary folder (Pictures, in the example shown in Figure 9-13).
- *Copy Folder Names from Camera:* Select this option to retain the folder structure of the memory card. That folder is placed inside whatever folder or subfolder you select via the other options.

Yowza. Don't ever say that the program developers didn't want you to have plenty of storage folder flexibility.

6. **Tell the program whether you want to rename the picture files during the download process.**

   If you do, select the Rename Files during Transfer check box. Then click the Edit button to display a dialog box where you can set up your new file-naming scheme. Click OK after you do so to close the dialog box.

7. **(Optional) Set a backup destination.**

   TIP

   This feature enables you to download photos to your primary drive and to a backup drive at the same time. To set up the dual transfer, click the Backup Destination tab, select the Backup Files box, and then use the other panel options to specify where you want the files to go.

8. **Click the Preferences tab to set the rest of the transfer options.**

   On this tab, you find more options that control how the program operates. Rather than cover all of them, which are explained quite nicely in the program's Help system (access it via the Help menu), I want to highlight just three critical options:

   - *Transfer New Files Only:* This option, when selected, ensures that you don't waste time downloading images that you've already transferred but are still on the memory card.
   - *Delete Original Files after Transfer:* ***Turn off this option***. Otherwise, your pictures are automatically erased from your memory card when the transfer is complete. Always make sure the pictures really made it to the computer before you delete them from your memory card. (See Chapter 8 to find out how to use the Delete function on your camera.)
   - *Open Destination Folder with the Following Application after Transfer:* You can tell the program to immediately open your photo program after the transfer is complete. Choose ViewNX 2 to view, organize, and edit your photos using that program. To choose another program, open the drop-down list, choose Browse, and select the program from the dialog box that appears. Click OK after doing so.

   Your choices remain in force for any subsequent download sessions, so you don't have to revisit this tab unless you want the program to behave differently.

9. **Click the Start Transfer button.**

   It's located in the lower-right corner of the program window. After you click the button, the Process bar in the lower-left corner indicates how the transfer is progressing. What happens when the transfer completes depends on the choices you made in Step 8; if you selected Nikon ViewNX 2 as the photo program, it opens and displays the folder that contains your just-downloaded images.

Processing Raw (NEF) Files

Chapter 2 introduces you to the Raw file format. The advantage of capturing Raw files — NEF files on Nikon cameras — is that you make the decisions about how to translate the original picture data into an actual photograph. You take this step by using a software tool known as a *Raw converter.* To process your NEF files, you have the following free options:

- **Use the in-camera processing feature.** From the Retouch menu, you can process Raw images right in the camera. You can specify only limited image attributes, and you can save the processed files only in the JPEG format, but still, having this option is a nice feature.

- **Process and convert in ViewNX 2.** ViewNX 2 also offers a Raw processing feature. Again, the controls for setting picture characteristics are a little limited, but you can save the adjusted files in either the JPEG or TIFF format, and TIFF is better at holding onto the original image quality than JPEG.

  TIFF stands for Tagged Image File Format.

The next two sections show you how to convert Raw files using your camera and ViewNX 2. If you're a dedicated Raw shooter, however, you may want to invest in a program that offers a bit more control over Raw processing than these two options. One program to consider is Nikon's own pro-level software, Nikon Capture NX2 (`www.nikon.com`). Other popular programs include Adobe Photoshop, Adobe Lightroom, Adobe Photoshop Elements (`www.adobe.com`), and Apple Aperture (`www.apple.com`). Visit the respective websites for details about each program; in some cases, you can download a free 30-day trial to find out before you buy whether the program is to your liking.

Processing Raw images in the camera

By using the NEF (RAW) Processing option on the Retouch menu, you can create a JPEG version of a Raw file right in the camera. Follow these steps:

1. **Press the Playback button to switch to playback mode.**
2. **Display the picture in the full-frame view.**

   If necessary, you can shift from thumbnails view to single-image view by pressing OK. Press OK twice if you're in calendar view. (Chapter 8 has details on these playback modes.)

3. **Press the *i* button.**

   You see the screen shown on the left in Figure 9-14.

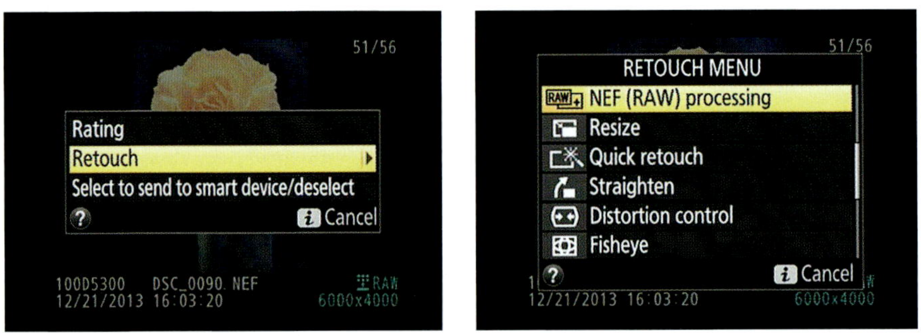

Figure 9-14: Select Retouch (left screen) and then scroll to the NEF (RAW) Processing option (right screen).

4. **Highlight Retouch and press the Multi Selector to right to display the Retouch menu.**
5. **Scroll to the NEF (RAW) Processing option (refer to the right side of Figure 9-14).**
6. **Press OK to display your processing options.**

   You see a screen similar to the one in Figure 9-15, which is where you specify which settings you want the camera to use when creating the JPEG version of the Raw image. If you press the Multi Selector down, you scroll to the second page of options, shown in Figure 9-16.

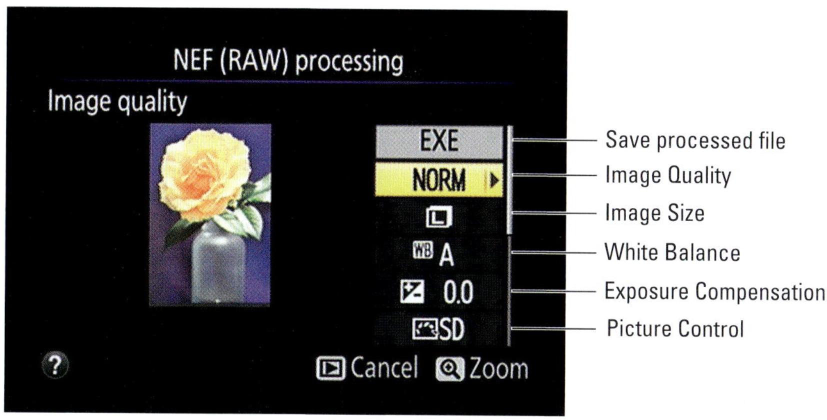

Figure 9-15: These Raw conversion options are on the first page of the menu screen.

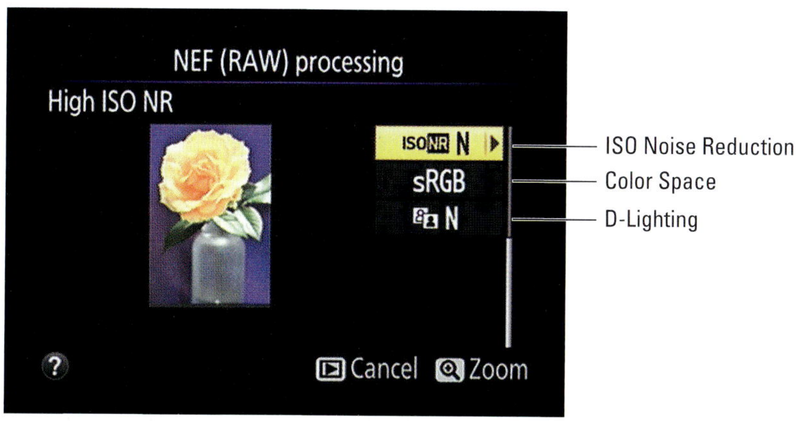

Figure 9-16: Press the Multi Selector down to scroll to the second page of conversion settings.

7. Set the conversion options.

Along the right side of the screen, you see a column offering the conversion options labeled in Figures 9-15 and 9-16. After highlighting an option, press the Multi Selector right to display available settings. After selecting a setting, press OK to return to the main Raw conversion screen. Or, if a triangle appears to the right of an option name, press the Multi Selector right to uncover additional options.

If you're not familiar with all the settings, the following list offers a few general recommendations and points you to the chapter where you can get more information:

- *Image Quality:* Choose Fine to retain maximum picture quality. See the Chapter 2 section related to the JPEG format for details on this option.
- *Image Size:* Chapter 2 explains this one, too. Choose Large to retain all the original image pixels.
- *White Balance:* Unless image colors appear to be wrong, stick with the default, Auto. Otherwise, experiment with each setting to see which one renders colors most accurately. Check out Chapter 5 for details about White Balance.
- *Exposure Compensation:* With this option, which I cover in Chapter 3, you can adjust image brightness. When using this feature for Raw conversion, you're limited to a range of –2.0 and +2.0; when shooting, you can choose from settings ranging from –5.0 to +5.0. Raise the value for a brighter image; lower it for a darker shot. The camera updates the preview to indicate how your setting will affect the picture.
- *Picture Control:* This option, detailed in Chapter 5, enables you to adjust color saturation, contrast, and image sharpness. As with the White Balance and Exposure Compensation settings, the screen updates to show you the effect of the selected Picture Control.
- *ISO Noise Reduction:* If your picture looks *noisy* — that is, marred by a speckled look — playing with this setting may help eliminate the flaw. See Chapter 3 for an explanation of this feature, which is designed to reduce the amount of noise in pictures shot using a high ISO Sensitivity setting.
- *Color Space:* This setting determines whether the camera sticks with the default color space, sRGB, or the larger Adobe RGB color space when converting your photo. Stick with sRGB until you digest the Chapter 5 section that details this option.
- *D-Lighting:* To brighten the darkest part of your picture without also brightening the lightest areas, try adjusting this setting. It's the post-capture equivalent of the Active D-Lighting feature that's available during shooting; see Chapter 3 for help with the option. To darken shadows, try setting the option to Off.

At any time, you can magnify the image by pressing the Zoom In button. Release the button to return to the normal display.

8. **After setting the conversion options, highlight EXE on the first conversion screen (refer to Figure 9-15) and press OK.**

   The camera records a JPEG copy of your Raw file and displays the copy in the monitor. The camera assigns the next available file number to the image, so the number of the original and the number of the processed JPEG don't match. The filename of the processed image begins with *CSC,* as do all photos that you create via the Retouch menu. You also see the little Retouch menu symbol (the box with a paintbrush) with the photo during playback.

TIP: You also can access the Raw processing tool by displaying the Retouch menu and then choosing NEF (RAW) Processing. The camera displays thumbnails of Raw images; use the Multi Selector to highlight an image and then press OK to get to the processing options.

Processing Raw files in ViewNX 2

In Nikon ViewNX 2, you can convert your Raw files to the JPEG format or, for top picture quality, to the TIFF format. Follow these steps to try it out:

1. **Open ViewNX 2 and click the thumbnail of the Raw file that you want to process.**

   TIP: You may want to set the program to Image Viewer mode, as shown in Figure 9-17, so that you can see a larger preview of the image. Just choose View⇨Image Viewer to switch to this display mode. To give the photo even more room, also hide the Browser panel, which normally occupies the left third of the window, and the Filmstrip panel that usually runs across the bottom of the window. Choose Window⇨Browser and Window⇨Filmstrip to toggle those window elements on and off.

2. **Display the Adjustments panel (refer to Figure 9-17).**

   Show and hide this panel and the Metadata panel by choosing Window⇨Edit or by clicking the triangle on the far right side of the window. You can then display and collapse the individual panels by clicking the triangles to the left of their names. (I labeled the triangles in the figure.) To allow the maximum space for the Raw conversion adjustments, collapse the Metadata panel, as shown in the figure.

3. **To display all available settings, choose All from the Adjustments drop-down list (refer to Figure 9-17).**

   You may need to use the scroll bar on the right side of the panel to scroll the display to see all the options.

4. **Use the panel controls to adjust the image.**

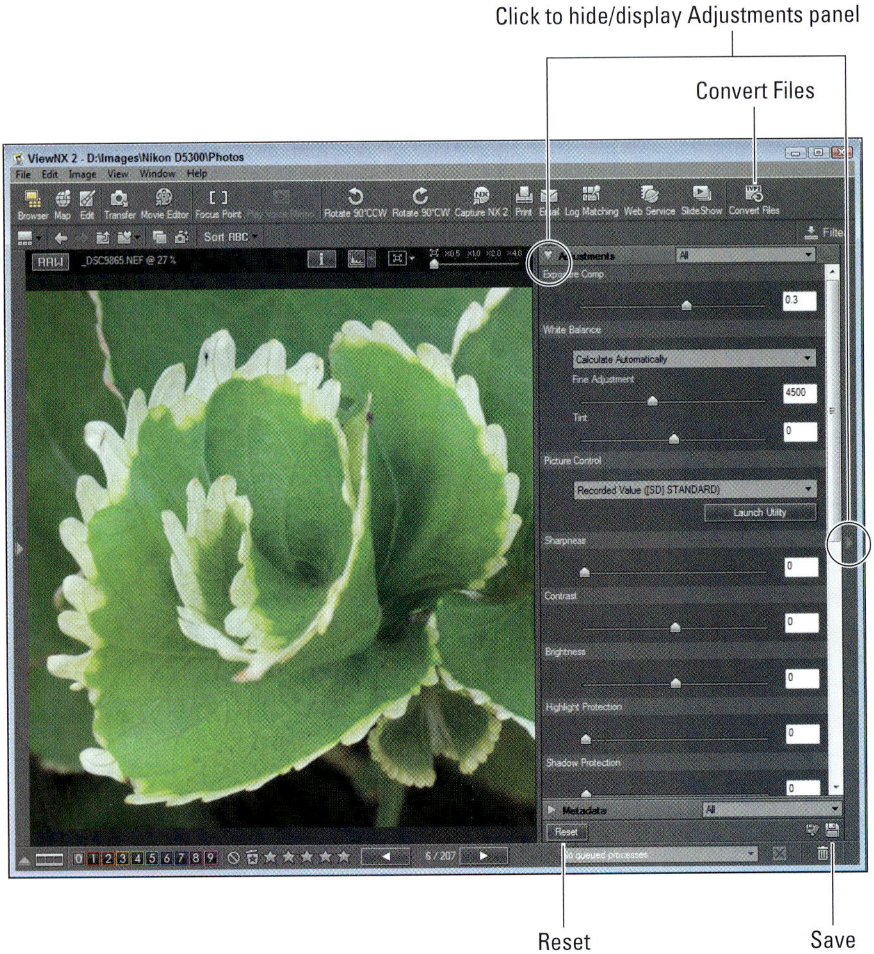

Figure 9-17: Display the Adjustments panel to tweak Raw images before conversion.

The preview in the image window reflects the default conversion settings chosen by Nikon, but you can play with any of the settings. If you need help understanding any of the options, open the built-in Help system (via the Help menu), where you can find descriptions of how each adjustment affects the image.

To return to the original image settings, click the Reset button at the bottom of the panel (refer to Figure 9-17).

5. **Click the Save button (refer to Figure 9-17).**

   This step stores your conversion settings as part of the image file but doesn't actually create the processed image file. Don't worry, though. Your original Raw data remains intact; all that's saved with the file is a "recipe" for processing the image, which you can change at any time.

6. **To save the processed file, choose File➪Convert Files.**

   You see the Convert Files dialog box, shown in Figure 9-18.

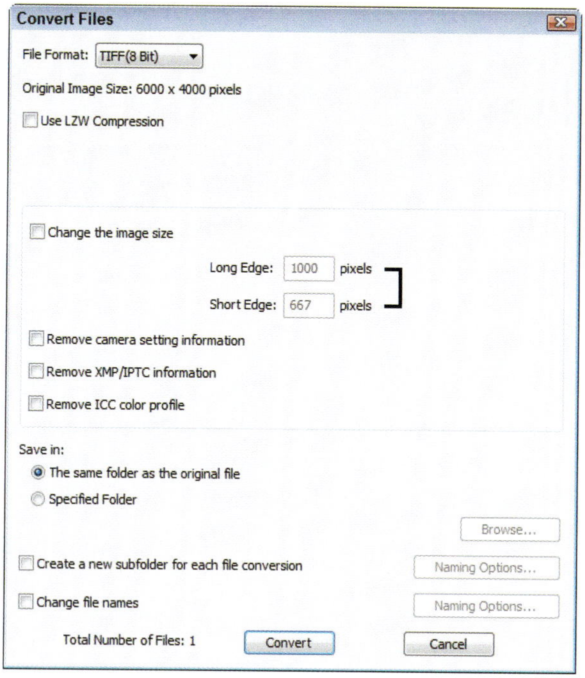

Figure 9-18: To retain the best image quality, save processed Raw files in the TIFF format.

7. **Choose TIFF (8 Bit) from the File Format drop-down list.**

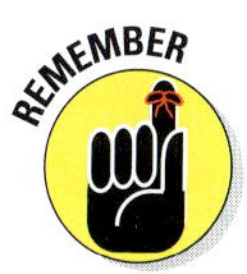

   TIFF is the best format because it retains your processed file at the highest image quality. (This format has long been the preferred format for print publication.) Don't choose JPEG; as explained in Chapter 2, the JPEG format applies *lossy compression,* thereby sacrificing some image quality. If you need a JPEG copy of your processed Raw image for online sharing — TIFF files won't work for that use — you can create one by following the steps laid out in the upcoming section "Prepping online photos using ViewNX 2."

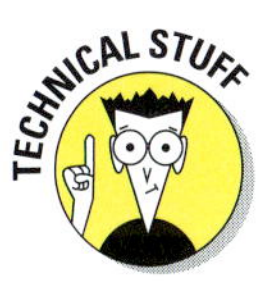

   As for the *8 Bit* part of the option name: A *bit* is a unit of computer data; the more bits you have, the more colors your image can contain. Although you can create 16-bit TIFF files in the converter, some photo-editing programs either can't open them or limit you to a few editing tools, so I suggest you stick with the standard, 8-bit image option unless you know your software can handle the larger-bit images.

8. **Deselect the Use LZW Compression option.**

   Although LZW compression reduces the file size somewhat and does not cause any quality loss, some programs can't open files that were saved with this option enabled, so turn it off.

9. **Deselect the Change the Image Size check box.**

   This step ensures that you retain all the original pixels in the processed image.

10. **Deselect each of the three Remove check boxes.**

    If you select the check boxes, you strip image *metadata* — the extra text data that's stored by the camera — from the file. Unless you have some specific reason to do so, clear all three check boxes so that you can continue to access the metadata when you view the processed image in programs that know how to display metadata.

11. **Select a storage location for the processed TIFF file.**

    You do this in the Save In area of the dialog box. Select the top option to save your processed file in the same folder as the original. Or, to put the file in a different folder, select the Specified Folder button. If you do, you see the name of the currently selected alternative folder below the button; change the storage destination by clicking the Browse button and then selecting the drive and folder where you want to put the file.

    TIP: By selecting the Create a New Subfolder for Each File Conversion check box, you can put your TIFF file into a separate folder within the destination folder. With this check box enabled, click the Naming Options button and then specify how you want to name the subfolder.

12. **Specify whether you want to give the processed TIFF a different filename from the original Raw image.**

    To do so, select the Change File Names check box, click the Naming Options button, and enter the name you want to use.

    If you don't change the filename, the program gives the file the same name as the original Raw file. However, you don't overwrite that Raw file because you're storing the copy in a different file format (TIFF). In Windows, the filename of the processed TIFF image has the three-letter extension TIF.

13. **Click the Convert button.**

    A window appears in order to show you the progress of the conversion process. When the window disappears, your TIFF image appears in the storage location you selected in Step 11.

TIP: One neat thing about working with Raw images is that you can easily create as many variations of the photo as you want. For example, you might choose one set of options when processing your Raw file the first time and then use an entirely different set to create another version of the photo. Just be sure to give each processed file a unique name so that you don't overwrite the first TIFF file you create with your second version.

Preparing Pictures for Online Sharing

Have you ever received an e-mail containing a photo so large that you can't view the whole thing on your monitor without scrolling the e-mail window? This annoyance occurs because monitors can display only a limited number of pixels. The exact number depends on the screen resolution setting, but suffice it to say that today's digital cameras produce photos with pixel counts in excess of what the monitor can handle.

Thankfully, newer e-mail programs incorporate features that automatically shrink the photo display to a viewable size. In Windows Live Mail, for example, photos arrive with a thumbnail link to a slide show viewer that can handle even gargantuan images. That doesn't change the fact that a large photo file means longer downloading times, though — and if recipients choose to hold onto the picture, a big storage hit on their hard drives.

Sending a high-resolution photo *is* the thing to do if you want the recipient to be able to generate a good print. However, it's polite practice to ask people if they *want* to print 11 x 14 glossies of your new puppy before you send them a dozen 24-megapixel (MP) shots.

For simple onscreen viewing, I suggest limiting your photos to fewer than 1,000 pixels on the longest side of the image. This strategy ensures that people who use an e-mail program that doesn't offer the latest photo-viewing tools can see the entire picture without scrolling the viewer window.

This size recommendation means that even if you shoot at your camera's lowest Image Size setting (2992 x 2000), you wind up with more pixels than you need for onscreen viewing. Some new e-mail programs have a photo-upload feature that creates a temporary low-res version for you, but if not, creating your own copy is easy. If you're posting to an online photo-sharing site, you may be able to upload all your original pixels, though many sites have resolution limits.

REMEMBER

In addition to resizing high-resolution images, check their file types; if the photos are in the Raw (NEF) or TIFF format, you need to create a JPEG copy for online use. Web browsers and e-mail programs can't display Raw or TIFF files.

You can tackle both bits of photo prep in ViewNX 2 or by using the Resize option in your camera. The next sections explain both methods.

Prepping online photos using ViewNX 2

For pictures already downloaded to the computer, you can create small-sized JPEG copies for online sharing using ViewNX 2. Just click the image thumbnail and then choose File➪Convert Files. When the Convert Files dialog box appears (see Figure 9-19), set up things as follows:

- **Select JPEG as the file format.** Make your selection from the File Format drop-down list.

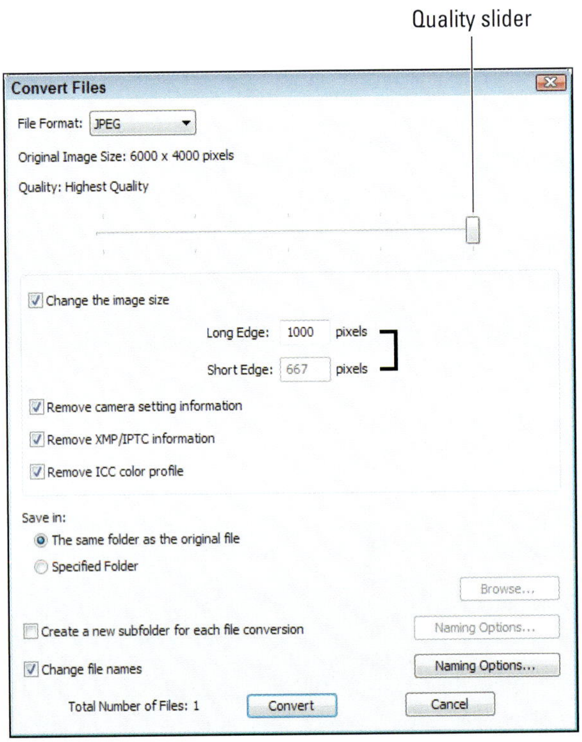

Figure 9-19: In ViewNX 2, select the Convert Files option to create a web-friendly version of a photo.

- **Set the picture-quality level.** Use the Quality slider (refer to Figure 9-19) to set the picture quality, which is controlled by how much JPEG compression is applied when the file is saved. For best quality, drag the slider all the way to the right, but remember the trade-off: As you raise the quality, less compression occurs, which results in a larger file size. (See Chapter 2 for more information about JPEG compression.)

- **Set the image size (number of pixels).** To resize the photo, select the Change the Image Size check box and then enter a value (in pixels) for the longest dimension of the photo. The program automatically fills in the other value.
- **Select all three Remove check boxes (refer to Figure 9-19).** Selecting these options removes unnecessary camera metadata, which reduces image file size.

The rest of the options work just as they do during Raw conversion; see "Processing Raw files in ViewNX 2," earlier in this chapter, for details.

WARNING!

If you're resizing a JPEG original, be sure to give the small version a new name to avoid overwriting that original.

Resizing pictures from the Retouch menu

TIP

The in-camera resizing tool, found on the Retouch menu, works on both JPEG and Raw images. With both types of files, your resized copy is saved in the JPEG format. You can get the job done in two ways:

- **Resize a single photo:** Set the camera to playback mode, display the photo in single image view (or select it in thumbnails or calendar view), and press the ***i*** button. On the screen that appears, select Retouch and press the Multi Selector right to display the Retouch menu, as shown on the left in Figure 9-20.

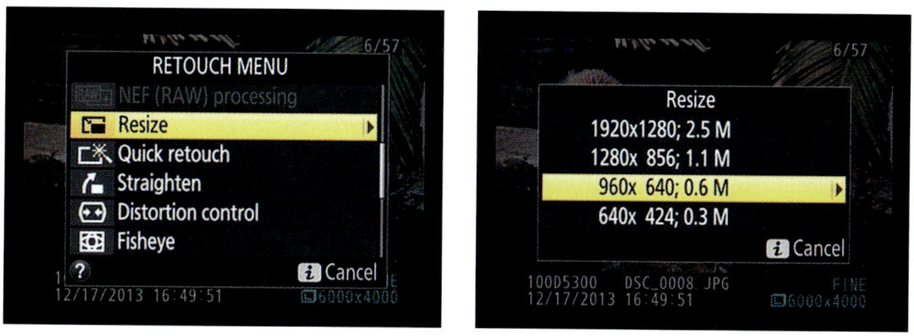

Figure 9-20: Use the Resize option to create a low-resolution version of a picture.

Select Resize and press the Multi Selector right to display possible image sizes (refer to the right side of Figure 9-20). The first value shows the pixel dimensions of the small copy; the second, the total number of pixels, measured in megapixels. Highlight a size and press the Multi Selector right. On the next screen, highlight Yes and press OK.

- **Resize a batch of photos:** Display the Retouch menu, choose Resize, and press OK to display the left screen in Figure 9-21. First, select Choose Size to set the pixel count of the small images. Then choose Select Image, as shown in the figure, to display thumbnails of your photos.

  Use the Multi Selector to move the yellow box over an image you want to resize, and then press the Zoom Out button to tag it with a resize icon (refer to the right side of Figure 9-21). Highlight the next photo, rinse, and repeat. After tagging all the photos, press OK to display the go-ahead screen; highlight Yes and press OK.

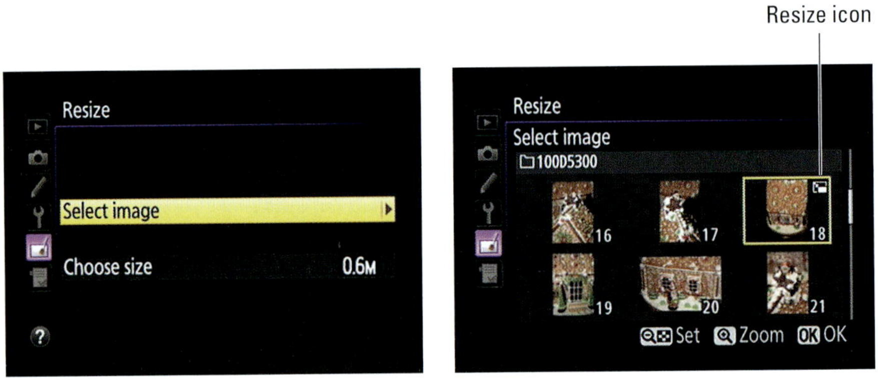

Figure 9-21: To resize a batch of photos, it's quicker to do the job via the Retouch menu.

In both cases, the camera duplicates the selected images and *downsamples* (eliminates pixels from) the copies to achieve the size you specified. The small copies are saved in the JPEG file format, using the same Image Quality setting (Fine, Normal, or Basic) as the original. Raw originals are saved as JPEG Fine images. Either way, your original picture files remain untouched.

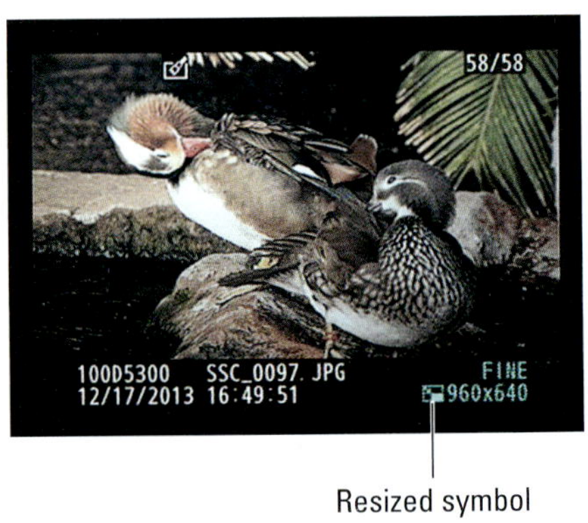

Figure 9-22: The Resize icon indicates a small-size copy.

Small-size copies appear during playback marked by a Resize symbol next to the file size (lower-right corner), as shown in Figure 9-22. The filename of the resized image begins with *SSC_* (or *_SSC,* if the original was captured using the Adobe RGB Color Space).

Taking Advantage of Wi-Fi Transfer

Your camera's Wi-Fi feature enables you to connect your camera wirelessly to certain "smart" devices: specifically, Android and Apple iOS-based phones, tablets, and media players (such as Apple's iPod touch).

Before you can enjoy this function, you must install the Nikon Mobile Wireless Utility app on your device. For Android-based devices, search for the app at the Google Play Store; for Apple iOS devices, head for the Apple App store. The application is free, but if you've never downloaded any apps, you have to register for an account and give a credit card number (required in case you ever want to download fee-based apps). Be sure to read the details on the download page to make sure that your device is running the required operating software to use the app.

After installing the app, you can perform the following functions:

- **Use the smart device to view photos that are on the camera memory card.** Depending on the size of your device, this enables you to get a little larger view of your photos than the camera's monitor offers.
- **Transfer photos from the memory card to the smart device.** You can then view the photos, upload them to Facebook or other social media sites, or attach them to e-mail or text messages via your device's normal wireless network or cell-based data connection.
- **Use the smart device to trigger the camera's shutter.** You see the live scene on your device screen, just as you see the scene on the camera monitor when you use Live View mode. Then you tap a button on your device to trigger the shutter release.

There are a few critical limitations to this feature:

- **Wi-Fi is for photos only.** You can't view, transfer, or shoot movies using your smart device.
- **You can't connect the camera to a computer via a standard wireless network.** The camera's Wi-Fi only works on a *peer-to-peer* basis: That is, the two devices must be able to talk to each other directly rather than over an intermediate network.
- **You can't adjust camera settings while the camera is connected to your device.** If you want to use your phone or tablet as a remote shutter trigger, you must select all picture settings *before* you connect the camera. If you need to change settings between shots, you have to uncouple the camera and the smart device, select the new settings, and then connect the two devices again. Boo.

- **The Wi-Fi feature is a battery hog.** The feature's insatiable appetite for battery juice is why Wi-Fi is disabled by default. The remote-shutter trigger function is also disabled automatically if the battery level on either the camera or the device drops below the level that the camera thinks it needs to perform its job. Long story short: If you routinely use the Wi-Fi functions, consider investing in a spare battery so that you don't run out of power during a shoot.

The next two sections provide a general overview of the Wi-Fi functions. Because the specific steps you take to use the app — and even the available app features — depend on your device, I can't provide full details on each function. However, if you head to the following Nikon web pages, you can download excellent, step-by-step instructions, complete with screen shots of where to tap to access the various app features:

- **Android:** `http://nikonimglib.com/ManDL/WMAU/index.html.en`
- **iOS:** `http://nikonimglib.com/ManDL/WMAU-ios/index.html.en`

Connecting the camera to your device

To connect your camera to your smart device, take these steps:

1. **Open the Setup menu, choose Wi-Fi, as shown on the left in Figure 9-23, and press the Multi Selector right to display the screen on the right in the figure.**

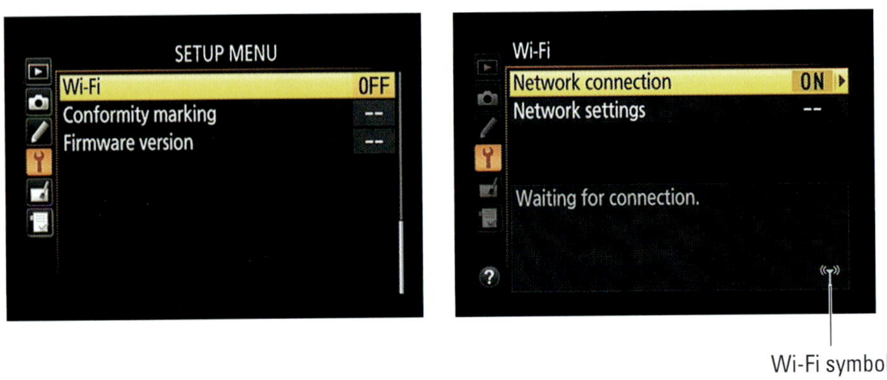

Figure 9-23: Enable Wi-Fi via the Setup menu.

2. **Select Network Connection, press the Multi Selector right, and choose Enable.**
3. **Press OK to return to the screen on the right in Figure 9-23.**
4. **Highlight Network Settings, as shown on the left in Figure 9-24, and press the Multi Selector right to display the screen shown on the right.**

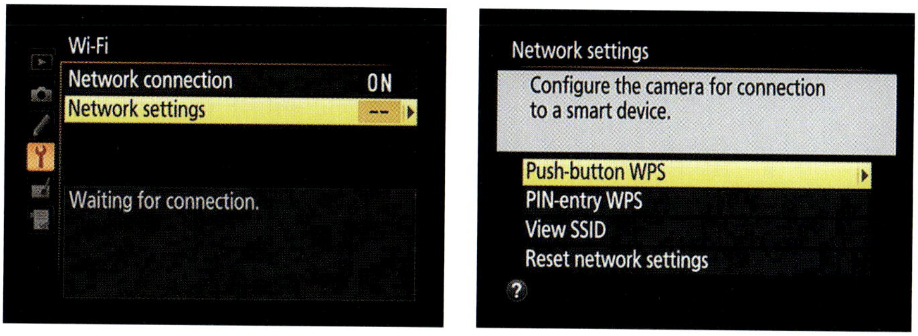

Figure 9-24: Here's the launch screen for configuring the camera to connect with your smart device.

5. **Select a connection option.**

   Which option you use depends on your device:

   - *Push-button WPS (Android only):* Some Android devices offer a WPS (Wi-Fi Protected Setup) feature that enables you to initiate a connection just by pushing a button. If your device has this feature, choose Push-button WPS from the screen shown on the right in Figure 9-24, and press the Multi Selector right. The camera displays a screen prompting you to press the WPS button on the device and begins searching for a connection. By default, the camera waits as long as two minutes to find the device; you can press OK to extend that timing.
   - *PIN-entry WPS (Android only):* If your device uses a PIN (personal identification number) for wireless security, select this option from the screen on the right in Figure 9-24 and press the Multi Selector right. On the next screen, enter the PIN and press OK to connect.
   - *View SSID (Android or iOS):* When you choose this option, you see the screen shown in Figure 9-25. Your camera is assigned an SSID number *(Service Set Identifier),* and, after a few moments, the SSID appears as an available network on your smart device. Select the camera's SSID on your device, and then choose the Connect option on the device.

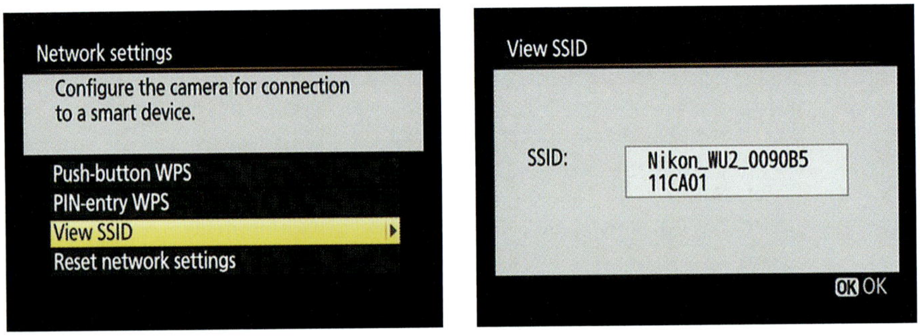

Figure 9-25: The SSID option works for both Android and iOS devices.

If the stars are in alignment and the devices connect, you see the confirmation screen shown in Figure 9-26. (It may take a few moments for the devices to shake hands. While the connection search is in progress, the Wi-Fi symbol labeled in Figure 9-26 blinks.) The same icon appears in the Information display and Live View display while Wi-Fi is enabled.

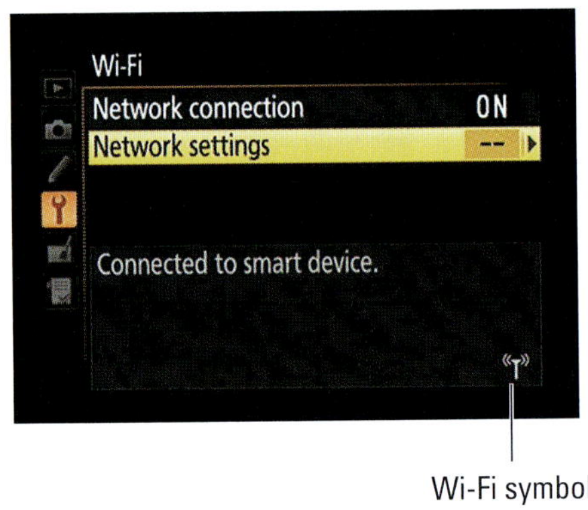

Figure 9-26: This message tells you that your devices are connected.

6. **Launch the Nikon Wireless Mobile Utility app on your device.**

   The initial app screen offers two main options: Take Photos and View Photos, as shown in Figure 9-27. (This figure and others to follow show how the app screens appear on my Android tablet; the design varies depending on your device and its operating system.) Somewhere on the screen, you should also see an icon that lets you access other app settings; usually, the icon looks like a little wheel. Again, for details, download and review the app user guide from the web addresses given in the preceding section.

7. **To sever the connection and turn off Wi-Fi, set the Wi-Fi option on the Setup menu to Off.**

Viewing photos on the smart device

After connecting your camera with the device and firing up the WMU app, tap View Photos on the smart device. You see a screen similar to the one shown on the left in Figure 9-28. Tap the option labeled Pictures on Camera. After a few seconds, thumbnails of your images appear, as shown on the right in the figure, and you can view your pictures using the same techniques you use to view photos that you take with your smart device. For example, you usually tap a thumbnail to display it in full-screen view and then swipe across the screen from left to right to view the next image.

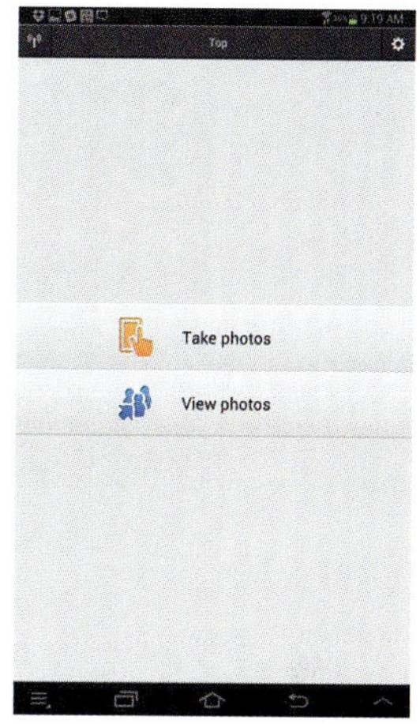

Figure 9-27: The initial app screen gives you the option to view or shoot photos.

Transferring photos to the device

While you're viewing your photos on the device, you can use options built into the WMU app to tag photos for transfer to the device. You can also set the size of the file you want to download. But an easier option is to use a camera feature that enables you to tag all photos you want to transfer. To try it out, open the Playback menu and choose Select to Send to Smart Device, as shown in Figure 9-29, and press OK. You see thumbnails of your images, as shown on the right in the figure.

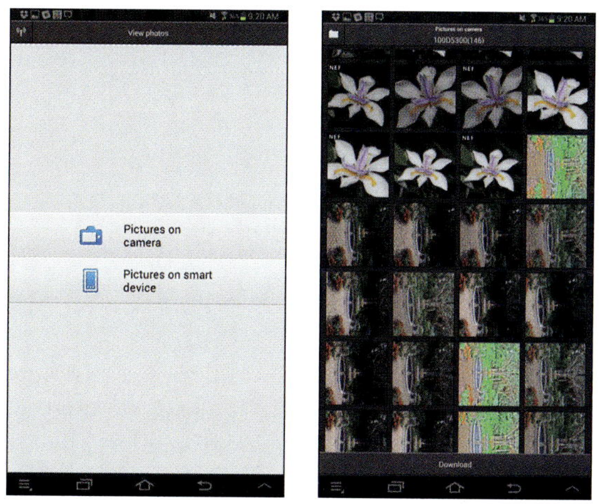

Figure 9-28: You can display thumbnails of photos stored on the camera's memory card.

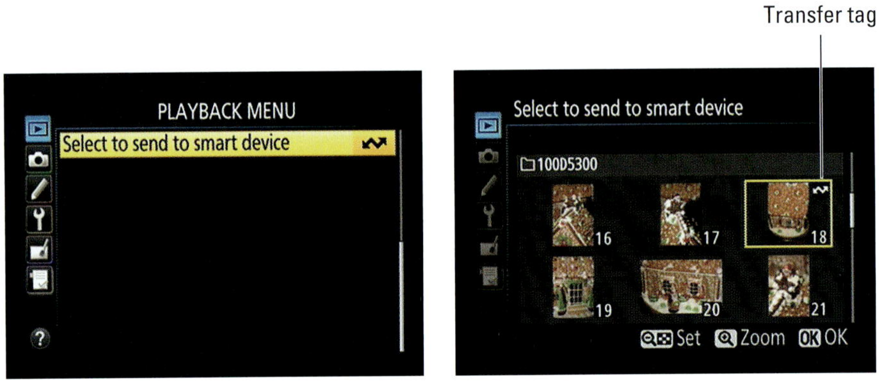

Figure 9-29: Use this menu option to tag a batch of files for transfer to your smart device.

To tag a photo for transfer, press the Zoom Out button. You then see a symbol like the one shown on the right in the figure. Press OK after choosing all your photos. Now when you select the option on the smart device that transfers photos, your tagged files are automatically downloaded.

During playback mode, you can tag an individual photo for transfer by pressing the ***i*** button, which displays the mini-menu shown in Figure 9-30. Select the Select to Send to Smart Device/Deselect option, as shown in the figure, to add the tag. (Choosing the option once adds the transfer tag; choosing it again removes the tag.)

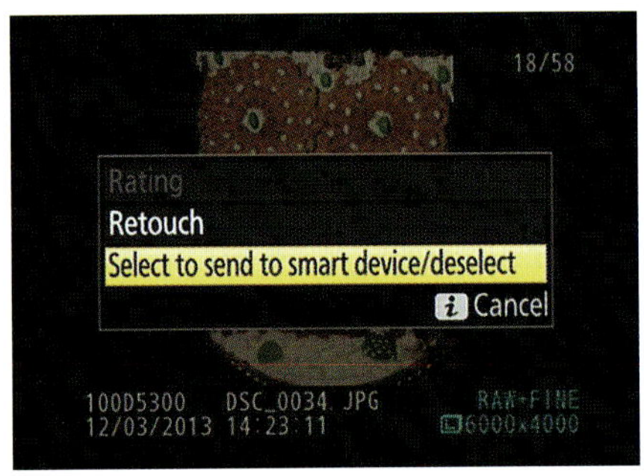

Figure 9-30: During playback, press the ***i*** button and then choose this option to tag a photo for wireless transfer.

If you shot the picture in the Raw (NEF) format, it is automatically converted to the JPEG format during the transfer process so that it's ready for online sharing.

Taking pictures via the smart device

To use your smart device as a remote shutter release, connect the devices, launch the WMU app, and then tap the Take Photos button (refer to Figure 9-27). The camera automatically shifts to Live View mode, and the live preview appears on the smart device screen, along with some shooting data, such as the shutter speed and f-stop, as shown in Figure 9-31. A focus box appears on the preview; tap your subject to place the focus box over it and set focus. (The exact focusing procedure depends on the current Live View autofocusing settings; Chapter 4 has details.) The focus box turns green when focus is achieved.

Make sure that the option at the top of the screen is set to the icon that shows a finger on the tablet; this tells the app that you want to use the tablet to trigger the shutter. Then tap the camera icon at the bottom of the screen to trigger the shutter release. (Again, the figure shows the screen as it appears on my Android tablet; the specific design may vary if you use a different device or operating system.)

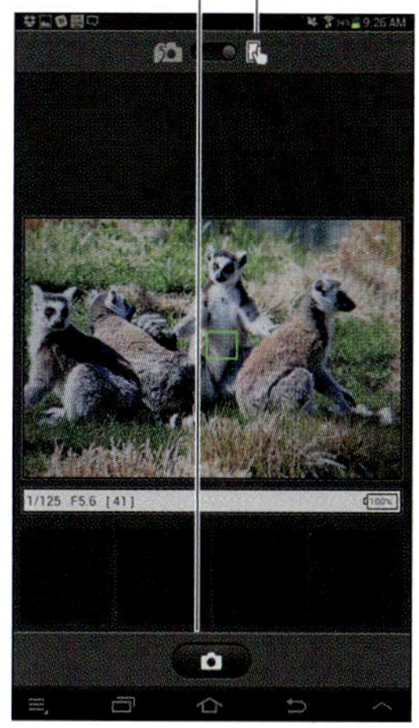

Figure 9-31: The Live View preview appears on the device screen; tap the camera icon to trigger the shutter.

Through the app options, you can specify whether you want the picture to be automatically downloaded after it's captured. You also can delay the shutter release by enabling the app's self-timer option.

Again, you must set all picture options *before* connecting the camera to the device; you can't change settings after the two devices are paired. Neither can you record movies this way; this function is for still photos only.

Exploring two special printing options

The camera offers two features that enable you to print directly from the camera or memory card:

- **DPOF (Digital Print Order Format):** With this option, accessed via the DPOF Print Order option on the Playback menu, you select pictures from the memory card to print and then specify how many copies you want of each image. Then, if your photo printer has a memory-card slot that's compatible with your camera's cards and supports DPOF, you simply pop the memory card into that slot. The printer reads the "print order" and outputs only the requested copies of the selected images. You use the printer's own controls to set paper size, print orientation, and other print settings.
- **PictBridge:** If you have a PictBridge-enabled photo printer, you can connect the camera to the printer by using a USB cable. The PictBridge interface appears on the camera monitor, and you use the camera controls to select the pictures you want to print. Using PictBridge, you specify additional print options from the camera, such as page size and whether to print a border around the photo.

For more information about both printing options, see the electronic version of the camera manual, provided on one of the CDs in the camera box.

Part IV
The Part of Tens

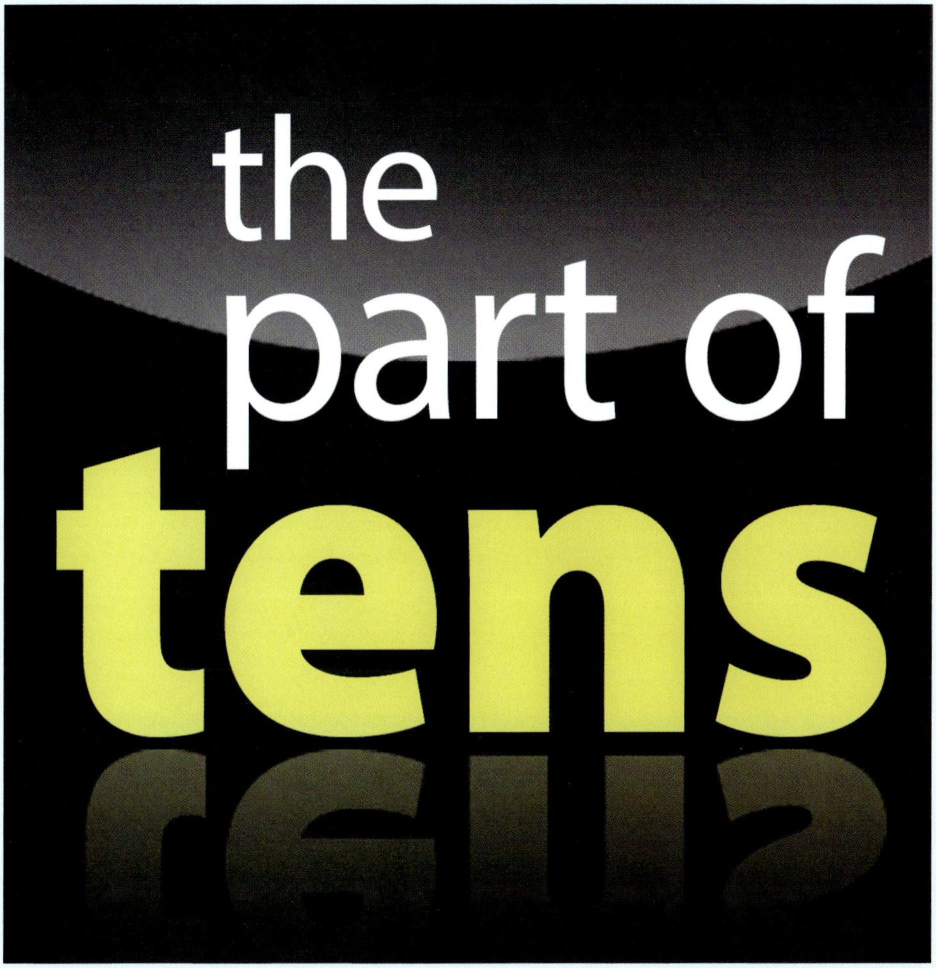

Enjoy an additional Part of Tens article about ten cool digital photography websites at www.dummies.com/extras/nikon.

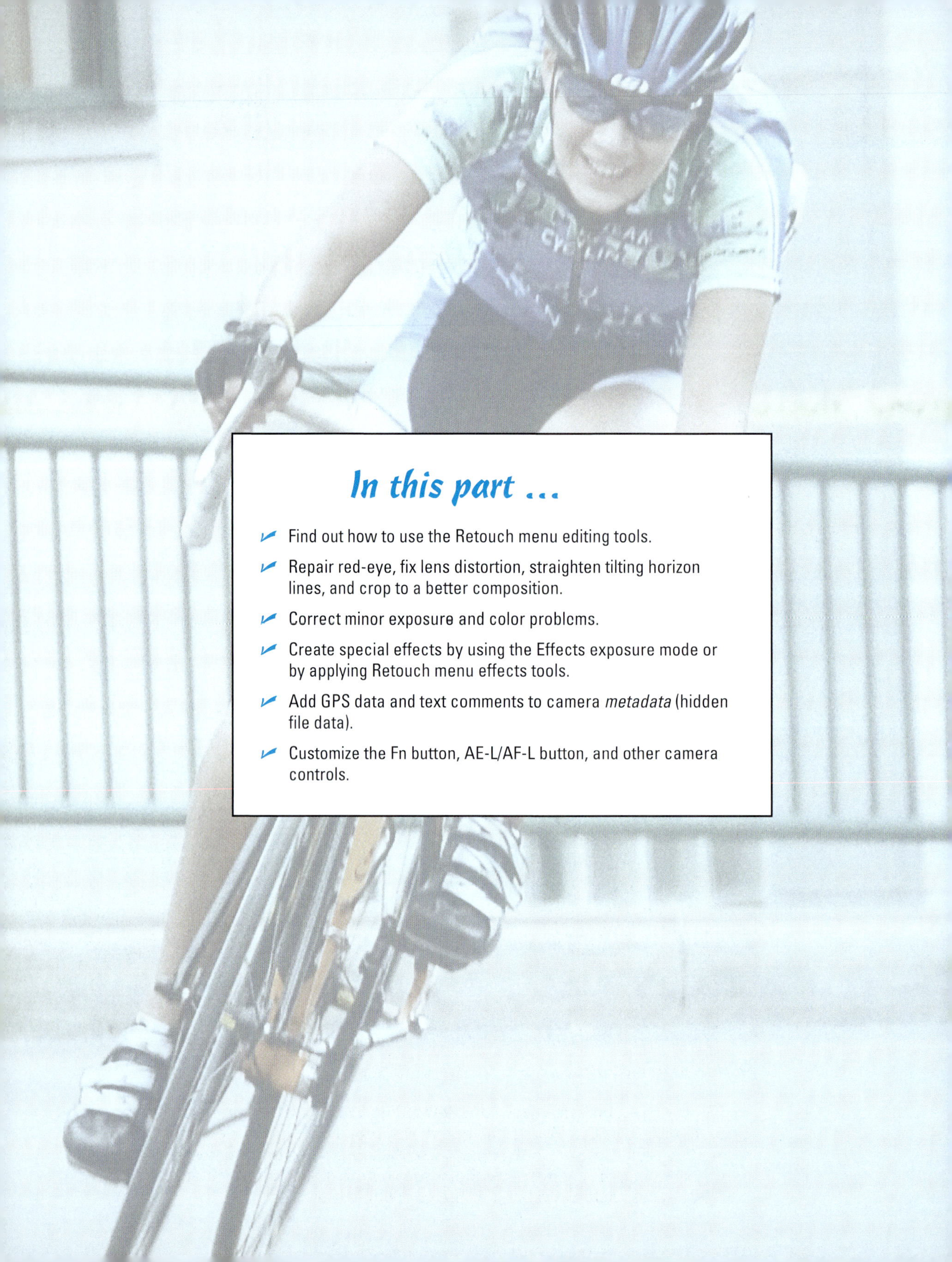

In this part ...

- Find out how to use the Retouch menu editing tools.
- Repair red-eye, fix lens distortion, straighten tilting horizon lines, and crop to a better composition.
- Correct minor exposure and color problems.
- Create special effects by using the Effects exposure mode or by applying Retouch menu effects tools.
- Add GPS data and text comments to camera *metadata* (hidden file data).
- Customize the Fn button, AE-L/AF-L button, and other camera controls.

10

Ten Fun (And Practical) Ways to Manipulate Your Photos

In This Chapter

- Applying Retouch menu filters
- Removing red-eye
- Correcting crooked horizon lines, lens distortion, and perspective
- Tweaking exposure, contrast, and color
- Cropping away excess background
- Creating a black-and-white version of a photo
- Having fun with special effects

Every photographer produces a clunker now and then. When it happens to you, don't be too quick to press the Delete button, because many common problems are surprisingly easy to fix. In fact, you often can repair your photos right in the camera, thanks to tools found on the Retouch menu.

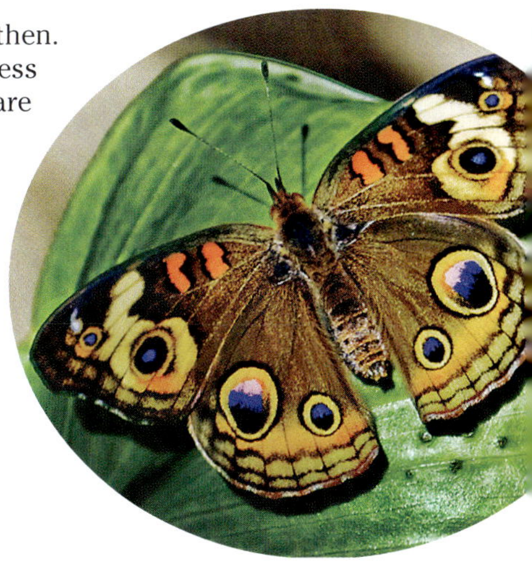

This chapter starts with the basics of navigating the Retouch menu and then provides specific instructions for using its photo-repair tools. Following that, I clue you in on a few special-effects tricks, including shooting in Effects mode.

Applying the Retouch Menu Filters

You can get to most Retouch menu features in two ways:

- **Display the menu, shown on the left in Figure 10-1, select a retouching tool, and press OK.** You're presented with thumbnails of your photos, as shown on the right in the figure. Use the Multi Selector to move the yellow highlight box over the photo you want to adjust, and then press OK to access settings related to the retouching tool.

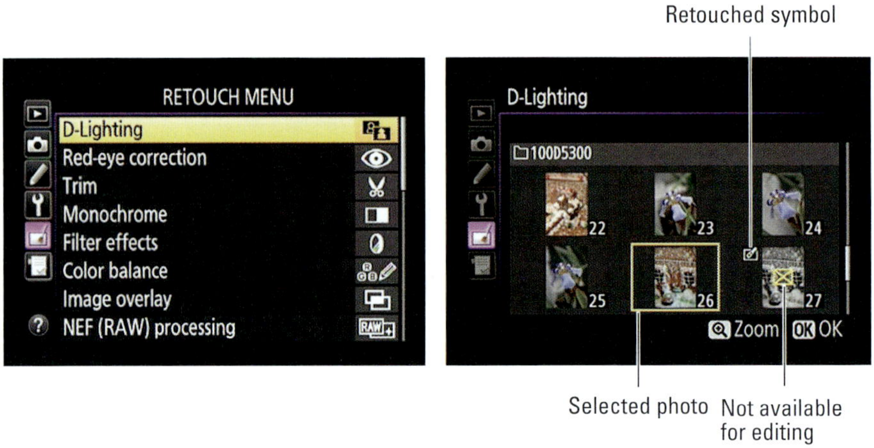

Figure 10-1: After selecting a Retouch menu option (left), press OK and highlight the photo you want to edit (right).

If a photo can't be altered, an X appears over the thumbnail, as in the lower-right corner in the figure. Normally, you get the no-go signal because you already applied a certain Retouch menu option to a picture. For example, you can't edit a photo after you crop it using the Trim tool.

- **Switch the camera to playback mode, display your photo in single-frame view, and press the *i* button.** The screen shown on the left in Figure 10-2 appears. Highlight Retouch and press the Multi Selector right to display the Retouch menu superimposed over your photo, as shown on the right. Select a tool and press OK to display options related to that tool.

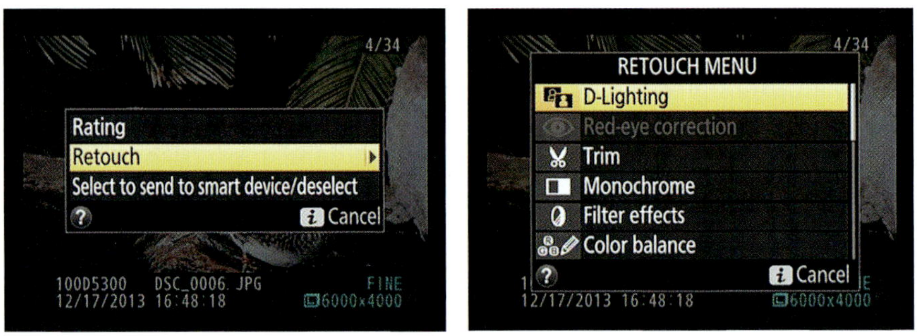

Figure 10-2: In single-frame playback view, press the *i* button to access the Retouch menu.

I prefer the second method, so that's how I approach things in this chapter, but it's entirely a personal choice. However, you can't use the ***i*** button method to access the Image Overlay menu item. That feature, which combines two Raw (NEF) photos to create a third, blended image, is available only when you display the Retouch menu by pressing the Menu button. (The last section in this chapter explains the Image Overlay feature.)

A few other facts to note:

TIP

- **Your originals remain intact.** When you apply a Retouch menu tool, the camera creates a copy of your original photo and makes the changes to the copy. A retouch symbol appears near the image thumbnails to tell you that you're looking at an altered photo (refer to Figure 10-1).
- **All Retouch menu tools work with either JPEG or Raw (NEF) originals except Image Overlay and NEF (Raw) Processing.** Those two tools work only with Raw files. See the Chapter 2 discussion about the Image Quality setting for an explanation of JPEG and Raw (NEF).
- **Retouched copies for all alterations except Image Overlay are saved in the JPEG file format.** The retouched copy uses the same JPEG quality setting as the original (Fine, Normal, or Basic). Retouched copies of Raw originals are saved in the JPEG Fine format. For Image Overlay, the retouched image is stored using the current Image Quality and Image Size settings. (Chapter 2 discusses the Image Size setting also.)
- **You can apply each correction to a picture only once.** The exception, again, is Image Overlay. If you save the composite in the Raw format, you can combine the composite with a third Raw image. In fact, you can keep combining photos until your memory card is full, if the urge hits you.
- **The camera automatically assigns the next available file number to the retouched image.** Make note of the filename of the retouched version so that you can easily track it down later. ***Hint:*** Filenames of pictures that you create via the Retouch menu start with the letters *CSC,* with one exception: Filenames of pictures that you downsized using the Resize option begin with the letters *SSC.* (If the Color Space option on the Shooting menu was set to Adobe RGB, as discussed in Chapter 5, a filename begins with an underscore followed by the three-letter code.)
- **When applying certain filters, you can press the Zoom In button to see a magnified view of the adjusted photo.** If so, you see the word *Zoom* along with a symbol that looks like the button at the bottom of the screen. (You can get a glimpse of this symbol in Figure 10-3.) Release the button to return to the two-thumbnail display.

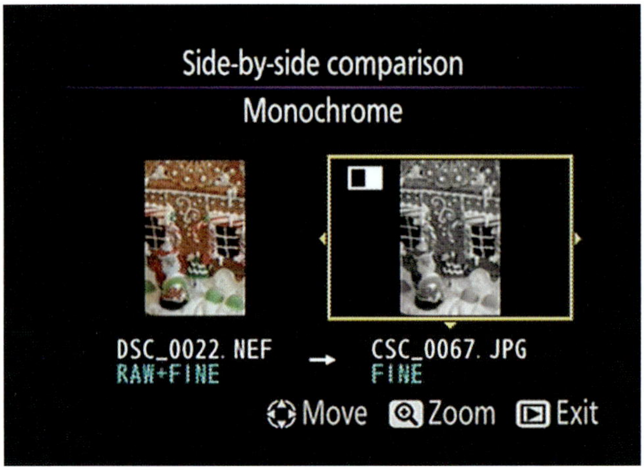

Figure 10-3: Use Side-by-Side Comparison to see whether you prefer the retouched version to the original.

- **You can compare the original and the retouched version by using the Side-by-Side Comparison menu option.** Start by displaying either the original or the retouched version in full-frame playback. Then press the ***i*** button, choose Retouch, select Side-by-Side Comparison, and press OK. You see the original image on one side and the retouched version on the other (refer to Figure 10-3). At the top of the screen, a label indicates the Retouch tool that you applied to the photo.

  These tricks work in Side-by-Side Comparison display:

  - If you applied more than one Retouch tool to the picture, press the Multi Selector right and left to display thumbnails that show how each tool affected the picture.
  - If you create multiple retouched versions of the same original — for example, you create a monochrome version, save it, and then crop the original image and save that — use a different technique to compare the versions. First, press the Multi Selector right or left to surround the After image with the yellow highlight box. Now press the Multi Selector up and down to scroll through the retouched versions.
  - To temporarily view the original or retouched image at full-frame size, use the Multi Selector to highlight its thumbnail and then press the Zoom In button. Release the button to return to Side-by-Side Comparison view.

  To exit Side-by-Side Comparison view, press the Playback button. The retouched photo appears on the screen.

If you want to view the original image in full-screen playback instead of the retouched version, use the Multi Selector to highlight the original while the Side-by-Side Comparison screen is active. Then press OK instead of the Playback button.

Removing Red-Eye

For portraits marred by red-eye, give the Red-Eye Correction filter a whirl, as shown in Figure 10-4. If the camera detects red-eye, it applies the filter and displays the results on the screen.

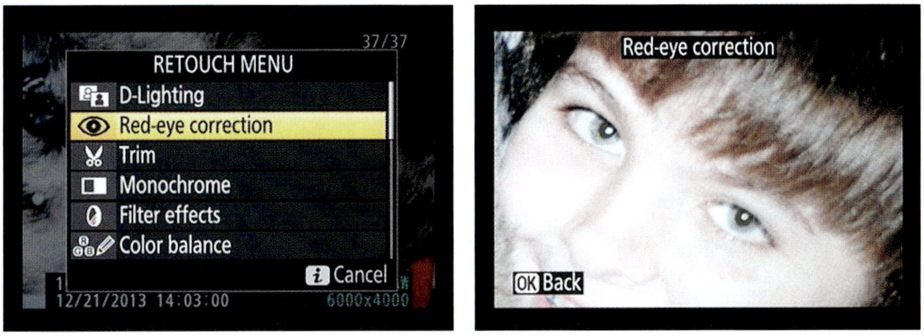

Figure 10-4: The Retouch menu offers an automated red-eye remover.

Press the Zoom In button to magnify the display, as shown in the figure, so that you can closely inspect the repair. Press OK twice if you're cool with the job the camera performed: The first press returns the display to normal magnification; the second makes the change official. To instead cancel the repair, press the Playback button.

Note that the filter can correct only red-eye; it can't fix animal eyes that a flash has turned white, yellow, or green.

Straightening Tilting Horizon Lines

I have a knack for shooting with the camera misaligned with respect to the horizon, which means that photos like the one on the left in Figure 10-5 often wind up crooked. Luckily for me, the Retouch menu offers a Straighten tool that can rotate tilting horizons back to the proper angle, as shown on the right.

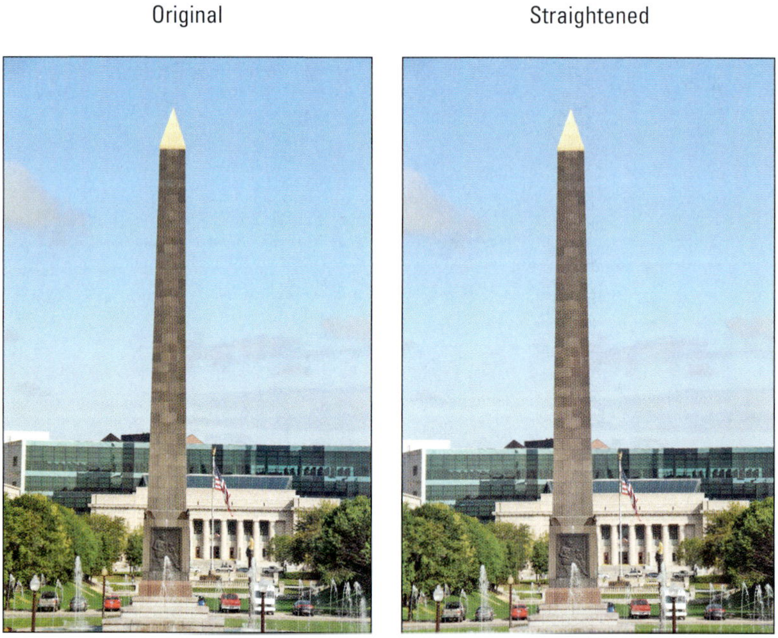

Figure 10-5: You can level crooked photos with the Straighten tool.

After you choose the filter from the Retouch menu, you see a screen similar to the one in Figure 10-6, with a grid superimposed on your photo to serve as an alignment aid. Press the Multi Selector right to rotate the picture clockwise; press left to rotate counterclockwise. Each press spins the picture by about 0.25 degrees. You can achieve a maximum rotation of 5 degrees. Press OK to create the straightened copy.

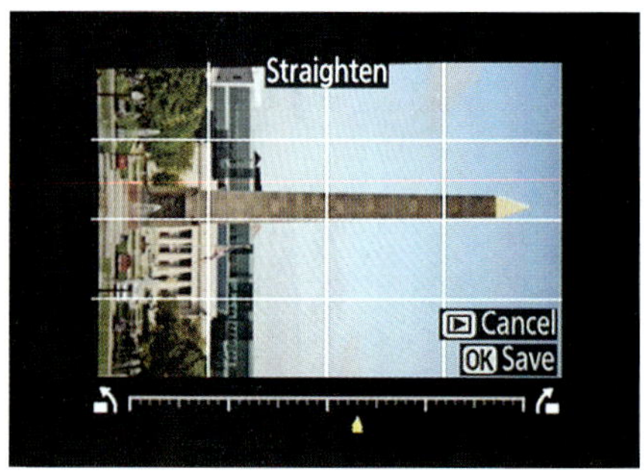

Figure 10-6: Press the Multi Selector right or left to rotate the image in increments of 0.25 degrees.

To achieve this rotation magic, the camera must crop your image and enlarge the remaining area — that's why the After photo in Figure 10-5 contains slightly less subject matter than the original. (The same cropping occurs if you make this kind of change in a photo editor.) The camera updates the display as you rotate the photo so that you can get an idea of how much of the original scene may be lost.

Removing (Or Creating) Lens Distortion

Certain lenses can produce a type of distortion that causes straight lines to appear curved. Wide-angle lenses, for example, often create *barrel distortion,* in which objects at the center of a picture appear to be magnified and pushed forward — as if you wrapped the photo around the outside of a barrel. The effect is easy to spot in a rectangular subject like the oil painting in Figure 10-7. Notice that in the original image, on the left, the edges of the painting bow slightly outward. *Pincushion distortion* affects the photo in the opposite way, making center objects appear smaller and farther away.

Slight barrel distortion After Distortion Correction filter

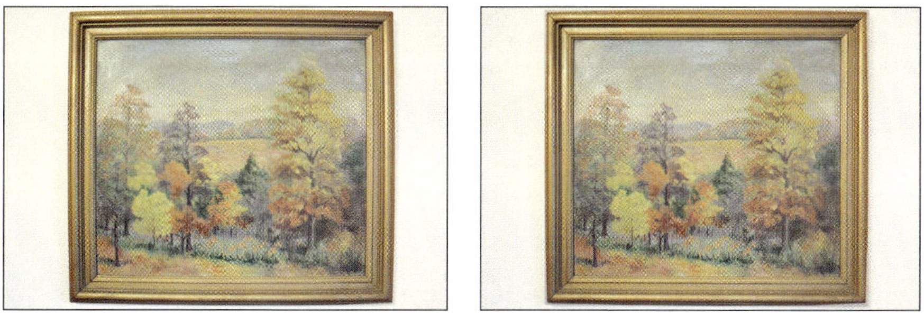

Figure 10-7: Barrel distortion makes straight lines appear to bow outward.

If you notice either type of distortion, try enabling the Auto Distortion Control option on the Shooting menu. This feature attempts to correct distortion as you take the picture. Or you may prefer to wait until after reviewing your photos and then use the Distortion Control tool on the Retouch menu to try to fix things, as I did for the second image in Figure 10-7. Less helpful, in my opinion, is a related Retouch menu filter, Fisheye, that creates distortion to replicate the look of a photo taken with a fisheye lens.

REMEMBER

With either filter, you lose part of the original image area as a result of the distortion correction, just as you do with the Straighten tool. So if you're shooting a photo that you think may benefit from these filters, frame your subject a little loosely.

Here's how the Retouch menu filters work:

- **Distortion Control:** After selecting the filter, as shown on the left in Figure 10-8, press the Multi Selector right to see the second screen in the figure. An Auto option is available for some lenses, as long as you didn't apply the Auto Distortion Control feature when taking the picture. As its name implies, the Auto option attempts to automatically apply the correct degree of correction. If the Auto option is dimmed or you prefer to do the correction on your own, choose Manual and press OK to display the screen shown in Figure 10-9. The scale represents the degree and direction of shift that you're applying. Press the Multi Selector right to reduce barrel distortion; press left to reduce pincushioning. Press OK to make your corrected copy of the photo.

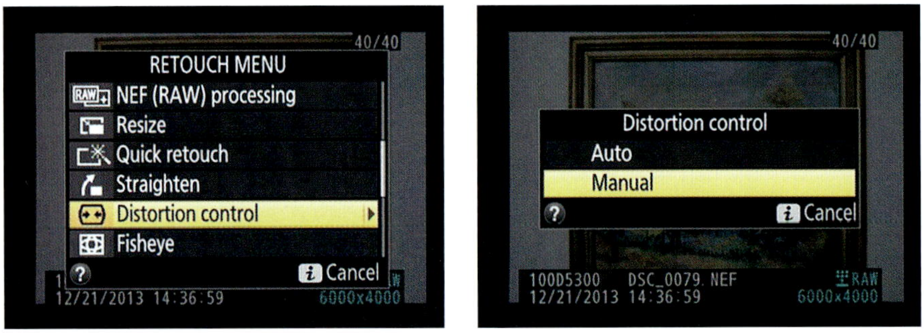

Figure 10-8: The Distortion Control filter can reduce barrel distortion.

- **Fisheye:** Select the filter and press OK to display a screen similar to the one in Figure 10-9, but with the word *Fisheye* at the top. Press the Multi Selector right or left to set the distortion amount and then press OK.

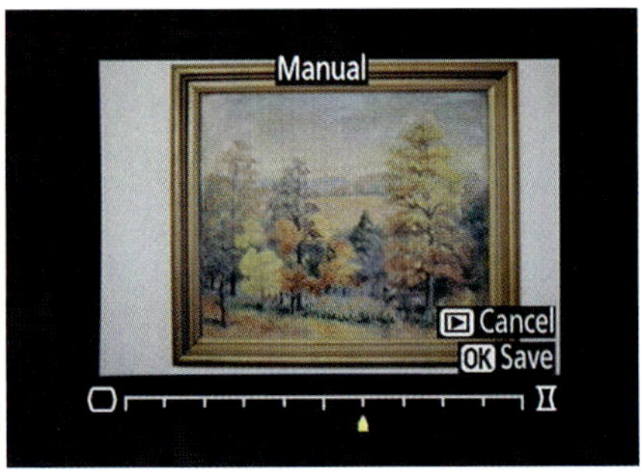

Figure 10-9: Press the Multi Selector right or left to adjust the correction.

Correcting Perspective

When you photograph a tall building and tilt the camera upward to fit it all into the frame, an effect that's referred to as *convergence* or *keystoning* occurs. This effect causes vertical structures to tilt toward the center of the frame. Buildings sometimes even appear to be falling away from you, as shown in the left image in Figure 10-10. (If the lens is tilting down, vertical structures instead lean outward, and the building appears to be falling toward you.) Using the Retouch menu's Perspective Control feature, you can right those tilting vertical elements, as I did to produce the right image in Figure 10-10.

Original After perspective correction

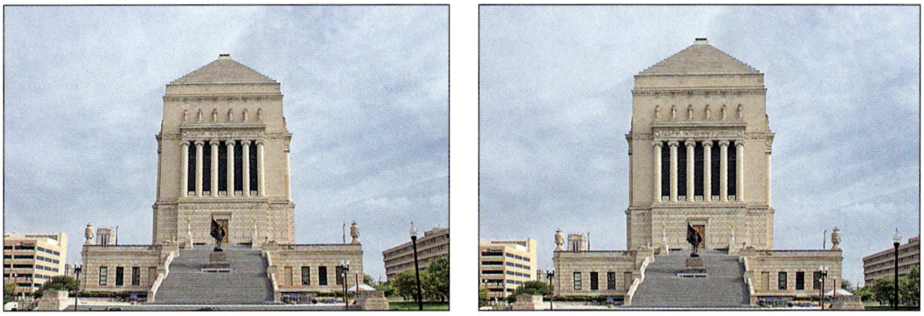

Figure 10-10: The original photo exhibited convergence (left); applying the Perspective Control filter corrected the problem (right).

Note, though, that as with the Straighten, Distortion Correction, and Fisheye tools, the Perspective tool results in some loss of area around the perimeter of your photo. So again, when shooting this type of subject, frame loosely — that way, you ensure that you don't sacrifice an important part of the scene due to the correction.

After you select the filter, you see a grid and horizontal and vertical scale, as shown in Figure 10-11. Press the Multi Selector left and right to move the out-of-whack object horizontally; press up and down to rotate the object toward or away from you. When you're happy with the results, press OK.

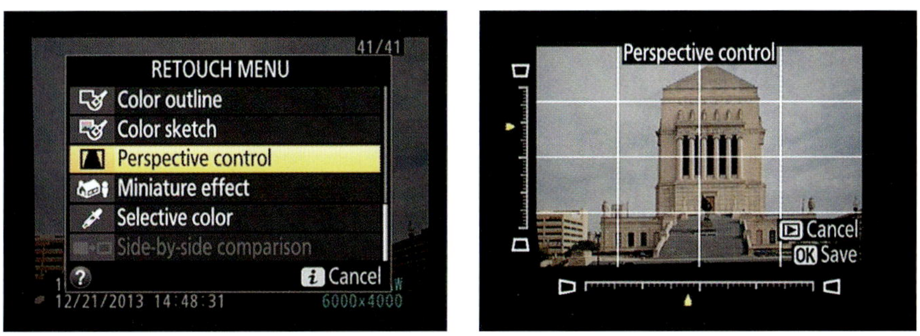

Figure 10-11: Again, use the Multi Selector to manipulate the image.

Manipulating Exposure and Color

You also have access to these Retouch filters that adjust exposure and color:

- **D-Lighting:** Chapter 3 explains Active D-Lighting, which brightens too-dark shadows in a way that leaves highlight details intact. You can apply a similar adjustment to an existing photo by choosing the D-Lighting filter from the Retouch menu. I used the filter on the photo in Figure 10-12, where strong backlighting left the balloon underexposed in the original image.

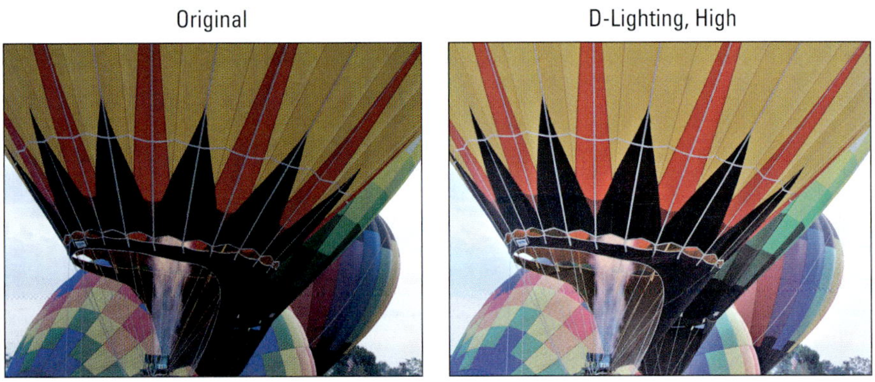

Figure 10-12: An underexposed photo (left) gets help from the D-Lighting filter (right).

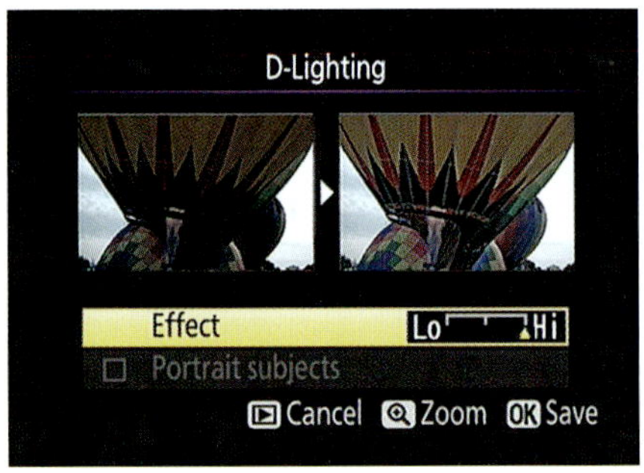

Figure 10-13: Press the Multi Selector right or left to vary the strength of the correction.

When you choose this filter, you see before-and-after views of the image, as shown in Figure 10-13. Press the Multi Selector left or right to adjust the Effect option, which sets the strength of the adjustment.

Also note the Portrait Subjects option, which is underneath the Effect option and dimmed in the figure. If the camera recognizes faces in the photo, you can select this option to limit the exposure adjustment to areas around the face (or faces). However, only three faces (maximum) are considered for this special exposure change. Also, you must have captured the photo with the Auto Image Rotation option on the Setup menu enabled. To see how things look with the portrait feature, highlight the option and then press the Multi Selector right to put a check mark in the option box. Don't like the results? Press left to remove the check mark and turn off the portrait adjustment.

WARNING!

You can't apply D-Lighting to a picture taken using the Monochrome Picture Control, introduced in Chapter 5. Nor does D-Lighting work on pictures to which you've applied the Quick Retouch filter, covered next, or the Monochrome filter, detailed a little later in this list.

- **Quick Retouch:** This filter increases contrast and color saturation and, if your subject is backlit, also applies a D-Lighting adjustment to restore some shadow detail that otherwise might be lost. As with D-Lighting, you can choose from three levels of Quick Retouch correction. And the same restrictions apply: You can't apply the filter to monochrome images or on pictures that you adjusted via D-Lighting.
- **Filter Effects:** Shown in Figure 10-14, the Filter Effects option offers filters that are designed to mimic the results produced by traditional lens filters. The first five are color-manipulation filters. The other two, Cross Screen and Soft (not shown in the figure), are special-effects filters; you can read about both later in this chapter.

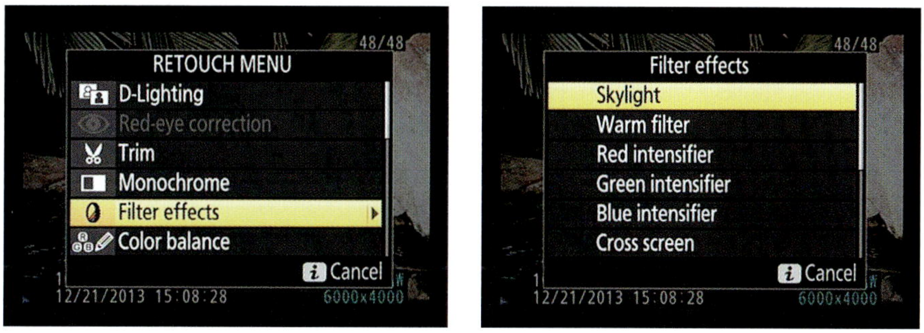

Figure 10-14: You can choose from filter effects that mimic traditional lens filters.

The color filters work like so:

- *Skylight filter:* Reduces the amount of blue to create a subtle warming effect.
- *Warm filter:* Produces a warming effect that's just a bit stronger than the Skylight filter.
- *Color intensifiers:* Enables you to boost the intensity of reds, greens, or blues individually. After choosing the intensifier you want to use, press the Multi Selector up or down to set the strength of the adjustment.

- **Color Balance:** Offering more flexibility than the Filter Effects options, this tool enables you to shift colors toward any part of the color spectrum. After you select the filter, as shown on the left in Figure 10-15, press OK to display the screen shown on the right. Shift image colors by using the Multi Selector to move the tiny black square around the color grid. In the figure, I moved the marker toward yellow, for example, to emphasize golden tones.

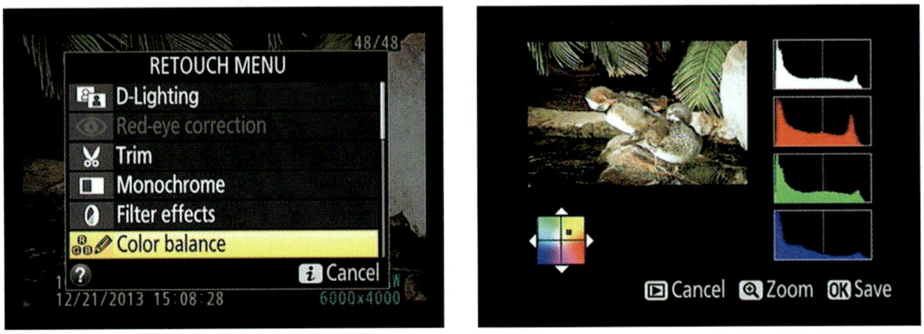

Figure 10-15: Press the Multi Selector to move the color shift marker and adjust color balance.

The histograms on the right side of the display show you the resulting impact on overall image brightness as well as on the individual red, green, and blue brightness values — a bit of information that's helpful if you're experienced in the science of reading histograms. Chapter 8 gives you an introduction.

- **Monochrome:** With the Monochrome Picture Control feature, covered in Chapter 5, you can shoot black-and-white photos. As an alternative, you can create a black-and-white copy of an existing color photo by applying the Monochrome option on the Retouch menu. You can also create sepia and *cyanotype* (blue and white) images via the Monochrome option. Figure 10-16 shows you examples.

  You can't apply certain Retouch menu options to your photo after you do the conversion; the D-Lighting, Quick Retouch, and Soft filters are among those that don't work on a monochrome copy. (Obviously, filters related to color adjustment also are no longer available.) So use those filters before heading to the Monochrome option.

  After selecting Monochrome from the Retouch menu, select the type of image you want to create (black-and-white, sepia, or cyanotype) and press OK. For the Sepia and Cyanotype options, you then see a screen that asks you to set the intensity of the tint; press the Multi Selector up and down to do so and then give the OK button one final push.

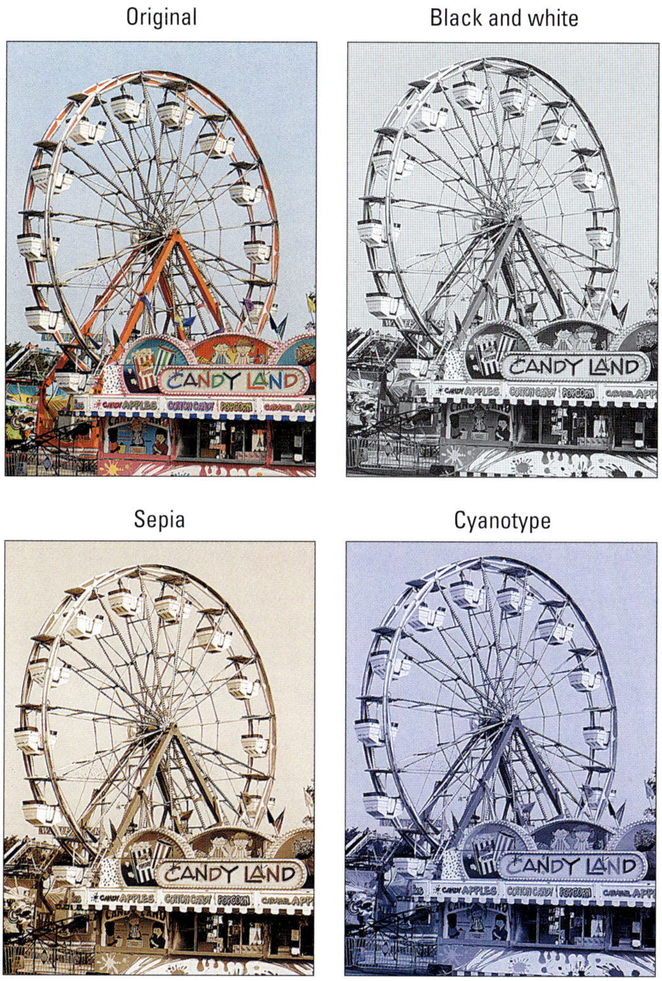

Figure 10-16: You can create three monochrome effects through the Monochrome tool on the Retouch menu.

Cropping Your Photo

To *crop* a photo means to trim away some of its perimeter. Cropping out excess background can often improve an image, as illustrated by Figure 10-17. When shooting this scene, I couldn't get close enough to fill the frame with the ducks, as shown on the left. So I cropped the image after the fact to achieve the composition you see on the right. Because I captured the photo using a high-resolution (Image Size) setting, I had plenty of pixels to allow enlarging the cropped photo. (Chapter 2 explains this issue in detail.)

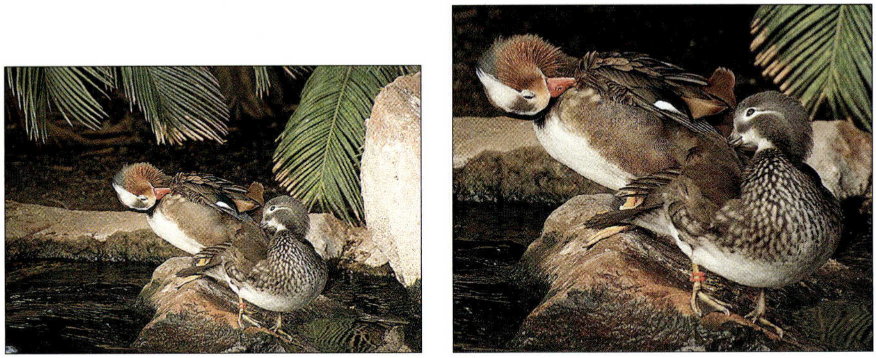

Figure 10-17: Cropping creates a better composition and eliminates background clutter.

WARNING!

With the Trim function on the Retouch menu, you can crop a photo right in the camera. However, always make this your *last* editing step because after you crop, you can't apply any other fixes from the Retouch menu.

To get the cropping job done, take these steps:

1. **Display your photo in single-image view and press the *i* button, select Retouch, and press the Multi Selector right.**

   The Retouch menu appears.

2. **Select Trim and press OK.**

   You see the screen shown in Figure 10-18. The yellow highlight box indicates the cropping frame.

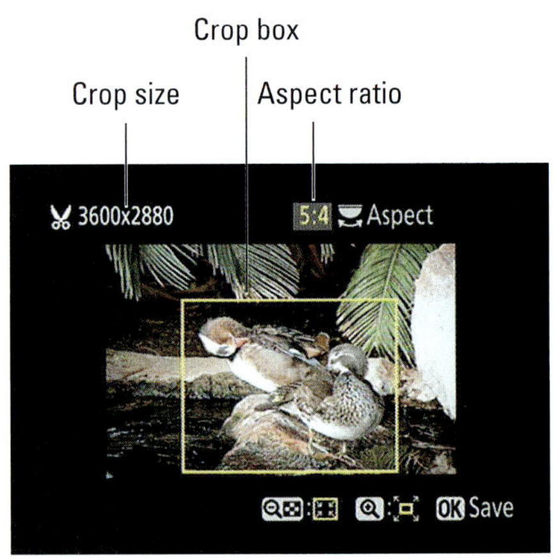

Figure 10-18: The yellow box indicates the cropping frame.

3. **Rotate the Command dial to change the crop aspect ratio.**

   You can crop to one of five aspect ratios: 3:2, 4:3, 5:4, 1:1, and 16:9. The selected aspect ratio appears in the upper-right corner of the screen.

4. **Adjust the cropping frame size and placement as needed.**

   For each aspect ratio, you can choose from a variety of crop sizes, which depend on the size of the original. The sizes are stated in pixel terms, such as 3600 x 2880. If you're cropping in advance of printing the image, remember to aim for at least 200 pixels per linear inch of the print — 800 x 1200 pixels for a 4 x 6 print, for example. The current crop size appears in the upper-left corner of the screen.

   You can adjust the size and placement of the cropping frame like so:

   - *Reduce the size of the cropping frame.* Press and release the Zoom Out button. Each press of the button further reduces the crop size.
   - *Enlarge the cropping frame.* Press the Zoom In button.
   - *Reposition the cropping frame.* Press the Multi Selector up, down, right, or left to shift the frame position.

5. **Press OK to create the cropped copy.**

   TIP: When you view the cropped image in Playback mode, a scissors symbol appears next to the Image Size readout (lower-right corner of the frame) to tell you that you're looking at a trimmed photo.

Applying Special Effects to Existing Photos

To alter reality beyond what you can achieve with the tools mentioned earlier in this chapter, experiment with these Retouch menu filters:

- **Cross Screen:** This filter adds a starburst effect to the brightest part of the image, as shown in Figure 10-19. To try it, select Filter Effects from the Retouch menu and then scroll down to the Cross Screen option.

  Using the options that appear along the right side of the screen, you can adjust the number of points on the star, the intensity of the effect, the length of the star's rays, and the angle of the effect. Use the Multi Selector to highlight an option, and then press right to display the available settings. Highlight your choice and press OK. To update the preview after changing a setting, highlight Confirm and press OK. When you're happy with the effect, choose Save and press OK.

- **Soft:** Also on the Filter Effects menu, the Soft filter blurs your photo to give it a dreamy, watercolor-like look. You can choose from three levels of blur: Low, Normal, and High.

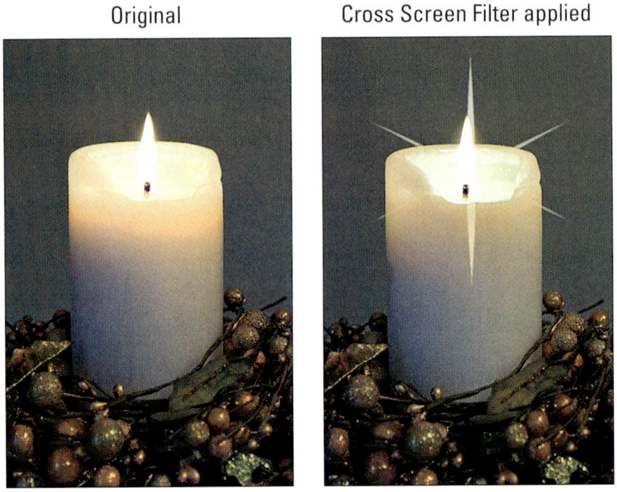

Figure 10-19: The Cross Screen filter adds a starburst effect to the brightest parts of the photo.

- **Color Outline:** Select this option from the Retouch menu to turn your photo into a black-and-white line drawing.
- **Color Sketch:** This filter creates an image similar to a drawing done in colored pencils; Figure 10-20 shows you an original (left) and its altered cousin (right). You can modify the effect through two options: Vividness, which affects the boldness of the colors; and Outlines, which determines the thickness of outlines.

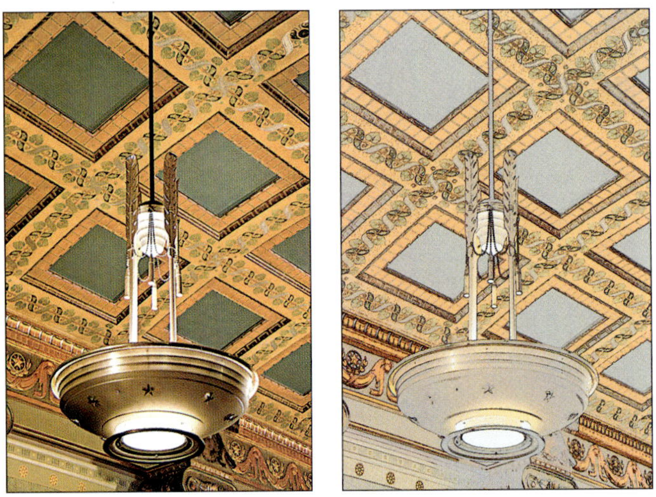

Figure 10-20: Color Sketch produces the effect you see on the right.

- **Miniature Effect:** Have you ever seen an architect's small-scale models of planned developments? The Miniature Effect filter attempts to create a photographic equivalent by applying a strong blur to all but one portion of an image, as shown in Figure 10-21. The left photo is the original; the right shows the result of applying the filter. For this example, I set the focus point on the part of the street occupied by the cars.

Original | Miniature Effect filter

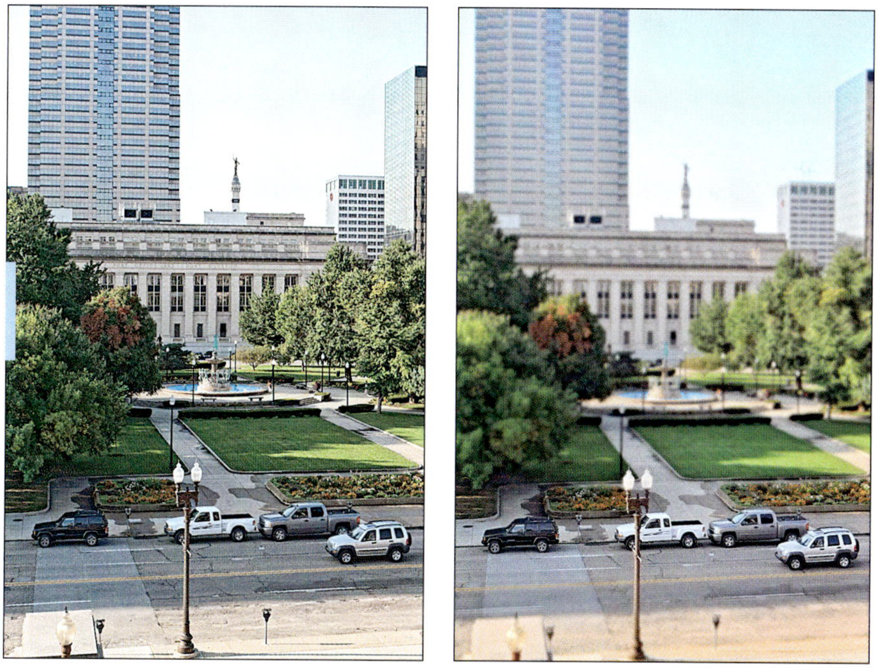

Figure 10-21: The Miniature Effect filter throws all but a small portion of a scene into very soft focus.

TIP

The Miniature Effect filter works best if you shoot your subject from a high angle — otherwise, you don't get the miniaturization result.

After choosing the filter from the Retouch menu, you see a yellow box over the photo, as shown in Figure 10-22.

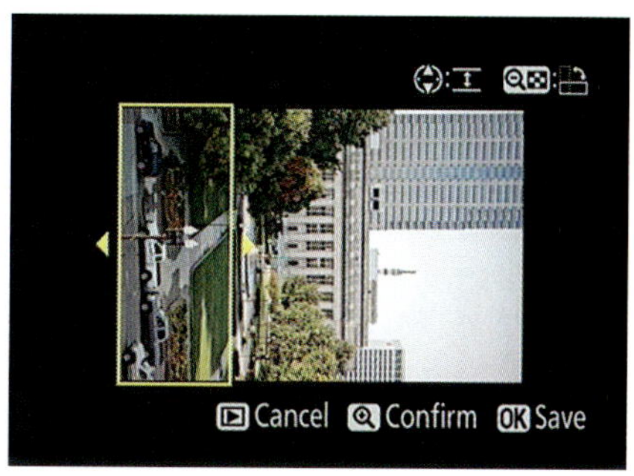

Figure 10-22: Use the Multi Selector to position the yellow rectangle over the area you want to keep in sharp focus.

The box represents the area that will remain in focus. Adjust its size and position as follows:

- *Rotate the box 90 degrees:* Press the Zoom Out button.
- *Position and resize the box:* When the box is oriented as shown in Figure 10-22, press the Multi Selector up/down to resize the box; press right/left to move it. If the box is oriented horizontally, use the opposite maneuvers. (The double-arrow symbol in the upper-right corner of the screen indicates which way to press the Multi Selector to resize the frame.)
- *Preview the effect:* Press the Zoom In button.

When you get a result you like, press OK to save a copy of the original with the effect applied.

- **Selective Color:** This effect *desaturates* (removes color from) parts of a photo while leaving specific colors intact. For example, in Figure 10-23, I desaturated everything but the yellows and peaches in the rose.

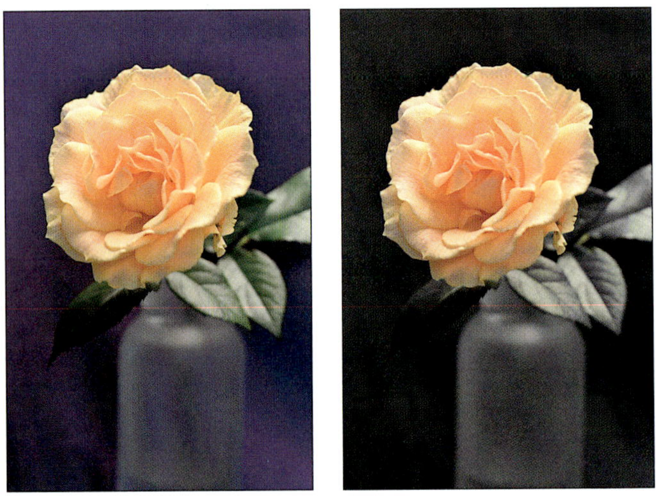

Figure 10-23: I used the Selective Color filter to desaturate everything but the rose petals.

After choosing the effect from the Retouch menu, you can select up to three colors to retain and specify how much a color can vary from the selected one and still be retained. Make your wishes known as described in this list of (loosely ordered) actions:

- *Select the first color to be retained.* Using the Multi Selector, move the yellow box (labeled *Color selector box* in Figure 10-24) over *the* color. Then press the AE-L/AF-L button to tag that color, which appears in the first color swatch at the top of the screen, as shown on the left in Figure 10-24.

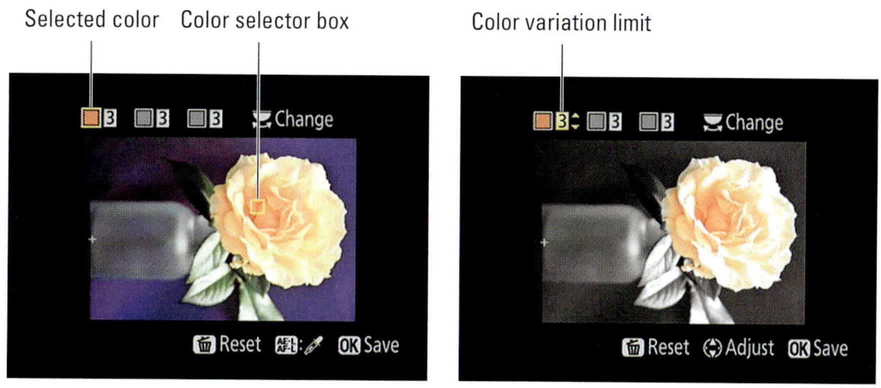

Figure 10-24: To select a color you want to keep, move the yellow box over it and press the AE -L/AF-L button.

- *Set the range of the selected color.* Rotate the Command dial to display a preview of the desaturated image and highlight the number box to the right of the color swatch, as shown on the right in the figure. Then press the Multi Selector up or down to choose a value from 1 to 7. The higher the number, the more a pixel can vary in color from the selected hue and still be retained. The display updates to show you the impact of the setting.
- *Choose one or two additional colors.* Rotate the Command dial to highlight the second color swatch and then repeat the selection process. To choose a third color, lather, rinse, and repeat.
- *Fine-tune your settings.* You can keep rotating the Command dial to cycle through the color swatch and range boxes, adjusting each as necessary.
- *Reset a color swatch box.* To empty a selected swatch box, press the Delete button. You can then move the yellow highlight box over a new color and press the AE-L/AF-L button to select it. To reset all the swatch boxes, hold down the Delete button until a message asks whether you want to get rid of all selected colors. Highlight Yes and press OK.
- *Save a copy of the image with the effect applied.* Press OK.

Shooting in Effects Mode

When you set the Mode dial to Effects, as shown in Figure 10-25, you can apply special effects on the fly: That is, the effect is added as the camera writes the picture to the memory card.

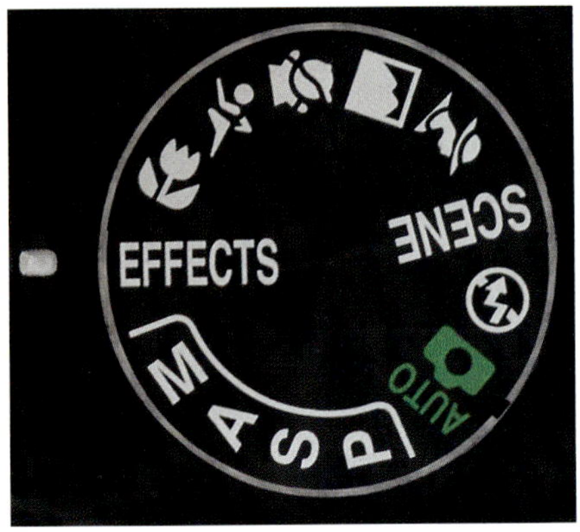

Figure 10-25: Effects mode lets you apply special effects to movies and still photos.

For still photos, I prefer to capture my originals sans effect and then work from the Retouch menu to alter them. That way, I wind up with one normal image and one with the effect applied, just in case I decide that I prefer the unaltered photo to the effects version. Shooting in Effects mode also brings up another problem: To create the effects, the camera puts most picture-taking controls, such as White Balance and Metering mode, off limits, just as it does when you shoot in Auto, Auto Flash Off, or Scene mode.

However, Effects mode does offer some artistic filters not available on the Retouch menu. In addition, it enables you to add effects to movies, which isn't possible on the Retouch menu. So even though I suspect that you won't find a use for the Effects mode very often, I'd be remiss if I didn't spend a little time discussing it.

As soon as you set the Mode dial to Effects, an icon representing the selected effect appears in the upper-left corner of the Information display, as shown on the left in Figure 10-26. Rotate the Command dial to cycle through the available effects, as shown on the right.

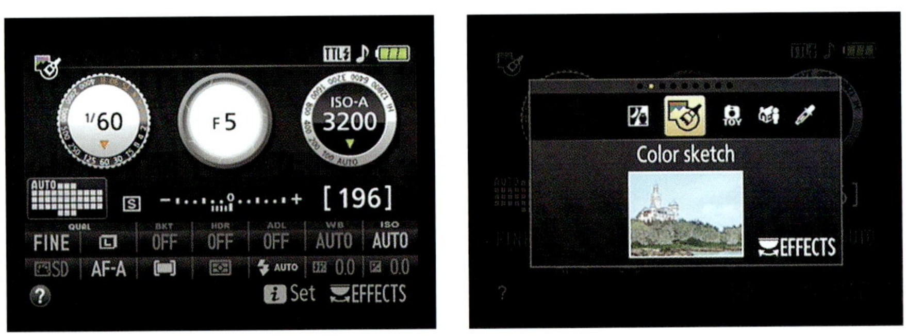

Figure 10-26: Rotate the Command dial to cycle through the effects.

TIP

Although the camera displays a thumbnail to indicate the result of each effect, you don't have to rely on that artwork: Instead, set the camera to Live View mode. For all but one effect, HDR Painting, the monitor then shows a live preview of each effect as you select it. You also need to use Live View mode to access the options that are available for some effects. To shift to Live View mode, just rotate the Live View (LV) switch on top of the camera.

Effects mode offers the following choices:

- **Night Vision:** Use this setting in low-light situations to produce a grainy, black-and-white image that resembles what you see with night-vision goggles. Figure 10-27 has an example. To achieve the grainy effect, the camera uses a high ISO Sensitivity setting — that high ISO produces noise, which results in the grainy look. How high the ISO climbs and, thus, how much noise becomes visible, depends on the ambient light.

  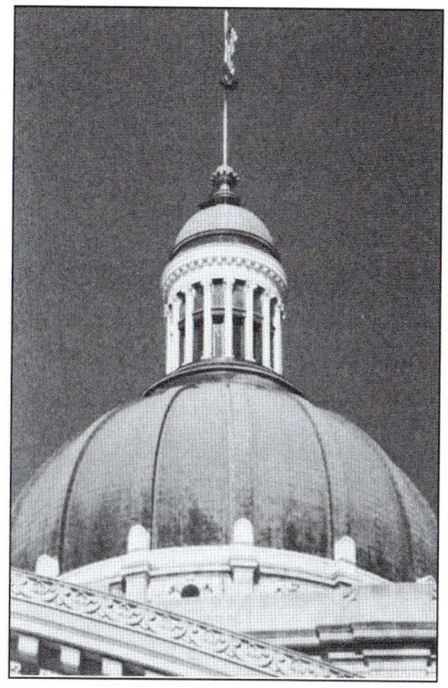

  Figure 10-27: The Night Vision effect creates an exceptionally noisy black-and-white image.

  A few critical points about Night Vision mode:

  - *Autofocusing is available only in Live View mode.* For viewfinder photography, you must focus manually.
  - *Flash is disabled, as is the AF-assist lamp.* The whole idea is to create a picture taken in little light, after all.
  - *Use a tripod to avoid blur.* A slow shutter speed is needed to capture the image in dark conditions, and you must be careful to avoid camera movement during the exposure. If your subject is moving, it can appear blurry even if the camera is on a tripod.
  - *You can capture the photo only in the JPEG format.* You select this setting via the Image Quality option on the Shooting menu. Raw (NEF) files aren't compatible with the Night Vision effect.

- **Color Sketch:** This setting produces the same effect as the Color Sketch filter on the Retouch menu (refer to Figure 10-20). Using Live View mode, you can adjust the same options available through the Retouch menu: Vividness and Color Outlines. Press OK to display the options; press the Multi Selector up or down to highlight the option you want to change, and press right or left to adjust the value for that option. Press OK again to hide the options and return to shooting. The camera remembers your settings and uses them any time you select the Color Sketch effect until you change them again.

Three points to ponder:

- *It's best to compose the image by using the viewfinder and then switch to Live View.* When the effect is selected, the Live View display updates very slowly, making it a pain to play with composition using the monitor.
- *Using the effect puts limitations on movie recording.* Movies recorded using this effect play back as a series of still images rather than as a standard movie. In addition, autofocusing during recording is disabled.
- *For still photos, you can shoot only in the JPEG format.* As with Night Vision mode, you can't create a Raw (NEF) file with this effect.

- **Toy Camera Effect:** This mode, also compatible only with the JPEG file format, is designed to create a photo or movie that looks like it was shot by a toy camera — specifically, the type of toy camera that produces images that have a vignette effect (corners of the scene appear darker than the rest of the image).

  In Live View mode, you can adjust the effect by pressing OK to access two options: Vividness, which affects color intensity; and Vignetting, which controls the amount of vignetting. After dialing in the settings you want to use, press OK to exit the setup screen.

- **Miniature Effect:** This one is also a duplicate of the one on the Retouch menu; Figure 10-21 shows an example of the result. Again, the filter works by blurring all but a small portion of the scene.

  REMEMBER

  To specify which area you want to keep in focus, first set the camera to Live View mode. In the center of the screen, you see a red focus frame; use the Multi Selector to center the frame over the area that you want to keep in focus and then press OK. Now you see horizontal markings that indicate the width of the sharp-focus region. Press the Multi Selector up or down to adjust the width of the in-focus region; press right or left to change the orientation of the box. When you achieve the look you want, press OK again.

  A few other limitations also apply: Flash is disabled, as is the AF-assist lamp. If you use the Continuous Release mode, the frames per second rate is reduced. You must set the Image Quality option (Shooting menu) to JPEG for still photography, and, when autofocusing, you can't use any AF-area mode except Single Point. (Chapter 4 discusses this autofocus option.)

  For movies, sound recording is disabled, autofocus is disabled during recording, and movies play back at high speed. (The high-speed playback means that a movie that contains about 45 minutes of footage is compressed into a 3-minute clip, for example.)

- **Selective Color:** Use this effect to create an image in which all but one to three colors are desaturated, just as when you use the Selective Color option on the Retouch menu. Figure 10-23 has an example.

  To choose the colors you want to retain and specify the range of similar colors that are included, switch to Live View and then press OK. At the top of the screen, you see three color-swatch boxes and a value next to each box. In the middle of the screen, you see a small white box, which is the color selector box. Set up the effect as follows:

  - *Choose a color to retain:* Frame the image so that the white selection box is over the color you want to preserve. Then press the Multi Selector up.
  - *Set the color range:* After setting the color, press the Multi Selector up or down to adjust the color range value. A higher value retains a broader spectrum of similar shades than the one you chose.
  - *Choose additional color to retain:* Rotate the Command dial to select the second color swatch box and repeat the process of choosing a color and setting its range value.
  - *Deselect a color:* Change your mind about retaining one of your chosen colors? Rotate the Command dial to highlight its color swatch and then press the Delete button. Or hold down the button for a few seconds to delete all your selected colors.

  After setting your color preferences, press OK to lock in your decisions and hide the options. The camera will use those settings any time you choose the Selective Color effect until you specify new settings. You can stay in Live View mode to shoot your photo or movie or exit Live View mode to take a picture using the viewfinder.

  Note that just as with the preceding Effects settings, you're limited to using JPEG as the file type when you use the Selective Color mode. Flash is disabled.

- **Silhouette:** Choosing this setting ensures that backlit subjects will be captured as dark silhouettes against a bright background, as shown in Figure 10-28. To help ensure that the subject is dark, flash is disabled.

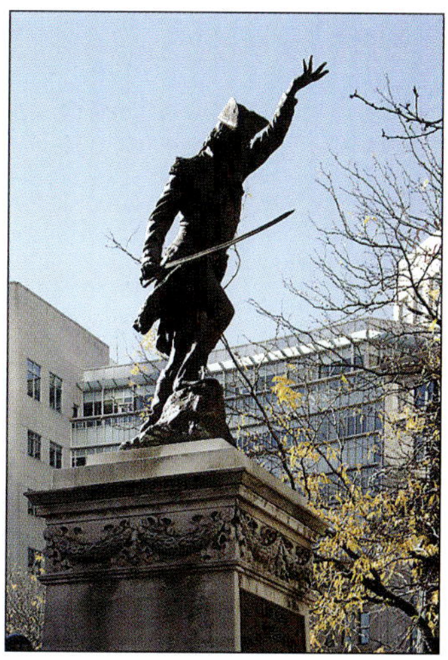

Figure 10-28: The Silhouette effect purposely underexposes backlit subjects.

- **High Key:** A *high key* photo is dominated by white or very light areas, such as a white china cup resting on a white doily in front of a sunny window. This setting is designed to produce a good exposure for this type of scene, which the camera otherwise tends to underexpose in response to all the high brightness values. Flash is disabled.

How does the name relate to the characteristics of the picture? Well, photographers refer to the dominant tones — or brightness values — as the *key tones.* In most photos, the *midtones,* or areas of medium brightness, are the key tones. In a high key image, the majority of tones are at the high end of the brightness scale.

- **Low Key:** The opposite of a high key photo, a low key photo is dominated by shadows. Use this mode to prevent the camera from brightening the scene too much and thereby losing the dark and dramatic nature of the image. Flash is disabled.
- **HDR Painting:** This option is a variation of the HDR (High Dynamic Range) feature that you can use when you shoot in the P, S, A, and M exposure modes, covered in Chapter 3. As with that feature, the camera records two exposures of the scene and then blends them together to create an image that has a higher *dynamic range* (range of shadows to highlights) than can be captured in a single frame. In this case, however, the result is a more obviously manipulated photo than when you use the HDR shooting option; colors are more intense, and details appear sharper (hence the *painting* part of the effect name).

  Just as with regular HDR mode shooting, this effect is limited to pictures that you shoot using one of the JPEG Image Quality settings (Fine, Normal, or Basic) and works well only for stationary subjects. Any movement of the subject or camera will result in a blurry mess. Also note that flash and continous (burst mode) shooting are both disabled.

After selecting an effect, you can exit Live View to take the picture using the viewfinder if you prefer. Or, to record a movie, remain in Live View mode and just press the red movie-record button to stop and start recording.

Two Roads to a Multi-Image Exposure

Your camera offers two features that enable you to combine multiple photographs into one:

- **Multiple Exposure (Shooting menu):** With this option, you can combine your next two to three shots. After you enable the option and take your shots, the camera merges them into one file. The shots used to create the composite aren't recorded and saved separately. The Multiple Exposure option isn't available in Live View mode.
- **Image Overlay (Retouch menu):** This option enables you to merge two existing Raw images. I used this option to combine a photo of a werewolf friend, shown on the left in Figure 10-29, with a nighttime garden scene, shown in the center. The result is the ghostly image shown on the right. Oooh, scary!

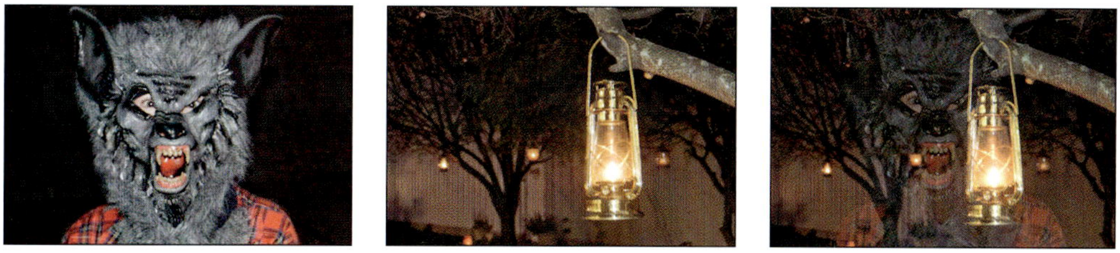

Figure 10-29: Image Overlay merges two Raw (NEF) photos into one.

On the surface, both options sound kind of cool. The problem is that you can't control the opacity or positioning of the individual images in the combined photo. For example, my overlay picture would have been more successful if I could move the werewolf to the left in the combined image so that he and the lantern aren't blended. And I'd also prefer to keep the background of image 2 at full opacity in the overlay image rather than getting a 50/50 mix of that background and the one in image 1, which only creates a fuzzy-looking background in this particular example.

However, there is one effect that you can create successfully with either option: a "two views" composite like the one in Figure 10-30. For this image, I used Image Overlay to combine the front and rear views of the antique match striker into the composite scene.

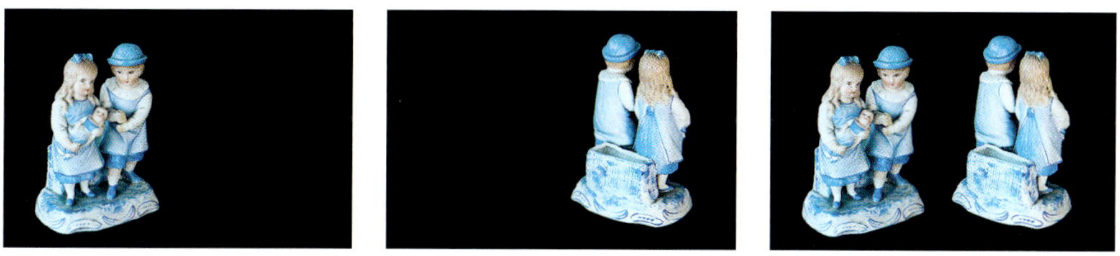

Figure 10-30: If you want each subject to appear solid, use a black background and position the subjects so that they don't overlap.

REMEMBER

For this trick to work, the background in both images must be the same solid color (black seems to be best), and you must compose your photos so that the subjects don't overlap in the combined photo, as shown here. Otherwise, you get the ghostly portrait effect like what you see in Figure 10-29.

To be honest, I don't recommend using Image Overlay or Multiple Exposure for serious photo compositing. Instead, do this kind of work in your photo-editing software, where you have more control over the blend. So in the interest of reserving space in this book for features that I think you will find much more useful, I leave you to explore these two features on your own. The electronic version of the camera manual (found on a CD that ships with your camera) explains the steps involved in using each of them.

11

Ten Special-Purpose Features to Explore on a Rainy Day

In This Chapter

- Tagging files with GPS data and image comments
- Creating your own menu and custom storage folders
- Altering the camera's automatic shutdown timing
- Customizing the Information display
- Changing the function of some controls

Consider this chapter the literary equivalent of the end of a late-night infomercial — the part where the host exclaims, "But wait! There's more!" The features covered in these pages aren't the sort that drive people to choose one camera over another, and they may come in handy only on certain occasions. Still, they're included at no extra charge, so check 'em out when you have a few spare moments.

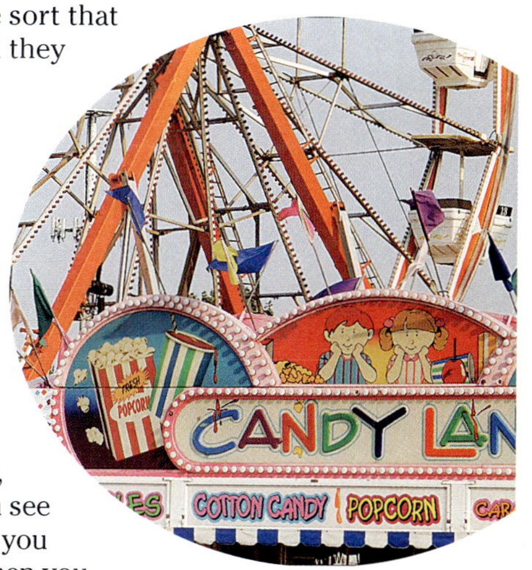

Tagging Files with GPS Data

Your camera's GPS (Global Positioning Satellite) device enables you to tag files with location data such as latitude, longitude, and altitude. During playback, you can view the information in the Shooting Data display mode, covered in Chapter 8. In Nikon ViewNX 2, the software that ships with your camera, you can even see a map that pinpoints the shooting location. (Of course, you need to be mindful of security and privacy concerns when you add this type of data to your files, because other people might be able to access the data when they view your pictures.)

To enable GPS tagging, select Location Data from the Setup menu, as shown on the left in Figure 11-1, and set the Record Location Data option to On, as shown on the right. The camera begins searching for a signal, and the satellite symbol labeled in the right figure starts to blink. The same symbol appears in the Information display and Live View display. When the symbol stops blinking, the signal is acquired and the data will be added to your next file.

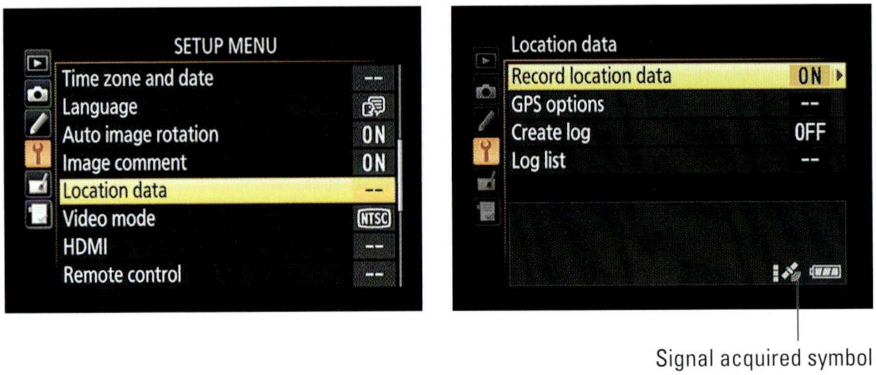

Figure 11-1: Enable GPS tagging via the Setup menu.

The other options shown on the right in Figure 11-1 enable you to control the following aspects of the system:

- **GPS Options:** Select this menu item to access these three settings:
  - *Standby Timer:* Normally, the camera saves battery power by turning off the exposure meter after a period of inactivity. But because problems can occur if the camera goes to sleep while the GPS unit is doing its thing, the Standby Timer option is turned off by default, and the meters never go to sleep when GPS is enabled. If you turn on the Standby Timer option, the camera shuts the meter off but extends the normal shutdown time by a full minute. (The normal shutdown time is determined by the setting of the Auto Off Timers option, explained in the upcoming section "Adjusting Automatic Shutdown Timing.")
  - *Set Clock from Satellite:* Select Yes to synchronize the camera's clock with the satellite's clock. You also can set the date and time via the Time Zone and Date option on the Setup menu.
  - *Update A-GPS Data:* The *A* in A-GPS stands for *assisted,* which simply means that the camera stores some data that helps the camera acquire satellite data faster. Occasionally, Nikon may release an updated A-GPS data file, and this menu item enables you to install the updated file.

The first step is to go to the Nikon website and download the file to a memory card. You then put the card in the camera, select the Update A-GPS Data option, and follow the prompts to copy the file from the card to the camera. If you're interested, type `http://nikonimglib.com/agps2` into your web browser's address bar. Full instructions for installing the file are found in the camera's electronic user manual, found on one of the CDs included in the camera box.

- **Create Log and Log List:** When GPS is enabled, turning these features on tells the camera to log its current position at periodic intervals, even when you're not shooting. Again, see the electronic user manual for full details on setting up, reading, and deleting logs.

TIP

A few other pointers to keep in mind:

- It may take a few minutes for the camera to find the signal. Your chances of acquiring a signal are best when you're outside, with an unobstructed view of the sky.
- If the satellite symbol contains only two boxes instead of the three you see in Figure 11-1, altitude data isn't being received and won't be recorded.
- Because the GPS system consumes battery power, disable it until you really need to use it. Note that a battery-level symbol appears with the satellite signal on the GPS control screen shown on the right in Figure 11-1.

Adding Hidden Image Comments

Through the Image Comment feature on the Setup menu, you can add hidden text comments to your picture files. Suppose, for example, that you're traveling on vacation and visiting a different destination every day. You can annotate all the pictures you take on a particular outing with the name of the location or attraction.

REMEMBER

The text doesn't appear on the photo itself; instead, it's stored with other *metadata* (hidden data, such as shutter speed, date and time, and so on). You can view the comment during playback in the Shooting Data display mode (see Chapter 8) or along with other metadata in Nikon ViewNX 2 (see Chapter 9). As with GPS data, keep in mind that other people who understand how to view metadata may be able to see your comments when viewing your photos.

Enable the feature via the Image Comment option on the Setup menu, as shown on the left in Figure 11-2. Press OK, highlight Input Comment, as shown on the right in the figure, and press the Multi Selector right to display the keyboard screen shown on the left in Figure 11-3.

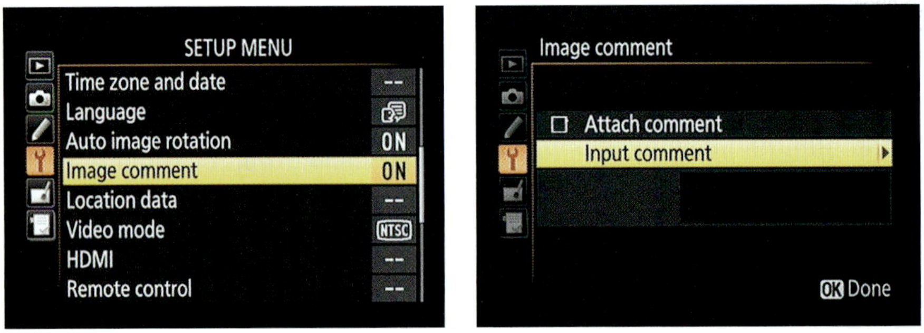

Figure 11-2: You can tag pictures with text comments through this feature.

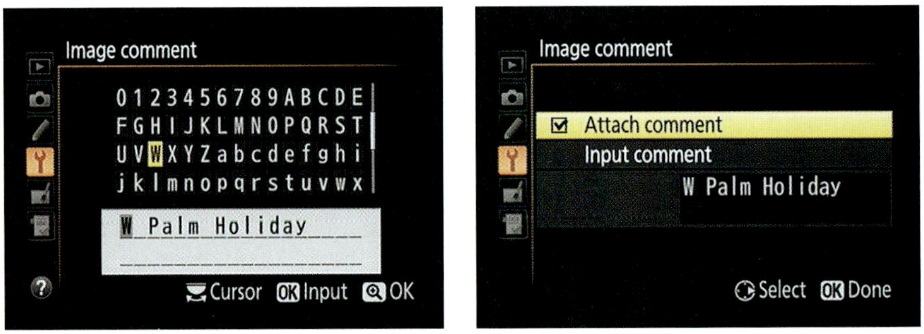

Figure 11-3: Select Input Comment and press the Multi Selector right; then highlight a letter and press OK to enter it.

Use these text-entry techniques to create your comment:

- **Enter a character:** Use the Multi Selector to highlight the character and then press OK. Your comment can be up to 36 characters long.

  Press the Multi Selector up and down to scroll the keyboard display and access additional characters.

- **Move the text cursor:** Rotate the Command dial.
- **Delete a letter:** Move the cursor under the letter and press the Delete button.

After entering your comment, press the Zoom In button to display the screen shown on the right in Figure 11-3. You should see your text comment underneath the Input Comment line. Highlight Attach Comment and press the Multi Selector right to put a check mark in the box, as shown in the figure, and then press OK. The Image Comment menu item should now read On (refer to the left side of Figure 11-2).

To disable the feature, revisit the Setup menu, select Image Comment, highlight Attach Comment, and press the Multi Selector right to toggle the check mark off. Press OK to make your decision official.

Creating Custom Image Folders

By default, your camera stores all images in one folder, which it names 100D5300. Folders have a storage limit of 9,999 images; when you exceed that number, the camera creates a new folder, assigning a name that indicates the folder number — 101D5300, 102D5300, and so on.

If you choose, however, you can create custom-named folders. For example, if you use your camera for both business and personal photography, you can set up one folder named DULL and one named FUN — or perhaps something less incriminating, such as WORK and HOME.

To create a custom folder, select Storage Folder from the Shooting menu and then highlight New, as illustrated in Figure 11-4. Press the Multi Selector right to display the same keyboard screen that appears when you add image comments (refer to the left screen in Figure 11-3). Use the same text-entry techniques described in the preceding section to enter a folder name up to five characters long.

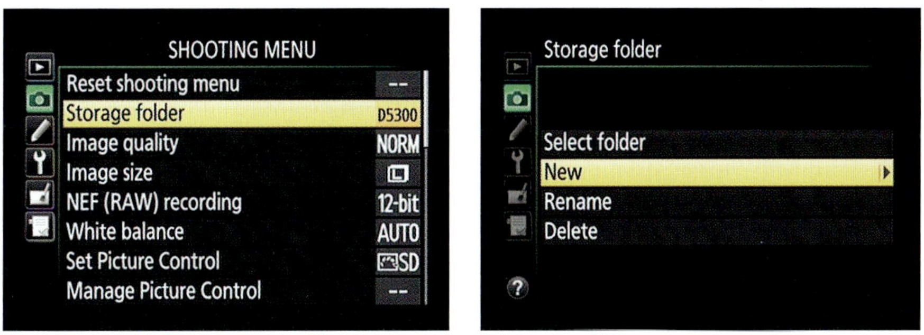

Figure 11-4: You can create custom folders to organize your images directly on the camera.

After entering your folder name, press the Zoom In button. You return to the Shooting menu, and the folder you just created is automatically selected as the active folder.

If you take advantage of this option, remember to specify where you want your pictures stored each time you shoot: Select Storage Folder from the Shooting menu, press OK, highlight Select Folder, and press the Multi Selector right to display a list of folders. Highlight a folder and press OK. Your choice also affects which images are displayed by default in playback mode; you can select a specific folder via the Playback Folder option on the Playback menu.

To rename a folder, use the Rename option on the Storage Folder screen (refer to the right screen in Figure 11-4.) Select Delete to get rid of empty folders on the memory card.

Creating Your Own Menu

Keeping track of how to access all the D5300's options can be a challenge, especially when it comes to those that you adjust through menus. To make things a little easier, you can build a custom menu that holds up to 20 of the options you use most frequently. Here's how:

1. **Display the My Menu menu, shown in Figure 11-5.**

   This menu shares a slot in the menu list with the Recent Settings menu. The menu icon for the My Menu menu is labeled in the figure. If the Recent Settings menu appears instead, scroll to the end of that menu, select Choose Tab, press OK, select My Menu, and press OK again. The My Menu screen then appears.

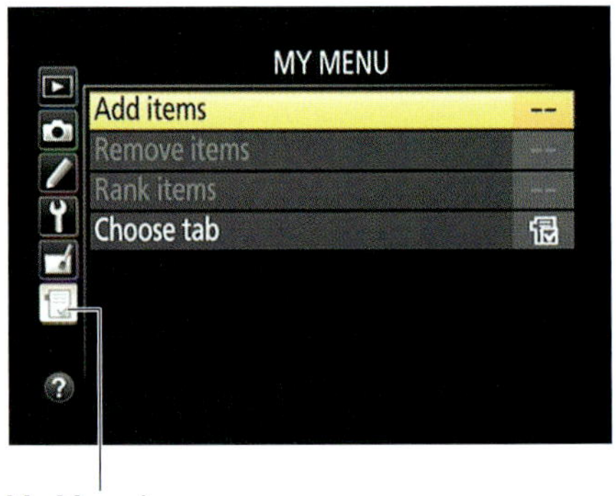

Figure 11-5: You can create a custom menu to hold up to 20 of the settings you access most often.

2. **Highlight Add Items and press OK.**

   You see a list of the other camera menus.

3. **Select the menu that contains an option you want to add to your menu and press the Multi Selector right.**

   You see a list of all available options on that menu. For example, I chose the Shooting menu to display the options shown on the left in Figure 11-6.

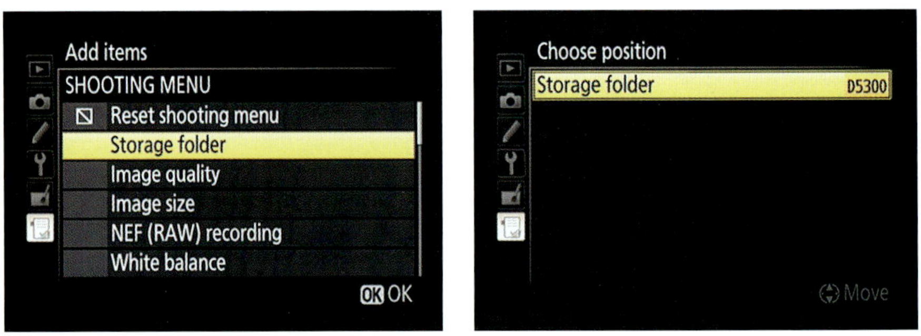

Figure 11-6: Select an item and press OK to add it to your menu.

A few items can't be added to a custom menu. A little box with a slash through it appears next to those items.

4. **To add an item to your menu, highlight it and press OK.**

   You see the Choose Position screen, as shown on the right in Figure 11-6, where you can change the order of your menu items. For now, just press OK to return to the My Menu screen; the item you just added appears at the top of the My Menu screen. (See the list following these steps to find out how to adjust the order of your menu items.)

5. **Repeat Steps 2–4 to add more items to your menu.**

   When you get to Step 3, a check mark appears next to any item that's already on your menu.

After creating your custom menu, you can reorder and remove menu items as follows:

- **Change the order of menu options.** Display the My Menu screen and highlight Rank Items, as shown in Figure 11-7. You see a screen that lists all your menu items in their current order. Highlight a menu item, press OK, and then use the Multi Selector to move it up or down the list. Press OK to lock in the new position of the menu item. When you're happy with the order of the menu items, press the Multi Selector left to return to the My Menu screen.

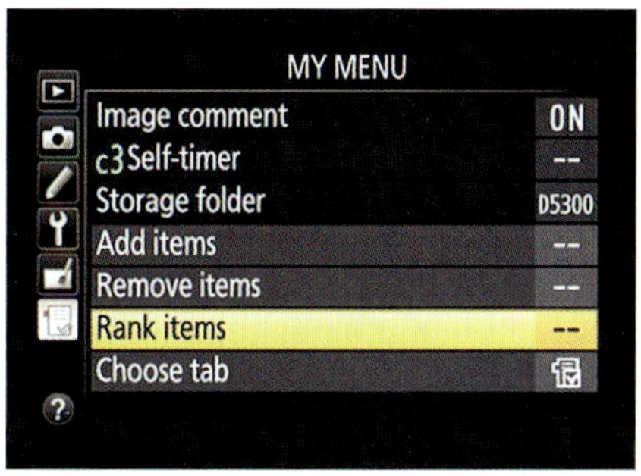

Figure 11-7: Choose Rank Items to change the order of menu items.

- **Remove menu items.** On the My Menu screen (refer to Figure 11-7), select Remove Items and press OK. You see a list of current menu items, with an empty box next to each item. To remove an item, highlight it and press the Multi Selector right. A check mark appears in that item's box. After tagging all the items you want to remove, press OK. You see a confirmation screen asking permission to remove the item; press OK to go forward.

Adjusting Automatic Shutdown Timing

When the camera is in shooting mode, its *standby timer* feature saves battery power by shutting off the Information display and viewfinder after a period of inactivity. Similarly, the camera limits the Image Review period (the length of time your picture appears immediately after you press the shutter button), the length of time the Live View display remains inactive, how long a picture appears in playback mode, and how long menus remain onscreen.

You can control the auto-shutdown timing through the Auto Off Timers option, found in the Timers/AE Lock section of the Custom Setting menu and shown on the left in Figure 11-8.

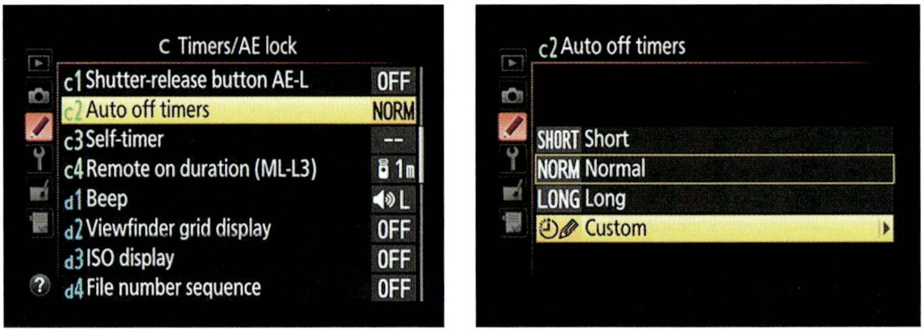

Figure 11-8: Customize auto shutdown timing here.

You get four choices, as shown on the right in the figure, which produce the following shutdown times:

- **Short:** Standby Timer (affects Information display and viewfinder), 4 seconds; Live View, 5 minutes; Image Review, 4 seconds; playback/menus, 20 seconds.
- **Normal (default setting):** Standby Timer, 8 seconds; Live View, 10 minutes; Image Review, 4 seconds; playback/menus, 1 minute.
- **Long:** Standby Timer, 1 minute; Live View, 20 minutes; Image Review, 20 seconds; playback/menus, 5 minutes.
- **Custom:** Choose this setting to specify delay times for the Standby Timer, Live View display, Image Review period, and Playback/menu display individually.

To disable Image Review altogether, head for the Playback Menu and set the Image Review item to Off.

Changing the Look of the Information Display

By default, the Information display appears as shown on the left in Figure 11-9, with the three large circular graphics representing, from left to right, the shutter speed, f-stop, and ISO settings. As you adjust the f-stop setting, the center of its circle grows or shrinks to represent the opening and closing of the aperture. (Chapter 3 explains apertures and f-stops.) If you prefer, you can switch to the simpler design shown on the right in the figure. You also can change the background color from black to blue or light gray.

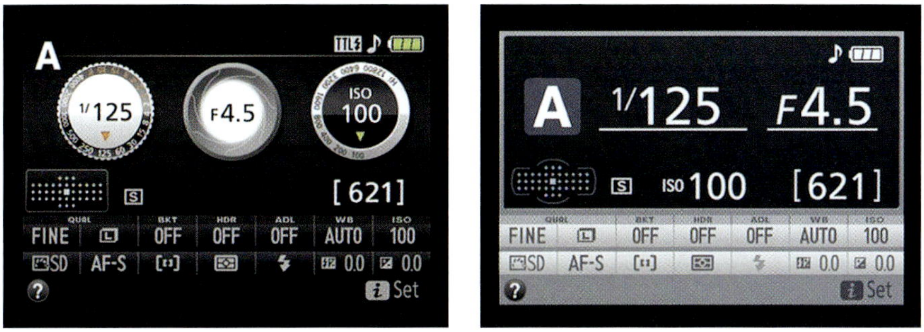

Figure 11-9: You can alter the display style of the Information screen.

Select the design via the Info Display Format option on the Setup menu, as shown in Figure 11-10. You can specify the design used for the P, S, A, and M exposure modes separately from the one used for the other modes.

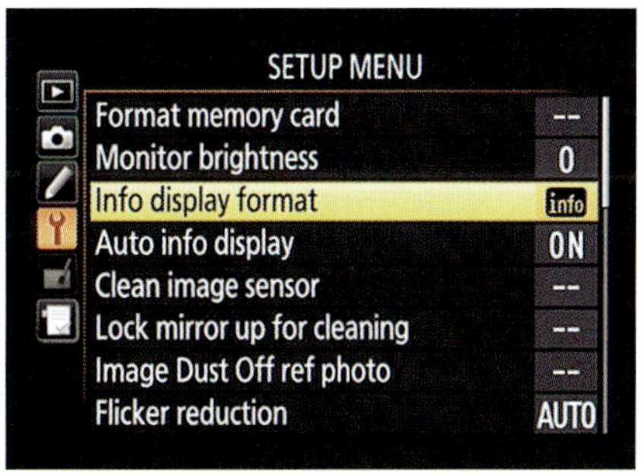

Figure 11-10: Modify the look of the display through this Setup menu option.

Keeping the Information Display Hidden

Just below the Info Display Format option on the Setup menu (refer to Figure 11-10), the Auto Info Display option offers another way to customize the Information display. When this option is On, as it is by default, the Information display appears whenever you press the shutter button halfway and release it. If you disable the Image Review feature (via the Playback menu), the Information display also appears after you take a picture.

Turn off the Auto Info Display option, and the Information screen appears briefly when you first turn on the camera, but after that, you must press the Info button to display it. Instructions in this book assume that you stick with the default setting (On). But because the monitor is one of the biggest drains of battery power, you may want to set the option to Off if you have a lot of shooting left to do and the battery is running low.

Customizing a Few Buttons

A few camera buttons can be modified to perform functions different from their default purposes. Again, instructions in this book assume that you haven't modified the buttons, but after you master your camera, you may want to take advantage of these options. You can customize the following buttons:

- **Function (FN) button:** Establish this button's behavior via the Assign Fn Button option, found on the Controls submenu of the Custom Setting menu and shown in Figure 11-11.

  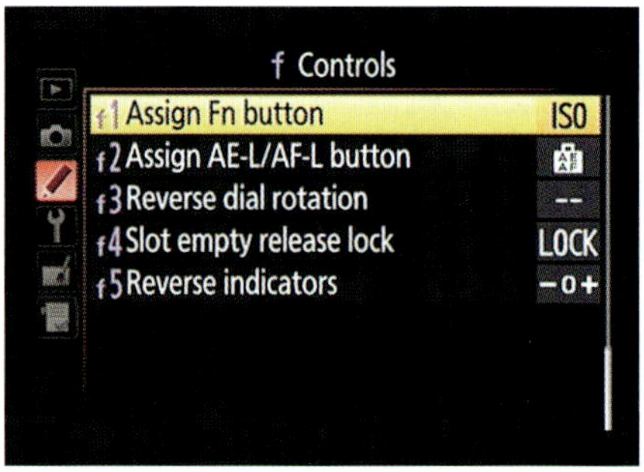

  Figure 11-11: You can assign any number of jobs to the Function button.

  Choose from these settings:

  - *Image Quality/Size:* Pressing the button while turning the Command dial cycles through available Image Quality and Image Size settings.
  - *ISO Sensitivity:* Pressing the button while turning the Command dial changes the ISO setting. (This is the default setting.)
  - *White Balance:* Pressing the button while turning the Command dial cycles through the available White Balance settings (available only when the Mode dial is set to P, S, A, or M).
  - *Active D-Lighting:* Pressing the button while turning the Command dial changes the Active D-Lighting setting (again, only in P, S, A, and M exposure modes).
  - *HDR mode:* Pressing the button while rotating the Command dial adjusts the HDR setting. See Chapter 3 for more about HDR.
  - *+ NEF (RAW):* This setting relates to the Image Quality option, introduced in Chapter 2. If you set that option to JPEG Basic, Fine, or Normal and then press the Fn button, the camera records two copies of the next picture you shoot: a JPEG version plus a second image in the NEF format. Note that this feature doesn't work when you shoot in Effects mode and select Night Vision, Color Sketch, Toy Camera, Miniature Effect, Selective Color, or HDR Painting as the effect.

- *Auto bracketing:* Pressing the Fn button while turning the Command dial lets you select a bracketing increment for AEB (automatic exposure bracketing) or white-balance bracketing. For ADL (Active D-Lighting) bracketing, you can use the button and Command dial to turn bracketing on and off. Bracketing, explained at the end of Chapter 3, is possible only in the P, S, A, and M exposure modes.
- *AF-area mode:* Pressing the button while turning the Command dial changes the AF-area mode, an autofocusing option you can explore in Chapter 4.
- *Viewfinder grid display:* Pressing the button toggles the viewfinder grid on and off.
- *Wi-Fi:* Pressing the button whisks you to the Wi-Fi option on the Setup menu.

- **AE-L/AF-L button:** This button is related to the autoexposure and autofocusing systems. You can set the button to perform the following functions via the Assign AE-L/AF-L Button option, found on the Controls section of the Custom Setting menu, just under the Assign FN Button option (refer to Figure 11-11):
  - *AE/AF Lock:* This is the default setting. Focus and exposure remain locked as long as you press the button.
  - *AE Lock Only:* Autoexposure is locked as long as you press the button; autofocus isn't affected. (You can still lock focus by pressing the shutter button halfway.)
  - *AE Lock (Hold):* This one locks exposure only with a single press of the button. The exposure lock remains in force until you press the button again or the exposure meters turn off.
  - *AF Lock Only:* Focus remains locked as long as you press the button. Exposure isn't affected.
  - *AF-On:* Pressing the button activates the camera's autofocus mechanism. If you choose this option, you can't focus by pressing the shutter button halfway.

- **Shutter button:** The Timers/AE Lock section of the Custom Setting menu offers an option called Shutter-Release Button AE-Lock, shown in Figure 11-12. This option determines whether pressing the shutter button halfway locks focus only or locks focus and exposure.

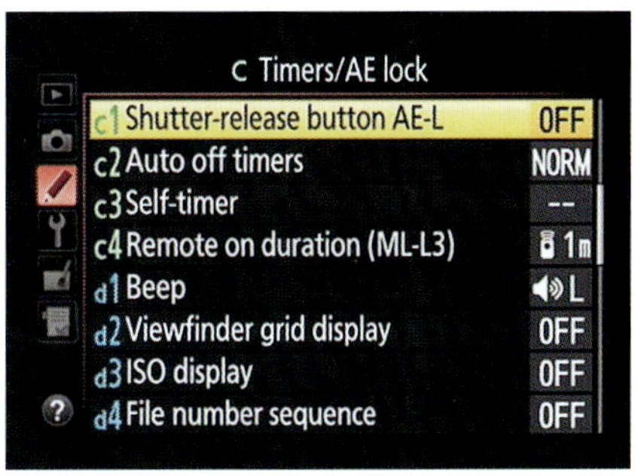

Figure 11-12: If you turn on this option, pressing the shutter button halfway locks exposure and focus.

At the default setting, Off, only focus is locked; exposure is adjusted up to the time you take the shot. If you change the setting to On, your half-press of the shutter button locks both focus and exposure. (Remember that you also have the option of using the AE-L/AF-L button to lock exposure and focus together, as outlined in Chapters 3 and 4.)

Reversing the Command Dial Orientation

When you shoot in the P, S, A, and M exposure modes, you rotate the Command dial to adjust shutter speed, aperture, and Exposure Compensation. By default, rotating the dial to the right raises the value that's being adjusted. If that setup seems backward to you, you can tell the camera that you prefer to rotate the dial to the right to lower the values.

To do so, cruise to the Controls section of the Custom Setting menu and choose Reverse Dial Rotation, as shown on the left in Figure 11-13. Press OK to access the second screen in the figure, where you can modify the dial orientation separately for Exposure Compensation and shutter speed/aperture adjustment. To reverse the dial orientation, highlight the setting and press the Multi Selector right to place a check mark in the box. In the figure, for example, I set the camera to reverse the dial orientation for both Exposure Compensation and Shutter Speed/Aperture. Note that the Exposure Compensation setting also affects the dial's performance when you adjust Flash Compensation.

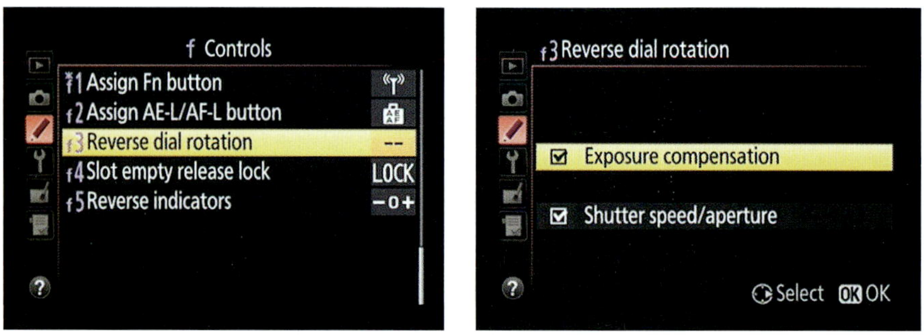

Figure 11-13: For people who like to go left when everyone else goes right, this option reverses the orientation of the Command dial.

Turning Off the AF-Assist Illuminator

In dim lighting, the camera may emit a beam of light from the AF-assist light, the little lamp just below the Mode dial, on the front of the camera. If that light could be distracting to your subject or others in the room, you can disable it by visiting the Autofocus section of the Custom Setting menu and setting the Built-in AF-Assist Illuminator option to Off, as shown in Figure 11-14. You may need to focus manually, though, because without the light to help it find its target, the autofocus system may have trouble.

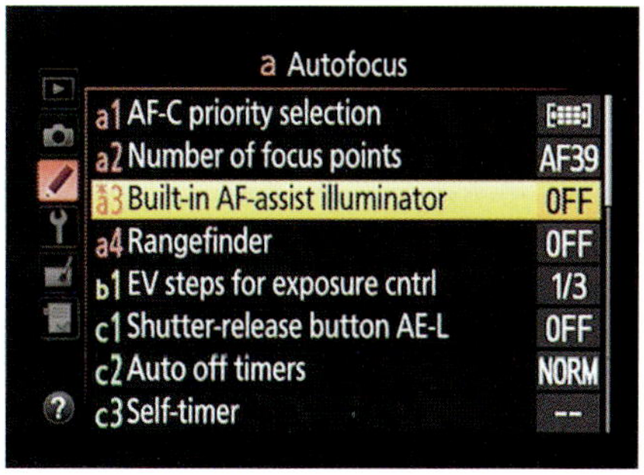

Figure 11-14: Turn this option off to disable the AF-assist lamp.

Appendix: Glossary of Digital Photography Terms

Turn to this glossary for a quick refresher on that elusive digital photography term that's stuck somewhere in the dark recesses of your brain and refuses to come out and play. For more information about a topic, check the book's index.

24-bit image: An image containing approximately 16.7 million colors.

Adobe RGB: One of two color space options available on your camera; determines the spectrum of colors that can be contained in the image. Adobe RGB includes more colors than the default option, sRGB, but also involves complications that make it a better choice for advanced photographers than for beginners.

AEB: Auto Exposure Bracketing, a feature that automatically records multiple exposures using different exposure settings.

AE lock: A way to prevent the camera's autoexposure (AE) system from changing the current exposure settings if you reframe the picture or if the lighting changes before the image is recorded.

aperture: One of three critical exposure controls; an opening in an adjustable diaphragm in the camera lens. The size of the opening is measured in f-stops (f/2.8, f/8, and so on), with a smaller number resulting in a larger aperture opening. Aperture also affects depth of field (the distance over which focus remains acceptably sharp).

aperture-priority autoexposure: A semiautomatic exposure mode, represented by the *A* on the Mode dial. The photographer sets the aperture, and the camera selects the appropriate shutter speed, to produce a good exposure at the current ISO (light-sensitivity) setting.

autoexposure: A feature that puts the camera in control of choosing the proper exposure settings.

bit: Stands for *b*inary dig*it*; the basic unit of digital information. Eight bits equals one *byte*.

bit depth: Refers to the number of bits available to store color information. More bits means more data.

bulb mode: A shutter speed setting that keeps the shutter open as long as you hold down the shutter button. Available only in the M (manual) exposure mode.

burst mode: Another name for the Continuous shooting Release mode settings, which record several images in rapid succession with one press of the shutter button.

byte: Eight bits. *See also* bit.

Camera Raw: A file format that records the photo without applying any of the in-camera processing or file compression that is usually completed automatically when saving photos in the other standard format, JPEG. Also known as *Raw*. Indicated by the file extension NEF on Nikon cameras.

color model: A way of defining colors. In the RGB color model, for example, all colors are created by blending red, green, and blue light.

color space: A specific spectrum of colors that can be rendered by a camera or another digital device. *See also* Adobe RGB, sRGB.

color temperature: Refers to the color cast emitted by a light source; measured on the Kelvin scale.

compression: A process that reduces the size of the image file by eliminating some image data.

contrast: The amount of difference between the brightest and darkest values in an image. High-contrast images contain both very dark and very bright areas.

crop: To trim away unwanted areas around the perimeter of a photo, typically done in a photo-editing program.

depth of field: The distance from the subject over which focus appears acceptably sharp. With shallow depth of field, the subject is sharp but distant objects are not; with large depth of field, both the subject and distant objects are in focus. Manipulated by adjusting the aperture, lens focal length, or camera-to-subject distance.

diopter adjustment control: The wheel next to the viewfinder that enables you to adjust the viewfinder to your eyesight.

download: To transfer data from your camera to a computer.

dpi: Short for *d*ots *p*er *i*nch. A measurement of how many dots of color a printer can create per linear inch. Higher dpi means better print quality on some types of printers; on other printers, dpi is not as crucial.

DPOF: Stands for *d*igital *p*rint *o*rder *f*ormat. A feature that enables you to add print instructions to the image file and then print directly from the memory card. Requires a DPOF-capable printer.

dSLR: Stands for *d*igital *s*ingle-*l*ens *r*eflex; one type of digital camera that accepts interchangeable lenses.

dynamic range: The overall range of brightness values in a photo, from black to white. Also refers to the range of brightness values that a camera, scanner, or another digital device can record or reproduce.

edges: Areas where neighboring image pixels are significantly different in color; in other words, areas of high contrast.

EV compensation: A control that slightly increases or decreases the exposure chosen by the camera's autoexposure mechanism. EV stands for *e*xposure *v*alue; EV settings appear as EV 1.0, EV 0.0, EV–1.0, and so on.

EXIF metadata: *See* metadata.

exposure: The overall brightness and contrast of a photograph, determined mainly by three settings: aperture, shutter speed, and ISO.

exposure compensation: Another name for EV compensation.

file format: A way of storing image data in a digital file; your camera offers two formats: JPEG and Camera Raw (NEF).

fill flash: Using a flash to fill in darker areas of an image, such as shadows cast on subjects' faces by bright overhead sunlight or backlighting.

firmware: The internal software that runs the camera's "brain." Nikon occasionally releases firmware updates that you should download and install in your camera (follow the instructions at the download site).

flash exposure (EV) compensation: A feature that enables the photographer to adjust the strength of the camera flash.

formatting: An in-camera process that wipes all data off the memory card and prepares the card for storing pictures.

frame rate: In a movie, the number of frames recorded per second (fps). A higher frame rate translates to crisper video quality.

f-stop, f-number: Refers to the size of the camera aperture opening. A higher number indicates a smaller aperture opening. Written as f/2, f/8, and so on. Affects both exposure and depth of field.

gamut: Say it "gamm-ut." The range of colors that a monitor, printer, or other device can produce. Colors that a device can't create are said to be *out of gamut.*

gigabyte: Approximately 1,000 megabytes, or 1 billion bytes. In other words, a really big collection of bytes. Abbreviated as GB.

grayscale: An image consisting solely of shades of gray, from white to black. Often referred to generically as a *black-and-white image* (although, in the truest sense, an actual black-and-white image contains only black and white with no grays).

HDMI: Stands for High-Definition Multimedia Interface, a type of port for connecting your camera to a high-definition television.

HDR: Stands for *h*igh *d*ynamic *r*ange and refers to a picture that's created by merging multiple exposures of the subject into one image using special computer software. The resulting picture contains a greater range of brightness values — a greater dynamic range — than can be captured in a single shot.

histogram: A graph that maps shadow, midtone, and highlight brightness values in a digital image; an exposure monitoring tool that can be displayed during image playback.

hot shoe: The connection on top of the camera where you attach an auxiliary flash.

image sensor: The array of light-sensitive "buckets" (technically called *photosites*) in your camera that collect light corresponding to three primary wavelengths: red, green, and blue. The amount of light collected is converted into digital information.

ISO: Traditionally, a measure of film speed; the higher the number, the faster the film. On a digital camera, it means how sensitive the image sensor is to light. Raising the ISO allows faster shutter speed, smaller aperture, or both, but also can result in a noisy (grainy) image. Stands for International Organization for Standardization, the group that devised the ISO standards.

jaggies: Refers to the jagged, stairstepped appearance of curved and diagonal lines in low-resolution photos that are printed at large sizes.

JPEG: Pronounced "jay-peg." The primary file format used by digital cameras; also the leading format for online and web pictures. Uses *lossy compression,* which eliminates some data in order to reduce file size. A small amount of compression does little discernible damage, but a high amount destroys picture quality. Stands for Joint Photographic Experts Group, the group that developed the format.

JPEG artifact: A defect created by too much JPEG compression.

Kelvin: A scale for measuring the color temperature of light. Sometimes abbreviated as *K*, as in 5000K. (Note that in computer-speak, the initial *K* more often refers to kilobytes, as described next.)

kilobyte: One thousand bytes. Abbreviated as *K*, as in 64K.

Live View: The feature that enables you to use the camera monitor rather than the viewfinder to compose your shots.

lossless compression: A file-compression scheme that doesn't sacrifice any vital image data in the compression process, used by file formats such as TIFF. Lossless compression tosses only redundant data, so image quality is unaffected.

lossy compression: A compression scheme that eliminates important image data in the name of achieving smaller file sizes, used by file formats such as JPEG. High amounts of lossy compression reduce image quality.

manual exposure mode: An exposure mode that enables you to control both aperture and shutter speed; enable it by setting the Mode dial to M.

manual focus: A setting that turns off autofocus and instead enables you to set focus by rotating the focusing ring on the lens.

megabyte: One million bytes. Abbreviated as MB. *See also* bit.

megapixel: One million pixels; used to describe the resolution offered by a digital camera.

metadata: Extra data that is stored along with the primary image data in an image file. Metadata often includes information such as aperture, shutter speed, and EV compensation settings used to capture the picture, and can be viewed using special software. Often referred to as *EXIF metadata;* EXIF stands for Exchangeable Image File Format.

metering mode: Refers to the way a camera's autoexposure mechanism reads the light in a scene. Modes available on your camera include *spot,* which bases exposure on a small area at the center of the frame; *center-weighted,* which reads the entire scene but gives more emphasis to the subject in the center of the frame; and *matrix,* which calculates exposure based on the entire frame.

monopod: A telescoping, single-legged pole on which you can mount a camera and lens in order to hold it stable while shooting. It does not stand on its own, unlike a tripod.

NEF: The acronym used for the Nikon Camera Raw format; stands for Nikon Electronic Format.

noise: Graininess in an image, caused by a very long exposure, a too-high ISO setting, or both.

NTSC: A video format used by televisions, DVD players, and VCRs in North America, Mexico, and some parts of Asia (such as Japan, Taiwan, South Korea, and the Philippines). Many digital cameras can send picture signals to a TV, DVD player, or VCR in this format.

PAL: The video format common in Australia, Brazil, China, and Europe.

PictBridge: A feature that enables you to connect your camera to a PictBridge-enabled printer for direct printing.

Picture Control: A setting designed to render images using different color, sharpness, and contrast characteristics; options include Standard, Neutral, Vivid, Monochrome, Portrait, and Landscape.

pixel: Short for *pic*ture *el*ement. The basic building block of every image.

pixelation: A defect that occurs whenever an image has too few pixels for the size at which it is printed; pixels become so large that the image takes on a mosaic-like or stairstepped appearance.

platform: A fancy way of saying "type of computer operating system." Most folks work either on the Windows platform or the Macintosh platform.

ppi: Stands for *p*ixels *p*er *i*nch. Used to state image output (print) resolution. Measured in terms of the number of pixels per linear inch. A higher ppi usually translates to better-looking printed images.

programmed autoexposure: A semiautomatic exposure mode, represented by the P on the Mode dial. The camera selects both f-stop and shutter speed, but you can select from different combinations of the two and access all other camera features.

Raw: *See* Camera Raw.

Raw converter: A software utility that translates Camera Raw files into a standard image format, such as JPEG or TIFF. Nikon ViewNx 2, provided free with your camera, offers this tool.

red-eye: Light from a flash being reflected from a subject's retina, causing the pupil to appear red in photographs. Can sometimes be prevented by using the Red-Eye Reduction flash setting.

Release mode: The camera setting that determines when and how the shutter is released when you press the shutter button. The default setting is Single Frame, which records one picture for each press of the shutter button. Other options include Continuous mode, which records a burst of images as long as you hold down the shutter button, and Self-Timer mode, which delays the shutter release for a few seconds after you press the shutter button.

resample: Adding or deleting image pixels. Adding a large number of pixels degrades images.

resolution: A term used to describe the number of pixels in a digital image. Also a specification describing the rendering capabilities of scanners, printers, and monitors; has different meanings depending on the device.

RGB: The standard color model for digital images; all colors are created by mixing red, green, and blue light.

SD card: The type of memory card used by your camera; stands for Secure Digital.

SDHC card: A high-capacity form of the SD card; stands for Secure Digital High Capacity and refers to cards with capacities ranging from 4MB to 32MB.

SDXC card: Secure Digital Extended Capacity; used to indicate an SD memory card with a capacity greater than 32MB.

sharpening: Applying an image-correction filter to create the appearance of sharper focus.

shutter: A light-barrier inside the camera that opens when you press the shutter button, allowing light to strike the image sensor and expose the image.

shutter-priority autoexposure: A semiautomatic exposure mode in which the photographer sets the shutter speed and the camera selects the appropriate aperture. Select it by setting the Mode dial to S.

shutter speed: The length of time the shutter remains open; or, to put it another way, the duration of the image exposure. Most often measured in fractions of a second, as in 1/60 second or 1/250 second.

slow-sync flash: A special flash setting that allows (or forces) a slower shutter speed than is typical for the normal flash setting. Results in a brighter background than normal flash.

sRGB: Stands for *s*tandard *RGB,* the default color space setting on your camera (and the one recommended for most users). Developed to create a standard color spectrum that (theoretically) all devices can capture or reproduce.

stop: An increment of exposure adjustment. Increasing the exposure by one stop means to select exposure settings that double the light; decreasing by one stop means to cut the light in half.

TIFF: Pronounced "tiff," as in a little quarrel. Stands for *t*agged *i*mage *f*ile *f*ormat. A popular image format supported by most Macintosh and Windows programs. Because it is lossless, it retains image data in a way that maintains maximum image quality. Often used to save Raw files after processing.

tripod: Used to mount and stabilize a camera, preventing camera shake that can blur an image; characterized by three telescoping legs.

UHS: A classification assigned to certain SD memory cards; stands for Ultra High Speed.

UHS-1: At present, the fastest-rated UHS-type card.

USB: Stands for Universal Serial Bus. A type of port for connecting your camera to your computer. Your camera ships with the USB cable necessary for the connection.

Vibration Reduction: A feature designed to compensate for small amounts of camera shake, which can blur a photo. Indicated on Nikon lenses by the initials *VR*.

white balance: Adjusting the camera to compensate for the color temperature of the lighting. Ensures an accurate rendition of colors in digital photographs.

Index

Numbers

• A •

• C •

• D •

• E •

• F •

• G •

• H •

• I •

• J •

• K •

• L •

• M •

• N •

• O •

• P •

Q

R

• S •

• T •

• U •

• V •

• W •

• Z •

About the Author

Julie Adair King is the author of many books about digital photography and imaging, including the best-selling *Digital Photography For Dummies.* Her most recent titles include a series of *For Dummies* guides to popular digital SLR cameras, including the *Nikon D7100, D3200, D5200, and D600s.* Other works include *Digital Photography Before & After Makeovers, Digital Photo Projects For Dummies, Julie King's Everyday Photoshop For Photographers, Julie King's Everyday Photoshop Elements,* and *Shoot Like a Pro!: Digital Photography Techniques.* When not writing, King teaches digital photography at such locations as the Palm Beach Photographic Centre. A native of Ohio and graduate of Purdue University, she resides in West Palm Beach, Florida.

Author's Acknowledgments

I am deeply grateful for the chance to work once again with the wonderful publishing team at Wiley. Heidi Unger, Jennifer Webb, Steve Hayes, Becky Whitney, Mary Corder, and Sheree Montgomery are just some of the talented editors and designers who helped make this book possible. And finally, I am also indebted to technical editor Dave Hall, without whose insights and expertise this book would not have been the same.

Publisher's Acknowledgments

Executive Editor: Steven Hayes

Project Editor: Heidi Unger

Copy Editor: Becky Whitney

Technical Editor: David Hall

Editorial Assistant: Annie Sullivan

Sr. Editorial Assistant: Cherie Case

Project Coordinator: Sheree Montgomery

Cover Image: Main image ©iStockphoto.com/shalamov; Camera and Back Cover images courtesy of Julie Adair King

Apple & Mac

Pad For Dummies,
th Edition
78-1-118-49823-1

Phone 5 For Dummies,
th Edition
78-1-118-35201-4

MacBook For Dummies,
th Edition
78-1-118-20920-2

S X Mountain Lion
For Dummies
78-1-118-39418-2

logging & Social Media

acebook For Dummies,
th Edition
78-1-118-09562-1

Mom Blogging
For Dummies
78-1-118-03843-7

interest For Dummies
78-1-118-32800-2

VordPress For Dummies,
th Edition
78-1-118-38318-6

usiness

Commodities For Dummies,
nd Edition
78-1-118-01687-9

nvesting For Dummies,
th Edition
78-0-470-90545-6

Personal Finance
For Dummies,
7th Edition
978-1-118-11785-9

QuickBooks 2013
For Dummies
978-1-118-35641-8

Small Business Marketing Kit
For Dummies,
3rd Edition
978-1-118-31183-7

Careers

Job Interviews
For Dummies,
4th Edition
978-1-118-11290-8

Job Searching with
Social Media
For Dummies
978-0-470-93072-4

Personal Branding
For Dummies
978-1-118-11792-7

Resumes For Dummies,
6th Edition
978-0-470-87361-8

Success as a Mediator
For Dummies
978-1-118-07862-4

Diet & Nutrition

Belly Fat Diet For Dummies
978-1-118-34585-6

Eating Clean For Dummies
978-1-118-00013-7

Nutrition For Dummies,
5th Edition
978-0-470-93231-5

Digital Photography

Digital Photography
For Dummies,
7th Edition
978-1-118-09203-3

Digital SLR Cameras &
Photography For Dummies,
4th Edition
978-1-118-14489-3

Photoshop Elements 11
For Dummies
978-1-118-40821-6

Gardening

Herb Gardening
For Dummies,
2nd Edition
978-0-470-61778-6

Vegetable Gardening
For Dummies,
2nd Edition
978-0-470-49870-5

Health

Anti-Inflammation Diet
For Dummies
978-1-118-02381-5

Diabetes For Dummies,
3rd Edition
978-0-470-27086-8

Living Paleo For Dummies
978-1-118-29405-5

Hobbies

Beekeeping
For Dummies
978-0-470-43065-1

eBay For Dummies,
7th Edition
978-1-118-09806-6

Raising Chickens
For Dummies
978-0-470-46544-8

Wine For Dummies,
5th Edition
978-1-118-28872-6

Writing Young Adult Fiction
For Dummies
978-0-470-94954-2

Language & Foreign Language

500 Spanish Verbs
For Dummies
978-1-118-02382-2

English Grammar
For Dummies,
2nd Edition
978-0-470-54664-2

French All-in One
For Dummies
978-1-118-22815-9

German Essentials
For Dummies
978-1-118-18422-6

Italian For Dummies,
2nd Edition
978-1-118-00465-4

Available in print and e-book formats.

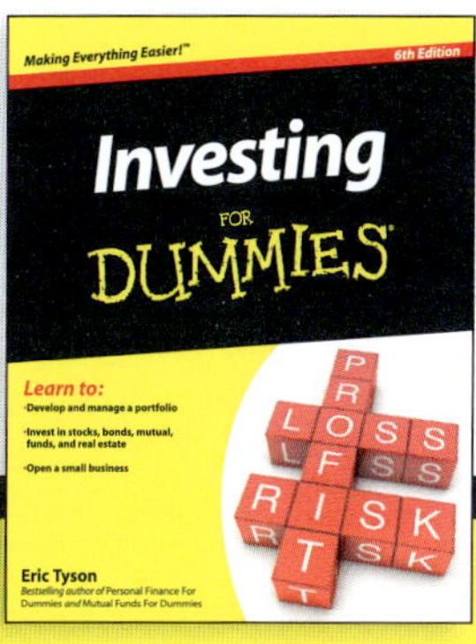

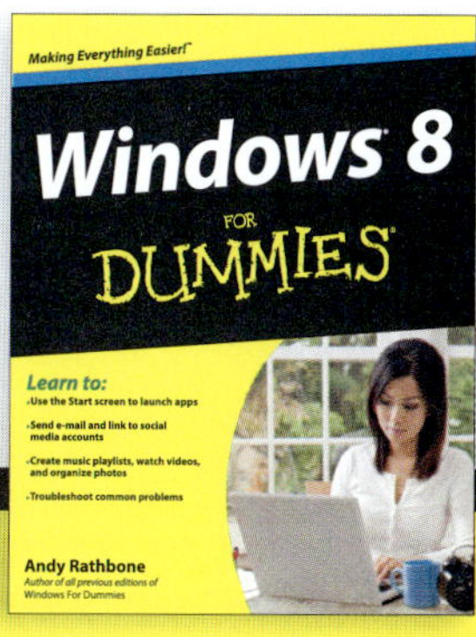

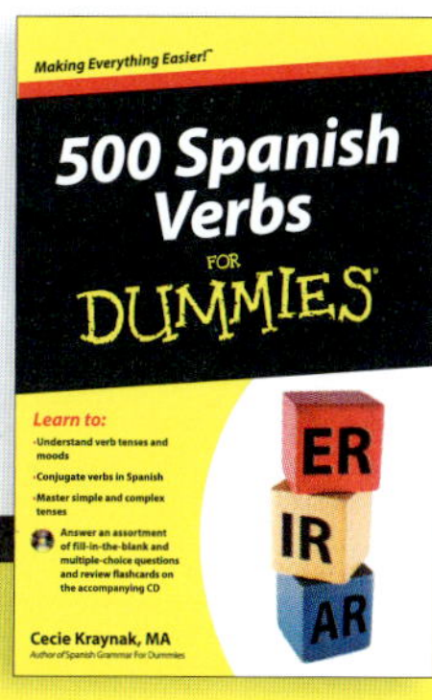

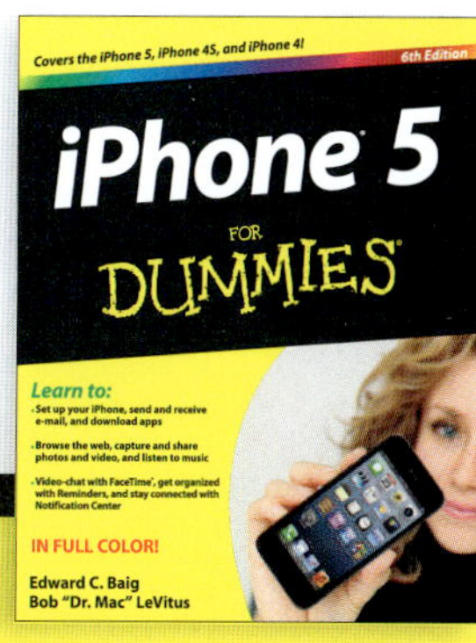

vailable wherever books are sold. For more information or to order direct: U.S. customers visit www.Dummies.com or call 1-877-762-2974.
U.K. customers visit www.Wileyeurope.com or call (0) 1243 843291. Canadian customers visit www.Wiley.ca or call 1-800-567-4797.

Connect with us online at www.facebook.com/fordummies or @fordummies

Math & Science

Algebra I For Dummies, 2nd Edition
978-0-470-55964-2

Anatomy and Physiology For Dummies, 2nd Edition
978-0-470-92326-9

Astronomy For Dummies, 3rd Edition
978-1-118-37697-3

Biology For Dummies, 2nd Edition
978-0-470-59875-7

Chemistry For Dummies, 2nd Edition
978-1-1180-0730-3

Pre-Algebra Essentials For Dummies
978-0-470-61838-7

Microsoft Office

Excel 2013 For Dummies
978-1-118-51012-4

Office 2013 All-in-One For Dummies
978-1-118-51636-2

PowerPoint 2013 For Dummies
978-1-118-50253-2

Word 2013 For Dummies
978-1-118-49123-2

Music

Blues Harmonica For Dummies
978-1-118-25269-7

Guitar For Dummies, 3rd Edition
978-1-118-11554-1

iPod & iTunes For Dummies, 10th Edition
978-1-118-50864-0

Programming

Android Application Development For Dummies, 2nd Edition
978-1-118-38710-8

iOS 6 Application Development For Dummies
978-1-118-50880-0

Java For Dummies, 5th Edition
978-0-470-37173-2

Religion & Inspiration

The Bible For Dummies
978-0-7645-5296-0

Buddhism For Dummies, 2nd Edition
978-1-118-02379-2

Catholicism For Dummies, 2nd Edition
978-1-118-07778-8

Self-Help & Relationships

Bipolar Disorder For Dummies, 2nd Edition
978-1-118-33882-7

Meditation For Dummies, 3rd Edition
978-1-118-29144-3

Seniors

Computers For Seniors For Dummies, 3rd Edition
978-1-118-11553-4

iPad For Seniors For Dummies, 5th Edition
978-1-118-49708-1

Social Security For Dummies
978-1-118-20573-0

Smartphones & Tablets

Android Phones For Dummies
978-1-118-16952-0

Kindle Fire HD For Dummies
978-1-118-42223-6

NOOK HD For Dummies, Portable Edition
978-1-118-39498-4

Surface For Dummies
978-1-118-49634-3

Test Prep

ACT For Dummies, 5th Edition
978-1-118-01259-8

ASVAB For Dummies, 3rd Edition
978-0-470-63760-9

GRE For Dummies, 7th Edition
978-0-470-88921-3

Officer Candidate Tests, For Dummies
978-0-470-59876-4

Physician's Assistant Exam For Dummies
978-1-118-11556-5

Series 7 Exam For Dummies
978-0-470-09932-2

Windows 8

Windows 8 For Dummies
978-1-118-13461-0

Windows 8 For Dummies, Book + DVD Bundle
978-1-118-27167-4

Windows 8 All-in-One For Dummies
978-1-118-11920-4

Available in print and e-book formats.

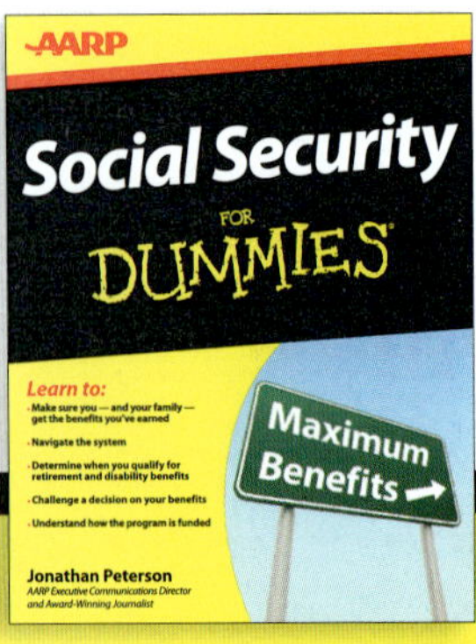

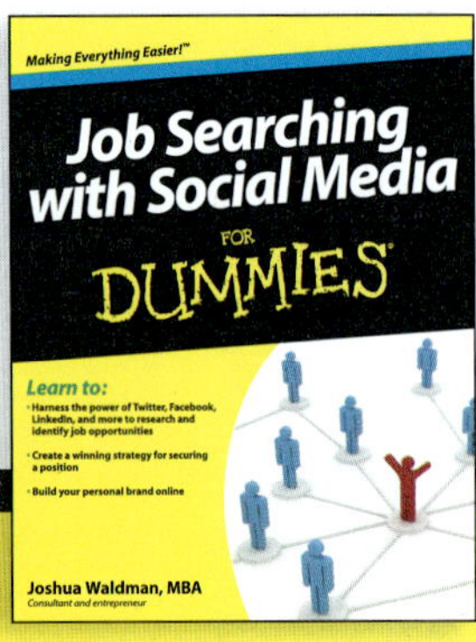

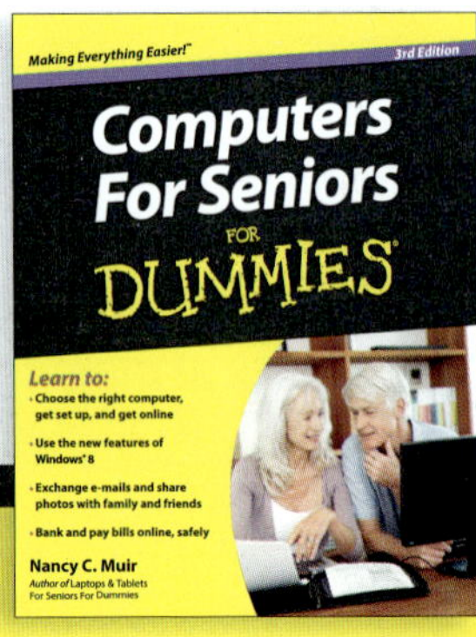

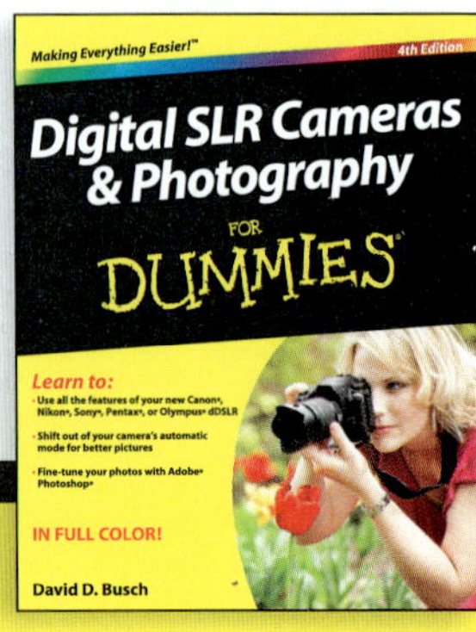

Available wherever books are sold. For more information or to order direct: U.S. customers visit www.Dummies.com or call 1-877-762-297 U.K. customers visit www.Wileyeurope.com or call (0) 1243 843291. Canadian customers visit www.Wiley.ca or call 1-800-567-4797.

Connect with us online at www.facebook.com/fordummies or @fordummies